"Qu'est-ce que le peuple? . . . . Le peuple est la masse de la nation, celle qui exerce le suffrage universel. Voilà notre maître à tous; et ces coteries qui s'appellent le peuple commettent un blasphême."

—Napoleon III

"Sämtliche Staaten haben ihre traditionelle Politik verlassen müssen, und die Richtung ihrer auswärtigen Politik ist mehr oder wenigster von den schwankenden Einflüssen der öffentlichen Meinung abhängig."

—Count von der Goltz

FRENCH OPINION on WAR AND DIPLOMACY

during the

SECOND EMPIRE

by

LYNN M. CASE

1972

OCTAGON BOOKS

New York

Reprinted 1972
by special arrangement with the University of Pennsylvania Press

OCTAGON BOOKS
A Division of Farrar, Straus & Giroux, Inc.
19 Union Square West
New York, N. Y. 10003

Library of Congress Catalog Card Number: 70-120242

ISBN 0-374-91302-1

Manufactured by Braun-Brumfield, Inc.
Ann Arbor, Michigan

Printed in the United States of America

In grateful tribute to an esteemed teacher
WILLIAM E. LINGELBACH

PREFACE

The study of French opinion during the Second Empire encounters many more difficulties than one on opinion during the
Third Republic[1] because in the former there was no freedom of the
press or elections until the last few years. Consequently, it would
require considerable temerity for a historian to undertake the task
for the Second Empire unless there were new types of sources to
justify such an effort. Such adequate sources, however, seem now
to be available, and the present author by their use feels that the
opportunity is at hand to extend our knowledge of French opinion
back from the period of the Third Republic to the equally important period between 1853 and 1870. Among the most important
sources for such a study are the voluminous secret reports to the
French government from the procureurs general and the prefects
and the equally valuable diplomatic dispatches of the foreign ambassadors and ministers residing in Paris.[2] The censored press,
however, plays a relatively minor role in this work because of its
comparative unreliability.

The importance of the period of the Second Empire likewise
requires such a study of opinion after it is found that satisfactory
sources are at hand. It was the period when the delicate balance of
power erected by the Congress of Vienna was badly dislocated by
the unifications of Italy and Germany; when Russia, Austria, and
France lost some of their weight and influence by the shifts of power
both in the Near East and in central Europe; and when the United
States began to emerge as a new power on the western horizon after
its expansion to the Pacific and its victories in the Civil War.
Furthermore, it was the period when the industrial revolution, passing to the European continent, transformed the power situation
within and between the various states. Recognizing these changing
situations, Napoleon III tried many times to obtain a new European
settlement and a restored equilibrium by the peaceful means of a
general congress. The refusal of the other powers to adopt this
method left no other alternative of adjustment than military conflict
and accounted for the many wars characterizing these two decades—
Crimean, Austro-Sardinian, Danish, Austro-Prussian, and Franco-
Prussian.

This was an era, too, when public opinion became a more
important factor in international politics. Constitutional monarchies
appeared in every country except Russia; the suffrage was liberalized

in England, France, Italy, and the German states; and the daily press was becoming a more widespread medium of opinion with the coming of the telegraph and the increase in literacy. All classes of society were bringing their influence to bear on both domestic and foreign policies.

Even with improved sources, such a work as this, like all historical efforts, has its limitations. A study of opinion deals with men's thoughts more than their actions, and with the thinking of men who have long ere this passed out of the living present. It is therefore with an increased measure of humility that a historian approaches such a task as this. It is because of these limitations that the present author deals only with the *major* diplomatic questions. Such questions as those of China, Syria, and Rumania did not evoke a sufficiently wide or sustained opinion to enable the historian to reproduce it. The author has devoted his attention, then, to those questions which aroused the interest of French opinion for periods long enough to permit some approximation of its reactions. Opinion on the American Civil War and the Mexican Expedition is omitted because earlier works have filled these gaps with varying degrees of adequacy.³ Furthermore, it must be understood that this is a study of opinion and not primarily one of the diplomacy itself. Because of the necessity for economies in the cost of publication the author also regrets that he has had to eliminate from his final text many details of a corroborative nature which would have enriched the account.

In some instances the author feels that this work only confirms previous rather vague estimates of opinion; but it confirms them, he believes, with a wealth of new documentary substantiation. In many other instances new fields are plowed for the first time or old estimates of opinion are found to need serious revision. Whether confirming, discovering, or revising, he hopes it may be helpful to reader and researcher alike for the period of the Second Empire.

In the long period of time required to collect and use the vast amount of material which stands behind this study, a period of time prolonged by the interruptions incident to service in the armed forces during World War II, the author has incurred many debts of gratitude to individuals and institutions both in America and abroad. The Social Science Research Council has furnished the author two grants-in-aid to help finance his research in France, England, Belgium, and Switzerland. The University of Pennsylvania has also generously supplemented the costs of research, writing, and publication by several grants from its research funds. Likewise, the Rice Institute supplied equipment for microfilming many of the sources. As is the experience of so many researchers in history, the author has enjoyed the wholehearted co-operation of the staffs of the following archives and libraries: the Archives Nationales, Bibliothèque Nationale, the departmental archives of Seine and Isère, and the archives of the Paris prefect of police in France; the Public Record Office in London; the Archives du Ministère des Affaires Etrangères in Brussels; the Archives Fédérales Suisses in Bern; and in his own country the Library of Congress, the National Archives, the New York Public Library, the libraries of the University of Pennsylvania, of Louisiana State University, of Cornell University, and of Syracuse University, institutions of scholarship in his own country of which he can be justly proud. However, certain individuals, whose untiring assistance and encouragement also merit them special mention, are Georges Bourgin, Abel Doysié, Robert Avezou, René Thalvard, and Marcelle Thalvard in France; A. Henri Lambotte and P. H. Desneux in Belgium; Leonhard Haas in Switzerland; and a host of his colleagues and friends in America: William E. Lingelbach, Roy F. Nichols, Jeanette P. Nichols, Gordon Wright, Oron J. Hale, Marshall Dill, Walter C. Richardson, L. Boone Atkinson, William Boyd, Robert Clark, and Nancy Nichols Barker. To all these obliging institutions and kind and helpful friends the author wishes to express his deep and lasting gratitude. The encouragement and help of his long-suffering wife, especially in the later stages of preparation, deserve a thanks all too inadequately expressed in words.

In conclusion he wishes to thank the *Public Opinion Quarterly* for permission to use parts of his article "French Opinion and Napoleon III's Decision after Sadowa," published in the *Public Opinion Quarterly* (XIII [1949], 441-461); and the American Historical Association for permission to use portions of his book *French Opinion on the United States and Mexico*, previously published under the auspices of the Beveridge Fund.

University of Pennsylvania   LYNN M. CASE

CONTENTS

ABOUT THE NOTES

The notes will be found on pages 278-316. In the text, referential notes are indicated by superior numbers in roman type; discussion notes by superior numbers in italics. In the note section, at the upper right-hand corner of each recto page and the upper left-hand corner of each verso page, will be found boldface numbers indicating the pages of the text to which the notes on these two pages refer.

CHAPTER I

WHENCE COMES THE VOICE?

After the enactment of the British Reform Act of 1832 and after the spread of the revolutions of 1848 throughout most of western Europe there remained little doubt that the people henceforth would have a share, along with their princes and their statesmen, in the formulation of both domestic and foreign policy. On innumerable occasions the diplomats after 1850 laid claim to certain objectives in their negotiations on the basis of the demands of public opinion. In their correspondence and confidences we even see on occasion that they remarked about the new force of opinion in public affairs. Napoleon III, elevated to power by consent of a plebiscite and devoted to the principles of popular sovereignty and universal manhood suffrage, was one of the foremost in recognizing the force of public opinion. In his speech at the closing of the Universal Exposition of 1855 he observed: "At the stage of civilization in which we are, the success of armies, however brilliant they me be,[1] is only transitory. In reality it is public opinion which wins the last victory."[2] The Duke of Morny, the emperor's half-brother and close advisor, in opening the session of the legislative body in November 1859, made a similar remark: "The rapid means of international communications, the [facilities for] publicity, have created a new European power with which all governments are forced to deal: that power is opinion."[3] Even the Paris envoy of the autocratic King of Prussia admitted that "all states have had to abandon their traditional policy, and the direction of their foreign policy is more or less dependent on the varying influences of public opinion."[4] If public sentiment was not an entirely new factor in the middle of the nineteenth century, it was at least by that time becoming recognized as a very important one.

The great problem was to know what public opinion really was, to know where and how to find it. Was opinion the electorate at the polls? Perhaps that is the broadest base on which to construct opinion. At least Napoleon III thought so. In a little unsigned note in his handwriting he has left us his idea of who the people and opinion were: "No, the people are the whole mass of the nation, those who exercise the universal suffrage. They are the masters of us all; and these little groups [*coteries*] who call themselves the people commit a blasphemy."[5]

One can but applaud this realistic and liberal interpretation, an interpretation which the emperor was to recognize in another way than by the official universal suffrage. But anyone who lives in a democratic state knows that on the morning after the elections there are about as many interpretations of the results as there were issues in the campaign. The people had spoken, but what had they said? The election returns were a combination of reactions to the many confusing issues and the many differing personalities of the candidates.

In the plebiscites of the Second Empire as well as in the elections for the legislative body, which took place every six years, a true electoral expression of opinion was thwarted. Although universal manhood suffrage was the rule, still the opposition was not allowed to campaign, and the press was coerced or censored. Besides, the government offered a list of official candidates, who were the only ones permitted to campaign. In 1851 the results were 253 official candidates elected and 8 from the opposition. The senate, or upper house, was appointed by Napoleon and dealt at first only with the unconstitutionality of laws and proposals for constitutional amendments. In 1860 and 1867 some relaxations were permitted in this rigid and "rigged" legislative system; but not until the parliamentary system was inaugurated in 1870 were the major restrictions lifted from the legislative houses. Again those of us who live in modern democratic countries have doubts about whether our legislatures reflect public opinion to any degree of accuracy. Certainly the legislature under Napoleon III could by no stretch of the imagination represent French opinion. Four years after the election of 1857 Cowley asked the emperor: "Did he think . . . . that the Legislative Body represented fairly the opinion of France? He seemed to think not."[6]

The Press and Opinion

Realizing the inadequacies of elections and legislatures to represent the real opinion of a country, many historians who are studying domestic or foreign policies come to rely on the expression of opinions in newspapers and magazines as a truer reflection of national sentiment. Indeed, so adequately did the press seem a reflection of opinion that in the vocabulary of historians press opinion and public opinion became almost synonymous terms, and detailed studies of the press were often published as analyses of "public opinion."[7]

And yet, as a result of American experience between 1932 and 1948, when in five successive presidential elections about 75 per cent of the newspapers found themselves on the losing side, we can no longer consider the press as a mirror of even electoral opinion, to say nothing of real opinion. The influence of governments and political parties, the ownership of newspapers by financial and industrial leaders, the outside business interests of publishers and editors, and the pressure of commercial advertisers—all tend to make the press of the modern industrialized democracy the voice of the favored few rather than that of the general public. Lucy M. Salmon, who made some exhaustive studies of the relation of newspapers to historical problems, concluded: "The very nature of the press prevents it from representing public opinion. . . . . The instability of the claim of any paper to represent public opinion is evident from an examination of its basis; the judgment of the press can not be regarded as final, and it is not altogether reasonable to hold it responsible for not doing what from its very nature, it can not do."[8] To a certain unknown degree this artificial press opinion sometimes creates, perhaps, a corresponding real public opinion.[9] Walter Lippmann in his analysis of public opinion seems to doubt, however, that the press either makes or even reflects it.[10]

The uncensored French press under the Third Republic, even in a less industrialized democracy, seemed to have suffered from what was called *la publicité financière*. Georges Boris, editor of *La Lumière*, asserted that "cabinets of all political complexions had, for the purposes of hushing up attacks, been paying considerable sums to newspapers and newspaper writers," that "blackmail, moreover, is the only means of subsistence for any number of small periodicals," that "newspaper opinion [in France] undoubtedly lies to the right of public opinion," and finally that foreign ideas of French opinion based on the French press are "often very far removed from reality."[11]

If the free press of the French Third Republic did not reflect opinion, the press of the Second Empire was an even sorrier instrument for registering popular thought. In addition to the many handicaps of the so-called free press, French newspapers during the reign of Napoleon III, at least until 1868, were subjected to a regime of stern censorship. Papers first had to obtain a government permit to be established; their editors and proprietors had to be approved by the government; they had to make a monetary deposit and pay a special tax on each number as well as increased postage rates. A newspaper was warned whenever it published an article that appeared merely "excessive, dangerous, or disagreeable"; after two warnings the paper, in case of a third offense, would be subject to a two-month suspension, which was usually fatal to its existence.[12]

In addition to censoring the press the government often influenced the press by special favors. These were shown particularly to the semiofficial journals, such as the *Constitutionnel, Patrie,* and *Pays,* which received certain government confidences in return for their co-operation. But this friendly persuasion was extended to other papers as well. One confidential note of the ministry of interior to the prefects said: "It is to be hoped that the departmental administration can help to increase the circulation of the *Revue contemporaine*."[13] On another occasion the prefect of Bouches-du-Rhône reported: "Of the five papers published in Marseilles only one defends the government. I have persuaded it to increase its size, develop its political and commercial coverage, and finally to have two daily editions. I anticipate a great success."[14]

In a direct and positive way, too, the government frequently gave instructions to the press, a practice even common under the Third Republic. On one occasion Moustier, the French foreign minister, assured the Prussian ambassador, Goltz, that he had not issued instructions to the press for the past eight days.[15] On another occasion Nigra, the Sardinian envoy, told of an article against his country, prepared by Cassagnac for the *Pays*, which was suppressed by the government.[16]

In addition to censoring and inspiring, the government also actually exerted other more subtle pressures on the press. Those which would follow the government line, particularly those in the provinces, were awarded the privilege of publishing the official administrative and judicial announcements and notices. Failure to hew to the government line could bring a sudden withdrawal of this special privilege and of the subsidy which went with it, a subsidy which frequently meant the difference between solvency and bankruptcy for the individual newspapers. Such a practice evidently was common enough that the prefect of Manche mentioned such a procedure in a rather off-hand way in one of his routine reports.

> The *Vigie de Cherbourg* [he wrote] generally neglects to publish the articles sent it by the administration. I had to warn the proprietor-manager of this sheet that if he persisted in a systematic refusal of semiofficial insertions of suggestions of a public interest, I should find myself obliged to withdraw the judicial announcements. "

The provincial newspapers were even more dependent and slavish toward the regime than were the Paris papers. The government kept a close watch on the provincial press as is witnessed by the instructions sent to the prefects on 12 July 1852 and 11 September 1853. But the minister of interior was dissatisfied with the results of these instructions which "do not give me all the necessary information to appreciate exactly the movement of opinion and the degree of influence exerted by each one of the organs of public opinion." Consequently in 1857 he gave the prefects a long form to fill out on newspapers, their circulation, and their opinions for the three years from 1855 to 1857 "to establish the exact status of these papers in the current month of May."[18] Furthermore, the administration had a regular system of syndicated articles sent to the subservient local papers. Such a system was publicly revealed by the London *Times* and the *Union de la Sarthe* on the occasion of the La Valette Circular. Let O'Meagher of the *Times* tell the story:

It is well known that . . . . there are bureaux in which a regular manufactory of leading articles is established, and whence those productions, carefully lithographed, are despatched to numbers of provincial papers. The *Union de la Sarthe* has just exposed this practice in an article entitled 'How Opinion is Formed,' in which it points out, as a thing to note and as a sign of the times, that on the same day and in many cases at the very same hour, there was published in a great number of provincial journals an article on the Lavalette circular which it is hardly necessary to say is by no means unfavourable to that document. The *Union de la Sarthe* says:

'The most curious thing with regard to this article, which, like the earthquake of the 14th of September, was repeated simultaneously from the north to the south of France, is not the article itself, for similar ones are daily written in the *Constitutionnel* and the *Pays*, but the emulation of the producing journals as to its paternity. In the *Journal de Chartres* the article is signed by Alph. Malteste; in the *Echo de la Mayenne*, C. Lenormand; in the *Union Bretonne* the author's name is Mounier; in the *Messager de la Sarthe* the father is called Dufau; the *Journal d'Alençon* pretends that it is J. Moreau; the *Journal d'Ile et Vilaine*, not daring to decide so disputed a point, publishes but does not sign; the *Journal d'Indre et Loire* heads the article with the safe and convenient form—"They write us from Paris." We might multiply examples indefinitely, but they would only increase the reader's perplexity. For in short, whatever M. de Lavalette's power of propulsion and persuasion, it is not easy to understand such unanimity of praise expressed upon the same day, in so many papers, and in terms so completely identical.' [19]

Certainly on these occasions the provincial papers did not represent provincial opinion nor even the opinion of their own editors, but rather that of a writer in a government bureau in Paris.

Yet, the ugliest aspect of press opinion during the Second Empire was the influence of outright bribery on its formulation. A public scandal developed when Kervéguen read a report before the legislative body of discoveries among the private papers of a certain Charles de Varenne, who was revealed to be a go-between in bribery arrangements with the Paris press in favor of Italy.[20] The evidence found recently in diplomatic correspondence rather confirms Kervéguen's charges. A few excerpts from this correspondence will revive and corroborate the charges:

(Beyens of Belgium) : For the papers what Kervéguen says is not new. It is the same for a hundred things which we could have done, half by [real] means [*moyens*], half by hopes, by favors which I could have done if they had given me the means— taking advantage of everything in doing some favors and in giving away 10,000 fr. if necessary . . . . . [21]

(Solms of Prussia) : If we want to take up the struggle emphatically, then the only thing that is left for us is to carry on the same with the same means, that is with significant sums.

Bismarck then allocated 5,000 francs a month to be used on the French press, and two months later Solms was writing:

I have contracted with M. Malespine, owner of the *Presse Libre* [!], for 1,500 francs a month, for which he puts his paper, of which he already circulates 20,000 copies, at our disposal. M. Malespine received money from us when he was still a collaborator on the *Opinion Nationale.*[22]

Nigra on 5 March 1859 reported that Guéroult asked for 200,000 lire from Sardinia to help him buy the *Messager de Paris.*[23] Villemessant, editor of *Figaro,* was frank and cynical enough to admit bribery when, to a group of friends, he exhibited an edition of his paper with the boast: "Here's the best number we've ever had; every line of it is bought and paid for."[24]

In the French press of the Second Empire power and money talked, but not the people. Under a system of censorship, favors, threats, syndicated editorials, and outright bribery this press emerged with the voice of Jacob and the hands of Esau. The public, however, was not as blind as Isaac, nor should historians be, who study French opinion during the Second Empire. Therefore in this work the press has been used sparingly and with caution.

The Procureur Reports

However much Napoleon III may have censored the press, rigged the elections, and controlled the legislature, he was very anxious to be well informed on the state of public opinion on both domestic and foreign affairs. Representing a less deeply rooted dynasty and living in a more democratic age, he had every reason to wish to keep his policy as closely in line with the desires of the people as was possible. The Austrian ambassador once remarked that "Louis Napoleon always will permit himself to be guided by what he believes to be the opinion, the interests, and the will of his country."[25] Yet, how could he be well informed on opinion when he undermined the normal channels of reaching the public? Recent researches in the Archives Nationales in Paris reveal that his government set up a thorough and continuous system of collecting information on public opinion through secret administrative reports. The confidential nature of these reports exonerates them from the charge, often made against newspaper articles, of distorting the facts to create a desired effect on the public. Just as with other sources, there may be inaccuracies or inadequacies in these reports—which will be pointed out below— but they seem to have furnished the imperial government, and incidentally the historian, with a relatively more reliable picture of the state of public opinion than could be given by the contemporary newspapers and periodicals. In order to understand more clearly the advantages of this type of source in a study of opinion, it might be well to consider in more detail the nature of the two important collections in question.

The reports of the procureurs general (*procureurs généraux*) were by far the best of the administrative sources for information on opinion. There was a procureur general assigned as part of the staff (*parquet*) of each of the twenty-eight[26] courts of appeals in France. He acted as the chief prosecuting attorney and provided for the criminal prosecution before the courts of appeals, and he supervised the prosecution and administrative personnel of the court, with a certain amount of authority over the prosecution personnel in the lower courts in his district. Below him was an advocate general, imperial procureurs, assistants (*substituts*), and justices of the peace. In addition to his regular duties the imperial government required that he send to the minister of justice (keeper of the seal) periodic reports on opinion and economic conditions in his district. In performing this duty he required all the hierarchy of these officials, from the justices of the peace on up, to furnish him political and economic data in their areas.

There was no doubt that the government wanted frank and accurate descriptions of opinion in these confidential reports. Rouher, as minister of justice, in his instructions of 24 November 1849, required "a reasoned appreciation of the moral and political situation . . . . on the first day of each month." In closing he added: "I do not need to suggest that you execute the present circular with the greatest precision and care; I am sure that you understand how important it is."[27] The report periods were changed to quarterly in 1852, to semiannual in 1853, and back to quarterly in March 1859.[28] Finally in the last-mentioned circular a great deal more emphasis and scope were given to these reports:

It will not suffice [wrote the minister of justice] for you to observe and report to me in a general way the state of public opinion; it is indispensable that I find in your communications evidence of a personal study and a clear and exact evaluation of everything characterizing the period in question and of anything revealing the tendencies and needs of the people. . . . . I attach a great deal of importance to these periodic communications.

I also think it to be of great importance that you give me the results of your observations on the principal economic questions with which the government and the country are concerned. Consequently I should welcome with great interest whatever you may have to report on the condition of industries in your district, the causes of their prosperity or decline [and] the condition of the workers employed.[29]

Henceforth the reports came in at quarterly intervals, except during the Austro-Sardinian War, when weekly reports were required between 15 May and 15 July. Thus the Austro-Sardinian War was the most thoroughly reported incident of the Second Empire.[30]

That the procureurs general took their instructions seriously and tried conscientiously to give an exact description of opinion is proved by innumerable remarks in their own reports, of which the following three are examples:

(Massot in Rouen): In my communications to Your Excellency on the moral and political situation as I see it, I do not set myself up as judge; I remain a reporter, and one of my first duties in this matter consists in observing with care all the great currents of opinion forming around me and in pointing them out then loyally and without reserve.[31]

(Chaix d'Est-Ange in Paris): I ask permission of Your Excellency to tell him frankly my thoughts on the attitude taken by the clergy in these circumstances. . . . . Anyway it seems to me useful that the government of the emperor be exactly informed on the state of opinion. Almost all my assistants have taken great care to furnish me documents on this subject, and these documents form the main part of the reports they transmit to me. My job then will be to mirror their conscientious investigations. In order to avoid useless repetitions, I have brought together into a single résumé the results of these conscientious investigations concerning the entire district.[32]

(De Leffemberg in Dijon): In drawing up this report every three months, I do not undertake to indicate political solutions. I consider myself simply as a witness, looking around and listening with all possible care and revealing with absolute honesty what I think I see and hear.[33]

The procureurs general not only said they were trying to be frank and honest in their reporting of opinion, but on many occasions they showed that they were telling the government that the people opposed the emperor's policy. This is indicated particularly when a vast majority of the reports revealed opposition to the Mexican expedition.[34] Again, too, they confessed that the people generally opposed the emperor's Auxerre speech in 1866.[35] Loiseau in Besançon wrote in 1859:

The heads of the courts' legal staffs [parquets] of Vesoul, Gray, and Lure tried hard to verify with the greatest care by their own personal investigations the information transmitted to them by the unanimous reports of the justices of the peace. They interviewed officials, industrialists, landowners, farmers, and plain workmen, and they did not meet one single person who showed the least sympathy for a war [a war which they knew was favored by the government].[36]

This report also shows how sometimes certain officials made a careful recheck on the information they received and how all classes were included in their surveys. But other individual procureurs general also represent examples of courageous reporting of hostile sentiments:

(De Leffemberg in Dijon): I studied and listened with all the attention of which I am capable to everything said or indicated around me and my assistants, and I believe to have perceived that opinion has not been carried away by the arguments of the orators of the government. It is hard for me [m'en coûte] to say it, but it is not right for me to keep still about what seems to me to be the truth.[37]

(Leclerc [advocate general] in Metz): I am too honest not to tell Your Excellency that this reception [of war rumors fostered by the government] was at first one of surprise, of disbelief, and in certain places of fright.[38]

It may have been hard for these men on certain occasions to be honest and frank, and some of their colleagues at times may have lacked the required courage; but they all gave clear evidence that they knew that their superiors were asking for the unvarnished truth. And the marginal notes in the ministry of justice showed the impatience of their superiors when their accounts smacked of slavish fawning. When Dessauret of Montpellier submitted a report replete with glowing terms about the government, a ministry official wrote in the margin: "It can't be possible that this report comes from M. Dessauret. No doubt he assigned its composition to some student of rhetoric." Again when Mourier indicated that the bishops of Savoy favored the government's policy, a ministry official scribbled in pencil, "How does he know?"[39]

Thus there poured into the ministry of justice every three months, sometimes more often, voluminous reports from each of the twenty-eight court-of-appeals districts of France, telling of opinion on domestic and foreign affairs, of moral conditions (disorderly conduct, drunkenness, prostitution),[40] and of economic conditions. Very few of the quarterly reports had less than ten pages;[41] some individual reports were ninety pages long; the average length was about twenty-five pages. Taken all together, this great collection forms a vast and detailed twenty-year Domesday Book of all of France during the Second Empire.[42]

There is an abundance of evidence that when these reports were received they were carefully read by officials of the government in Paris. Their pages are replete with red-penciled underlinings; their margins abound with lines, checks, and comments. Particularly in the period between 1866 and 1869, when various crises arose, the passages dealing with foreign affairs were copiously underlined. A delay in the dispatch of one report caused the following expression of impatience:

> I beg you to hasten the dispatch to the chancellery of your report on the moral and political situation in your district during the last quarter of 1859. I absolutely must have this document to complete a digest of the descriptions by the procureurs general of the present state of public sentiment over the whole extent of the empire.[43]

Frequent digests, accompanied by many illustrative extracts, were prepared for higher officials, presumably for the emperor. One entire carton (368) is set aside for digests and extracts for the period between 1853 and 1863. There are also five other cartons filled with special reports on the Election of 1863 and two with special reports on Agitation Relating to the Roman Question (1860-1861).[44] No marginal notes are found on these digests or extracts to give us an actual clue that the emperor saw them, but these were evidently the draft copies of digests and extracts for the emperor.

There can be little doubt, however, that these were prepared for the emperor and seen by him in their final draft. Speaking of the procureur reports on the Army Bill, Vautier affirms that "information coming from Alsace was sent directly to the emperor."[45] On an earlier occasion in October 1862, when the cabinet debates waxed hot on the questions of withdrawing French troops from Rome and when Thouvenel and Persigny lectured the emperor and their colleagues on public insistence on withdrawal, the emperor arose and said, "I also, Gentlemen, feel the pulse of France twice a day; I know her sentiments, and I shall not abandon the pope."[46] While he was not specific here on how he felt the public pulse, the emperor acknowledged that he was constantly receiving information on opinion. The circumstances and the evidence, then, all point to the probability that Napoleon III was familiar with the information coming from these procureur reports. The minister of justice was not directly interested in public opinion as far as his duties were concerned; the administration of justice, based upon law and evidence, could

disregard opinion more than any other ministry. Yet time after time
the circulars of the minister demand more and better reports on
opinion; and again and again digests and extracts were prepared.
It must have been for some one higher up who had a more general
interest than the keeper of the seal. That some one could hardly have
been anyone except the emperor himself.

The Prefect Reports

However, not content to have just one administrative source on
opinion, the emperor also required a continuous series of reports
from his prefects. The prefects, appointed by the minister of interior,
are the chief administrative officials of the eighty-eight (in 1860) departments of France. In the fulfillment of their duties they might
be expected to make such constant and varied contacts with the
populace, either directly or through the medium of their subordinates,
that they would have an intimate knowledge of the trend of public
thought.[47]

By frequent and repeated instructions the ministers of interior
continued all during the Second Republic and the Second Empire
to demand regular reports from their prefects and to criticize those
they received. From 1848 to October 1852 they asked for monthly
reports; from October 1852 to December 1854, bimonthly reports;
from December 1854 to 18 November 1859, quarterly reports. In
November 1859 the prefects were ordered to send in reports three
times a month; from December 1860 to April 1865, twice a month.
From April 1865 to the end of the empire they were monthly reports.
The circular of 13 December 1860 exemplifies one of these instructions as well as the critical attitude of the government.

On several occasions [wrote the minister of interior] my predecessors have
complained about the irregularity with which several of your colleagues sent in their
reports, and, since taking over the ministry, I have already noticed it myself.

I can not urge you too strongly, Mr. Prefect, to show the greatest punctuality
in the dispatch of your report at the precise times I am indicating for you. The
regularity which I am requiring of you is indispensable if I am to be able to
evaluate early enough the general situation in the Empire as a whole.[48]

On one occasion in June 1866, before the outbreak of the Austro-
Prussian War, the prefects were called in to Paris for immediate
information on opinion concerning intervention in the pending war.
Their reports were evidently so hostile to the government's contem-
plated intervention that they were sent back to see that their mayors
of the communes made a thorough recheck on the previous findings
of the police.[49]

The ministry not only criticized the lack of promptness but also
the superficiality of information. In one communication the minister
of interior wrote the prefect of Ain:

The subprefect of Trévoux has dealt with all the questions raised in the
directive, but perhaps he should have gone into them in more detail and especially

explained to me more fully the political situation, the trends of public opinion in his *arrondissement*.[50]

Thus independently of the procureur reports the government was being inundated with prefect reports on opinion every month or even more often. These documents form series F^1cIII in the Archives Nationales. There is about one carton for each department with the documents unbound, merely tied together by a cloth band.[51]

There was certainly evidence from German sources that the government was receiving and using the prefect reports. Goltz, the Prussian ambassador, wrote that La Valette was becoming more favorable to the pope "partly as a result of the prefect reports on the attitude of the country." A year later another Prussian representative, Solms, wrote that he received this information directly from La Valette: "In his capacity as minister of interior he [La Valette] received from all sides and from all departments the most exhaustive reports on the feeling of the French people, and he could assure me that in France the people wished for nothing more heartily than for peace."[52] We know, then, that the prefect reports were studied by the minister of interior and that even foreigners knew of their existence.

A comparison of these prefect reports with those of the procureur reports as to their relative values as sources on opinion will also reveal the nature of the prefect reports. In fact the prefect reports are much inferior to the procureur reports in several respects. They are much shorter in length; from 1865 to 1870 they were merely four-page printed forms filled out with the briefest possible remarks.[53] For the period between September 1859 and November 1865, constituting one-third of the Second Empire's duration, the prefect reports are lost or destroyed.[54] Furthermore, there are no digests, extracts, or economic reports.

Because of their inferior value the prefect reports have not been used as extensively in this work as have those of the procureurs general. The present author believes that he has seen and used almost all of the extracts in the procureur reports dealing with foreign relations. As to the prefect reports, he selected fourteen departments scattered in all parts of France and representing rural, commercial, and industrial areas and utilized their reports.[55] Such reports served as a sort of check on the other sources used.

A system of police reports on opinion, assembled and digested by the Paris prefect of police, was another source of information for the imperial government. Unfortunately, most of these reports seem to have been destroyed in the Commune fires of 1871 and were not available for this study. What makes this loss a particularly heavy one is that the procureurs general in Paris did not give as much detail on opinion in the city as they did in that of the surrounding areas, evidently supposing that the emperor was already well informed on Paris by his prefect of police. Consequently, by a strange inversion from those who base their study of opinion on the Paris press, we have more report material on the provinces than on Paris itself.

Another deficiency from which both the procureur and prefect reports suffer is that they are not very full after October 1868. These officials evidently believed, as did later historians, that a free press reflected opinion because, when censorship was relaxed in 1868, their reports become much scantier. On a prefect report of 1868 from Isère, at the place on the form where the heading "Opinion of the People" appeared, an official of the ministry of interior wrote: "Not necessary, special reports."[56] Likewise the same attitude appeared among the procureurs general. De Prandière in Lyons wrote in 1869: "What good does it do to try to analyze and describe the impressions and tendencies which every day in all forms and directions are freely and publicly proclaimed?"[57] So slim and uninformative are the procureur reports after October 1868 that they are not filed with the other district reports, but altogether in carton 389. These deal mostly with the elections in 1869 and very little with foreign affairs.

In writing a history of public opinion, we have to realize eventually that we are seeing it through the eyes of some intermediary. Just as with the press, we must finally ask the question whether the procureurs general may be a poor class of men from whom to get evidence on opinion. Narrowed by their specialty and accustomed to being one-sided in pleading cases, they would seem to be the type which would find it difficult to give an objective analysis of general sentiment. Their connections with the government would make the opposition groups hesitate to confide their views to them or their agents. Furthermore, these officials were appointees and would hesitate to bite the hand ;that fed them. Lord Cowley, the British ambassador, once observed that "French functionaries are so much in the habit of stating that which they think will be agreeable to their superiors, that too much reliance must not be placed on their opinions."[58] The fact, too, that they were of the upper bourgeoisie might make them inclined to neglect peasant and labor opinion.

Of course the procureurs were human, with loyalties and prejudices like any other group of human beings. Their inquiries and those of their subordinates may not have plumbed every depth of French opinion, and their evaluations after their surveys may have at times erred as much as did George Gallup in 1948. But what more can we ask than that they should in the long run make a mighty and sincere effort to seek out the truth and set it down as they thought they saw it? The procureurs general, at least, did that much. By their instructions and by their replies we must be convinced that an earnest job was intended, an earnest job that covered all of France and all of twenty years. Nor was it intended that they give merely the opinion of their own class. "What effect do the principal events of each quarter produce on the different classes?" they were asked by the minister of justice.[59] Nearly all the reports had their information broken down by classes and by political groups. When a rare report left the suspicion that it contained guess-work rather than genuine search, the official in Paris would show his impatience by some such remarks as these: "Here's a report that did not cost much effort." "Then all that up above is not the opinion of his district, but his own." "He's the only pr. g[al] who reports any such public sentiment."[60] Nor could the people of the various classes have been very reticent in the face of these informal or disguised interviews because the reports abound with hostile comments and uncomplimentary remarks.

The prefect reports may have serious gaps and scanty contents; they may be valuable more as a check or a confirmation. But the procureur reports, by their detail, by their completeness, by their ring of sincerity, are in many respects superior, as a source for public opinion, to the sampling methods of the Gallup Poll.

Diplomatic Documents

The foreign diplomatic representatives in Paris were also vitally interested in the reactions of the French public to matters of foreign policy. Their means of sampling opinion were often crude and inadequate, but it is obvious from their correspondence and memoirs that they devoted a great deal of attention to opinion. Their dispatches included many clippings from newspapers, usually to show the curious twist some paper was taking, for they knew of all the distortions which resulted from censorship and bribery. Their other sources were equally dubious: the salons, the clubs, the gossip of the diplomatic corps, the Bourse, the confidences of government officials. Seldom did the diplomats get right down to the grass roots. Beyens of Belgium did seem to have a contact with some one in the office of the prefect of police and by that source was able to get nearest to the opinion of the common people. Perhaps it is for that reason that Beyens appears to be the best of the diplomatic observers. At least for middle and upper class opinion their testimony in dispatches and books is an important source.

The foreign office archives in all important countries, except those of Germany and Russia, are now open to historians for the period of the Second Empire. In the preparation of this work those of Great Britain, Belgium, Switzerland, and the United States were used. The Prussian documents are found in the collection of *Austwärtige Politik Preussens*, the Sardinian documents in the *Car-*

teggio Cavour-Nigra, Austrian and south German documents in Oncken's *Rheinpolitik Kaiser Napoleons III.* There are also special collections of private unpublished papers of some of these diplomats,
such as the Cowley letters to Russell and Clarendon in the Public
Record Office, the Beyens-Lambermont correspondence in the Belgian
foreign ministry archives, the Bigelow papers in the New York
Public Library, and Rouher's Cerçay papers in the French foreign
ministry archives and the French National Archives. Among the
printed materials are also the memoirs, diaries, and letters of many
important diplomats and other contemporaries (listed in the Bibliography). One nondiplomatic foreign observer whose accounts of
opinion are frequent and important was O'Meagher, the London
Times Paris correspondent. His almost daily articles to the *Times*
are full of analyses of press and opinion. Of course the legislative
debates are found in the *Moniteur Universal* (up to 1869) and in
the *Journal Officiel* (after 1868).

The voices of the French people of the Second Empire have
have also "gone with the wind." Yet the fallen leaves, blown by
that wind and found again scattered in archives and published collections, in private letters and memoirs, in newspapers and debates,
still yield up blurred and dimmed recordings of yeas and nays, of
hopes and fears, of loves and hates from out of that long-lost past—
but a past which, by some mysterious amalgam of memory, still
remains a part of the living present.

CHAPTER II

THE CRIMEAN WAR

The dispute in the Near East began in 1850 with France's revival of her claims to be the protector of Roman Catholic interests in the Holy Places of Jerusalem and Bethlehem. By the capitulations of 1740, conceded by the sultan of the Ottoman Empire, the Roman Catholic monks had received the keys and possession of the more important Christian religious shrines, and France had obtained recognition as the protector of the Latin (Roman) Christians and their shrines in that area. Then during the period of the French Revolution and its aftermath French influence and Latin Christian activity had greatly decreased in the Holy Lands, while Greek Christians, backed by Russia as their political protector, obtained the ascendancy and the custody of the Holy Places. Not until 1850, when the French Republic had a clerial legislature and a strong executive, were the French and Latin claims reasserted. The sultan's response in February 1852 was to return some of the custody and rights to the Latin Christians.

But, when Russia immediately protested, the sultan secretly issued another firman in favor of the Greek Christians and nullified most of the concessions given to the Latin-French party. This contradiction between the two concessions came to an issue in Jerusalem where the local Ottoman commissioner adhered to his earlier instructions in favor of the Latins. Then Russia brought heavy pressure to bear on the Porte by sending to Constantinople in 1853 an impressive mission headed by Prince Menshikov. In an arrogant and threatening manner Menshikov peremptorily demanded of the sultan a treaty granting to the Greek Christians the custody of the Holy Places and to Russia the protectorate over all Greek Orthodox Christians in the Ottoman Empire. On the advice of the British and French ambassadors the sultan yielded on the Holy Places but refused the protectorate. Menshikov thereupon left Constantinople in ostentatious anger, and in July 1853 Russia proceeded to occupy the sultan's principalities of Moldavia and Wallachia until satisfaction could be obtained.

This occupation, of course, endangered the European balance of power, which in turn led Great Britain and France to concentrate their Mediterranean fleets at Besika Bay just outside the Straits.

Austria was also alarmed by this Russian occupation on her door-step, but, being on friendly terms with the czar, she offered a mediation plan called the Vienna Note. This, instead of a treaty, was to be sent by the sultan to the czar acknowledging the czar's right to be concerned over the Greek Christians and promising their protection according to assurances in previous treaties. The czar was willing to accept this; but the sultan, on the advice of Sir Stratford de Redcliffe, the British ambassador, insisted that the protection be "by the Sublime Porte [Turkey]."

Russia's refusal to accept this amendment led to the sultan's declaration of war in October 1853 because of the continuation of the Russian occupation of the two provinces. And this state of war in turn seemed a justification to the British and French for the entrance of their fleets into the Straits and their anchorage before Constantinople.

The Sinope Incident

As long as the Eastern question was one of the custody of a few ancient holy shrines 1700 miles away, it was not only very secondary in the eyes of the foreign ministry and the emperor but definitely unimportant as far as political observers and commentators were concerned. As to the general public, few people even knew that such a dispute existed. However, when the news of Menshikov's impressive mission reached Europe, their attention was aroused, and the Eastern question became one of the general topics of the day.

Yet, even after this turn of events the general public, outside business and journalistic circles, still took little interest in Eastern affairs, or, if it did momentarily, it quickly lapsed into a mood of unconcern again. One indication of this lack of concern was very infrequent mention of the subject in the reports of the procureurs general and the prefects during the first half of 1853. These local officials in the departments not only took an interest themselves in current political questions, but they had also been specifically instructed to report the interests and trends of public opinion.[1] Yet their reports before July contained very little mention of the subject, and after 1 July they usually indicated a general lack of concern.[2]

Indeed, during the greater part of the year 1853 the peace-loving business circles were only mildly alarmed by the signs of impending conflict and with the exception of the *Assemblée Nationale*, the press generally was anti-Russian and favorable to the working agreement with Great Britain. But these reactions were restricted to a limited group of businessmen, journalists, and government officials. For the rank and file of the general public the Eastern question was greeted usually with apathy and lack of interest.[3]

A little more excitement was injected into the Eastern question in the last month of 1853 by the famous Sinope incident. On 30 November a Russian naval squadron in the Black Sea attacked a Turkish fleet anchored in the harbor of Sinope on the north coast of Asia Minor. Almost all the Turkish ships were sunk, half their sailors were killed, and the city partly destroyed by fire. The stir this attack caused in the chancelleries of western Europe was due largely to the fact that they had believed that Russia had agreed to the neutralization of the Black Sea. Now she had made it an area of warfare and had done it almost within view of the French and British combined fleets at Constantinople. It thus became quickly a question both of balance of power and of prestige. With these considerations in mind the French government, in agreement with the British, issued a circular (29 December) explaining that the combined fleets had been ordered into the Black Sea to enforce its neutralization.

The news of Sinope reached Paris on 11 December, and it has been said that the outcry of anger it aroused led directly to the outbreak of war a few months later. The *Times* correspondent declared that "the effect produced here [Paris] has been very great indeed, and the comments to which it gave rise cannot be passed over in silence."[4] La Gorce asserted that "the news from Constantinople was greeted without any reflection, and, imagination combined with reality, the public impression everywhere gave vent to an immense murmur of anger and pity."[5]

The first public reaction was revealed, of course, in the press. Here all shades of press opinion seemed united in condemning Russia.[6] But Napoleon III's reaction was even more violent than that of the press.

A burst of indignation [reported the *Times* correspondent] first followed that announcement [on Sinope], and I believe that for one whole day the Emperor was fully determined to undertake alone, if necessary, the task of protecting the Turks from future outrage in the Black Sea, if not of avenging those they have already endured. . . . . He declared on another occasion that, in the Eastern question, as it stood, there was but one course for him to follow, and that was *le sentier d'honneur*— the path of honor—and that he was determined to do so, even if he did it alone and unaided.[7]

Lord Cowley also obtained the same impression in his conversation with the emperor.[8] It is not surprising, then, that Napoleon III should interpret the press reaction and his own as that of opinion in general when he wrote his official protest to the czar.

The Sinope event [he declared] was for us as humiliating as it was unexpected. . . . . No longer was it our policy which had received a setback, it was our military honor. The cannon shots at Sinope resounded painfully in the hearts of all those in England and in France who have a strong feeling of national dignity . . . . . Hence the order given to our squadrons to enter the Black Sea.[9]

Sinope therefore did obtain a decided and unanimous reaction from the press, and it created the usual decline on the stock exchange.[10] But was the emperor justified in interpreting his own feeling and that of the press as the sentiment of general public opinion? What did the reports of the procureurs general and the prefects reveal as to the popular reaction to the Sinope incident? Curiously enough, after all the sound and fury in the press and in government and business circles, there was still almost no reaction to the Sinope incident among the common people. Out of all the procureur reports in January 1854 only one even mentioned a specific reaction to Sinope, and this one (from Aix) indicated more indifference than excitement, which would explain the absence of comments in the others.[11] Of the fourteen prefect reports consulted from departments carefully selected to represent the different geographical and economic areas, only six even mentioned public reaction to Sinope, and only one of these six indicated any real concern. This exception was from Gex, near Lyons, where the prefect reported that "except for concern which was caused by the possibility of war in Europe public opinion continues to offer all the symptoms of calm." This statement certainly had no resemblance to the thunder of the newspapers.[12]

All of this lethargy mingled with a pervading silence is in marked contrast with the impressions, described above, of O'Meagher of the *Times* and of La Gorce. One is left with the suspicion that La Gorce, like Emperor Napoleon, was reading into the public mind what he and his associates were saying to each other, while the *Times* correspondent was reporting as public opinion what he heard in government circles. Indeed, the Swiss minister, Barman, seemed to have had his ear down closer to the grass roots when, in reporting on public reaction to the news from Sinope, he remarked that "in France public opinion is not very susceptible, and the newspapers are not in a position to stir it up."[13]

The Outbreak of War

Only two months elapsed between Sinope and the rupture of diplomatic relations and less than three until the declaration of war. During this three-month period there were several diplomatic efforts either to avoid the fatal trend or to justify the positions of the powers. England and France protested Sinope and announced the entrance of their fleets into the Black Sea. Nesselrode for Russia countered with a complaint of Turkey's offensive action in the Black Sea and a protest against the Allied fleets. Napoleon III wrote a personal letter to the czar on 29 January asking for Russian withdrawal from the Principalities, Allied retirement from the Black Sea, and direct negotiations between Turkey and Russia. Before the czar's reply came, Russia broke off relations with the two Western powers because the fleets were not withdrawn from the Black Sea. Then on 19 February the czar's reply rejected the reciprocal withdrawal proposal. It needed only an Anglo-French ultimatum (14 March) and a Russian disdainful refusal to reply to bring the declaration of war by the two Western allies on 27 and 28 March.

If the Sinope incident had difficulty in arousing the general public, it will be interesting to observe whether the rapid descent to actual war caused any more positive public reactions and whether these reactions may have influenced in any way the fateful course of events.

La Gorce, a contemporary and a leading authority on this period, felt that the public was mute on the approaching war although he had previously claimed it was aroused over the Sinope affair. "While the voice of opinion in England was loud," he wrote, "just to the same extent it was veiled and muffled in France." "The press," he added, "either badly informed or afraid, remained silent."[14] In this estimate of the situation La Gorce is only partly right. To be sure there was very little significant discussion of the issue of war and peace in the press. Where it did appear, press opinion was inclined toward war, an attitude that was certainly not in harmony with general opinion. The press neither reflected opinion nor influenced it. Thiers expressed it well when he said: "If we had a free press and a tribune, I could rouse all France against Russia in a fortnight. But when he [Napoleon III] thought that opinion was against him, he destroyed all the means of influencing it. No one attends to what is said by his nominees in the Chamber; no one reads his paid newspapers."[15]

Turning from the press to the administrative sources of opinion, we find unfortunately that the reports of the procureurs general and the prefects give us relatively little information on war sentiment in January and February. What indications they do reveal are as contradictory as those of the press. The prefect in Alsace indicated that the radical republicans (*hommes de désordre*) were hoping for war. As for the majority he merely said they were "concerned," and business, he thought, would prefer war to the present uncertainties. The procureur general at Dijon likewise noted the desire of this same element for war and the apathy of the rural population on the question. From Lorraine the procureur report was more definite on general opinion:

> The circular of the minister of foreign affairs of 30 December last [wrote Gérando from Metz] has been favorably received by the upper classes of society, the only ones among whom political life is still manifested. This circular seemed to correspond to a feeling of justice and of national interest so evident that it obtained the approbation of diverse opinions. Whatever may be the apprehensions they may feel for the maintenance of the general peace and the secret hopes that party spirit may feel, the government can count entirely on the people of my district. At least up to now they are not seriously alarmed by the prospects of war. Their calm reflective patriotism . . . . understood the necessity of such a worthy attitude as Napoleon III has taken on the Eastern question and would not be lacking in support if he is obliged to back it up by force of arms.[16]

Yet this prowar sentiment of some groups in the northeast was not shared by people in the southwest. The procureur general and the prefect at Bordeaux reported that business circles did not like the uncertainties created by the threat of war. Only a small opposition group took hope from the prospects of an armed clash. In the Montpellier area business interests were disturbed by the dangers of war and alarmed at the hopes of the revolutionary elements. Massot, the procureur general at Toulouse, gave a much clearer and detailed picture of sentiment in this southwestern region:

> The vast majority of men concerned over the events in the East, strongly desire [désire avec vivacité] a peaceful settlement. . . . . The current of opinion does not run toward war, but it would allow itself to be channeled in that direction . . . . . The preceding indications apply almost exclusively to the educated classes . . . . . The real war for the masses, the kind they would understand best, would be a continental war. They are even a little astonished under the present circumstances to see us allied to the English whom they do not distinguish much from the Russians when we speak of the enemy. Nor are our southern provinces as spontaneously militaristic as, for example, the eastern regions of France. . . . . It cannot be said that the war would be popular, but it might become so later.

The merchants of Marseilles were also just as averse to war. This antiwar sentiment of the southwest was likewise seen in Normandy and Touraine. Rabou reported from Caen that "all eyes are turned towards the East: they fear war, and this apprehension paralyzes big industry," while the prefect at Tours stressed the bourgeois longing for a peaceful solution.[17]

The most we can glean from the Paris press and the reports from the provinces is that opinion was divided. The general prevalence of an outright prowar or antiwar sentiment was not clearly indicated.

A consultation of the soundings and observations of French contemporaries and of the foreign diplomats then residing in France, on the other hand, seem to reveal a definite and overwhelming aversion to a declaration of war. All during the critical month of February, Nassau Senior, a frequent English visitor to France, was interviewing French leaders (mostly of the Orleanist opposition) for their views on the impending war and the public reaction. His conversations with Thiers and Guizot bring out that these two elder statesmen were hostile to Russian policy and saw a war as the only solution. Yet these same men felt that opinion was not favorable to such a step. Guizot affirmed that there was "no public enthusiasm," and Thiers declared that the Legitimists, many of his own fellow Orleanists, and even some of Napoleon III's Bonapartist followers disliked the idea of a war against Russia and a French alliance with England.

> All the Royalists are against it [said Thiers]. They cannot bear to see Louis Napoleon fortified by the English alliance, and the more discreditable the compromise is to the country, the better it will please them, because it will be more

discreditable to him. The bourgeoisie cares only for its material interests and for a *paix à tout prix*. And of the small number of persons whose motives are patriotic, many are weak enough to believe that English interests are those really at stake, and that we have little to do with the matter. Even if he [the emperor] were virtually to give up all that we have been negotiating for, such a capitulation would be well received in France.[18]

Then up spoke Baron Rivet, who was to become famous later under the Third Republic for his presidency resolution in favor of Thiers. He maintained there would be a great outcry against war taxes. "Before a year is out," he predicted, "war will have become so unpopular that he [Napoleon III] will choose to think himself forced to escape from it by a separate peace, which he will buy by sacrificing his allies, perhaps by joining the enemy." One of Louis Napoleon's former cabinet members under the Second Republic, Léonard Faucher, also shared this gloomy view of opinion.

> Among the masses [he observed] the war and the famine have shaken him [the emperor's hold] frightfully. . . . . In Paris we make some allowances for the difficulties of his situation. . . . . But the provinces are exasperated. . . . . I do not believe he knows the severity of the famine, or that he suspects the hostility of public opinion.

Another former minister under Louis Philippe, Pierre Dumont, denounced Napoleon's letter to the czar as definite evidence that the former promoted the war. He then went on with this somber picture of opinion:

> The French public . . . . cares little about the matter in dispute and is anxious only to get out of the quarrel by any means whatever before more money has been spent and more speculators have been ruined.
> . . . . I have just been in the provinces; the country people whose votes gave that man [*celui-ci*] his throne, are unanimous against the war. 'That's going to bring on taxes,' says one. 'What's going to become of our boys?' says another. 'It's a long way off,' they all repeat.[19]

While these liberal Orleanist estimates of a uniformly antiwar opinion may be suspected of showing a partisan bias, the analyses by the foreign diplomats nevertheless give abundant confirmation of the views of Senior's friends. The dispatches of the Belgian minister, Firmin Rogier, between 6 January and 14 February revealed a continued dislike for the prospects of war. He noted the decline of quotations on the stock market with the entrance of the fleets in the Black Sea and with the publications of Drouyn de Lhuys's circular and the czar's letter to the emperor. On 23 January he wrote: "As I have already . . . . written you several times, public opinion is very much alarmed."[20]

This adverse reaction of the business world is also noted by Rogier's American and Swiss colleagues. Sanford noted that Drouyn de Lhuys's circular "produced a sort of panic here," and Barman reported in March that "alarm is very strong in business circles; a large number of failures have been announced here and in London, and they think a great many more are to be expected."[21]

In his diary for the day of 7 January the Austrian ambassador recorded that "the nation is indifferent, the middle classes fear the war, and the politicians of the former political parties [Legitimist and Orleanist] criticize the government for not having taken Russia's side on the Eastern question as the Restoration did." Twelve days later he noted that "public concern . . . . is increasing every day."[22]

When Kisselev departed, he left behind him in the Russian embassy a subordinate official, Poggenpohl, who undertook on his own initiative a little polling of the public on the boulevards and in the theaters of Paris. His account, while detailed and colorful, would seem prejudiced if it did not at the same time conform in general to the picture given by other observers:

> The attitude of public opinion in France [he wrote] is far from being hostile to us. Just recently on the Paris boulevards they were selling several broadsides . . . . containing songs against our emperor [the czar] which were in as bad taste as they were in bad style and language. Standing around smoking my cigar, I tried several times to find out just what was the public reaction. The very few people who even consented to buy them threw them away in disgust after reading one line. Several times I heard some of them exclaim, 'What trash!' I attended the play *Etoile du Nord*, which was a great success, and the audience applauded wildly when Peter the Great gave that fine speech to his soldiers . . . . . Indeed, there is nobody outside those in government circles, neither nobles, bourgeois, bankers, nor shopkeepers, who do not look on this war with regret and fear and who do not speak in our favor. Louis Napoleon is feared. They recognize his great Machiavellian ability but are ashamed of him and detest him. The lower classes are not concerned about anything, and the soldiers march off only because they have to.[23]

That this Russian official was not exactly whistling in the dark was confirmed by the testimony of the British themselves, who were about to become the allies of France. Greville recorded in his diary the impression prevailing in government circles in London:

> The accounts of the distress in France, the stagnation of trade, and the financial embarrassments, and the consequent alarm that prevails as well as suffering, make it very natural that the [French] Government should shrink from plunging into a war the duration of which is doubtful, but the expense certain.[24]

At the same time Lord Cowley was writing from the British embassy frantic alarums about the attitudes of the French people. "I cannot repeat too often," he warned Clarendon, "that the idea of war has become so unpopular that I do not wonder at the Emperor wishing to back out."[25] This pessimistic estimate was likewise duplicated by Sir Henry Ellis, a retired British diplomat in Paris, who told Senior in February that "the war is more than unpopular . . . . it is universally detested."[26]

Surely La Gorce was wrong when he said opinion was shrouded and mute. If shrouded, it was like a ghost, haunting the village squares and the city streets, whose apparitions were discerned, through the murky fog of prefabricated news, by a multitude of clairvoyants. Among these were the procureurs general and prefects, the Orleanist political leaders, and friend and foe and neutral in the diplomatic corps. And all of them, except the officials in Alsace and Lorraine, bore witness to French public opposition to the prospective war.

But mingled with this opposition to war was also a profound dislike of an alliance with England. There were too many memories of the eighteenth-century wars and the wars of Napoleon. Many of the people who were currently supporting Napoleon III did so through their devotion to the Napoleonic legend. Yet this and the Anglo-French commercial and naval rivalries kept alive a hostile feeling toward the British. Consequently the advocates of the alliance— the *Siècle*, the *Débats*, and the *Revue des deux mondes*—had a very hard row to hoe, but they remained undaunted.[27]

Although this limited advocacy was not too convincing to the French, it at least impressed the Austrian and American diplomatic representatives. Hübner asserted that Kisselev was wrong in thinking that the alliance would be just an idle fancy, and Mason, noting the "extraordinary harmony" between the French and British, felt certain that the ancient prejudices had ceased to exist.[28]

Actually, however, such harmony was conspicuous by its absence on the eve of the war, and the dislike of an English alliance contributed to the unpopularity of the war itself. In spite of the pro-English attitude of the Orleanist *Débats* and *Revue des deux mondes*, most of the Orleanists and Legitimists showed a great dislike for and distrust of England. The Legitimist *Union* insisted that England was merely trying to seduce France into supporting British interests, and the Legitimist *Assemblée Nationale* drummed constantly on this same theme.[29] Sainte-Aulaire told Senior to his face that he believed this was England's quarrel and tried to make him distrustful of France by warning that if England tried to train the French navy, it might one day be turned against the British. The liberal Orleanist, Cousin, spoke in the same vein to Senior and declared frankly that he preferred the preservation of the Russian navy for future use against the British. Such an attitude was prevalent enough to alarm Thiers, a pro-British Orleanist. "All the Legitimists and all the Orleanists," he complained to Senior, "are striving to make us distrust you and you distrust us." And Sir Henry Ellis, the retired English diplomat, came running to Senior with the same story:

> The few friends of the English alliance are in great alarm [he reported]. The Emperor's fidelity to you is attacked both by threats and solicitations. . . . . La Cour [former French ambassador to Constantinople] tells everybody that the rejection of the Vienna note by Turkey was suggested by Lord Stratford; [and] the French public believes this.[30]

Baron Beyens of Belgium added his testimony to that of others. He learned that anti-English plays were increasing in popularity in the provincial cities. "In France," he said, "the alliance could not be popular; too many bad recollections still separated the two nations more widely than the English Channel."[31] Finally even the British ambassador became convinced of the predominance of the anti-English sentiment.

> You have no idea [Cowley wrote to Clarendon] how the tide of public opinion is setting against us here, and it is spreading to the Emperor's entourage. 'What business have we with an English alliance? It has always brought us bad luck!' is in every one's mouth. Then the old story of France being engaged on an English question, that we want Egypt, etc., etc.
>
> . . . . As for me, I am supposed to be the incarnation of war itself, merely because I say that it would be dishonorable to abandon Turkey and truckle to Russia.[32]

If the British ambassador had to make such a bitter admission, contrary to all his highest hopes, there is little doubt but that the Legitimist-Orleanist campaign had borne fruit in turning a large segment of the French public against the English.

This strong tide of opinion against war and against the British was bound to have its influence on the emperor and the government. As the war crisis became more acute in mid-January 1854 and public antiwar sentiment became clearer, the Austrian ambassador and the Belgian minister both noted a growing concern in official circles. "The uneasiness of government officials," Hübner noted, "is increasing daily." In a personal note to the Belgian foreign minister Firmin Rogier confided that "among all my [diplomatic] colleagues and the political leaders with whom I have occasion to speak there are perhaps not more than three who still have hopes of avoiding war."[33]

This alarm was vigorously expressed in a meeting of the French council of state and council of ministers, which had been called by the emperor to consider the Russian protest note which arrived about 23 January. Russia was demanding an explanation of the presence of the western fleets in the Black Sea and assurances of their prompt withdrawal. Napoleon III demanded the separate opinion of each minister on what reply he should give. We do not know all that went on in these cabinet discussions, but some rumors leaked out. Persigny, the minister of interior, was for a forceful policy side by side with England. But at least two members present (Bineau, minister of finance, and Fould, councillor of state) were for some sort of accommodation with Russia. Bineau was reported to have threatened to resign if war broke out because he thought, considering the present state of opinion and business conditions, it would be impossible to raise the necessary funds for the war.[34] Lord Cowley also received intimations of this opposition when he reported a few days later about anti-British sentiment "spreading even to the emperor's entourage."[35]

While the emperor, according to Faucher, declared in the meeting that he could not break with England, he was evidently impressed by the public opposition and the debates among his advisors. Cowley in alarm reported home that Napoleon definitely wanted "to back out."[36] At least the emperor wished to prolong the diplomatic phase of the dispute by writing an appeal directly to the czar. This became his famous letter of 29 January. That this move was inspired by antiwar opinion he freely confided to Hübner on the same day. "Every government [the emperor declared] must consider public opinion. But public opinion looks for moderation in the sovereign. So I have given proof of moderation by writing a letter today to Emperor Nicholas . . . . . "[37] On the same evening at a ball at the Palais Royal, Rogier noted that the occasion was not very gay. All the court and the government notables seemed very uneasy, and the emperor himself told Rogier that the situation was most obscure.[38]

The antiwar sentiment of opinion was unmistakable, and its sobering effect on the emperor and his imperial court was noticeable to many reliable observers. But the czar's uncompromising reply made the war inevitable in spite of its unpopularity. From here on it is merely a matter of tracing the fluctuations of opinion during the years of reverses, delays, and costly victories until at last peace again returned in a momentary blaze of glory for the French.

Early Months of the War

Between the time of the rupture of diplomatic relations (4 February) and the declaration of war (27 March) the French government tried in several ways to elicit public support for the impending war. First a translation of the British documents on England's prewar negotiations with Russia was published on 5 February; and then a similar collection of French documents was issued in the newspapers and in pamphlet form during the same month.[39] These were attempts to convince world opinion that France and Britain had done all they could to bring their disagreement with Russia to a peaceful solution and to reveal Russia's ambitions and her recalcitrant attitude.

This part of the campaign seems to have been successful. From all parts of France there came approbation of the prewar negotiations. Leaving out of consideration the inspired semiofficial press, we see the two leading Orleanist organs, the *Revue des deux mondes* and the *Débats*, approve the government's earlier efforts.[40] Of course the democratic *Siècle* was already convinced of the righteousness of France's cause, but Havin, its editor, added a comment of interest on their respect for opinion:

The almost meticulous care that each government took to show the justice of its course, not only to its own nationals but also to foreigners, reflects the greatest respect for human life, the greatest respect for opinion, which, in spite of all efforts, still remains the queen of the world.[41]

Those administrative reports which spoke specifically about the prewar documents all testify to a favorable public reaction, and these come from many different sections of the country. The prefect report from Finistère (Brittany) was perhaps the most sweeping in its favorable estimate of opinion:

> The upper class is unanimous in rendering homage to the wisdom and moderation of the Emperor. *All men of all shades of opinion, without exception,* are agreed in recognizing . . . . that the Eastern question was admirably handled, that His Majesty did all he could to avoid war.

The upper classes of Alsace approved the "wise and energetic conduct of Eastern affairs," those of Franche-Comté "applaud the skillfulness of the negotiations," and similar sentiments were described by the prefects of Ain and Gironde. The prefect in Limoges affirmed that "the efforts of the government to assure peace . . . . had the unanimous approval of men of the most contradictory political opinions."[43]

Then, in addition to the publication of the dispatches between ambassadors and foreign ministers, the French government published Napoleon's letter of 29 January to Nicholas I in the *Moniteur* of 14 February. The urgency of using this letter to influence opinion is underlined by the fact that it was made public before the czar had had a chance to reply. Cowley said the official explanation was that erroneous press reports of its contents had to be spiked by the revelation of its actual terms, but he also learned that they wanted its publication before the French people read the hostile debates in the British parliament.[44] In it was found the veiled threat of the two allies:

> . . . . If Your Majesty desires a peaceful settlement as much as I do, what would be simpler than to declare that an armistice will be signed today, that things will return to diplomatic negotiations, and that all troops will be withdrawn from the places where warlike motives had sent them. . . . . If Your Majesty adopts this plan agreed upon by the Queen of England and myself, quiet will be restored, the world will be satisfied . . . . . But if Your Majesty counters with a rejection, then France and England will be obliged to leave to the fortune of arms and to the hazards of war what could be decided today by reason and justice.[45]

Here was an offer and a challenge which the French people were allowed to read before the answer had been received.

The diplomatic observers found the public reaction generally unfavorable. The Belgian and Swiss ministers both reported that the letter caused a big stir, alarmed the stock market, and convinced people generally that the czar would reject it.[46] Cowley was particularly alarmed at the response to the published letter:

> I cannot exaggerate [he wrote Clarendon] . . . . the bad impression produced on all persons with whom I have conversed by the publication of the Emperor's letter to the Emperor of Russia. I have met with no one who has attempted to defend it. Those, including the ministers, who do not blame it, take refuge in silence.
> . . . . I should add that when the letter first appeared, people were so convinced that the answer to it must have been received and was unfavorable or that the letter could not have been published that the funds fell 3 per cent. There are not wanting those who declare that the Emperor was persuaded to give his letter publicity to have a very different effect upon the public securities and who have suffered severe losses in consequence.[47]

The comment of Napoleon's Orleanist opponent, Dumon, was very caustic. "This letter crowns the whole," he cried to Senior, "it throws on him the responsibility of the war, and that responsibility will crush him."[48] Even the semiofficial *Constitutionnel* limited its comments to reporting a "deep impression caused in Paris and the provinces" by the letter. It devoted the rest of its remarks to praising the emperor for taking the public into his confidence.[49] Only the American minister reported a favorable response. "The publication," he wrote, " . . . . appeared to be received by all parties with satisfaction approaching enthusiasm."[50]

While Mason's impression contradicted those of his colleagues, it was even more positive than the administrative reports from the provinces. Three prefects were about as noncommittal as the *Constitutionnel* had been. In Ain the impression was said to be "strong, the effect startling"; the prefect at Bordeaux said that the letter had "clarified" the subject; while the one in Rouen noted "a deep and lasting effect." Only from three other departments of the fifteen consulted was there some moderate approval reported: The subprefect at Trévoux (Ain) said everybody considered the letter a chef d'oeuvre. In the department of Meuse the letter had "excited the most patriotic sympathies of the country people." Nothing was said about the other classes. The people of Manche (Cotentin peninsula) "rendered homage to the language of the emperor's letter."[51] Napoleon III must have been keenly disappointed at the signs of disapproval countered only by the damning of faint praise.

Entering thus into the first war of his reign with such a hostile or unenthusiastic public attitude, the emperor felt impelled to make a particularly convincing defense of his policy and a strong appeal for public support in his speech of 2 March delivered before a joint session of the reconvened parliament. At the very beginning of the part of his speech dealing with foreign affairs he tried to make very clear the fact that he had done everything humanly possible to avoid a war.

Last year [he said], in my opening speech, I promised to do all in my power to maintain peace and to reassure Europe. I have kept my word. To avoid a conflict, I have gone just as far as honor will permit. (Unanimous agreement.) Europe now knows beyond a shadow of a doubt that if France draws the sword, it is because she has been forced to do it.

Like so many statesmen in similar positions on the eve of other wars he tried to persuade France and all Europe that he had no selfish ulterior motives but rather the highest of moral impulses in accepting the Russian challenge. Then he turned to meet the traditional antagonism against France's new ally, England.

Now England, our ancient rival, tightens the bonds of an ever closer alliance with us because the ideas we defend are at the same time those of the English people.

From England he turned to the German powers to show that there was a general condemnation of Russia.

Germany, who had retained a rather defiant attitude [toward France] because of the memory of bygone wars and who for that reason had for the last forty years shown perhaps too much deference to the policy of St. Petersburg, has already reassumed an independent outlook and freely decides on what side her interests lie. Austria especially, who cannot look indifferently on impending events, will join our alliance and thereby will confirm the moral and righteous character of the war we are undertaking. (Applause.)

After making this rather hazardous prediction about Austria, he tried to meet another current opposition argument about France fighting England's war.

France has as much as or even more interest than England in seeing that Russian influence does not spread indefinitely to Constantinople, for to rule over Constantinople is to rule over the Mediterranean. And none of you, Gentlemen, I believe, will say that England is the only one who has a great interest in that sea which washes upon three hundred leagues of our shores. Besides, that policy of ours does not just date from yesterday. For centuries every national government in France has followed it; I will not desert it now. (Loud applause.)

Don't let them ask any more what business we have over there in Constantinople. We are there with England to defend the cause of the sultan and indeed at the same time to protect the rights of Christians. We are there to defend the freedom of the seas and our rightful influence in the Mediterranean. We are there with Germany to help her preserve her position there, which another is trying to reduce, to assure her frontiers against the preponderance of a too powerful neighbor . . . . . (Prolonged applause.)

Then the speech ends with a final appeal to the public opinion of the nation.

On this solemn occasion, Gentlemen, as on all those occasions when I need to appeal to the country, I am sure of your support, (Yes! Yes! the deputies shout) for I have always found in you the generous sentiments animating the nation. So, fortified by that support, by the nobility of our cause, by the sincerity of our alliances and confident especially in God's protection, I hope soon to have peace which cannot again be disturbed by one man with impunity.[52]

Thus the emperor in his war speech began and ended on a note of peace, rather clear acknowledgment of his sensing the antiwar sentiment of the people.

Although one cannot put too much trust in the official *Moniteur* when it reports "applause" and "shouts of approval" by the legislators, there is no doubt that the speech was well received by Napoleon's handpicked parliament. The American minister confirms that "it was received with great enthusiasm by those to whom it was addressed."[53]

As to the reaction to the speech outside the chambers, it does not seem to have been quite so unanimous. O'Meagher, the *Times* correspondent, in his reading of the Paris papers and in his conversations with informed people found that it gave rise "to very varied criticism." "On the whole," he added, "the effect is favourable, with the exception that the allusion to the Austrian alliance is not considered as being positive enough."[54] Of course the semiofficial press gave its obsequious approval. But even the hostile Legitimist and Ultramontane paper, the *Univers*, came out in support of the declaration of war.[55] But another opposition paper (Fusionist: Legitimist-Orleanist), the *Assemblée Nationale,* struck a sour note. While owning that all must now unite in support of the war, the editor went on to say that the speech took up questions which he neither could nor would discuss. He regretted, however, that the war had been undertaken and feared that the Ottoman Empire would not survive the war, whichever side won.[56] Although this was a mild and covert attack on the government, the authorities pounced on the paper immediately and suspended its publication for two months.[57] This was to be a warning to the press on its freedom to discuss war issues but also is a reminder to historians on the unreliability of the badgered press as a reflection of general opinion.

In addition to describing the favorable legislative response to the speech the American minister also described, perhaps regretfully, the growth of Anglo-French comradeship.[58]

The secret reports from the prefects, however, also confirm O'Meagher's and Mason's impression of a favorable public reaction. The report on opinion in Dauphiné (Grenoble) is typical and perhaps the most detailed of those consulted. The prefect of Isère made the following report after a tour around his department:

> I was very happy to find—and it was the salient fact of my inspection trip—that everywhere in the countryside the Eastern war is understood with an astonishing accuracy. The mayors of the rural communes as well as their inhabitants are convinced that justice is on the side of France, and the government can count on the vigorous support of opinion on the question of the war. . . . . The interests of Russia are weakly defended in a few rare drawing rooms, and even there only in a lukewarm manner. . . . . The conduct of the czar appears to [the Legitimists] to be just as condemnable as it is senseless and in their opinion it is the duty of Europe to chain up this crazy man (the exact word of a Legitimist).

This general attitude in Dauphiné is also confirmed by the procureur general in the province.

But from other parts of the country came prefect reports of similar reactions. From Normandy the prefect of Seine-Inférieure noted public pride and renewed patriotism at seeing France reassume world leadership. The prefect of Manche informed the government that "public opinion . . . . knows that the struggle is imposed by the gravest and most legitimate interests." "All shades of opinion," he added, "are agreed in rendering homage to the language [of the Emperor] so full of nobility and frankness." From Brittany the report was the same. In Ain department, near Lyons, it was observed that the patriotic and national feeling of the masses applauded the emperor's policy. Likewise a favorable prefect report was received from Bordeaux. Only from Versailles and the industrial suburbs of Paris was any dissatisfaction noted. Here the declaration of war alarmed the merchants and industrialists, but they accepted the war as unavoidable under the circumstances.[59]

Thus in the early months of the war antiwar sentiment changed to resignation or to patriotic support of a conflict which Frenchmen held had been thrust upon them. The emperor's speech, tuned to these varying moods, gave occasion not only for rallying support but for observing its intensity.

Discouragement in 1854

The first nine months of the war were none too impressive as to progress toward victory. Austria on 2 June 1854 called upon Russia to evacuate the Principalities, and later in the same month the Russians complied with the understanding that it would encourage Austria's neutrality. This move greatly perplexed the Anglo-French allies who had massed forces and supplies for a Danubian campaign. After some hesitations and uncertainties the Western allies in August chose the Crimea as their new theater of operations and Sebastopol with its naval base as their objective. However, before French forces embarked for the Crimea they were swept by a severe cholera epidemic which took five thousand lives (12 per cent of the whole force), and large quantities of their supplies were consumed by a great fire in Varna.

Once in the Crimea the Allies soon came to grips with the Russians in a series of bloody battles of Alma, Balaklava, and Inkermann, which were costly to both sides but indecisive. Then all of the severities of winter set in with biting cold, heavy rains, and muddy terrain. The ensuing suffering was heightened both by lack of fuel, food, and warm uniforms for a winter campaign and by an unusual hurricane which struck the camps. The result was a new wave of sickness. Some men contracted dysentery, pneumonia, scurvy, typhus, or cholera; others suffered from frozen limbs and attendant infections or amputations. The serious cases evacuated to Constantinople alone amounted to twelve thousand. Among the evacuees was Marshal de Saint-Arnaud himself, commander of the French expedition, who was a victim of the continuing cholera epidemic. He died on 29 September during the voyage back to France.[60]

The tragic news from the Crimea as well as the lack of any decisive military progress was bound to replace the initial mild support of the war with a mood of discouragement. As early as 14 August 1854 Charles de Mazade noted a general discouragement and impatience over the lack of progress.[61]

In the midst of this discouragement came, what was worse, a false report of the capture of Sebastopol. A Tartar dispatch carrier had brought the news from Constantinople to Vienna. The government was so anxious to counter the disgruntled mood of the public that it unwisely publicized the news on 3 October before it was confirmed. Announcing that the news came from the French ambassador in Vienna, the government's statement in the *Moniteur* added cautiously, "The government has not yet received direct and official news of the capture of Sebastopol." The public would naturally be led to believe that it was only a matter of confirmation. This belief would also be fortified by an announcement on the same page of the *Moniteur* that the Austrian foreign minister had sent his most sincere congratulations "for the striking success of our troops in the Crimea."[62] While the congratulations might very well have referred to the battle of Alma (20 September), the vagueness of the wording left the impression that even a neutral country was convinced of the fall of Sebastopol. The government bungled the affair further when it learned that Sebastopol had not fallen. To cushion the embarrassing news, it published the congratulations of the Austrian emperor himself two days before the admission of the falsity of the Sebastopol report. Then on 6 October came the cryptic two lines in the *Moniteur:* "The Tartar's story is denied direct from Bucharest."[63]

Napoleon III was not wrong in anticipating an adverse reaction by the public to the official credence given the false news. Henri Dabot, a lively, ubiquitous lawyer in Paris, tells us in his diary of the dashed hopes in the French capital.

During the day [30 September] the Salle des Pas Perdus[64] was full of joy and excitement; this evening the theaters are illuminated. The people are not illuminating, however; they are no doubt awaiting the official confirmation of the news.

6 October 1854. The news was false; they believed in it enough to be very dejected on learning officially of its falsity.[65]

Mazade noted that there was great disappointment when the report was denied;[66] Taxile Delord wrote later:

When the truth became known, everybody appeared dismayed as if we had just suffered a defeat; the public forgot Alma; it seemed even that no one was willing to accept as compensation the series of successful maneuvers and progressive advances which brought the Allies almost in view of Sebastopol.[67]

On hearing of the costly and indecisive battles of Balaklava and Inkermann in late October and early November, La Gorce records that at Paris a very strong feeling of discouragement developed with a realization that this conflict was going to drag out into a long war. People began to wonder whether the gains to be won by the war would equal the losses to be sustained.[68] The Swiss minister declared: "Serious concern prevails in the populace, which was not prepared for such stubborn resistance on the part of the Russians. Trade and industry, which up to now had endured the burden of events, are now very affected by it."[69] At the end of the year Henri Dabot, looking back on the past twelve months, recorded in his diary the discouraged mood of Parisians:

Doleful year's end. Because of the Crimean war everybody is sad in spite of the recent victories at Balaklava and Inkermann. The siege of Sebastopol goes on; our poor soldiers suffer horribly from cold in the trenches; the thoughts of every one are tortured by the memory of the famous winter of 1812 which was the salvation of Russia and the beginning of our disasters.[70]

a rather ugly thought on top of such an indecisive year.

The earliest reports of the procureurs general for January 1855 (reporting on the previous six months) also seemed to confirm this ominous mood of the public. The report from the generally hostile district of Bourges came in first (sent on 28 December). In it the procureur general noted that opinion was very much concerned over the war and was impatiently counting on an early victory.[71] A few days later Massot reported from Rouen on "impatience at the failures of the campaign in the Crimea and the prospects of . . . a long war."[72] And the third report to arrive, from Dijon, was even more discouraging. De Marnas wrote: "If difficulties continue, if the war drags out for a considerable length of time, perseverance will become wearied and this premature weariness will become a source of discontent, a veritable complaint against the government."[73] The story from the procureur general of Aix was in a similar vein.[74]

By the end of the month the rest of the procureur reports and some prefect reports had been received, and seven more (eleven in all) revealed dissatisfaction with the progress of the war. In the north the feeling in Paris and Brittany seemed similar to that in the Rouen area of Normandy. Although the procureurs general in Paris and Rennes (Brittany) reassured the minister of justice that the alarm was not general, they indicated certain signs of discontent. In Paris and in the nearby department of Eure-et-Loire the war was exciting the greatest concern. Bodan wrote from Rennes that "concern was strong and profound over the complications in foreign policy (negotiations with Austria) and the dangers and sickness in the army." "In the city of Rennes," he continued, "the delay in the siege of Sebastopol [underlined by pencil in the ministry] and the military operations undertaken in the East, badly understood and interpreted, had appeared to give hopes to the Socialist party which has held a few meetings." Besançon, to the east of Dijon (already noted), also showed signs of impatience. Likewise in the less enthusiastic southwestern France there was evidence of the same dejected mood. From Bordeaux came reports of "burning solicitude," "painful uneasiness," "fear" of increasing conscription, and of Legitimist satisfaction with the "prolonged siege of Sebastopol." And the prefect at this port similarly pointed out "the excessive impatience of the [Bordeaux] public concerning the events of the war." In Poitiers there was "impatience at the results of the siege of Sebastopol" and in the Vendée an uneasiness over finding farmhands to replace the sons who had gone off to war. In only two reports, from Haut-Rhin and Agen, was there any semblance of satisfaction.[75]

Discouragement in 1855

The French public, which had experienced a general disappointment over the lack of progress in the war during 1854, found little encouragement during the first nine months of 1855. There is nothing so depressing as quickened hopes suddenly dashed by reverses. Just as in the case of the false news of the fall of Sebastopol in 1854, this was also the character of developments in the Crimean War between March and September 1855. On 2 March, Czar Nicholas I, who had been in the minds of the French the personification of Russian belligerency and intransigence, had died. Yet his successor, Alexander II, who had been reputed to be unfavorable to the war, showed no signs of reversing his father's policy. This attitude was particularly confirmed in the negotiations at Vienna between March and June of 1855. Russia rejected the neutralization of the Black Sea and even the limitation of her naval power in those waters. As a last desperate attempt Lord John Russell for Great Britain and Drouyn de Lhuys for France drew up in Vienna a compromise plan of naval balance which, if rejected by Russia, they hoped would lead Austria to join the allies in the war. To the consternation of the negotiators the compromise plan was rejected by their own governments, and Drouyn de Lhuys was left no other alternative than resignation. This diplomatic failure was followed by military failures. A small success at the Mamelon-Vert on 7 June was overshadowed by a severe defeat at Malakoff eleven days later in which the British and French suffered 4,900 casualties.

The effect of the unfortunate and unprofitable winter on the mood of the French public was very unfavorable. "It was humiliating for France," wrote Delord, "to be forever besieging a fortress as in the days of Louis XIV; public opinion was astonished at the slowness of the siegè of Sebastopol."[76] Nassau Senior was back in France again, inquiring about the effect of the war during the winter on Napoleon III's popularity. Duvergier gave him a very gloomy report: "At first, while all was smiling, it [the war] did him good. But that has been worse than undone during the last four months. Though we have no news correspondents, we have letters from the army, and their contents are terrible." On the following day he put the same question to Moritz de Mohl, the German economist who was at that time studying French industry and who had had a good opportunity to observe business opinion. Mohl only confirmed Delord and Duvergier.[77]

Knowledge of these trends, particularly as indicated by the procureur reports of the previous January, made Napoleon III very uneasy. Finally in February he decided to go to the Crimea in person and hasten the capture of Sebastopol. However much discontent existed on the progress of the war, a definite adverse reaction greeted this proposal. The procureur general in Amiens declared:

The announcement of the [proposed] departure of the emperor for the theater of the war has been a touchstone for the feeling of the country. The first reaction was one of great and general concern. Even the parties least disposed to gratitude toward the man who has saved them have become seriously afraid of the dangerous misfortunes to which . . . . the emperor might expose himself. . . . . This attitude has been particularly that of a portion of the Legitimists.

On the other hand the Socialists in Amiens were reputed to be glad to be rid of the emperor's presence.[78] The Republican-Socialist ("anarchist") group in Orleans was also accused by the local procureur general of wishing the emperor would carry out his Crimean plan. Rouland in Paris noted that "public opinion was aroused by the plan for the emperor's departure," and the ministry penciled this passage on receipt of it.[79] Likewise the prefect of Ain (near Lyons) reported the public alarm caused by the news of the emperor's projected departure. He warned that the Socialists were ready to act and that refugees in Geneva would swarm back into France with such encouragement.[80]

If even the Legitimists showed alarm at the prospects of the emperor's departure, it is not surprising that the emperor's own followers should have become concerned. "At the first intimation of the plan," remarked La Gorce, "there was in the monarch's entourage one vast rumble of disapprobation and alarm; these servants of this prince, usually so quick to disagree among themselves, were united this time in a unanimous agreement."[81] Baroche, the president of the council of state, also reported that when Napoleon III tried to reassure them by suggesting Marshal Vaillant as regent instead of Prince Napoleon, "the silence of the ministers was the only reply."[82] Cowley in his correspondence related that the ministers were alarmed and that there was actual panic in the town. Intimations of the impending imperial departure were in fact fortifying the urge for peace. Any terms now, the British ambassador feared, would be acceptable to bring the French army home.[83] Cowley's estimate was confirmed by Persigny when he told Lord Malmesbury that "the Emperor must be stopped at any cost from going to the Crimea even if we have to make peace." Magne, the minister of finance, insisted that the emperor's departure would bring on a financial collapse. "All the creditors of the state will demand their money, and no one will give it financial support."[84]

The emperor found that his proposed Crimean trip, inspired in part by public impatience, had only increased the uneasiness in the country. The remedy had been worse than the disease. He therefore finally gave up the idea.[85]

The news of the death of Nicholas I arrived in France late on 2 March, and the immediate reaction was a hope that the change of ruler in Russia would mean peace. The next day government bonds experienced an almost unprecedented rise of five francs, and all other investments went up in proportion—a sure sign of optimism whether justified or not.[86] In the salons which Hübner frequented people were congratulating themselves that peace would be aided by the czar's death.[87] Both the Swiss and Belgian ministers confirmed Hübner's impression of the salons and suggested a similar reaction among the people in Paris.[88] But in the procureur reports of four months later only the one from Nancy noted a public inclination to interpret the czar's death as a prelude to peace.[89]

However, within two days after the arrival of the news, opinion was already beginning to have its doubts. O'Meagher wrote to the *Times:*

> The great question which occupies our minds is whether his death is likely or not to lead to peace. Opinions are divided on this point. The more sanguine do not hesitate to regard that event as a solution of all our difficulties; others consider it on the contrary as a new complication. Some feel convinced that peace is all but made; while others cannot help foreseeing new dangers from a new reign.[90]

A week later disillusion had set in completely, with the aid of the government's semiofficial paper, the *Constitutionnel.* On 12 March Ceséna wrote in its columns:

> With the man dead, still there remains the people, the system, and the tradition. Whatever his name, the sovereign who reigns in St. Petersburg is always the czar; and the czar is neither Nicholas or Alexander. It's rather the thought of Catherine, of Peter, in fact of Russia. Emperor Alexander, just by succeeding Nicholas, cannot change the policies of his ancestors nor smooth out the difficulties of the situation.[91]

This sobering view was echoed by the Orleanist, Charles de Mazade, who noted that Alexander had promised to carry out the policies of his ancestors and could not very well make a peace gesture while Sebastopol was under full attack.[92]

This press reaction had its influence on the public in general. The Swiss minister gave a detailed picture of the later dejection:

> The hopes for peace [he wrote], which the czar's death had inspired, have, if not completely vanished, at least appreciably diminished. I have never seen in this country, even though notorious for its hasty impressions, such a sudden and emphatic change. After a little reflection they have become convinced that nothing has changed in the traditional policy of Russia, even though she has a ruler who is less adroit, less firm, and endowed with less prestige.[93]

At least one report noted the same reaction in the provinces. From the Vendée the prefect wrote that "they had hoped at first that this unforeseen event would bring an end to the war but, although the people want peace, they no longer believe in it today."[94]

On the heels of the dejection over Alexander II's disinclination to make peace and the failure of the Vienna negotiations in the spring of 1855 came the news of the defeat at Malakoff. La Gorce gives us a vivid description of what he thought was the French reaction:

> From one end of France to the other the emotion [evoked by this news] was extreme. There was no explosion of anger or frightened outcry, but a painful anxiety in every heart . . . . . Disapproval of the war was overwhelming by its very moderation. Nothing was heard except a grave and restrained murmur, a pitiable, almost respectful wail, through which could be detected at times the heartrending cry of mothers calling for their lost sons.[95]

This description is eloquent and may well have reflected La Gorce's own reaction and that of his close acquaintances. But La Gorce asserts that "the newspapers were silent,"[96] and we know that the procureur reports were not yet available to historians at the time of his writing. It is therefore doubtful whether he had any sound basis for determining the sentiment "from one end of France to the other" or "in every heart." It would be difficult to prove that there was "no explosion of anger or frightened outcry" in all of France.

Turning away from such flights of fancy, however intuitive they may have been, we find that some papers and periodicals did not remain silent. While the *Débats* did mention the defeat without any subsequent comment,[97] the *Constitutionnel* tried to alleviate anticipated discouragement. "The most valiant armies," wrote Ceséna, "in the course of their most glorious campaigns have had their misfortunes and reverses. Some great and decisive battles had been won the night before and lost the morning after. Everything depends on the success at the eleventh hour and in the last battle."[98] Not too much comfort could be gained from such observations.

Mazade in the *Revue des deux mondes* was more outspoken. After recalling the disastrous winter in the Crimea and the outbreak of epidemic, he went on to discuss the latest reverse at Malakoff. A victory there would have hastened peace, he thought. Now the war would have to drag on. He even reviewed the losses sustained in the battle. Two weeks later he was back again on the same distasteful theme. He noted significantly that public opinion had its influence everywhere, even in France, and complained that there had not been force enough at Malakoff to sustain the attack. The capture of Malakoff, he thought, would not be decisive, but the strength of allied arms would thereby be demonstrated in victorious fashion. It must be tried again.[99] The fact that Mazade and the *Revue des deux mondes* were strong supporters of the war only emphasized all the more their keen disappointment at the turn of events.

The foreign observers in France seem to confirm that the attitude of Mazade was representative of the general public. Greville, who was in Paris at the time, recorded in his diary that "this failure has cast a great gloom over Paris."[100] The Belgian minister described the discouragement thus: "The telegram published yesterday by the *Moniteur* has made the worst of impressions. They were expecting news of a striking success, and General Pélissier announces to the government a costly reverse. June 18th seems to be an unlucky day for France [also date of Waterloo]."[101] The Swiss minister also noted the "bad impression" caused by the Malakoff news and added that the lack of details had given free rein to the most pessimistic imaginations.[102]

If this fragmentary evidence on Paris seems to indicate discouragement in the capital, what sort of reaction occurred in the provinces? Here again the evidence is fragmentary. Only four procureur reports in July 1855 specifically mentioned Malakoff, but these four are distributed all the way from the north to the south in eastern France (Amiens, Nancy, Besançon, and Aix). Only one of these reports, that from Aix, shows any favorable attitude of the people. From there the procureur general wrote: "I can happily assert from the various points in my district that far from exaggerating the results of the setback on June 18th, they had only seen in this event an ordinary incident of a war of siege and that confidence in the success of our arms had remained the same." Later on in his report, however, he does hint at some impatience. "If they all are impatient to hear of new successes, they also do not doubt the [eventual] triumph of our arms."[103] The situation was therefore probably not all sweetness and light even in Aix.

But farther north the attitude became more grim. The report from Besançon was forthright in its frankness.

If we look to the bottom of things, the situation is no longer the same [under-lined by pencil in the ministry]. The vicissitudes of the war in the East . . . . make the biggest impression at the moment, furnish a text for the sullen opposition, and find a useful auxiliary in the instability of public opinion. The telegraphic reports from the Crimea every day read with avidity by an anxious crowd, produce the most contradictory reactions. The feeling of absolute security of one day gives way to discouragement on the next. . . . .They are not without apprehension over the outcome of the Crimean campaign, and our latest reverse there has given us a chance to see how easily opinion lets itself go from confidence to discouragement.[104]

From Nancy in Lorraine the procureur general reported that the setback of 18 June had embittered opinion and that the dema-gogues were not missing the opportunity of exploiting this feeling.[105] While the procureur general in Amiens asserted that the people in general were cheerfully supporting the war, he admitted that there was a sullen and discontented minority who fed upon the defeats, the hopeless prospects of any real constructive results from the war, the epidemics, and the economic dislocation.[106]

Naturally the Malakoff defeat would be expected to have an adverse effect on opinion. Likewise the dictatorial regime discouraged newspaper editors and the man in the street from giving public vent to their feelings. Yet from the fragmentary evidence on Paris and the provinces it is possible to discern the prevalence and the degree of a further decline of war spirit in the middle of 1855 as a result of the defeat at Malakoff.

The shock of the Malakoff defeat again trailed off into a long period of sullen discouragement lasting all summer. Rogier, the Belgian minister, gave one of his best discriptions of this continuing disgruntled mood.

The insignificance of the recent telegraphic dispatches [he wrote], sent by General Pélissier and published by the *Moniteur,* is not of a nature to satisfy the impatient curiosity of the public and does not fulfill the promise, so often renewed, that a great blow is about to be struck. It is to be feared that the confidence of the country in a definite triumph may be a little weakened by the delays and ever-reappearing difficulties of this siege that is unparalleled in military annals.[107]

But it was in this summer of continuing war that a new crop of reports came in from procureurs general and prefects. An examination of these gives ample confirmation of Rogier's account. The procureur general at Bordeaux wrote:

> The prolongation of the war [he said] nevertheless begins, I must not conceal, to cause a certain weariness to appear [previous five words underlined in pencil] in one part of the population. But it is noticeable that it is neither the agricultural nor laboring classes who seem to feel it so much. It is rather the business and leisure classes which are troubled by it [the war] in their transactions and specu- lations and which hope most devoutly for a return of peace as a vital factor in their prosperity.[108]

The report of the prefect at Bordeaux was almost identical.[109] The procureur general near Marseilles, while asserting that Malakoff did not discourage his area very much, went on to reveal an unwhole-some morale in many quarters.[110] Similar reports of war-weariness were received from almost every part of the country. Listed from north to south, here are the cities from which the reports came: Rouen, Douai, Caen, Amiens, Metz, Bar-le-Duc, Tours, Orleans, Besançon, Lyons, Riom, Limoges, and Toulouse.[111]

From only three cities—Grenoble, Rennes, and Saint-Lô—were the reports encouraging in regard to morale. A typical one from Grenoble said:

> In all classes of society the necessity of war sacrifices is understood, and the hopes for success animate and support everywhere the energy of our people. When the adjournment of [the conferences of Vienna] destroyed their hopes of peace, this news was treated in our departments without impatience or discouragement.

The reports from Rennes and Saint-Lô were in similar terms.[112] But of the reports mentioning morale sixteen showed a continued decline and only three a favorable and patient attitude. In all of these reports were found discussions of subversive activities of Legitimists and Republicans, playing upon the war discouragement to undermine the popularity of the imperial regime.

The Urge for Peace

The depressed spirits of the French people, only slightly relieved by the distractions attending Queen Victoria's state visit to Paris in August, were definitely lifted by the genuine news of victory in Sep-tember. On the eighth the combined French and British forces had finally made an all-out assault on the fortifications outside Sebastopol. The British were repulsed at the Grand Redan, but the French finally took full possession of Malakoff. Thereupon the Russians evacuated Sebastopol, and the allies reached their long-sought goal.

The first news arrived in Paris by telegraph on 9 September, telling only of Malakoff's capture. After the false news in 1854 the people hesitated to celebrate without further confirmation. Then towards the evening of the next day the guns of the Invalides boomed forth the news of some great triumph, and the papers and bulletins announced the fall of Sebastopol itself. La Gorce says that it was only after several days with repeated confirmations that skepticism yielded to rejoicing.[113] But the Belgian minister tells us that right after the sound of the guns the boulevards came alive with great excitement, which continued far into the night. Buildings and houses immediately began to illuminate, and Paris was in the throes of a great celebration.[114] The festivities continued with increasing tempo for several days, for M. Dabot waited until the 13th before he recorded: "Immense joy . . . . Malakoff taken . . . . Sebastopol has been evacuated." Then on the following day, Friday, he described the great *Te Deum* at Notre Dame Cathedral, attended by the emperor. "A great throng of people," he recorded, "overflowing all the streets, screamed and shouted with joy." "The whole day was filled with rejoicing, all the theaters were opened with free admission. . . . . In the evening a fairy land of lights. Even the poorest quarters were illuminated."[115]

And in the provinces the festivities were as joyous as in Paris. From the Vendée also came a picturesque account of its reception of the news.

> The news of the capture of Sebastopol [recounted the prefect] spread through the department with incredible speed. The towns and little hamlets illuminated spontaneously. The following Sunday the occasion was celebrated with the greatest rejoicing, the illuminations were still more brilliant because they had had time to prepare them. Even the isolated houses and farms [in the country] were lighted up, in almost every commune great bonfires were lighted to cries of Long Live the Emperor! From the heights of the Pouzauges Mountains the Vendée looked all afire.[116]

The celebrations in the Vendée seem to have been typical of the rest of France. Similar reports came from the departments of Manche, Seine-Inférieure, Seine-et-Oise, Indre-et-Loire, Finistère, Ain, and Gironde and from the procureurs general in Caen, Douai, Amiens, Nancy, Dijon, Aix, and Toulouse.[117]

Obviously there was more to the celebration of the fall of Sebastopol than that of a victory. The event carried with it the implications of an imminent peace. Mérimée had told Senior six months before that "while Sebastopol stands, peace is impossible; and also if it falls, peace will follow immediately."[118] When the fortress city fell, the Austrian ambassador also thought peace was near, but the Belgian minister averred that "this opinion is not generally shared."[119] Even the American minister felt that opinion was confused and in doubt about the immediate peace probabilities after the victory.[120]

However dubious the diplomats may have been, the press was more outspoken in its anticipations and demands. Saint-Ange in the

Débats hopefully remarked: "But let's look for the military and political consequence of [the] event." And Mazade in the *Revue des deux mondes* thought that "Russia will now be inclined to make peace." But the incorrigible *Assemblée Nationale* inferred the same direction of thought in a much more violent manner. It insisted that peace should have been made the previous April when Drouyn de Lhuys had been compelled to resign and that the blame for all the bloodshed since then rested directly on the shoulders of the allied governments.[121] The inference was plain: if not before, certainly now.

Likewise the prefect reports seemed to corroborate these hints for peace. From Versailles and the Paris suburbs came the unqualified statement: "There are signs of a desire to obtain as soon as possible an honorable peace worth of France . . . . . The considerable expenses of the war . . . . trouble their thoughts a little; the heavy casualties have caused a bad impression." Another prefect reported that "in the city of Bordeaux, whose prosperity depends especially on trade, the most prevailing wish is in favor of peace."[122]

This talk and the expectant atmosphere could not escape the emperor. It is very likely that they corresponded with his secret inclinations. Chevalier, who could not be thought to be anti-British, expressed positive views on this subject to Senior, who recorded them thus:

Chevalier believes the Emperor to be anxious for peace . . . . because the war is unpopular, and the English alliance equally so, as tending to prolong it. French vanity was interested in taking Sebastopol, but now that is done, the war is supposed to be carried on merely for English objects, the preservation of India, and the annihilation of Russia as a naval power.

And Cowley warned the foreign office that "His Majesty is fast coming to the conviction that public opinion in France will not support him much longer in this war."[123]

At least the emperor found an opportunity to express publicly his inclination toward an early peace and thus to sound out opinion two months before the next semiannual procureur reports. This was in a speech officially closing the Universal Exposition of Fine Arts and Industry which had been held in Paris during the summer and autumn of 1855. On this occasion the emperor declared:

At the sight of so many marvels spread out before our eyes, the first impression is a desire for peace. Only peace, in fact, can develop still more these remarkable productions of human intelligence. You must all then wish with me that this peace may be swift and lasting.

But to be lasting, it must definitely solve the question which compelled recourse to arms; to be swift Europe must assert herself, because without the pressure of general opinion conflicts between powers tend to be prolonged. If, on the contrary, Europe decided to declare [unequivocally] who is right and who is wrong, it would be a great step toward a solution.

At our present stage of civilizatoin the success of armies, however brilliant it may be, is only momentary. In reality it is only public opinion which invariably wins the final victory.[124]

"Peace" and "opinion," these then were the themes of his first major address since Sebastopol. It was an appeal as much to British and Austrian as it was to French opinion. The British at this time seemed inclined to continue the war for victories of their own and for more severe terms on Russia; and as for Austria, her intervention in some form was necessary to make the peace "swift."

There were thirty thousand people present at this closing ceremony. Many were English, among whom was the Duke of Cambridge, the queen's representative; but there were many from other countries as well. The *Times* correspondent left us a detailed description of the response of the audience and the city to the emperor's words:

> The acclamations [he wrote], the repeated and enthusiastic applause from more than 30,000 people, both French and English, was an unmistakable proof how this spirit went with him in all he said. This time at least there can be no mistake as to the Emperor's reception, and if any doubt on the point existed hitherto, a visit to the Exhibition yesterday would have shown how well that extraordinary man knows how to speak to the popular heart and the popular interests at the same time, and how faithfully he is responded to. Copies of the speech were posted up in the mairies of the arrondissements of Paris, and the results of my inquiries are that the industrial classes are most favorable. Its precision and clearness strike them forcibly; they see that the Emperor is not desirous of war for the sake of war.

He concluded, however, with a remark, colored by British proclivities, that "there are few who regard it as decidedly warlike or decidedly pacific."[125] Yet, Mazade in the *Revue des deux mondes* noted that there was one word (peace) "which strongly impressed all minds . . . . and responds to a general instinct."[126]

It is difficult to determine the effects of the speech itself on the provinces because by the time the reports came in, other events had supervened to crowd out the speech itself. But two reports mentioned the speech specifically and revealed a pacific reaction to it. A report from Besançon stated that the people "above all else want peace" and that the emperor's speech was "acclaimed with enthusiasm in all parts of the district"; while the people in Toulouse "were all given over joyously to the unexpected hopes of an imminent peace; and their gratitude goes out to the initiative of the emperor's powerful appeal to Europe on the closing day of the Universal Exposition."[127]

Nevertheless, whether or not it was elicited by the emperor's speech, there was plenty of evidence of peace sentiment in France during the last months of 1855 and the early weeks of 1856. The British, who did not want to be rushed into too lenient a peace, were downright alarmed at the situation. Nothing illustrates this more than a report (January 1856) from the Duke of Cambridge who was then in Paris on a military mission.

> France wishes for peace more than anything else on earth [he wrote], and this feeling does not confine itself to Walewski or the Ministers—it extends itself to all classes. The Emperor alone is reasonable and sensible in this respect, but his position is a most painful one, and he feels it very much. The fact is that public opinion is much more felt and more loudly expressed in this country than anybody

in England at all imagines. No doubt the Emperor can do much that he wishes, but still he cannot go altogether against a feeling which so loudly expresses itself on all occasions, without thereby injuring his own position most seriously.[128]

All during these months, while secret negotiations were going on with Austria on the five-point ultimatum and during its considera- tion by Russia, French opinion was confirming more and more this estimate of the duke. Other observers were noting it as much as he and Cowley. The Belgian minister declared that peace sentiment "dominated the entire country"; Barman of Switzerland affirmed that "everybody wants peace"; and Mason wrote to Washington that both the French and their government yearned for this result.[129] O'Meagher of the *Times* reaffirmed his undoubted belief in a great desire for peace, and Mazade in the *Revue des deux mondes* openly avowed the impatience of the public for confirmation of their hopes.[130]

While a few of the prefects and procureurs general reported that opinion would support the government in peace or continued war, they all agreed in stressing that peace was the universal desire in their regions. This estimate is found particularly in the reports from the departments of Seine-Inférieure, Haut-Rhin, Ain, and Vendée and from the judicial district of Rennes, Caen, Rouen, Douai, Amiens, Metz, Besançon, Dijon, Riom, Orleans, Nîmes, and Toulouse.[131] Such strong and universal feeling in all classes and in all regions the emperor was not going to be able to ignore. Fortunately, he did not have to ignore it because the Russians accepted the ultimatum in mid-January.

The news came to Paris on 17 January and was posted up in the Bourse first of all, whence the main impetus for a peace policy had come. Stocks immediately jumped five francs. "Paris has gone mad," wrote Cowley in disgust, "people kissed each other in the streets yesterday when peace was talked of, and they treat Hübner [Austrian ambassador], whom they consider a sort of demigod, with ovations."[132] Hübner, while not mentioning the ovations in his direc- tion, confirmed Cowley in other respects: "In the evening many buildings were illuminated; people were seen in the streets kissing each other and shedding tears of joy. But there were some disgruntled people, like the British ambassador, and a few speculators who had played for a market decline were stunned."[133] Even cotton went up on the Le Havre market, so happy were the traders.[134]

The press, uninhibited by censorship on this item of news, was almost unanimous in its rejoicing. Everywhere except in the *Siècle*. This democratic and anticzarist journal was incredulous and warned the two allies to be on their guard against Russian duplicity.[135]

One could not expect the provinces to be unhappy over the Russian acceptance of terms after they had shown their unequivocal desire for peace before the acceptance. Most of the reports were written before the news of Russia's acceptance was known or at least too late to determine public reaction. Only five of them mentioned the good news, but they all confirmed the happiness of the populace. Indeed, these reports went further: they showed that the people were considering the first steps to be, in effect, also the last step. Negotiation had to mean peace.

In fact [the procureur general wrote from Amiens] peace seemed included in Russia's pure and simple acceptance of the four [sic] propositions made by Austria and agreed to in advance by the allies. That is the interpretation given from the very beginning by public opinion to this as fortunate as it was unexpected news. . . . . The tendencies of our new society are peaceful. Peace today is popular.

The procureur general in Rouen pointed out that the people there had such confidence in the government that they would believe, if peace were not made, that the government just did not want it. So, he concluded, "peace has become by slow stages almost an absolute obligation." And this last line was heavily penciled in the office of the minister of justice. "They look upon the peace as already concluded," declared the prefect of Manche. And it was the same again in the judicial districts of Orleans and Riom.[136] This did not mean that the people would have approved a too generous peace, but they just did not believe that France had to offer such terms.

Thiers in his sour attitude toward the government still did not regret the opening of negotiations, but he once had said that "without a press and a tribune public opinion cannot be expressed or even formed."[137] In this instance he was wrong; public opinion formed itself and expressed itself. And its outward manifestations corresponded with the government's secret soundings: an honorable peace if possible, but peace.

The Peace Congress

The Congress of Paris, as the French called it, held its first sessions on 25 February 1856. As was customary, all its sessions were secret, and the public did not know of, nor express an opinion on, the debates which went on behind closed doors. Finally a month later, 30 March, the treaty was signed with a quill plucked from an eagle in the Paris zoo, and the public was allowed to know that that part of the deliberations was completed. During the following month a session was held to condemn the conditions in the Neapolitan, Papal, and Austrian-occupied parts of Italy; a treaty was signed concerning neutral rights on the seas, blockades, and privateering; and finally an alliance was concluded by Great Britain, France, and Austria to guarantee the fulfillment of the peace terms and the integrity of Turkey. The main peace terms, as revealed on 29 April, provided for the neutralization of the Black Sea; the transfer of southern Bessarabia from Russia to Moldavia; the autonomy of Moldavia, Wallachia, and Serbia; an international administration of the

Danube; and Turkish assurance of good treatment of Christian subjects.

While ignorant of the deliberations in the congress, the public did reveal certain sentiments during the period of the negotiations. Of course, having been urging peace since the fall of Sebastopol, the people naturally continued to desire the conclusion of a peace treaty in this conclave.[138] But there were other significant manifestations, such as the pro-Russian feeling which seemed to appear particularly after the Russian acceptance of the five points. Attention has already been given to some courtesies and complimentary remarks concerning the Russians after Sebastopol.[139] But this same attitude was revealed more fully in connection with the Russian delegates to the congress, Prince Orlov and Baron Brunnow.

A first-rate controversy arose between the allies over the arrival of Baron Brunnow, who preceded Orlov. He arrived at the Gare de l'Est at 10:00 P.M. on 12 February: on that much all accounts agree. However, the *Times* correspondent added: "Some groups were collected at the terminus to see him." The Belgian papers, which were not censored, furnished more details, saying that a crowd awaited him on the platform and presented him with a bouquet as he stepped down from the train. That considerable pro-Russian talk was going the rounds in Paris at that time is evidenced by an entry in M. Dabot's diary of 10 February. Dabot was usually on hand for most public demonstrations and had a keen ear for marketplace gossip. On this occasion, although he missed the train, he picked up this bit of Paris conversation:

> There is not the least hatred between the French and Russian armies. The Russians reserve their hate for our allies, the English. When French and Russian officers meet they show each other the highest marks of esteem.[140]

The English were evidently disconcerted over this incident and the attendant Paris gossip. The *Times* remarked that "even before breaking with England, France is already allying with her former enemy." And on the day the English read of Brunnow's arrival, Queen Victoria, in her letter commending her delegate, Clarendon, to the emperor, wrote at great length on the two allies resisting Russia's divisive efforts.[141]

On the same day that Napoleon III received this letter, he was faced with another embarrassing circumstance. Each of the delegates, as he arrived, would have to be officially presented to the emperor and assured a cordial welcome. Brunnow had arrived but was the delegate of an enemy state with whom there was not even an armistice. Yet the emperor, resolved to improve relations with the new czar and have as much cordiality as possible in the conference, determined to receive Brunnow in the same manner as the delegates of his allies.[142] This would certainly not be reassuring to the English.

Therefore Napoleon set in motion a series of events to mollify his principal ally. He invited Lord Clarendon to dinner on the evening before Brunnow's presentation. After the dinner he detained him for a two-hour conversation. The first thing he said was: "What a charming letter you brought me from the queen!" Then he went on to state "that he would give Baron Brunnow and Count Buol [the Austrian delegate] to understand that if they thought the Alliance could be disturbed by them, they would find themselves greviously mistaken and that it would be a waste of time to try to alter any conditions upon which he had agreed with the English Government."[143]

Then as if to make a public demonstration of these reassurances he had the *Constitutionnel* publish a denial of the railroad-station scene on the same day he received Brunnow. Declared the *Constitutionnel:* "It is needless to insist on the absurdity of these stories which are completely untrue. M. de Brunnow arrived in Paris at 10 o'clock at night, when the terminus was deserted, and immediately, without being in any way remarked, entered the carriage of M. de Seebach, the Saxon minister."[144]

Then a newspaper controversy gave him another opportunity to quiet the English. The *Débats* had published an article arguing that the neutralization of the Black Sea should not include the dismantling of Russia's naval arsenal at Nikolaevsk, up the Bug river. The next day the *Siècle* published a counterblast, saying it would be little assurance to Turkey to destroy the naval establishments at Sebastopol and leave those at Nikolaevsk, intact. Napoleon immediately seized upon the *Siècle* article and gave it his blessing by republishing it in the *Moniteur* just two days after his conversation with Clarendon. "It has produced a certain sensation in the public," remarked the *Times*. But a further sensation was produced by the fact that the *Constitutionnel*, jealous of the *Moniteur's* privileged position, claimed that the editor of the *Moniteur* had made a mistake. He was supposed to have republished a *Siècle* article reflecting an earlier *Times* article which had bitterly criticized France for moving toward Russia. Either article, if it had been published in the *Moniteur*, would have served the same purpose; but the *Moniteur* was not going to let the *Constitutionnel* make it look ridiculous. Therefore on 22 February the *Moniteur* replied:

The *Constitutionnel* is mistaken in attributing to an error the *Moniteur's* insertion of an article from the newspaper, *Siècle*. We profit by this occasion to reaffirm that the *Moniteur* is the only government paper. If an error creeps into its columns, it would not leave it to others to correct it.

Error or no error, this latest teapot tempest of the Paris press gave the government a double opportunity to show the English it was trying to counteract certain trends in public attitudes.[145]

But newspaper maneuvers were not going to stem the pro-Russian tide. This was shown in the way the Paris public acted toward Prince Orlov, the principal delegate. Even before his arrival innumerable anecdotes were being circulated about his exploits. His daguerrotype pictures were on display in the windows of all stationery shops, and groups of curious kept up a constant vigil in front of the Russian embassy on rue Faubourg Saint-Honoré to watch his coming and going.[146]

Two days before the congress Orlov was formally received by the emperor with surprising cordiality considering the breach of diplomatic relations and the state of war. "Fiction," said Mazade, "gave place to reality" and "this universal courtesy, which is one of the signs of contemporary civilization, especially of French civilization, made Paris for the time being a neutral city."[147]

Neutral city was hardly the proper term. No such popular interest was shown Lord and Lady Clarendon. Orlov was invited to all the social functions, and no affair was considered very elegant without his presence.[148] On the very evening after his court reception he attended an elaborate American celebration of Washington's birthday at the Hotel du Louvre at which most of the delegates of his enemy countries were present.[149] At the Opera he was the main attraction; all eyes turned toward him and lingered on his three diamond-bespangled medals, indicating by their portraits of three successive czars the continuing importance of Orlov at the court of St. Petersburg. "In a word, Orlov was in style; he enjoyed a veritable vogue in a very good-humored Paris," Charles-Roux affirmed.[150]

Then the formal opening of the congress came at 1:00 P.M. on 25 February at the ministry of foreign affairs. An enormous crowd gathered outside the building to see the delegates arrive; and Dabot said they were looking "particularly for Count Orlov, a man of superb physique and stature."[151]

Not only did the people belie Napoleon's assuring gestures to the English, but the emperor himself in various ways showed his inclination to be especially friendly to Orlov. On receiving the Russian delegate for the first time, he endeavored to flatter him by asking him (the defeated enemy): "Well, will you accord us peace?" Orlov, who had been instructed to build up Franco-Russian friendship, answered courtesy with compliment: "Sire, I come to ask you for it."[152] One version of the rest of the interview, as Mérimée related it to Senior, was as follows:

> I am sorry [Orlov went on] that this mission has been given to me, for I am no diplomatist, and I know that I have none but enemies to meet in the congress. Under such circumstances I throw myself on Your Majesty's protection, being well convinced that you are a generous enemy, if you still are an enemy, and that you do not wish Russia to be seriously injured or humiliated, and to enable you to protect me I will tell you what are my instructions. They are to *contest* everything,

but to *insist* on nothing. Peace is absolutely necessary to us. I trust in your magnanimity that you will not force us to buy it too dearly.[153]

This version may be exaggerated or even apocryphal, but it is not far removed from the spirit of their relationship. From then on it was a veritable love-feast between the two. Orlov was invited to the Tuileries for a concert the next evening, to Walewski's reception after the opening session, and to a play at the palace on the 28th. Napoleon III began to assume more and more the role of an arbitrator. When he chatted at length with Clarendon, he would soon find occasion to do the same with Orlov. At several points during the congress he settled disputes in the spirit of magnanimous impartiality.[154] In the great military review of 1 April Orlov rode directly behind the emperor and Prince Napoleon and ahead of all other mounted guests and received with the emperor the plaudits of the crowds along the routes.[155] The semiofficial *Constitutionnel* gave a laudatory account of Orlov and Brunnow in its number of 2 March. Although this was one of a series on all the delegates, no effort was made to restrain the special effusiveness of this article. And this complimentary article was echoed with even greater fervor in the next number of the *Revue des deux mondes*.[156] In the meantime the legislature met for its regular session, and here again the emperor from the tribune proclaimed to all the world his generous sentiments:

The Emperor of Russia, inheritor of a situation that he had not created, seemed animated with a sincere desire to put an end to the causes which had brought on this bloody conflict. He resolutely accepted the proposals transmitted by Austria. Once the honor of his arms had been satisfied, it was to honor himself as well, to defer to the clearly expressed will of Europe.

Then he added, as if to remind himself of his mediating role, "Let us be ready to draw the sword again, if necessary, or to extend the hand of friendship to those we have loyally fought."[157]

As to the provinces, the only report specifically showing a trend toward Russia was the one from Aix (and Marseilles), cited above, which recounted the sympathetic treatment the Russian prisoners received.[158] But another a year later from Agen at least showed how much the British were disliked:

We were able to observe [wrote the procureur general] that France, less forgetful than good policy advises and more faithful to old instincts and previous antipathies than concerned with contemporary necessities, had no very cordial disposition toward the English alliance. The stories brought back from the Crimea by our officers and soldiers and especially the presumptious language of the English statesmen and generals have erased with a strange uniformity what during the war the comradeship in arms and the common sacrifices and perils had established as fraternal appearances between the two people. Our national susceptibilities were more than justly wounded by British haughtiness and their unjustified pretension at predominance on the battlefield. They forget the great interests of western civilization still to be safeguarded by the union of the two flags, and they endure this haughty friendship more from necessity . . . . than from confidence and affection.[159]

Hübner was right when he confided to his diary: "The fact is that the Russians are gaining a great deal of ground here."[160] But much of that ground was beyond the Tuileries Gardens, even beyond the walls of Paris.

Outside the movements of Orlov and the emperor's legislative speech, the first real news of the congress came with the announcement of the signature of the treaty on 30 March. On the previous day Clarendon wrote Victoria that he could not now postpone the ceremony, since "every preparation is [already] made for illuminations, not alone at Paris, but throughout France, as all the Prefects have been informed of the [impending] signature."[161] Finally at one o'clock bulletins were posted on the walls throughout the city, and the crowds began to throng the streets, cocking their heads to get confirmation from the cannon of the Invalides. At two the salvos began, 101 of them, and the whole capital went wild. Tears of joy were noticed in the more emotional groups. Flags went up on the boulevards, including many Russian flags! (a state of war still existed until after ratification). People gathered outside the foreign ministry and cheered and shouted as each delegation left. Then at night, according to the Swiss minister, "the illuminations were more general than I had ever seen them in Paris." One feature of the illuminations was a transparency of Alexander II lighted from behind in a darkened window of a Russian printshop on the Boulevard des Italiens. It attracted large crowds during the whole evening. Then the illuminations were repeated on the following night.[162]

After such emotion-filled celebrations for Sebastopol, Russia's acceptance of negotiations, the birth of the new prince, and the signing of the peace, the final ratification of the peace and the publication of the terms[163] on 29 April came as a dull thud of anticlimax. One could hardly celebrate the peace all over again: it had already been celebrated three times. But the evaluation of the treaties by the people in the provinces, at least as reported three months later, was very simple. To them the quality of peace was not strained; it too fell, like the gentle dew, from heaven. They did not count up on their fingers—neutralization, demilitarization, internationalization, freedom of the seas, end of coalitions. They just beheld peace and saw that it was good. The joy expressed in all the reports could have referred as much to the signing as to the terms later published—both happened in the six months period of the procureur reports.

There were two reactions, however, which emerge from the general level of satisfaction. One was the exultation over France's new place in world affairs. The people in the Grenoble district, said the procureur general, "have understood that, in signing the treaty in Paris, the emperor became the arbiter of the destinies of the world and that his greatness becomes France's greatness." In Seine-et-Oise the inhabitants rejoiced that "France had been put back at the head of the nations of Europe." Such "vain boasts and foolish words" were likewise repeated in the accounts from Aix, Metz, Agen, Dijon, and Poitiers.

The second noticeable reaction was the increased popularity of the emperor in the country. From the urban region of Lyons, the procureur general wrote: "I do not believe that for a whole century has governmental authority been so solidly implanted and so respected as it is today. That is especially true in our departments where men of leisure are rare." Similar statements of the popularity of the emperor and the eclipse of the opposition came from Bordeaux, Agen, Grenoble, Colmar, Limoges, Toulouse, Riom, Metz, Besançon, and Saint-Lô.[164]

" 'Tis an ill wind that bloweth no man to good." And the war had blown France to good, even beyond the treaty terms, for her people, gagged and terrorized by a new regime born of a *coup d'état,* had finally found their voices again, however faint and hoarse, and breathed new courage. The adversity of war had loosed their tongues and bestirred their pens on issues which did not involve too much the life or death of the existing regime. From the sharp-eyed pro-cureurs general and prefects with their cohorts of eaves-dropping subordinates, from the cautious editorial pages, from the confidences to foreign personages had come genuine expressions of opinion, revealing the moods, thoughts, hopes, and fears of an unfree nation at war.

History has disagreed over who was responsible for the Crimean War, whether it was Nicholas I, Strafford de Redcliffe, or Napoleon III. But of this there is no doubt: it was not caused by the pressure of French public opinion. As La Gorce has said, it was not one of those wars growing out of an accumulation of national rivalries and hatreds. The French and Russian common people hardly knew each other.[165] Except for a few politicians and journalists, hardly any one realized there was a dispute over the Holy Places. This was so true that the French government could retreat on that issue without any fear of public condemnation. Likewise, in regard to the subsequent phases of the Eastern question, the people did not understand them and showed little interest in them. Obedient to their newly acquired habit, they tended to remain mute. Even when the Sinope incident occurred and the English public and the French emperor became aroused, the French people continued in their unconcern.

But after the Sinope attack the people became aware of the European implications of the Eastern hostilities and the dangers of a possible general war involving France. Then, and only then, did they begin to show some positive reaction. And this reaction was far from contributing to the outbreak of war, for it clearly indicated opposition to France's involvement. To the extent that it compelled the emperor to move with more caution public opinion probably delayed France's war declaration.

Yet the war inevitably came at the end of a sequence of events which are so typical of the chaos of our international system of states. The French people then had to accept rather grudgingly a *fait accompli* of war and of an alliance with a traditionally unpopular partner. However, at this point patriotism and love of military glory produced general support of the war effort. But there was no deep-seated conviction or determination. When the hot sun of casualties, sufferings, expenditures, and lack of victories began to beat upon the half-hearted war spirit in 1854, it wilted into deep discouragement. And this sullen mood became more and more apparent as the same lack of victories continued through the first two-thirds of 1855. The war was neither accepted nor waged with enthusiasm.

Of course nearly all Frenchmen rejoiced when peace came, and they could be expected to get satisfaction from old humiliations avenged and new prestige acknowledged. But considerable evidence points to the conclusion that they would have taken peace without these premiums. The victory, the peace, and France's heightened prestige also gave the emperor's regime greater popularity and stability. At the same time a prompt reconciliation with the Russians became evident, and the old French dislike for their English allies reappeared.

Among the French people the stronger opposition to the war came from the business men and peasants. The Legitimists (Bourbonists) were in many instances even sympathetic with Russia, but they had no influence on policy. Nor did Republican circles have much influence, and they were frequently more favorable to a war against the czarist autocracy, the persecutor of Poles and Jews. The working classes in the cities in some instances and the newspaper *Siècle* therefore showed less opposition to the war and more war support. Yet when the period of discouragement came, the opposition could not refrain from seeing their silver lining in the cloud: defeat would no doubt mean the overthrow of the imperial regime. Some reports even indicated instances where Legitimists and Republicans tried to capitalize on the general slump in morale. Finally the victorious peace silenced these dissidents and dashed their hopes.

As in most societies the bourgeoisie was more assertive and probably more influential. But by the system of reports the attitude of the common man was also known. The emperor even hinted that he might mobilize the latter against the former if he had to continue the war. But the common man proved to be as peace-minded as the bourgeoisie. Thus in 1856 Europe found peace—to use Napoleon's own words spoken at Bordeaux in 1852—"because France wants it, and, when France is satisfied, the world is at ease."

CHAPTER III

AN ITALIAN WAR IN THE MAKING

Napoleon III had declared publicly in 1852 that the empire meant peace, and yet within a year and a half France was in the Crimean War. Exactly six years later this "peaceful" empire was again at war, this time as an ally of Sardinia against Austria. All three of these governments share in the responsibility for the latter conflict; but the main blame must rest with Napoleon III, for it was he who took the initiative in arranging the Plombières interview and conspired for the provocation of a war.

The motives prompting the French emperor deliberately to plot a war are obscure and confused. However, it was clearly a traditional French policy to remove Austrian predominance in Italy, and Napoleon III was anxious to have a more active and successful foreign policy than that of his predecessor. To him, too, the national movements seemed destined to inevitable success. If such was the case, France could at the same time weaken Austria and gain the alliance of a new national state by aiding the Italian unification movement.[1]

By 1855 the French emperor found the Kingdom of Sardinia to be in a position to contribute a considerable share toward the effort of liberating Italy, thus making the French task seem much easier. Likewise the Piedmontese (in Sardinia) and other Italian nationalists looked to him, because of his earlier Italian sympathies, for aid against Austria and showed disappointment that neither at the Paris peace conference of 1856 nor since had he done anything important to further their cause. To us with the hindsight of ninety years it seems as if it could have been only a matter of time before these two discontented and ambitious states would have joined in a common effort toward their mutual goal.

The event in 1858 that precipitated such a rapprochement was the attempted assassination of Napoleon III by Orsini, a patriotic Italian fanatic who felt that the French emperor should be punished for his apparent abandonment of the Italian cause. While on trial for the crime the accused wrote a letter to Napoleon III in which he pleaded for aid to Italy.[2] Whether the emperor was frightened by the prospect of other attacks on his life, as some unsympathetic commentators imply, or whether he merely became convinced that the time had finally come to adopt an active policy for the liberation of

51

Italy, he began forthwith to set in motion the chain of events which led directly to war. It is even suspected that his prefect of police, Piétri, suggested the letter to the accused. At least the emperor seemed much affected by it and set about making immediate use of it to influence public opinion. He allowed Jules Favre, Orsini's attorney, to read it during the trial; the official journal, the *Moniteur*, published it; and he even sent another of Orsini's letters to the Sardinian prime minister, Cavour, for publication in Italy. The significance of such publicity moves was not lost on the shrewd Italians; they could be sure that more developments would follow soon.

Although Orsini was allowed to go to his death on 13 March, the expected developments began to appear within two months when the emperor invited Cavour to Plombières for conversations. The plan drawn up on that occasion by the two conspirators provided for a defensive alliance against Austria; the provocation of Austria until she committed an aggression; the marriage of Prince Napoleon, cousin of the emperor, to Princess Clothilda, daughter of Victor Emmanuel; the Sardinian annexation, after a successful war, of most of northern Italy; the French annexation of Savoy and Nice as compensation; and the establishment of an Italian confederation bereft of Austrian influence.[3]

At several points during the Plombières conversations Napoleon showed his concern for French opinion. "The war must be undertaken," he insisted, "for a nonrevolutionary cause which can be justified in the eyes of diplomacy and still more in the eyes of public opinion in France and in Europe." When the two plotters finally decided to make the cause of war an outbreak in Modena, the emperor thought that "it would be popular not only in France but also in England and in the rest of Europe, since that prince is considered, rightly or wrongly, the scapegoat of despotism." Again in speaking of the pope, he remarked: "I must treat [him] carefully . . . . in order not to arouse the Catholics in France against me."[4]

Newspapers and New Year's Greetings

In spite of Napoleon's concern for opinion, there was not much manifestation of it concerning the events above described as far as they applied to the larger aspects of foreign relations. The people were shocked at the attempted assassination, and not even the publicity given by the emperor to Orsini's letter was enough to gain opinion to the idea of a reduction of Orsini's sentence to imprisonment. Because the plot had been hatched in England, there was also a wave of anti-British sentiment which became so serious that it led to the downfall of the Palmerston ministry. But in the light of subsequent events and the quick subsiding of the excitement the Anglo-French incident does not deserve a detailed development here. Of course the details of the Plombières negotiations would have elicited a wide reaction if they had been made public; but they remained hidden even from Napoleon's own ministers for some time,[5] and the whole story was not generally known until 1883. Not until November 1858 was there a sufficient indication of intentions to stimulate general public reaction to something tangible.

One of these early indications was an article in the *Presse*, attributed to the inspiration of Prince Napoleon and perhaps tolerated by the emperor as a trial balloon. The article, appearing on 22 November over the signature of Géroult, mentioned rumors of an Austrian alliance with the reactionary princes of Italy and her movement of troops toward Piedmont. "We don't like war," he concluded, "and we hope some day it will disappear from the face of Europe; but we would like to see one more, and that one directed against Austria." Such hopes and accusations were also echoed a few days later by another imperialist paper, the *Patrie*.[6]

The stock market, the most sensitive barometer of business opinion, showed an immediate reaction by the decline of quotations all along the line. Soon, too, a newspaper controversy arose, as some took the *Presse* and *Patrie* to task. Prévost-Paradol in the *Débats* wrote: "No one will accuse us of being partial to Austria, nor still less of indifference to Italy; but we could not see without astonishment this glib talk of declaring war on a power allied[7] to France without being able to bring up any complaints serious enough to justify war in the eyes of civilized nations."[8]

Having at least presented the possibility of war to the public, the government tried to quiet the resulting alarm by an indirect denial of intentions. This could be easily and willingly done by the ministers because they did not share in the emperor's secret. On 29 November Renée wrote in the semiofficial *Constitutionnel*: "This unexpected press campaign has produced on the public an effect of surprise and excitement which has not yet subsided. . . . . The papers which started this flurry only expressed on this occasion their own particular views. The government of the emperor has nothing to do with this dispute."[9] But the alarm continued and spread until finally the *Moniteur* also felt it necessary to give an official denial to the implications.[10] And poor, deluded Walewski, the foreign minister, repeated to the Prussian ambassador, Hatzfeld: "With some people in France there may be some vague feelings in regard to Italian affairs, but these are only disembodied ideas. . . . . There is no substance to any of it, and the French government does not even think of stirring up or favoring complications concerning Italy."[11] How little Walewski seemed to have realized that these ideas were already embodied in the mind of the emperor himself and in an unwritten agreement with Cavour!

But the public, suspicious that where there was smoke there must be some fire, continued uneasy. "The articles which the imperial government has found necessary to insert in the *Moniteur* and the *Constitutionnel*," wrote the Belgian minister, "have not attained their intended purpose and have not been sufficient to calm the fears that the rumors have aroused of a future clash in Italy."[12] Only in one provincial report, from Marseilles, did there appear a reaction to this controversy, and this seemed to confirm the views of the Belgian minister. The prefect of Gironde wrote: "Public sentiment has asserted itself definitely against the war which certain papers like to presume to be imminent. . . . . They continue . . . . to be concerned with this grave question whose solution they hope they'll find in the emperor's opening speech to the legislature."[13]

In spite of Walewski's reassurances, he and the French public were being softened for coming events by the emperor's hot-and-cold treatment. Having been cooled by the *Moniteur's* disavowal, the public was given another heat treatment on New Year's Day. The emperor, as usual on that day, held a diplomatic reception; and, as he approached Baron Hübner, the ambassador of his "ally" Austria, he remarked audibly: "I regret that our relations with your government are not as good as in the past; but I beg you to tell your emperor that my personal feelings are not changed."[14] Hübner was stunned, but so was the French public. This time the heat came by electric shock. Baron Beyens observed: "These words were heard, whispered, and commented upon by all those present. Immediately circulated by the diplomats in the gatherings of important people, it made the rounds of Paris like a trail of ignited gunpowder, and the telegraph made it resound throughout Europe. Next day the Bourse felt the effect as if at the announcement of future complications."[15] In his little diary under 2 January lawyer Dabot noted: "Great alarm is spreading in Paris. . . . . They think they have everything to fear."[16] Both Viel Castel and Reuss, another Prussian representative, affirmed the "excitement of the Paris public" before any publication of the incident had appeared in the press.[17]

But on 4 January, as if to step up the temperature, the semi-official *Constitutionnel* published the full statement and added that "commented on in public, [it] has produced a certain emotion." Rumors then became reality, and the other papers felt free to give countercomments. Veuillot in his clerical *Univers* deplored any move that would lead to a break or even to an estrangement with Austria.[18] Prévost-Paradol in the *Débats* was critical of the incident because the public could not know how far the ill-feeling had gone between the two countries and because such remarks tended to encourage disorder and excitement in north Italy. Friends of Italy and newspapers, he thought, should not arouse these unconfirmed hopes.[19]

The Belgian and American ministers gave rather detailed accounts of the whole affair:

> The few words addressed by the emperor to Baron Hübner [Rogier remarked], ... thanks to excited comments, have received a very exaggerated interpretation and meaning which was not, I believe, in the mind of the august speaker. The spreading alarm has again come to life worse than ever; and the government bonds have taken another downward turn. One would think that the war was already declared and that the armies were by now in the field.[20]

His American colleague was even more specific:

> The incident [wrote Mason] has had the effect of depressing the Bourse to an unprecedented extent and in the comments of the Paris press, while professing not to be alarmists, the Editors generally attribute a grave significance to these words and the public mind seems to be impressed with the belief that a war is impending, to commence between Austria and Sardinia but which will probably involve all Europe. No allusion has been made in the *Moniteur* to the affair. On the especial causes of the interruption of good relations between France and Austria, there does not seem to be a very clear understanding on the part of the public, but there has been a want of accord on many questions. . . . .There seems to be a general apprehension that war will soon take place.[21]

By 7 January the reaction had become so strong and adverse and the alarm so intense that Napoleon III was forced to give some reassurances by a statement in the official *Moniteur*. It was time for another dash of cold water. "For some days now," the *Moniteur* parroted, "public opinion has been excited by alarming rumors, to which the government must bring a halt by declaring that nothing in our diplomatic relations justifies the fears these rumors tend to arouse."[22] With this cue the cold water came in a flood. The *Constitutionnel* observed that "far from being threatening [the emperor's words] contained an indication of good will toward the Emperor of Austria and of regret that any difficulties could arise between the two governments."[23] The *Pays* and the *Patrie* joined in the semi-official chorus, and Rogier observed that these editorials "have contributed not a little in restoring some calm to opinion and checked the disordered decline on the Bourse."[24]

The French ambassador in London told Malmesbury that there was "no apprehension of a war *at present* as public opinion in France, especially in the large towns, had been so strongly pronounced against a war that it was impossible."[25] Malaret, his secretary, also told the British foreign secretary "that public feeling in France against a war is tremendous and most openly expressed."[26] At the end of the month Forcade in the *Revue des deux mondes* added his warning to the emperor: "Public opinion, however poorly informed it may be, has shown itself to be peace-minded in its general and unequivocal expression. Present-day France likes peace, wants it, and would agree to war only if it was shown the necessity by a foreign aggression or by a question of honor."[27]

The reactions of the people in the departments were well summarized by a revelation made to the Belgian minister. "They assert,"

Rogier wrote, "that the reports addressed by the prefects to the minister of interior on the state of public opinion in their departments are all in agreement, except in one instance ['the one from Seine-Inférieure'], to show the opinion of the people to be against war." In general there was only one inaccuracy in this estimate, and that was the exception. The prefect of Seine-Inférieure had also reported that opinion "desires and believes that peace will be preserved."[28]

There were also many witnesses to the effect the public reaction had on the emperor. "The panic," said Cowley, "which this state of things has created has shown H. M. that his country is not disposed to go to war, and he accordingly hesitates to know what to do." Likewise his Prussian colleagues reported that the "various outspoken opinions in France against war have obviously not failed to make a definite impression."[29] At a dinner on the night of 7 January the emperor, with tongue a little in cheek it must be imagined, confided thus to the Belgian minister:

> It was for me a matter of great astonishment how the public gave itself over to unreasonable alarm in recent days. Did it have any serious justification? Certainly not. You need only to seek the cause in that swift mobility of impressions which distinguish the French from all other people. From confidence and exaggerated enthusiasm, they fall back almost without transition into a no less extreme discouragement and panic. A little careful and thoughtful examination of the situation would have determined that, if political difficulties exist, they can be solved otherwise than by an immediate recourse to arms.[30]

Again, when the emperor was chatting with General Delarue he "expressed his surprise at the effect caused in France by his remarks to the Austrian ambassador." The general rather boldly chided that "the excitement would not very easily be allayed, as a war would affect too many interests." Rothschild was in the room, and when the emperor's remarks had been whispered around to him, he muttered (*sotto voce*):

> The emperor does not know France. Twenty years ago a war might have been proclaimed without causing any great perturbation. Hardly anybody but the bankers held stock exchange or commercial securities, but today everybody has his railway coupons or his three-per-cents. The Emperor was right when he said 'the Empire meant peace,' but what he does not know is that the Empire is done for if we have war.[31]

Lord Granville spent the last week of January in Paris where he also had a conversation with the emperor on the whole burning question. In spite of the fact that Napoleon had just signed the alliance with Victor Emmanuel, the emperor assured Granville that he was not committed to the King of Sardinia. Granville went away with the impression "that the question is adjourned for the present, owing to the clear manifestation in France, but much more so to the unanimous tone of the German and English press."[32]

A Wedding and a Pamphlet

In all this furor and excitement Napoleon III had not forgotten the stipulation about the marriage between Prince Napoleon and

Princess Clothilda. It took some time to persuade the father and daughter to accept the rather unsavory Prince Napoleon as a bridegroom. Finally, however, their resistance was overcome and the plans made just in time to give the French public another hot shot in the arm. On 14 January the *Moniteur* announced that Prince Napoleon was making a short trip to Turin, and away went the Bourse and the public around and around again in a dizzy swirl of anguish.[33] Our man in the street, M. Dabot, jotted down in his little diary under 15 January: "Stocks slump . . . . marriage of Plon-Plon with Princess Clothilda . . . . to get the emperor's protection against Austria."[34] Then came the official announcement that General Niel in the name of the emperor had asked for the hand of Clothilda for Prince Napoleon, followed the next day by the *Moniteur's* report of the betrothal with an accompanying falsehood that the event was not coupled with any alliance.[35] The *Constitutionnel* slavishly perpetuated the lie on the following day and ridiculed the tumbling Bourse and the trembling public. Just because somebody was getting married, they thought the fighting was going to start tomorrow; just because a general was asking for a fair lady's hand, they thought he was supervising Sardinia's fortifications. Foreigners would laugh at the French for becoming so easily alarmed. Could they not put their trust in the high intelligence and enlightened patriotism of the emperor? Then ominously—even if war did break out, did they not know that France was powerful enough to fight?[36]

On 3 February the newly married couple came home to Paris, and this time it was the public which furnished the ice water for the occasion. All the world, especially France, loves a lover, but this love match was different. It takes the London *Times* correspondent to give us a full picture of the event:

By what I hear from various persons who were at the Louvre yesterday, and in the line of the Prince's cortege from the Railway Terminus to the Palace of the Tuileries, nothing could be more indifferent, or even colder, than the demeanor of the crowd. What surprised most people, no cries were heard, and hardly even was the silent courtesy of taking off the hat paid. None of the official shouters in the service of the police appeared to be present; and, if there were any, they certainly did not perform their peculiar duty—they were mute and motionless. These persons are on such occasions sent in small bands to shout, and it is easy to distinguish their fabricated enthusiasm from the spontaneous signs of contentment or approval. But they were either absent or silent yesterday. Some imagined the orders were that the claque should not be employed, and that no cries should be uttered, lest they should give rise to counter-cries of 'Vive la Paix.' I repeat merely the remarks of several persons who were present, and one person was heard to reply to a Sergent de Ville, who expressed his surprise at the silence that prevailed, '*Il n'y a pas d'ordre.*' In fact, from all one hears, it would seem that the reception was icy. Independently of any feeling towards the Prince himself, it may be wondered at that in an assemblage of Frenchmen of every class the presence of a young and attractive lady did not produce some external mark of respect. Her tender years, her countenance, serious if not sad, the fatigue depicted on her features, hurried by sea and land from Turin to Paris, her strange position—all might well give her a claim to more than sympathy. The truth is, it is not from anything like dislike to the Princess Clothilda that she and her husband were received so coldly, but from the feeling that this alliance is merely the equivalent paid by Victor Emmanuel for French aid and the pursuit of his scheme is reflected on the innocent Princess, whose hand is regarded by them as the guarantee for them. Otherwise, the daughter of Victor Emmanuel was spoken of with a sort of sympathy, and, though no cries were uttered, the disapproving silence meant no disrespect to her.[37]

The British ambassador, who was at the scene of sullen welcome, confirms this account. "Not a cheer, not a wave of the handkerchief," he reported. Dabot the lawyer also noted that "Princess Clothilda . . . . is received without enthusiasm by the very disturbed Parisians." "We do not greet the little one," one workman said, "because she brings us war."[38]

The reports from the provinces did not deal much with the marriage. No doubt the delicacy of this dynastic affair inclined the government officials to avoid the subject. But also by the time they wrote their reports, so much more of importance had occurred that the marriage had been partially forgotten by them and their public. Only twice was a mention of the marriage found, these in the reports of Aix and Colmar.[39] Whether on the sidewalks of Paris or in the reports from the provinces, the marriage and the alliance it represented seemed to have been given at least the silent treatment.

The very next day after the arrival of the newlyweds the public was again put into a dither of excitement by the appearance of a pamphlet entitled *L'Empereur Napoléon III et l'Italie* with a well-known imperial ghost writer, La Guéronnière, designated as author.

The emperor, who had been opinion-conscious at Plombières, had meditated from that very moment on the issuance of a pamphlet which would give direction to public thought. He knew that if the plot were ever to be carried out, a great deal of work would have to be done on opinion. So, after Cavour's departure he called in La Guéronnière, his favorite pamphleteer, and made him privy to the conspiracy. He now wanted a brochure prepared, he said, which would show how the *status quo* was impossible in Italy both from the Italian and French points of view and which would sketch a plan of confederation for the Peninsula. He was in no great hurry. On the diplomatic and military questions he would make available to him documents from the foreign office and from, presumably, army intelligence. It would be up to La Guéronnière to search out the historical background of the confederation idea.

For this last purpose the faithful ghost writer on 12 August sought out Eugène Rendu, a well-known writer and Italophile, who was at that moment composing a paper for a session of the Academy of Moral and Political Sciences entitled *Italy and the German Empire*. In a sense La Guéronnière passed on the writing of the rough draft to Rendu, who in a few days and nights composed a complete work.

But the emperor delayed in calling La Guéronnière back. Two

months went by until finally on 2 November the emperor's secretary wrote him to stand by. The two joint authors hurriedly went over their chef-d'oeuvre again. But it was in November that the press controversy broke out, which may have been Napoleon III's temporary substitute for the pamphlet; or, if he were not responsible for the *Presse* article, he may have decided that one trial balloon at a time was enough. At least La Guéronnière was again kept on the waiting list.

Then after the wild excitement over his New Year's greetings to Hübner, the emperor invited La Guéronnière to dinner on 10 January, asked how the work was coming, briefed him on the latest diplomatic developments, and said he would want him back some morning soon. From 20 January until the eve of the publication La Guéronnière was frequently in the emperor's office, reading the text and revising it at the dictation of His Majesty. Napoleon praised highly the general content of the work, but he made many and quite detailed revisions. He added passages on England and Germany and on the impossibility of papal reforms while Austria was in Italy. Section X was entirely the emperor's addition of the estimate of Austria's military situation in Italy. "Every sentence of the brochure was scrutinized and weighed by the emperor," Rendu declared. He eliminated references to the preservation of states and dynasties in Italy. "If we are to wage war," he said, "we will naturally have to change many things." So sensitive was he on the subject of assassination that he struck out the phrase "the dagger of Ravaillac" and replaced it by the less suggestive words "the premature death of the king." And finally he himself added the famous and threatening words: "We ardently hope that diplomacy may accomplish before a conflict what it will certainly do after a victory."[40] Finally on 3 February, while the pamphlet was actually running off the printing presses, Napoleon III called together his council of ministers and told them that a manifesto on the Italian question would appear on the morrow. They were all caught off-balance, they were stupefied, but no one dared risk the disfavor of the ruler by protesting.[41]

Here, then, we are able to see in detail just how methodically and deliberately the emperor prepared propaganda for the public, weighed its words, and timed its appearance—all with the idea of influencing opinion toward the plighted and inevitable event.

The brochure appeared on the morning of 4 February, the day after the sullen reception of the imperial bride and bridegroom. "Behind the windows of all the bookstores," noted Dabot, "are displayed copies of a pamphlet by Arthur de La Guéronnière." "It was," he was told, "inspired by the emperor." "From the avidity with which it is sought," wrote the *Times* correspondent, "the present edition will, I am sure, be soon exhausted." He also said that most people attributed it to the emperor. Rogier reported that three or four thousand copies were bought up in a few hours. It reflected, he likewise affirmed, the ideas of an *"Auguste Personnage."*[42] Without benefit of a panel of judges the pamphlet became the book-of-the-month selection as soon as it hit the streets, and few had any illusions about its real authorship.

And what did those avid people read as they opened its covers? Here is the gist of the premeditated bombshell. Italy, the source and center of civilization, harbored two movements, one revolutionary, the other national. The national movement was legitimate. It was approved by England, Germany, and even Austria before the latter won the war in 1849. Now England outstripped France as the champion of Italian national independence. But France had a great tradition to make her a leader in this question. Napoleon I believed it was France's role to help free these nationalities. If he had conquered them to free them, his successor would free them without conquering them. "If France, who wants peace, were forced to wage war . . . , the war . . . . would have no other aims than to prevent revolutions by giving legitimate satisfaction to the needs of people." Thiers wished as much for Italy. As to Rome, if France withdrew her forces, Austria or revolution would move in. Italy should have a federation with Rome as capital, with the pope as president, with a reformed lay government for the Papal States, and an Italian army under Piedmontese leadership as the protector of pope and confederation. Now Austria cannot reform Italy; she can only hold it by force or get out. War or the force of European public opinion will be the only means to make Austria withdraw from the Peninsula.[43]

The reception the pamphlet received was no different from that given to the press controversy of November 1858 or to the New Year's greeting. O'Meagher of the *Times* wrote home:

> It is the great, I may say the absorbing, topic of the day. Hardly anything else is talked of . . . . . It is looked upon as a threat to Austria, and everyone asks how Austria will reply, and whether Sardinia will consider it as a signal to begin. . . . . Among the commercial public generally it has added to the panic and on the Bourse it has fallen like a fulminating shell as the stocklists of yesterday and today abundantly show."

Likewise the Belgian minister gives us a similar account of public reaction:

> The effect produced by this brochure [he wrote] has been perhaps the opposite from what they expected. First the bourse was alarmed by it, and all its stock quotations continue on a swift downward course. Then the political men found, not without reason, that the *war pen* overlooked too readily the treaties which bind governments, and it appeared to them that the plan for an Italian confederation which it proposes was a utopia and an almost impracticable undertaking. This appeal to opinion, after which, if it is not heeded an armed conflict may ensue, has not then calmed the concern of the public, which remains very great, and which will only increase until the opening of the legislative session.[45]

Reuss, the Prussian ambassador, had two interesting reports to give.

Speaking of the public reaction, he remarked that "public opinion spoke out almost unanimously against the principles contained therein." Then in another report he reproduced Walewski's comments, which are intriguing when we know now of his presence in the ministerial council of 3 February: "He told me . . . . that he regretted the publication of this brochure, whose ideas and principles were completely in contradiction with the thoughts of the emperor [!] and his government. . . . . There was consequently nothing in common between the government and this lucubration of some writer."[46] The son of Napoleon I could lie as roundly as the nephew,[47] and the latter no doubt would have only pulled his mustaches with a sly smile had he heard the word "lucubration." But even a close friend at court, Viel Castel, admitted that the pamphlet "had a most detestable effect."[48]

Strangely enough there was scarcely any sign of reaction to the pamphlet in the reports from the provinces. Its main effect had evidently been in the capital. Then, too, it had come out right after the periodic reports of the procureurs general and the prefects. By the time another set had been sent in, other developments had intervened to attract the attention of provincials and administrators alike.[49]

Pax Vobiscum

Evidently it was time to quiet the excitement again. Several reports and articles had said the public would look to the emperor's opening speech to the legislature for a sign that the emperor intended peace, and on this occasion he evidently decided not to disappoint it. Three days after Paris was flooded with a disquieting pamphlet, the emperor with a most serious mien delivered from the throne what was, in the light of his alternating disturbing and quieting campaign, one of the most cynical and amusing speeches ever made by a ruler.

However [he declaimed], there has ensued at intervals, in the midst of the peace and general prosperity, a vague uneasiness, a muffled agitation, which, without any very definite cause [!], influences certain people and affects public confidence. (Movement among the legislators.)

I deplore these periodic discouragements without being too surprised . . . . .

The emotion which has just been aroused, without any appearance of imminent danger, should rightly be a surprising manifestation; because it is an indication at one and the same time both of too much distrust and too much fear. They seem to doubt, on the one hand, the moderation of which I have so often given proof, and on the other, of the real power of France. Fortunately the mass of the people are far from succumbing to such moods. (That's true! That's true!)

. . . . What has been my constant policy? Reassure Europe, obtain for France her rightful rank, closely cement out alliance with England, and regulate the degree of our intimacy with the other continental powers of Europe according to the proximity of our respective views and to the nature of their relations with us. (Applause.)

That is why, on the eve of my third election, I said at Bordeaux, 'The Empire means peace,' hoping thus to prove that if the heir of Emperor Napoleon reascended the throne, he would not begin an era of conquests again, but he would usher in a system of peace which could only be disturbed for the defense of great national interests. (Much excitement. Prolonged applause.)

After commenting on his good relations with England, Russia, and Prussia, he came to the problems of Austria and Piedmont.

The cabinet of Vienna and mine, I say regretfully, have often found themselves in disagreement on important questions, and a great spirit of compromise was necessary to solve them . . . . .

With that state of things there was nothing extraordinary about France's further rapprochement with Piedmont, who was so faithful during the [Crimean] war and so loyal to our policy in time of peace. The happy union of my well-beloved cousin Prince Napoleon with the daughter of Victor Emmanuel is not then one of those unusual events for which a hidden reason must be found, but the natural consequence of the community of interests between the two countries and the friendship of two sovereigns. (Applause.)

For some time the condition of Italy and her abnormal situation, where order can be maintained only by foreign troops, has justly alarmed diplomacy. That is, however, no sufficient reason for thinking there will be a war. Let some wholeheartedly call for war without any legitimate reason, let others in their exaggerated fears, try to show France the perils of new coalitions. But I shall remain steadfastly in the path of right, justice, and national honor; and my government will not let itself be led astray or intimidated, because my policy will never be either provocative or pusillanimous. (Repeated shouts of Long Live the Emperor! resounded throughout the hall.)

Away then with false alarms, with an unjust and intentional mistrust. Peace, I hope, will not be troubled. Take up again then with calm assurance the habitual course of your labors. (Sensation.) [50]

On the next day the speech by Morny, as president of the legislative body, appeared to reinforce some of the peaceful aspects of the emperor's speech or, perhaps, indirectly to remind the emperor that he should not get too far out of line with opinion. The gist of Morny's remarks was that in these times nothing can be accomplished without the concurrence of public opinion and that nothing could be more efficacious than the influence of the elected representatives of the country. [51]

The Belgian minister had the impression that the emperor's speech "leaves the friends of peace with the hope that all existing difficulties can be solved by diplomatic means." "The closing words of the speech," he added, "were greeted with prolonged applause." [52] Prince Albert, who was usually well informed from British sources of information, summarized their impressions of French public reaction thus: "In Paris the public seem to be furious at being treated from the very throne with contempt for putting one and two together and getting three as the product; and seeing what care has been taken to avoid all express promises not to break the peace, and to respect existing treaties, they are in no way satisfied with the Speech, neither are they willing to go back to work, as the speech enjoins them." [53]

All the prefect reports consulted for this study, which mentioned the imperial speech, registered provincial opposition to war. But all save one (from Maine-et-Loire) indicated a favorable effect made by the speech. The procureur general in Riom, in his report, gave this more detailed description of a favorable public attitude:

I must not conceal from Your Excellency [he wrote] that they [the war rumors] have in general been greeted by the population with regret. They are frightened by the evils which it would bring in its wake. Italy no doubt excites honorable sympathies, but the revolutionary passions of which it is the principal center in recent years alarm the friends of order and moderated liberty . . . . .

The eloquent and forceful words spoken by His Majesty last February before the great state assemblies have reassured opinion. The echos from Auvernge as well as from the entire world have vibrated at the noble accents of that powerful voice. [Both paragraphs were marked with pencil in the office of the minister of justice.]

Similar favorable reports on the speech came from the prefects of Haut-Rhin, Ain, Finistère, Vendée, and Haute-Vienne, as well as from the procureurs general of Nancy, Colmar, Bourges, Grenoble, Agen, and Pau. But from Maine-et-Loire came a courageous report, the only negative one in regard to the speech. Its prefect declared: "The emperor's speech before the legislative body was at first well received and interpreted in a peaceful sense. Later they found it rather belligerent and indefinite. They would like to see an end to uncertainty, which displeases the peace people very much as well as that small number of those who are not afraid of the prospects of war."[54]

Indeed, business circles, which had been grumbling privately about the trend toward war, finally decided to do something about it.

A certain number of chambers of commerce in the departments [reported the Belgian minister], justifiably alarmed at the prevailing and persistent war rumors, decided to express their fears on this subject by petitions which they would have presented directly to the emperor and which show what harm and what losses would be suffered by all the trade activities by such a long period of uncertainty. It seems certain that instructions were sent to the prefects to stop such manifestations because they were considered illegal and impolitic.

Delord substantiates this account; and La Gorce goes further by indicating that the petitioners then circumvented the emperor and took their complaints to a more sympathetic official, Walewski, begging him in this crisis to bring all his influence to bear on the emperor in the cause of peace.[55]

The emperor learned, too, in no uncertain terms that his ministers and advisors were against his war policy. Greville recorded in his journal at the end of January: "Granville is just come back from Paris, where he spent a week; he saw and conversed with everybody, beginning with the emperor and ending with Thiers. All the ministers he talked to, Walewski, Fould, and Rouher, are dead against war, Morny the same."[56] And Viel Castel in his memoirs wrote that the emperor was opposed not only by his ministers but also by his ambassador to England (Persigny), the president of the legislative body (Morny), and his own aide-de-camp (General Fleury). Fleury was quoted as saying: "As a soldier, Sire, I love war, but in this matter I beg Your Majesty to consider how detrimental it would be to the interests of France and to your dynasty."[57] Even Empress Eugénie disagreed with her husband on this issue.[58] And Cavour's personal representative in Paris, Nigra, had to admit that "a quiet war continues to be waged against the emperor's ideas by those around him."[59]

This "quiet war" finally led Prince Napoleon to resign his position as minister for Algeria in protest against the peace faction.[60]

Preparing Opinion for War

Even before this heated council session, Napoleon III could see that almost all opinion was against him. Yet instead of bending to it, he was resolved, as Pourtalès said, to try to bring opinion around to his point of view. Soon after his speech to the legislature he wrote to Victor Emmanuel: "But all that [military preparation] takes time and especially a lot of caution because even in France public opinion needs to be developed and made to understand all the interest the country should have in seeing a free and sincerely allied people on its borders."[61] From this moment forward the emperor began in earnest to prepare the French public for the inevitability of war. A few days after his letter to the Sardinian king he instructed the prefects to have the local newspapers accustom their readers to the prospects of an unavoidable war and inspire in them a blind loyalty toward the emperor. They were to be assured that, if war came, it would be a defensive one for a just cause.[62] Three weeks later, on 4 March, Napoleon called in one of his loyal journalists, Granier de Cassagnac, and there in his office they drew up together an article for the *Moniteur* which would supplement the campaign in the local papers. The famous *Moniteur* article of 5 March, however, interlarded hopes for peace with a definite avowal of commitments to Sardinia. Like his legislative speech, this article denounced certain papers which were spreading vague and absurd rumors. "The emperor has only promised the King of Sardinia one thing," began the amazing line, "to defend him against an aggression by Austria." The article concluded on a hopeful note that the questions in dispute were already being handled by diplomatic means and that there was no reason to fear results detrimental to peace.[63] After the war was over, the empress reminisced to Count Arese: "The emperor himself was at one moment against his own people, and he found it necessary to revive in them a feeling of generosity and glory in order to have a war accepted by a country still weary from the terrible experiences of a previous one."[64]

The months of March and April were watched, then, for signs of this hoped-for trend toward public support of the war policy. The next reports of several prefects revealed in rather transparent fashion that they were trying to carry out their instructions. The prefect of Finistère replied in April that from the very first he "took pains to let them get a glimpse of the fact that a war was possible, even probable, in spite of the emperor's efforts to avoid it." His colleagues in Haute-Vienne and Gironde gave similar assurances of valiant efforts.

These prefects may have been boastful of the job they were doing, but that a job was underway there was no doubt.[65]

Yet, despite the press campaign, the people still wanted peace. A week after the *Moniteur* article the Belgian minister noted: "The fears of a future inevitable war persist and spread among the people. The Bourse and commercial affairs continue to feel their effects."[66] Mérimée, an Italian sympathizer, complained in disgust:

> They only think of the effect the war can have on bonds and railroad stocks. It goes without saying that no one thinks of glory or humanity. The emperor appears to be rather wrought up over the general cowardice, and he tells us what he thinks of us in rather harsh terms, and, my faith, we certainly deserve it. Fortunately the army has an entirely different attitude. All the officers would like to be in the advance-guard in order to be the first to see the *donne* and eat macaroni.[67]

The observation of the Prussian ambassador showed that after the second *Moniteur* article Napoleon III was between two fires. While Pourtalès still affirmed that "public opinion . . . . was opposed to the idea of a war in Italy," he also noted that "today what Emperor Napoleon has most to fear is the unpopularity, especially in France, of any movement of retreat" which "will be exploited, here, by numerous enemies of the present regime."[68] On the other hand Nigra, the Piedmontese special envoy, thought he saw some "improvement" in opinion. "The *Moniteur* article," he declared, "produced a reaction against the idea of peace at any price."[69]

Only four procureurs general seem to have noted provincial public reactions to the *Moniteur* articles in spite of the fact that special instructions had also been sent to these officials to watch "what reception opinion gave to the rumors of war."[70] The procureur general at Metz was more frank and detailed in his report, but in general it was favorable:

> I am too sincere [he wrote] not to tell Your Excellency that this reception was at first one of surprise, incredulity, and, in certain places, fear. But little by little these varying sentiments were replaced by a uniform reaction of absolute confidence in the profound wisdom of the emperor, soon heightened still more in reading in the *Moniteur* the notes of 5 and 15 March. This language, so noble, so dignified, so firm, so imbued with moderation and frankness, produced an immense effect. When they saw that the German press replied to them with insults and calumnies, they became angry. When they also learned that our neighbors were arming in spite of genuine and peaceful assurances, they only wanted one thing: that France arm too so as to dominate them more by her attitude than by her past resentments, so as to be ready to fight them and beat them in case they have to.

Such a description, beginning with frankness and changing to abject flattery, does not leave us too sure of a developing acquiescence in war. But the general picture is confirmed in the reports from Bourges, Colmar, and Pau.[71] While the paucity of provincial attention to the articles in the *Moniteur* weakens the value of the four favorable reports, it must be remembered that much more important events were monopolizing public attention by the time the April reports were being written.

In the meantime diplomatic negotiations were moving on apace, with some steps known and some not known by the public at large. England, alarmed by the threatening signs of the times, offered her "entirely cordial intervention" between France and Austria. Cowley, her ambassador at Paris, after briefing himself on the latest developments in French policy, proceeded to Vienna and obtained Austria's adhesion to a four-point program: evacuation of the Papal States, reforms in the Italian states, peace guarantees to Sardinia, and new treaties between Austria and her satellite duchies. Agreement appearing too dangerously close, Napoleon III then began to insist on a European congress, which would officially revise the Italian settlement of 1815. Russia co-operated by issuing a congress invitation, and England and Austria felt obliged to accede. Then followed a dispute over attendance and disarmament. Austria wanted the exclusion of Sardinia from the congress and her prior disarmament. Just as agreement seemed possible on the basis of the admission of all Italian states and the reduction of Austrian, Sardinian, and French armaments, Austria issued an ultimatum to Sardinia demanding her unilateral disarmament and thus presented Cavour and Napoleon III with the very situation they wanted—an unreasonable Austrian demand and a resultant Austrian aggression.

The news of the congress proposal became known to the French public in the third week of March, and the favorable reception it received merely underlined the persistence of the general desire for peace. Rogier wrote to Brussels: "Those who despaired of the situation now give themselves over to confidence. It is as if they were saying: 'I foresaw it all the time—a war with Austria in favor of Piedmont was impossible. Away then with misgivings and hurrah for diplomacy.' "[72] Similar peace-loving optimism was shown in the reports from the procureurs general and prefects in April. From Toulouse the procureur general wrote: "Today everybody attributes to the prudence of the emperor the prospective meeting of the European congress. No one has any doubt but that under such auspices there will come out of those solemn deliberations a state of things favorable to civilization, to world peace, to the welfare and repose of Italy and to the honor and glory of France." Favorable reactions to the congress were also reported by the procureurs general from thirteen other districts scattered in every part of France. Only the report from Aix-en-Provence was dubious of the congress's success: "The people wanted a congress and now are looking forward to it, but without being completely reassured on the outcome of the deliberations. Will Austria be resigned to the necessary concessions? They dare not hope she will; and hence the great uncertainty in their minds and the complete stagnation in business."[73]

These prevailing attitudes were confirmed by the prefects. From

Bordeaux the report was sanguine: "The news of the calling of a congress for the settlement of Italian affairs was greeted with intense satisfaction by Bordeaux business. They hope very much that peace will be the result." Echos of these sentiments came also from Haut-Rhin, Vendée, Seine-Inférieure, and Allier. But a sour note was struck in the report from Maine-et-Loire where the people "rather generally fear that the future congress may not succeed in achieving the much desired peace." Thus, while there was not unanimity of optimism, there was again reflected a unanimity of peace sentiment.[74]

An interesting report from the procureur general at Besançon not only stressed this unanimity but revealed the careful way information was gathered and rechecked. On 9 April he wrote to Paris:

The heads of the court's legal staffs [les chefs du parquet] at Vesoul, Gray, and Lure have taken pains to verify carefully by personal investigations the information furnished them by the unanimous reports of the justices of the peace. They interviewed officials, industrialists, landowners, farmers, and plain workmen, and they have not met one person who showed the least sympathy for war in the interest of Piedmont or even Italy.[75]

This careful consultation of different classes of the population in Besançon is merely one instance of what was done in many other judicial districts and departments. Thus, as in Besançon, we can also discern over the nation as a whole from the other reports cited above the varying views of the different parties and classes. The Bonapartists, except for Prince Napoleon and a few of his friends, the clergy and their clerical supporters, the Legitimists, the Orleanists, the bourgeoisie, and the peasantry remained hostile to war in spite of propaganda and pressure. On the other hand, the working classes in the cities were divided between indifference, peace, and war; but a decided majority of them were for war, as was their clandestine Republican party. If then, the emperor had, like Diogenes, taken his lantern and searched the country over for some sign of support for his war policy, he would have become a very weary and disillusioned man.

The sixteen months preceding the outbreak of the Austro-Sardinian War were filled with many curious contrasts and contradictions, which could almost be termed inexplicable were it not for one man, Napoleon III. Here was an emperor who was nearly assassinated by a fanatic of the Italian cause and who then espoused that cause to the extent of plunging his country into war. Here was a ruler, boasting universal suffrage and plebiscites, anxious for periodic reports on opinion, who went contrary to an almost unanimous opinion for peace. Napoleon III is coming more and more to be known as an idealist and humanitarian, and yet here he allowed his idealism, or his ambition, to make him a conspirator, a liar, and a cheat. He blew hot and cold to his people in the vain hope of conditioning them for the war. He lied to his ministers, to his legislators, to his diplomatic corps,

to Queen Victoria, but most of all to his people. And all this deception
did not succeed, since he was suspected of war-mongering by Frenchmen and foreigners alike. Under the spell of this suspicion his strongest
political supporters opposed him vigorously and stubbornly, and his
most dangerous political enemies, the democratic Republicans, aided
and abetted him.

It is hardly necessary to look back and analyze opinion. Very
few distinctions need to be made. All classes, all parties (except the
Republicans), all regions—north, south, east, and west; urban and
rural—were opposed to war. Business, finance, commerce, agriculture,
labor, church, civil service, ministers, foreign governments, even the
empress, could not prevail against a mysterious obsession and the
birdcalls of Cavour and Prince Napoleon.

At one moment it looked as if a congress were going to preserve
peace and still attain the aims of "that man" (*celui-ci,* as he was
called in the salons). But he shrewdly discerned that none of the
foreign governments would tolerate the European revisions he
wanted. Therefore he killed the congress idea with kindness and left
it to Austria to give it the *coup de grâce.* And thus the war came: for
in this world of perpetual international anarchy it is so easy to make
a war and so hard to make or keep the peace.

CHAPTER IV

THE AUSTRO-SARDINIAN WAR

The rumors of war of the past six months were suddenly transformed into war itself by the news published in the *Moniteur* of 23
April. It told of the Austrian ultimatum demanding that Sardinia
reduce her army to its former peacetime size and dismiss her volun-
teer corps. Austria's reasons for such an ill-advised step seem to have
been that she could expect no favorable solution from a congress
apparently stacked against her and that she could not afford to keep
her mobilized troops indefinitely on a war footing. The war party in
Vienna succeeded in persuading Francis Joseph to find a more favorable solution in a quick and decisive war.

Of course Cavour and the Sardinians were delighted with the
ultimatum, since Austria gave them the pretext of aggression they

had been seeking for so long. Similarly, in France more active and open military preparations could begin at once. To increase the authorized size of the army from 100,000 to 140,000 it was necessary to go before the legislature. The legislative discussion likewise gave an opportunity to make public statements and condition the definitely antiwar opinion for the future hostilities. Walewski, the foreign minister, went before the legislative body with a long review of the prewar negotiations. He said nothing about the Plombières interview but recounted France's peaceful policy of supporting Cowley's mission, disarmament, and the congress. Previously an opponent of the war plans, he concluded his speech with an appeal to arms: "If Sardinia is threatened, if, as everything seems to indicate, her territory is invaded, France cannot hesitate to answer the appeal of an ally with whom are joined common interests and traditional sympathies." Morny, President of the Council of State, then requested the enlargement of the army and the authorization of a war loan. Also an opponent of the war, he now tried to rally the antiwar legislature to support of the war by a vigorous speech.

His words were greeted with applause and cries of *Vive l'Empereur*, but the laws were not voted until several members took occasion to criticize the recent course of events. The Bonapartist members—Lemercier, de la Tour, and Plichon—protested against keeping the legislature in the dark until it was presented with a *fait acompli*. Jules Favre spoke for the small Republican opposition. He countered the government contention of Austria's precipitation of the war by saying this was the emperor's war, and he honored him for it. This war must be for the independence of Italy, and he asked for confirmation of his statements. Baroche, the government spokesman, arose and denounced Plichon's statements as giving comfort to the enemy, but ignored Favre's queries.[1] The Belgian minister remarked that the legislative body greeted the proposal for an increased army with cries of *Vive l'Empereur* but responded to the request for the loan of 500,000,000 francs with silence.[2] Nevertheless both measures were passed.

A week later the emperor himself issued a proclamation after Austria had invaded Sardinian territory and war had been declared. In it he blamed Austria for starting the war and added: "Either she must dominate up to the [French] Alps or Italy must be free to the Adriatic. I want no conquests [for France]. . . . . The aim of this war then is to restore Italy to the Italians and not just to have her change masters, and we will have on our borders a friendly people who will owe us their independence." Then to reassure those fearing revolution or threats to the pope's temporal power, he made the further declaration: "We are not going to Italy to foment disorders or to disturb the authority of the Holy Father, whom we have restored to his throne, but to free him from that foreign pressure which weighs on the whole peninsula and to help establish order there based on the satisfaction of legitimate interests."[3]

The Old War Spirit

However peaceful opinion had been up to 22 April, it greeted the Austrian ultimatum with angry resentment. The procureur general of Nancy declared: "The insane aggression of Austria has set everybody against her; in all eyes she is the one who wanted the war and started the fire; she draws on herself the ire of the strongest supporters of peace." Indeed, from thirteen judicial districts or departments, located in all regions of France, came specific reports of similar denunciations of Austria.[4]

Guizot's son-in-law, De Witt, told Senior that in his region of Val Richer the bourgeoisie, which had previously blamed Napoleon III, "now believes Austria to be at fault and is reconciled to him." Likewise Mérimée found Paris changed from antiwar to prowar sentiment because they considered Austria to be the aggressor.[5]

The emperor, who had been so concerned with the development of opinion before the war, became even more preoccupied with its attitudes during the war. Before he left for the fighting front he therefore instituted one of the most thorough systems for checking opinion that France had during the Second Empire. On 12 May his minister of justice sent a circular to all the procureurs general urging them "to redouble their vigilance and firmness during the entire period of the emperor's absence and to send him at the end of each week [instead of each quarter] a summary report of political events and manifestations of public opinion as seen in your district."[6] Thus there exists for the Austro-Sardinian War an almost continuous account of opinion on all events and from all parts of France.

And it certainly must have been a great comfort to the newly organized government under the regency of the empress to learn from these early reports that there had been an almost complete reversal of opinion. From twenty-five of the twenty-seven judicial districts[7] of France came definite descriptions of a noticeable shift from peace to war sentiment. Only the regions of Metz and Limoges noted enough opposition to make a change not very apparent. In addition seven prefect reports received in April and May noted the same prowar trend in Seine-Inférieure, Seine-et-Oise, Meuse, Ain, Isère, Bouches-du-Rhône, and Gironde. A typical initial report was one from the procureur general in Orleans:

Public opinion at first very opposed to war, as I pointed out in my last report, has suddenly changed in a most gratifying way. Even those who reproached the emperor for unwisely engaging France in a war of no value to her now consider war in Italy as justified and necessary. It is even a rather strange spectacle to see the mobility with which the French mind, suddenly becoming belligerent, has come out for the policy of the emperor and is now confident of the outcome of the war and of the success of our arms.[8]

This changeableness of opinion is confirmed by three other non-official observers. "Parisians are so changeable in their impressions," Rogier declared, "that this war, whose very possibility caused serious anxiety, today when they see it as a certainty, welcome it with a sort of satisfaction." O'Meagher of the *Times* thought the French were so fickle and changeable that they reminded him of Prudhomme when he said: "I swear to defend the institutions of my country and, if need be, to combat them." Writing again to Panizzi, Mérimée exclaimed: "We're a funny nation! I wrote you two weeks ago that there was only one man who wanted war, and I told you the truth. Today you can take the opposite to be true. The Gallic instinct has been stirred. Now we have an enthusiasm which has its magnificent and its frightening aspects. The people accept the war with joy; they are full of confidence and spirit."[9]

The center of gravity of French opinion on the war may have shifted sharply, but that did not mean that opinion was unanimous. The prowar majority sentiment may also have been rather uniformly distributed throughout France, but it differed widely among the various political and social groups.

Among the bourgeoisie there was the greatest divergence of opinion. They had previously feared the effects of war on business, and some still let those fears dominate them. Others, resigning themselves to the unavoidable, succumbed to the patriotic fervor of the moment. This prowar sentiment of the business classes was more apparent in the north in the urban centers of Angers, Paris, Rouen, Douai, and Nancy. The procureur general in Douai, for example, wrote that "the reawakening of the military spirit is most noticeable among those who had been the strongest for peace; the bourgeoisie and the people are generally unanimous in this sentiment." The bourgeoisie of the Paris region was reported to have frankly accepted the war under the circumstances of its coming; and Mérimée, on his return to the capital, found it reconciled to it.

However, the business classes of the east and south were so unenthusiastic as to be almost hostile. The procureur general in Lyons reported: "Among the merchants . . . . a prudent reserve is noted. They will rejoice at any victories, but they will complain more or less bitterly if the hoped-for successes do not materialize." In Limoges there seemed to be even less enthusiasm:

> The merchants, the big bond-holders and landowners are not much happier than the Legitimists. The war is upsetting to business, checks its expansion. Furthermore, to them the Italians appear unworthy of sponsorship . . . . .
>
> Such are the impressions of the bourgeoisie: they will not conspire against the emperor; they do not want any military reverses; but, if it were possible, without too much danger, to restore the Orleans dynasty, they would bless the Lord if He aided this desired result.[10]

From the southernmost district of Pau the procureur general reported: "The bourgeoisie takes very little part in the enthusiasm;
they are not hostile, but they keep an expectant attitude. They have
no sympathies for Italy; they are far from the theater of war; they
do not sufficiently understand its interests and importance." Not far
different were the reports from the eastern cities of Amiens, Rheims,
Nancy, Metz, and Grenoble."[11]

As to the farmers in the country and the workers in the cities the
sentiment seemed almost unanimous. All reports from procureurs
general and prefects which specifically mentioned these classes described them as thoroughly in favor of the war. However, De Witt,
from his observation, divided the peasants into three groups: those
who had sons disliked the war; those who had horses to sell were
delighted at the prospects of high prices; those who had neither were
indifferent.[12]

On the other hand the clergy was almost as much opposed to
the war as the common people were in favor of it. Maurain, of course,
gave a detailed treatment of its attitudes. He concluded: "But it does
not seem that in the west or in the rest of France the clergy tried to
incite the people against the war. Disgruntled, it more or less let its
feelings appear in its sermons, remarks, and *Te Deum* celebrations.
These were more spontaneous manifestations of ill-humor than deliberate attempts to stir up opinion."[13] And the administrative reports
generally confirm Maurain's conclusions. The procureur general of
Angers gives a rather good picture of a cross section of clerical
opinion:

> The clergy is also divided [he said]. The wiser ones justify the government
> and recognize what it has done . . . . for religion. The majority is and will remain
> hostile. The ultra-Catholic party had actively exploited the possible dangers to
> the Holy See in a conflagration in Italy. If these anxieties were sincere, the emperor's
> proclamation and the declaration of the minister of worship would have calmed
> them; but the perils to the papacy are a theme of opposition convenient to
> maintain; and the extreme part of the clergy, together with the associations using
> charity for their ultramontane propaganda, persist in predicting that the pope will
> be the victim of revolution. Where does this propaganda line [*mot d'ordre*] come
> from? I don't know. I see, though, that it is spread by men known for their
> theocratic views. Deplorable error of the clergy . . . . . The vast majority of the
> country detests these ultramontane pretentions and passions. In associating itself
> with them the clergy is alienating all sensible men.

Thus it was in most parts of France. Most bishops and a few priests
of Gallican persuasion were circumspect and moderate, but the rank
and file of the priests and the Jesuits were ultramontane and violently
opposed to the war.[14]

Strangely enough political and not moral or humanitarian reasons mainly prompted these ordained ministers of Christ. It was rather
from the ranks of the lay intelligentsia that a humanitarian regret
appeared. The procureur general of Bordeaux, in an entirely different
section of his report remote from his comments on the clergy, added

these observations: "I often hear this thought expressed with sadness that in a civilized century like ours we have to resort to gigantic combats, to terrible human butchery, whose proportions, still more extensive during the last century, take us back to the colossal battles of the middle ages. But these are only the reflections of a small number of philosophic minds, more lofty, more educated, and more moral perhaps than the others."[15]

The Legitimists (Bourbon royalists) were closely linked with the views of the clergy, and of course many of the ultramontane clergy had Legitimist leanings. Here again was found a very strong tendency to oppose the war. The Legitimists not only sympathized with the Austrian monarch and the rulers of the Italian states, including the pope, but they opposed nationalism and the revolutionary impulses associated with it. Every report from the fourteen judicial districts which specifically mentioned the Legitimists in this period declared that they were opposed to the war after it had begun. Many of the procureurs general accused them of hoping for an unfavorable outcome of the war in order to bring a Bourbon restoration after another Bonapartist downfall. Such accounts come from Amiens, Douai, Nancy, Angers, Besançon, Lyons, Grenoble, Limoges, Montpellier, Pau, Poitiers, Toulouse, and Riom. Mérimée, however, who was a partisan of Italy, had a kinder word for some Legitimists in Paris. "Many rich young men are in the army," he wrote, "and Legitimists say that, whatever happens, one must defend the flag." Strange expression, when it was particularly the tricolor to which the Legitimists had objections.[16]

At the opposite end of the French political spectrum from the Legitimists were the Republicans. And the Republican attitude toward the war was also the opposite of the Legitimists. A small fraction of Republicans were noted in Pau, Riom, and Lyons who disliked the war because they thought victory might consolidate the empire permanently. But the majority faction in these areas and the Republicans in eleven other districts, in whose reports they were mentioned, were solidly behind the war effort and its most extreme objectives. A report from Lyons gives us a picture of the unequal division of Republican sentiment:

The Republicans are divided [wrote the procureur general], and the great majority rally around the government, which defends the liberties of oppressed peoples and which is trying to assure their independence.

At La Croix Rousse the Republicans are divided now between patriots and 'Austrians.' The former, much more numerous, admire the emperor and openly express their wish for victory. The rest still remain hostile and hold themselves aloof.

The Republican situation in Lyons was duplicated in Caen, Paris, Orleans, Besançon, Bourges, Grenoble, Limoges, Toulouse, Agen, and Aix. The attitude of the Parisian Republicans soon became apparent also in the public demonstrations during the first weeks of the war.[17]

The Soldier's Farewell

Once the war was declared, many events occurred which gave occasion for the outward expression of public feeling. One of the earliest of these occasions was the departure of the troops. The soldiers in and around Paris began to march to the Lyons railway station (*Gare de Lyon*) on their way to the front. All of these troop movements were followed by sympathetic and excited crowds, which showered flowers upon the men and handed them bottles of wine. And of course there were those heart-warming and morale-building scenes of fair young ladies running into the streets to kiss the departing heroes. A regiment of Zouaves all had bouquets of lilacs in their guns. People marched with them, keeping step with the music. And the shouts of the Republicans and workers along the line were loud and lusty: "Kill all the Austrians you can!" "Down with the Emperor of Austria!" "Long Live the Line!" "Long Live the Emperor!" "Long Live Napoleon!"

The troops seemed as joyful as the populace. They wrote chalk signs on the cars: "Excursion trains for Italy and Vienna." The Zouaves in particular were shouting, "No more guard-room duty!" But sometimes they showed how ignorant they were, even about who the enemy was, for on one occasion the troops were shouting, "We're going to thrash those blackguard Piedmontese!"[18]

In the provinces the send-offs were as enthusiastic and boisterous as in Paris, as the following procureur report from Riom will testify:

> The departure for Italy of the 54th Regiment of the Line which was garrisoned at Clermont was the occasion for a sort of ovation. The crowd converged on the railway station to acclaim them, and the train was greeted with the same acclamations when it passed through Riom.
>
> The warmest greeting was given to the 2nd Dragoons, which also left Clermont for the same destination, by all the places in my district through which it went.
>
> In spite of some heartaches and tears of certain families, the return of soldiers to active duty is carried out with great spirit. The young soldiers, called to the colors by conscription, share the enthusiasm of their older comrades.

Similar scenes were reported again and again in Aix, Marseilles, Rouen, Versailles, Besançon, Grenoble, Toulouse, Montpellier, and Lyons; and no doubt, whether reported or not, each arrondissement and each highway and railroad center had the same warm gestures of farewell. All France seemed in labor, bringing forth whole armies of young men destined for an Italian rendezvous.[19]

Even more than the departure of the troops, Napoleon III's departure from Paris on 10 May was the occasion for a public display of sentiment. And this procession to the Lyons Station was in great contrast to the sullen crowds on the arrival of Prince Napoleon and his bride.

The line of march of the imperial procession was well advertised in advance, and hundreds of thousands of people crowded the designated avenues. The first contact of the emperor's carriage with the waiting throng was at the palace gate opening on the Place du Palais Royal. Here the eyewitness account of lawyer Dabot gives us a dazzling description of the scene:

> Departure of the emperor for Italy; it is impossible to give any idea of the enthusiasm with which he was greeted when in field uniform, with tunic and kepi, he emerged from the great portal of the Louvre opposite the Palais Royal. I was right next to the gate, on the front row as usual, at the risk of being crushed. An overwhelming acclamation of Long Live the Emperor! Long Live Italy! arose. The sovereign's face was radiant with joy. The immense crowd began to sing the Marseillaise; I was thrilled to the very depths of my being [entrailles], and I ended up by sharing in the common joys and hopes.

The procession turned right and proceeded slowly down Rue de Rivoli with the curbs, sidewalks, entrances, balconies, and windows packed and jammed with waving, shouting, and shrieking humanity. But even that was nothing in comparison to the greeting he received farther on, on the Rue Saint-Antoine. This was the revolutionary workers' quarter—had been since the great revolution of 1789. Up to this point during the Second Empire these people had been repressed and sullen. Now for once they had a cause, and they let themselves go in the wildest manner. Every master, workman, and apprentice, their wives and children, as well as Republicans far and near in and out of Paris swarmed by the hundreds of thousands into the Saint-Antoine quarter. Tricolor flags flew from all the buildings and windows; many poor people had succeeded in obtaining cheap paper flags. The yells and screams which arose were deafening. Once in a while one could make out the cries: "Long Live the War! Long Live the Emperor! Long Live Italy!" The cries became more familiar, if more endearing: "We'll behave while you're gone! We'll guard the empress!" The crowds got into the street, trying to follow the procession; the lines broke; the procession slowed down; women and children reached for the carriage, children were extricated from beneath the horses of the Cent-Garde, who managed somehow, though, to keep the way open for the carriages.

Finally, they arrived at the Place de la Bastille. Here was another unforgettable scene. This square, so wide you can hardly read signs on the opposite side, was again packed solid with a pushing, howling, delirious mob. A continuous roar rose to the vaulting sky. Again the crowd broke the lines, surrounded the carriage, their hands outstretched to clasp those of their departing sovereign. The emperor beamed with pleasure; he had no fear, for at that moment he was among friends. He shook hands, waved, saluted. The workmen encircled the horses; they started to unharness them; they wanted to draw the emperor themselves. And it was the emperor who extricated himself this time. He spoke a few words: The time is short; the enemy is waiting; help make way for me to go. The crowd gave way.

On he moved to the equally tumultuous Rue de Lyon, to the
Gare de Lyon, to the train platform. All the way a sea of yelling,
scrambling, weeping, worshiping Frenchmen. The station was overflowing, the tracks and platforms were lost under a carpet of people.
There was hardly room for the court and the dignitaries. The platform
sheds resounded with cries of "The Emperor! Long Live the Emperor!" Several times he came out to the door of the train to wave
and nod his head. Finally the train began to move; the cars seemed
to be gliding silently through an inferno of ear-splitting sounds,
through a storm of flying papers and waving arms and flags. Napoleon III was off to war, his war, with the thundering cheers of work-
ing-class, Republican Paris still ringing in his ears.[20]

Eyes Across the Alps

Observers of opinion before the war had noted considerable
indifference among the common people toward the rising disputes
over Italy. This attitude had also changed with the coming of the
war. Their sons were now in battle array before a powerful foe on
the plains of northern Italy. Their emperor had gone hence to command their gathering forces. Great and decisive battles were impending on whose outcome the fate of France and the imperial dynasty
depended. The issues were no longer academic, they were real.

In Paris the people were buying maps of northern Italy. They
recognized the old familiar places made glorious by the victories of
an earlier Napoleon; and, as the armies began to move and come to
grips in bitter struggle, they pinned miniature flags from point to
point to follow the progress of the campaign.

In Besançon "the bookstores could hardly keep up with the
demand for maps and charts." "The masses," remarked the procureur
general, "think only of Italy, and their enthusiasm increases day by
day." "With the arrival of war dispatches, crowds gather around the
bulletin boards. New illustrated papers, such as the *Italie*, the *Journal
de la Guerre*, the *Bulletin de l'Armée*, and the *Zouave*, which appear
in great numbers, find a big sale and are read with intense eagerness.
Public opinion has no other interests." Outside Besançon, the same
official later reported, "the rural people buy up old newspapers from
the city," and "after the arrival of the rural postman, they gather
around the mayor or teacher, who reads the papers subscribed to by
the commune." People passed around their letters received from
the officers in the army. And when the soldiers' mail was delayed
by service difficulties, the families became very worried; rumors
began to spread that orders from higher up were holding up the
mail, presumably because of bad news or bad army morale.

To the north of Besançon in the Alsacian area of Colmar "they
snatch the public news sheets from each other, and on every hand

they read to each other their letters which arrived before the official bulletins." And around Lyons to the south the city and country people were avidly reading the details of the battles and circulating their private letters from hand to hand.

In southern France there was the same stimulation of the public mind. The newspapers in Provence had greatly increased their number of subscribers. Around Toulouse the local papers had more than doubled their circulation; and rural communes, which had never before seen newspapers, were now receiving them and reading them excitedly. In the region of Bordeaux, reported the procureur general: "The people are all in Italy in mind and spirit. They continue to follow with a curiosity, which time has not been able to diminish, the movements of our armies. Workers take out group subscriptions to local papers, and during the lunch hour one of them reads them to the others."

Although such manifestations of interest were not specifically noted by other procureurs general, we can be quite sure that this sort of stimulated interest in eastern and southern France and in the capital would also appear to some extent in other areas of the north and west. Thus, while Napoleon III basked in the glow of Milan's tumultuous welcome or shuddered at the sights of death and bloodshed on the battlefield, he well knew that the eyes of France were upon him. He'd better make good.[21]

Ten days after the emperor left Paris, he was able to report back to his expectant people a minor victory in the engagement at Montebello. Naturally the country rejoiced at this good news, but not much official attention was given to the event beyond the army communiqués.[22]

But on 4 June a full-scale battle was fought and won at Magenta, a victory which opened the province of Lombardy to the Franco-Sardinian forces and led to Napoleon III's triumphal entry into Milan two days later. On this occasion official celebrations combined with the popular rejoicing. At eight o'clock in the evening of 5 June the people of Paris heard loud salvos of artillery, which could mean only that some great victory had been won. Official bulletins were hastily posted at some points, and the news began to spread like wildfire. By the time it was dark, buildings were already brilliantly illuminated, and the crowds were beginning to swarm the boulevards. At nine Eugénie and her new cousin-in-law, Clothilda, took a carriage and drove joyfully down the Rue de Rivoli and through many of the principal boulevards, receiving the exultant plaudits of the milling throngs. By ten o'clock fireworks and bonfires lit up the sky in every direction.

Two days later there were more official celebrations. A solemn *Te Deum* was sung at Notre Dame in the presence of the empress and other members of the imperial family. Again Eugénie received ovations from the holiday crowd. The buildings were decked out with French and Sardinian flags, and the theaters as usual opened their doors to free performances. Méry composed a song to commemorate the occasion, Auber set it to music, and Gueymard sang it lustily at the Opéra. At the Opéra Comique a play hastily written by Saint-Georges and accompanied by music by Halévy made a great hit.

As soon as the news of Magenta had been received in Paris, the minister of interior relayed it by telegraph to the prefects of all the departments. On the next day the *Constitutionnel* reported the reactions: "The news was received everywhere with inexpressible enthusiasm. All the telegrams are announcing that the people are taking a holiday, flags are being raised on the houses, and illuminations are under way." Other reports of great elation with both wild and solemn celebrations came in from ten judicial districts of France, representing the northern, central, and southern parts of the country. At least the rejoicing of the people was genuine and general, and hopes that the war would soon be over were already being expressed.[23]

Then on 24 June came the second great victory, Solferino, and again the inhabitants of town and country went wild. Grandguillot wrote the following description of the Paris celebration in the *Constitutionnel:* "It was not only the boulevards, the wide monumental streets, which were flooded by the lights and overrun by the shouting crowds. One needed to see the poorer quarters: the smallest street, the most obscure blind alley was transformed, lighted, glittering. Men, women, and children each in his own way expressing his joy, his enthusiasm, and his hopes. This was, in the widest sense of the word, a real national celebration."

The most elaborate description of provincial rejoicing came from the procureur general of Besançon:

In all the eleven years that I have directed the staff of this court, I have never witnessed an enthusiasm comparable to that which the victory of Solferino aroused in my district. Hardly had the first bulletins been posted on the walls of Besançon than the flags began to come out of the windows as if by magic. The commercial court had just started its session; but the excitement was so great that it had to suspend its proceedings. Such an immense crowd gathered around the posted bulletins that the traffic was almost halted in front of the buildings occupied by the newspaper offices. In the evening the city was splendidly illuminated . . . . . At nine o'clock the choral society of the Enfants du Doubs marched to the prefecture in a torchlight parade and serenaded the prefect. More than 3,000 people, shouting Long Live the Emperor!, pressed into the inner courtyard of the prefecture, whose gate had been opened, and their shouts redoubled after a stirring speech by the prefect. Then the crowd went in good order to the headquarters of the 7th Division, and there again they cried Long Live the Emperor! This completely spontaneous manifestation made a very deep impression.

I myself visited different sections of the city. The illuminations were general and brilliant, especially in the suburbs and the workers quarters. There were several transparents reading 'Long Live Napoleon III, Father of his People, Protector of Nations!' To the very end of the smallest alleys the poorest houses were lighted in all the windows on every floor. . . . . We heard some groups of men say:

'We illuminated yesterday for the emperor; today we want to give a lesson to the Austrians of Besançon'—alluding to those who had refrained from illuminating the night
before, several of whom were out of town. . . . . There is in the lower classes an
extreme resentment and a feeling of irritation against the upper classes and
the clergy, who are not very sympathetic toward the war.

Similar scenes, with their local variations, were reported from Rennes,
Rouen, Amiens, Douai, Nancy, Dijon, Lyons, Aix, Bastia (Corsica),
Toulouse, and Bordeaux.

Yet there were also Legitimist "Austrians," unhappy about the
victory, in the judicial districts of Rennes, Rouen, Douai, Angers,
Orleans, Nancy, Metz, Colmar, Lyons, Aix, Toulouse, Pau, and Bordeaux. But at Dijon the Legitimists and Republicans both were
shouting Long Live the Emperor! Also in the district of Agen the
Legitimists joined in the celebrations; and one Republican, encounter-
ing a well-known Legitimist in a cafe, hailed him with the words:
"Well, red and white, we're both done for! The cannon of Magenta
have killed us."

Even among the government supporters, however, there was
some dissatisfaction after Solferino. In the regions of Paris, Rennes,
and Rouen they were openly complaining that a full week after the
battle there were no official details. People were actually getting
worried over the possibility that the losses were extremely heavy or
that something had gone wrong since the battle. A few days later,
when the statistics were published, the procureur general of Rennes
noted: "When they learned of the number of killed and wounded,
everywhere it cast a great pall of gloom and made people hope that
an honorable peace would soon come to crown a glorious war." In
Agen there was severe criticism of the emperor for exposing himself
unnecessarily in the battle. We have never questiond his courage, they
complained, so he does not have to endanger the whole imperial
regime by trying to prove it to us.[24]

Opinion Anticipates the Peace

Within thirteen days after the Solferino victory, which took
the French only halfway across Austria's north Italian possessions,
the armistice of Villafranca was announced. It was so unusual for
two enemy emperors to meet and draw up an armistice, especially
when the war had just begun and the current campaign was only
half over, that some historical accounts have perpetuated the impression of great surprise. La Gorce said that this "*coup de théâtre*"
was "so unforeseen," "in the French camp, the impression was one
of surprise." Debidour called it "a peace which astounded all Europe."
Even the progovernment *Constitutionnel* said that the "unexpected
news" caused "the greatest amazement in Paris"; while the Orleanist
Débats likewise mentioned that the peace was greeted with joy and

surprise. And lawyer Dabot noted in his diary that "the bulletins [of
the armistice] are read with some surprise."[25]

But there is considerable evidence to make one think that the
French public was right abreast of, if not ahead of, Napoleon III
with the idea of peace at the halfway mark. Even before the battle
of Magenta a report from Toulouse said that people "also ardently
desire peace in the near future."[26] After the battle of Magenta the
procureur general in Aix, speaking of the large Legitimist group in
Provence, remarked: "At every step [in the campaign] they ask for
peace. For them Magenta should be the extent of our glory. Our
military honor is satisfied. There is nothing else now to do but
negotiate." Indeed from the departments to the east and southeast
of Paris, if the procureur general is to be believed, all the people
wanted peace after Magenta. "In fact," he wrote, "the general wish
is that the war be ended quickly, so that it may not last, if possible,
beyond one campaign. They greet each victory with a hope for peace,
and I find that expression unanimous in the reports of my assistants
from Auxerre, Châlons, Etampes, Epernay, Arcis-sur-Aube, and
Rheims." Even the *Constitutionnel* whetted these desires when, in
announcing the Magenta victory, it hinted: "There's little doubt that
we may be soon reaching the goal that we proposed in taking up
arms." And Cowley was as positive as the reports from Auxerre and
Rheims. "There was a momentary enthusiasm on the arrival of the
first successes," he wrote Russell, "but all that the people now desire
is that it should terminate, for they do not comprehend its object
and have no real sympathy for Italy."[27]

But after Solferino the idea of an immediate peace was so widespread that it would almost seem that the emperor was under the
spell of telepathic communications from his subjects. The procureur
report from Lyons is typical of the eighteen reports from eleven areas
of France:

Already in on-the-spot commentaries they spin out the results of the great
victory on the Mincio [Solferino]. 'Peace is made.' 'Italy is freed to the Adriatic.'
'Venice has chased out her oppressors.' 'Austria, humiliated and defeated, accepts
our conditions.' . . . . 'Our political horizon is cloudless.' [Eleven days before
Villafranca negotiations were begun.]

Thus these eighteen reports (from Rennes, Caen, Rouen, Amiens,
Napoléon-Vendée, Metz, Lyons, Riom, Toulouse, Agen, and Bordeaux), together with two newspapers and the British and Neapolitan
ambassadors, all "anticipated" Villafranca. Seven of these reports
were sent to Paris early enough to be known by the emperor in Italy
before he even started his Villafranca negotiations. (These passages
were heavily underlined with pencil and marked in the margin.) It
is doubtful that French opinion suggested the idea to Napoleon III,
but it is certain that they strengthened the conviction of the regency
government in Paris that peace should be made soon and reassured

both it and the emperor that they would not be out of line with opinion if a quick peace were made. At least Napoleon's sudden inspiration to make a quick armistice at Villafranca was neither an original idea nor a great surprise; many humble people had already thought it out almost down to the last detail. How could they be surprised, then, if they merely read their own thoughts on the bulletin board, unless they might have been surprised that the emperor had had the same thoughts as theirs?[28]

Opinion was particularly anxious for peace in order to avoid the spread of war to Germany and Prussia. Indeed, considering the unreliability of sovereign states in the states system, no country should dare to commit itself to a large war in one direction without assurances that its other neighbors would not attack it from other directions. These assurances Napoleon III thought he had obtained before he entered the Austro-Sardinian War. With Russia he had a neutrality treaty; the English public, shocked at Austria's aggression, he was sure, would not tolerate intervention, and its government had no mind to intervene; the Prussian prince regent, strongly disliking Austria, indicated he would not move along the Rhine. Besides, the French emperor had hopes that Russia would actually restrain Prussia if the latter threatened France. With these reassuring considerations he put most of his eggs in the Italian basket.

But events did not work out quite as smoothly as he anticipated. German nationalist opinion became wrought up against France and in favor of Austria and, through the Confederation Diet, forced Prussia to lead a German mobilization movement along the Rhine. As this developed, Russia showed clearly that she would only use diplomatic, not military, pressure on Prussia. The situation became so critical in late June that Russia warned France to make peace quickly, and Eugénie wired the emperor in great alarm. This situation, then, was *one* of the major factors which brought about the Villafranca armistice.

At present another element of this factor is known which made it all the more urgent to sign an armistice: the French people became as fearful of a war with Prussia as did their emperor. They had jumped on the war bandwagon with the feeling that this would be a short, localized war. Any development toward a general war or a two-front war with Prussia would be very much opposed by them, and they would hold the emperor accountable if the Italian war got out of hand. This was no imaginative suspicion in Napoleon's mind; he had plenty of hard facts and evidence to back it up.

Even before the emperor left for the front, several signs indicated that public support was predicated on localizing the war. The prefect of Gironde wrote on 30 April that "they hope that the emperor's policy will succeed in getting the foreign powers to be disinterested in the question and in localizing the war." In like vein the prefect in Marseilles said the people "hope that the war can remain limited to Italy"; and the prefect in Rouen remarked that people "expect and hope that, restricted to this territory, the war will be of short duration." The procureur general of Paris confirmed these prefects in noting that business circles were perturbed over the war's becoming European. In the *Débats* Camus also expressed the hope of a localized war.

The emperor, however, had hardly arrived in Italy before his people were all stirred up over developments in Prussia. The Prussian lower house made a report which imputed to France ulterior motives affecting Germany. Immediately the *Constitutionnel* tried to deny this and reiterated that France was only opposed to Austria in Italy and was taking action only against her *Italian* possessions. But the semiofficial paper was only anticipating what was going to alarm the public. And the public began to show its concern, especially along the eastern border. In Nancy people feared a German nationalist uprising and counted on the emperor to arrange to have Russia as a counterweight to Prussia. The Legitimists in Besançon were making the people uneasy by talk of Prussian action along the Rhine and a possible rupture of diplomatic relations by Bavaria. In Rouen people were "especially worried by what Germany may do." The upper bourgeoisie of Paris was "somewhat concerned to see the attitude of the German Confederation and the possibility of a European war." Likewise the business classes in Yvetot and Le Havre were uneasy about possible "incidents which could, by complicating the war, make it a European one." The region of Bourges, the procureur general said, would remain calm "if the war was restricted to its present limits" and "if France did not have to face any new enemies." The government knew, before the battle of Magenta was ever fought, that the main concern at home was an attack from Germany.

Then in the month of June came Prussian mobilization of several army corps along with further agitation in the other German states, and French alarm became acute. The reports of the border areas are significant. From Besançon came these comments:

> The unforeseen attitude of Prussia and the mobilization of her army corps begin to impress opinion strongly. They notice a strange connection between all the war preparations across the Rhine, the voyage of the King of the Belgians to London, the delay in the return of Count Pourtalès [Prussian] to Paris, and the retreat of the Austrian armies. One wonders whether Prussia . . . . may be disposed now to become the center of a crusade against France on the side of Austria and to issue an ultimatum to our victorious armies.

From Nancy came a similar cry of alarm. Yet both border areas around Nancy and in Alsace showed a certain amount of defiance toward Germany and a willingness to have a war with them with the understanding, of course, that they would have "Russia as an ally." The

Gortchakov circular in the middle of June gave them some hope that Russia could be counted on.

But another Lorraine area around Metz did not share at all in this spirit of bravado. "In the [arrondissements] along the frontier," remarked the procureur general of Metz, "where the remembrance of the invasions of 1814 and 1815 is still keen, they anxiously await the outcome of the rearmament activities of the neighboring powers." Indeed Nancy and Colmar were the only districts which showed some willingness to accept the German challenge. In thirty-three different reports from almost three-fifths of the districts in France[29] definite mention was made of a fear of a war with Prussia and an insistence that the war continue to be restricted to Italy. A report from Pau on 2 July is a good example of this general attitude. Its procureur general wrote: "It would be giving you an erroneous picture of the situation, Mr. Keeper of the Seal, not to inform you that even among many of our most loyal people [Bonapartists] there are some today who seem worried over the . . . . menacing attitude of Germany and the rearming Prussia has just ordered."

The emperor knew how hard it had been to get the country to accept this local war in Italy. Now he and his advisors knew in no unmistakable terms that the country wanted a quick peace and no war with Germany and certainly no general war. Fleury tells us that the empress always had tried to give the emperor the impressions of the public on events,[30] and Walewski took care to let the emperor know that Prussian mobilization "caused a rather big sensation here."[31] Therefore, when the German situation became more critical and Russia showed she would not take up arms, Napoleon III did hasten to negotiate the armistice; and among the considerations included in this cause of the sudden cessation of hostilities must be placed the emperor's knowledge not only of the attitude of Prussia and Russia but also the attitude of his own people.[32]

In addition to fear of Prussia, French clerical opinion was concerned over the harm that the war might bring to the interests of the pope. Before the Austro-Sardinian War, Austria had stationed troops in the Romagna, the northern province of the Papal States, to help the pope to maintain his authority there. But as the campaign progressed and as Austria felt the need of using her troops elsewhere, she withdrew this force northward on 11 June. Almost immediately the province rose in revolt against the papal government, joined the rest of north Italy on the side of Sardinia, and accepted a Sardinian commissioner as a temporary executive. This event had repercussions throughout the Catholic world, but especially among the French clergy and its clerical party. The relation of this public reaction to the armistice of Villafranca is also a subject which deserves careful consideration.

Napoleon III had been well informed on the attitude of the clericals. He knew their hostility toward an Italian war before its outbreak, and he knew that they were the principal group opposed to the war in the early weeks. We have repeated evidence that he was concerned about the clerical attitude as the war developed. In his proclamation of 3 May he had tried to reassure French Catholics that France was not going to Italy "to foment disorder or to upset the authority of the Holy Father."[33] With the same aim of calming this group he had made a cabinet shift before he left for the front by putting the Duke of Padoue in the ministry of interior in the place of Delangle, because the former was well known as a decided clerical. The empress, who also had clerical sympathies, was made regent, and the members of the teaching orders were exempted from military service. "The government tried," said Maurain, "by its acts as well as by its words, to give confidence to the clergy."[34] After the emperor's departure Delangle, now minister of justice, issued the circular asking his procureurs general for weekly reports on opinion.

It can be easily imagined then how disturbed and embarrassed Napoleon III was when he heard of the uprising in the pope's territory of the Romagna on 11 June. He insisted upon Victor Emmanuel's rejection of the dictatorship offered him by the Romagna insurrectionists. To Gramont, ambassador to the Vatican, he wrote: "I cannot recognize an event [Romagna revolt] which, in the eyes of Europe, complicates our situation."[35]

Since weekly reports on opinion were by then being sent in, it is interesting to see the public reaction concerning the events of 11 June. Up to within a few days before Napoleon made his Villafranca decision, fifty different reports were sent in from the provinces, and not one of them reported sympathy for the insurgent Romagnols, except from a few isolated uninfluential Republicans. Yet these insurgents were fighting on the side of France. On the other hand twelve of these reports were positive and some even detailed about the great alarm appearing among the French Catholics and the clergy. In Bordeaux the procureur general described this reaction:

The movements in Romagna and especially the offer of the dictatorship to Victor Emmanuel by that part of the Roman states also stirs opinion, especially the clergy, who considers it the first blow at the temporal power of the Holy Father. If this dictatorship were accepted, it would be feared that ecclesiastical influence, in general not very favorable to the war in Italy, might become even more openly hostile. Many people reveal a fear that eventuality [hostility] might come to pass.

From Rouen came this report: "What is going on in the Papal States begins to alarm them [the upper classes]. They have full confidence in the emperor, but they wonder whether events may not go beyond his plans and whether, after victory, he may not have to call upon all his energy to impose his wisdom on our allies." In Besançon "the clergy did not like the news from Rome." It was certain that the opposition in Brittany "would exploit the outbreaks which have just occurred in Bologna and other parts of the Legations."[36] In Toulouse the revolt caused concern. "The clergy especially looks with alarm on anything that could threaten the integrity of the Holy Father's temporal power." The procureur general in Nancy took the tactful approach of complimenting the emperor and Victor Emmanuel for rejecting the dictatorship. From Angers the procureur general wrote: "I shall limit my remarks to Your Excellency by saying that the attitude of the Legitimists and clergy is becoming more and more hostile." And the same general tenor was found in the reports from Douai, Bourges, Lyons, Aix, and Pau between 11 June and 2 July.[37]

The big question, of course, is whether the government paid any attention to these reports and whether this demonstration of opinion had any influence on Napoleon's decision to end the war. Maurain is positive that the Romagna was not a factor in the making of the armistice. "Neither he [the emperor] nor those who were around him at that time, notably Fleury, ever mentioned it. The numerous notes taken by Baroche on the council of ministers held during the Italian war contain no allusion to the conduct of the clergy; it was therefore not a concern of the empress and her ministers, who had many other reasons for wanting peace. Hence it does not seem that the clerical agitation could have contributed appreciably to the decision taken by Napoleon III."[38]

It would seem amazing, after all the concern for clerical opinion, before the war and right down to Victor Emmanuel's rejection of the dictatorship, that the regency paid no attention to it and that French Catholic opinion did not have considerable influence on the emperor at the time of Villafranca. Indeed, in this instance it seems as if Maurain may have relied too heavily on the possibly incomplete notes of Baroche because there does exist a great deal of circumstantial evidence to indicate that clerical opinion was a definite factor at Villafranca in spite of the fact that the emperor and others did not allude to it immediately after the event.

One paper found in the Tuileries after the fall of the Second Empire contained the minutes of a cabinet meeting of 14 May in which the hostile attitude of the Paris clergy *was* discussed. The Archbishop of Paris, who was present, promised that he would see that prayers for the emperor would be included in the church services during the war.[39] If Baroche's notes failed to mention this incident in a cabinet meeting, they may very well have failed to mention the same topic on later occasions. Moreover, if the cabinet discussed the clerical attitude before the Romagna revolt of 11 June, how much more likely it was that it considered the subject after the Romagna revolt. Therefore Baroche's silence is not at all conclusive as to the cabinet's failure to consider the clergy before the Villafranca armistice. Furthermore, out of the twelve reports from the procureurs general received before 3 July seven had the passages on clerical opinion heavily underlined with pencil and marked in the margins by some one in the minister of justice's office. It is hard to believe that this same minister (who had asked for special weekly reports) would not bring this carefully noted clerical opinion to the attention of the cabinet and the empress, especially when he knew it would re-enforce his and her own opinions.

Another reason to believe Maurain is wrong in considering that clerical opinion "was not a concern" of the emperor and his ministers is a conversation Walewski had with Lord Cowley twelve days after the Romagna revolt. Cowley reported it as follows:

> The Emperor, he [Walewski] said, wished to insure the greatest amount of benefit to the [Romagna] populations that could be given without endangering [?] the Pope's authority, but he would not conceal from me, he said, that the Emperor would be very gentle in his dealings with the Pope. Not that H. M. in reality cares one farthing for H. H., but he is afraid of offending the French clergy and thereby weakening his own position at home, if he does anything that can be considered an act of hostility to the Pope.

In a dispatch three days later Cowley said that "there are many people who think that his [the emperor's] fears of the clergy are exaggerated—his uncle and cousin among the number—but in the Empress the Pope has a very warm partisan."[40] The emperor then was so concerned over the clericals that some thought his fears exaggerated. This fact, together with the empress' warm partisanship, could hardly make it seem that clerical opinion was ignored at this stage.

But, in addition to this indirect evidence, we have direct evidence of attention given to clerical opinion. Although General Fleury, who was Napoleon III's aide-de-camp and emissary to Francis Joseph, does not mention in his *Souvenirs* the Romagna and Catholic opinion in connection with the Villafranca negotiations, his son, Count Fleury, in his *Memoirs of Empress Eugénie* shows that Catholic opinion was a preoccupation of those at court in Paris. The younger Fleury and his mother were both very close to the empress at that time, and the count claimed to have utilized papers and statements of Eugénie in his *Memoirs*. In discussing the uprisings in Tuscany, Parma, Modena, and the Romagna, Count Fleury wrote: "All these facts reached the Empress in Paris some time before they reached the Emperor in Italy, and she always made haste to send him her impressions of the event, *as well as the impressions of the public* [author's italics] and those about her, feeling that such information might be useful to him in making up his own mind as to what should be done under the circumstances."[41] Further on in his *Memoirs*, in discussing the eve of Villafranca, he wrote: "In the meantime, the Emperor, *informed of the state of public opinion in Paris* [author's italics], Germany, and elsewhere, was becoming very anxious concerning the future." He then quotes a letter from Napoleon III to Eugénie in which the emperor gave the reasons for his decision to negotiate. The letter mentioned the heavy casualties, the arrival of distraught relatives of soldiers, the overpowering heat, the threat of a typhus epidemic—"all these and *many other reasons*."[42] The reasons given in the letter were obviously minor ones, the "other reasons" were the important ones—concern over Prussia and the French clericals.

In at least two messages sent between the Romagna revolt and the Villafranca armistice Walewski warned Napoleon III of hostile clerical opinion. When the papal nuncio in Paris hinted that the pope might flee from Rome if he did not receive reassurances on the Romagna revolt, Walewski wrote the emperor: "I am convinced that from the point of view of internal policy, this would be one of the most unfortunate events which could happen to Your Majesty." Five days later in the interest of placating opinion and the pope Walewski urged Napoleon III "to disapprove in strong terms all attempted insurrections which have been undertaken against the government of the Holy Father."[43] Debidour affirmed that "the empress and minister Walewski addressed to him [the emperor] the most alarming reports on the state of the empire" and told him that "discontent was increasing . . . . especially in the wealthy classes and the rural population deeply attached to the church." Albert Thomas also asserted that "the Empress and Walewski . . . . dispatched telegram after telegram to the emperor" concerning clerical alarm.[44] One such telegram from the empress five days after the Romagna revolt read: "The Legations [Romagna] cause concern. Mr. Wki [Walewski] must have already written by mail. I have too. Please simply tell [us?] whether the king [Sardinian] has accepted the dictatorship and whether this fact does not violate recognized neutrality."[45]

Walewski was also frantically writing to the French minister in Turin as well as to the emperor at headquarters. Cavour wrote to Prince Napoleon: "Walewski in his dispatches to Prince de la Tour d'Auvergne goes Gramont still one better. He calls down the thunderbolts of heaven upon me. I hardly know how to answer such strange arguments."[46] Gramont was the French ambassador to the Vatican, and his and Walewski's thunderbolts had to do with the Romagna revolt.

Thus Cowley, County Fleury, Cavour, Debidour, Albert Thomas, the empress, and Walewski himself all concurred that Catholic opinion was very much the concern of the government in Paris and that the emperor was being bombarded with alarming warnings on that subject before his negotiations at Villafranca. This evidence would seem to overweigh Maurain's reliance on the silence of the Baroche papers.

So far we have seen the Catholic alarm in France from the
reports of the procureurs general and the government's frantic communications to the emperor on that subject. Now the question remains
whether Napoleon III ignored these warnings and acted upon entirely
different impulses. Obviously the Prussian threat was the important
preoccupation, but did it monopolize the emperor's attention to the
extent that he did not take French Catholic opinion into account?
There is now evidence that the emperor was concerned with the
Romagna as well as with Prussia just before the Villafranca armistice,
although he did not mention it in July as one of his reasons for peace.
On 1 July he wrote Prince Napoleon: "Certainly I should like to
have the military occupation of Bologna [in the Romagna], but if
I took the initiative in such a move, I would have against me all
Catholic Europe. So we must have patience."[47] Correspondence on
the subject was going to Walewski as well as coming from him. Just
before the first armistice negotiations Cavour wrote to General La
Marmora: "I think we have finally come to an accord with the emperor
on the Roman question. He wants to leave the Marches to the pope
and deprive him of the Romagna. This is evidently the result of dispatches which he has addressed to Walewski and to me. The arrangement appears acceptable."[48] But Walewski did not interpret these
ideas as favorably to Sardinia as did Cavour. Cowley had a conversation with Walewski at this time and related it to Russell. "The
only difference [wrote Cowley] between Persigny's language to you
and Walewski's to me respecting the conditions on which the Emperor
should make peace is with regard to the Papal States, no part of
which, according to Walewski, does the Emperor wish to alienate
from the Pope, though he is willing to minimize [?] the pnt. as
much as possible."[49] Apparently there was then a two-way correspondence on the Romagna between Paris and the field headquarters.

Then when Napoleon began to make soundings with the European
powers for peace, Cowley wrote: "The readiness to accept an armistice
here however implies something wrong, which I will endeavor to
fathom."[50] When he did fathom it, he reported the causes were: the
emperor's horror at the battle casualties, the Italian apathy for the
cause, and his "distrust of the intentions of the King of Sardinia and
Cavour."[51] This latter distrust referred to the Sardinian desire to
annex the duchies and the Romagna. A month later Cowley obtained
a very emphatic confirmation of the Catholic factor in the emperor's
motivation from Walewski. This is what he reported to Russell:

'If the day comes [declared Walewski] when the Pope shall say you must help
me further or I will go, the Emperor's decision is taken. Assist the Pope he must,
or he might lose his own throne. It will no longer be a question of external but of
internal policy, before which, whatever our wishes may be, we must bow. The
French Clergy would unite to a man to force the Emperor's hand, and as the
Clergy has an immense influence over the peasantry from which the Emperor derives

principally his title to power, he must give way to them.' . . . .There are Frenchmen [Cowley continued] who think that the power of the clergy is overrated by the Emperor, but be that as it may, it is probable that H. M. will not put it to the proofs if he can help it.[52]

Certainly the emperor was not inclined to put it to the proofs on 6 July by eschewing an armistice and continuing the war. Indeed, in his letter to the pope on 31 December he publicly admitted the Catholic factor in his desire for the armistice: "One of my most earnest concerns during as well as after the war [he wrote Pius IX] was the situation of the States of the Church, and certainly among the strong reasons which impelled me to make peace so quickly must be listed the fear of seeing revolution [Romagna and duchies] assume greater proportions every day."[53]

But even after the Villafranca negotiations had begun, more and more reports kept coming in showing the hostile reaction among the clergy and their Catholic followers toward the events in the Romagna. Twenty-five reports between 8 July and 8 September from eighteen different judicial districts of France all emphasized this shift of opinion, while none indicated any favorable reaction to the Romagna affair. Warnings and advice poured in from all over France. Together with the reports before 6 July from Rennes, Douai, Bourges, Aix, and Pau there were in all twenty-three out of the twenty-seven judicial districts reporting a strong clerical and Catholic opposition developing toward the war because of the Romagna affair.[54]

On the eve of the Villafranca armistice, then, there had been at least three distinct manifestations of public opinion. The earlier war enthusiasm was rapidly changing to a desire for an early peace. The fear of Prussian intervention and a general war involving all Europe was haunting the upper classes in all parts of France as soon and as much as it was the government and the emperor. And finally the Romagna revolt, growing out of the Italian conflict, was alienating the clergy, the devout Catholic laymen, and the peasantry, on all of whom the imperial regime counted for its main support. Nor were these public reactions occurring in a vacuum. They were noted and reported long in advance of Villafranca, even transmitted to the emperor at the front. By the emperor's own admission as well as by the testimony of contemporaries the rising protests of the Catholic clergy and their followers became one of the important considerations in the decision to seek an armistice.

The Armistice of Villafranca

The Preliminaries of Villafranca were developed in three stages. General Fleury, Napoleon III's aide-de-camp, went first to the headquarters of Francis Joseph on 6 July and obtained a cessation of hostilities until 15 August. On 11 July Napoleon III himself met the Austrian emperor at Villafranca where the two men alone agreed on the terms of a final peace settlement. The third meeting in the afternoon of the 11th was between Francis Joseph and Prince Napoleon, who brought a written version of the morning's oral understanding. Agreement was reached on disputes concerning minor details, and signed copies of the Preliminaries were exchanged through the medium of Prince Napoleon.

Twice during these negotiations reference was made to public opinion. Napoleon III said that opinion required more than just a cession of Lombardy. Some settlement of the entire Italian question must be included. Francis Joseph chided him a little when he said, "Believe me, dynasties are not established by having recourse to such bad company; revolutionists overturn, but do not construct." The French emperor did not take offense at this, and the Austrian emperor in turn agreed to an over-all Italian settlement. Again Prince Napoleon brought up French opinion in his discussions. Whereupon Francis Joseph countered: "You talk to me of public opinion in France. Do you think there is none in Austria?" Obviously a weather eye was cocked at opinions all around as the terms of the Preliminaries of Villafranca were drawn up.

These terms as agreed upon provided that Lombardy be ceded to France for transfer to Sardinia; that the Austrian princes be allowed to return (without armed support) to Modena and Tuscany if they would grant a general amnesty; that Venetia was to be retained by Austria; that the pope was to institute "indispensable" reforms in his states; that a confederation of Italian states be organized with the pope as honorary president; and that the Austrian emperor have membership in the confederation for the state of Venetia. Since Sardinia would receive only Lombardy, Napoleon III did not ask for the annexation of Savoy and Nice, but he still clung to his favorite idea of a European congress to ratify an all-round settlement of the Italian question. The terms of Villafranca were published on 12 July for all the world, including Frenchmen, to judge.

The first public announcement of an armistice, that of 8 July, merely mentioned a temporary cessation of hostilities. The *Constitutionnel* said that commissioners still had to meet to agree on the duration and the details, and the *Moniteur* suggested that it was only a truce and did not necessarily mean the end of the war.[55]

With such cautious statements it is not surprising that the public's initial reaction was more hesitant and expectant than enthusiastic. The Prussian minister described the mood well when he said that the news of the truce "has been greeted here by the public with joy" and that "generally it is hoped that out of this truce peace may emerge."[56] The same hopeful, but wary, crossing of fingers appeared in the provincial reports. In the Besançon district, for example, there was no fond rejoicing. "The armistice . . . .," remarked the procureur general, "has been very favorably received . . . . but they fear that Austria may not consent to submit to the sacrifices indicated in the emperor's speech before His Majesty's departure for Italy and that the negotiations may encounter insurmountable difficulties." Nine other reports revealed the same optimistic caution. Only in Rennes, Limoges, and Grenoble was there unadulterated rejoicing at the earliest armistice news.[57]

But the announcement of the actual peace terms four days later, with the official accompaniment of cannon salvos and illuminations, set off a momentary explosion of popular celebrations and rejoicings. At 1:30 P.M. the cannon of the Invalides boomed a hundred times, announcing the conclusion of peace. In Paris it caused an "immense sensation," said the *Constitutionnel*, and at night the entire city was illuminated. The procureur general confirmed this Paris reaction and added, concerning the surrounding departments, that "illuminations and public rejoicings gave vent to the feelings of all classes of the population in several cities, notably in Troyes, Joigny, Versailles, Rambouillet, and Châlons-sur-Marne." From Lyons the Belgian consul reported: "All classes join [in the rejoicing], public buildings and private buildings are bedecked with flags. It cannot be concealed that the joy is universal without distinction of opinion. Such scenes of jubilant celebrations were also noted by newspapers and procureurs general in Rouen, Amiens, Le Havre, Cherbourg, Compiègne, Lille, Roubaix, Bourges, Besançon, Lyons, and Bordeaux.[58]

But after the first flush of celebrating the peace the public began to get down to the more difficult task of analyzing the terms. And here there was evidence of more sober and less unanimous thoughts. The new situation fulfilled the predictions of the procureur general of Bourges, who was sure that opinion would disagree on the details of the peace terms.[59] Disagreements were at first noticeable in the press reaction, although here the fear of running afoul of the minister of interior caused less striking disagreements than in the public at large. Of course the governmental *Constitutionnel* led off with a paean of praise for the peace terms. The imperialist *Pays* was just as enthusiastic in almost the same terms. As to Venetia, it said that the Austrian emperor would become merely one Italian prince subject to the decisions of the Italian diet. "All legitimate interests are satisfied."

The clerical papers were mixed in their reactions. Although the *Correspondant* worried about the pope's temporal power, Veuillot in the *Univers* called the peace "a double stroke of conscience and of genius." He marveled that the peace came on the day of St. Elizabeth, the patron saint of peace. On the other hand the *Ami de la Religion* made rather inferential attacks on the terms. Austria may have lost Lombardy, but it was more a ball and chain than a jewel. Was it worth all of Piedmont's effort to get it? The paper had thought Italy was going to be freed to the Adriatic, but presumably events spoke louder than words.

The *Débats* made great sport of the *Univers*. People had been discussing a great deal what may have been the causes of the sudden peace. Now we know, declared the *Débats:* the faithful, praying in the churches on St. Elizabeth's day, instantaneously brought it about. In a more serious vein the paper said it had hoped for the liberation of Venetia, but its changed position was an important gain. At least it would not be incorporated in the German Confederation, and no general war would be involved now in trying to pursue the matter further.

The democratic *Siècle* was sorely disappointed. It would have preferred a war to the bitter end, but even it was reasonable: "Our disappointment does not make us exaggerate things; we are not insensible to the increased territory Piedmont receives. It becomes a respectable power, and, if it remains faithful to its policy, it may one day become the center of Italian unity." Thus the press adjusted itself to the existing situation with circumspect decorum.[60]

But the rank and file of the people of France, while they had to be circumspect too, were quite open and outspoken in their favorable and adverse estimates of the peace settlement. Between 12 July, when the terms were first made known, until 9 October thirty-nine provincial reports were received which analyzed the popular reception of the terms. Twenty-six of these showed a definite division of opinion with one or more groups of opinion opposed to the peace terms. The procureur general of Toulouse remarked: "There are, however, even among the friends of the government, some politicians or fanatics who think we have not done enough for Italy or for the Italians in the duchies." In Brittany there was also grumbling over the fate of Venetia. "But, although there may have been isolated and entirely individual critics," said the procureur general, "the great majority of the Breton population applauds without reserve the conclusion of peace." In Provence, several days of calm reflection were necessary before hesitations gave way to general satisfaction. The Alsatian population seemed particularly hostile to the peace. The procureur general wrote with painful surprise:

I must say that the dispatch announcing the accord negotiated between the two sovereigns has not encountered among our people the warm and sympathetic reception that one might expect. The successive victories of Magenta and Solferino had left the impression that even more decisive successes were in store. A feverish exaltation took possession of the people. The impatience to win the goal made them lose sight of the difficulties involved in attaining it. Only reflection and a knowledge of the dangers to the country inherent in the continuation of the war has modified little by little this first impression.

Eighteen out of twenty-seven districts in France (Rennes, Vendée department, Rouen, Paris, Angers, Orleans, Nancy, Metz, Besançon, Dijon, Ain department, Riom, Allier department, Lyons, Aix, Nîmes, Toulouse, and Agens) showed a strongly divided opinion on the peace; Colmar and Bastia at one time were reported almost entirely opposed to the terms; while only Bourges, Bordeaux, and Caen seemed predominantly favorable. Thus is revealed how difficult it is to please the people. Before the war they were against war; before the peace they wanted an early peace; now that they had their early peace, large numbers of people in all parts of France grumbled about it.[61]

The widespread disagreement over the peace terms reveals the different attitudes of the various classes and political groups in France. The peasants were the most satisfied of all; they would see their sons return soon and could be sure of retaining those still at home. The clergy, too, were in general favorable to the settlement because they thought, mistakenly, that the pope was now safe and would regain the Romagna. But the Legitimists were about evenly divided: some pleased at the generous terms granted to Austria and at the setback for the antipapal revolutionists, others critical of the possible difficulties coming after the peace.

In the cities the bourgeoisie revealed divided opinions. A great majority were favorable because it would mean a restoration of normal business and less taxes. But a few, especially the smaller shopkeepers, shared the liberal sentiments of the Italian nationalists and wished, now that the war was safely over, that the war might have been continued at least until Venetia was taken. On the other hand the city workers and Republicans were almost unanimously hostile to the Villafranca terms. They wanted the war pursued in the interest of both the Italian and Hungarian revolutions, and perchance until disaster might have brought the downfall of the French imperial regime. The basic attitudes of the groups had not been changed but merely applied to the new raw material at hand.[62]

Sour Postwar Moods

Napoleon III's departure from Italy was in great contrast to his arrival. Although Victor Emmanuel II tried to perform to the end his duties as a grateful host with as much royal courtesy as possible, he was unable to carry the people with him. In Turin they closed the shutters on their windows as the emperor passed through; in some windows appeared portraits of Orsini. At the opera, attended by the emperor, a popular ballerina by the same name of Orsini was greeted by the audience with cries of Long Live Orsini! As he went to the station, the streets were almost deserted except for a few paid cheerers. Both he and Victor Emmanuel heaved deep sighs of relief as his party crossed the border.

His return to Paris on 17 July was also in great contrast to his
departure in May. No previous announcement, no public welcome,
no ovations—he just quietly slipped through the capital and resumed
his control of the government at Saint-Cloud. Already bitter over his
Italian send-off, he became deeply disappointed over what he learned
of the French reaction to the peace arrangements. On the following
morning Walewski told Cowley that the emperor "is a little *préoccupé*
at the manner in which his Preliminaries of Peace have been received." A week later Cowley wrote again: "H. M. is dreadfully cut
up at the criticism made on his peace. Mme Walewska (no bad judge)
says that she has not seen him smile since his return, and she has
been living at Saint-Cloud."[63]

Soon after his return the two houses of the legislature and the
council of state went to Saint-Cloud to congratulate the emperor. He
utilized this occasion to try to justify his policy of making peace.
So sensitive was he to public criticism of this policy and so anxious
was he to defend himself that he launched into a detailed apology,
which seemed a little out of place under the circumstances. He pointed
out that after Solferino the war had entered a more protracted stage
of laying siege to strong fortresses, which could not be turned except
by violating neutral territory, that Europe was "armed and ready to
challenge us" whether we succeeded or failed, that the effort would
have been "way out of proportion to the anticipated results." "I
should have had to seek help from revolutions." Such sacrifices could
have only been demanded if our very independence was at stake.
He made war, he said, for the independence of Italy; he made peace
for the interests of France.[64]

Two days later, in a rather abrupt statement to the diplomatic
corps, he declared that in making the early peace he had belied the
unjust accusations of the rest of Europe that he intended to overturn
the status quo of the continent or to unleash a general war.

Evidently the diplomats understood the remarks in the way
they were intended, for Rogier commented: "All in all, the impression that the diplomatic corps carried away from this interview was
that the emperor did not show his usual calm and benevolent attitude
and that he did not try to conceal his resentment at the position assumed during the war by several of the great and small powers."
Cowley elaborated a bit more: "The Emperor was very sulky at the
reception of the diplomatic corps today and contrary to his usual
custom hardly said a word to anyone."[65]

The diplomatic corps was evidently somewhat uneasy after the
audience, and the over-jittery Bourse had another seizure of palpita-
tions. Malmesbury recorded that "the tone of his speech [to the
diplomatic corps] was considered so unsatisfactory that the funds
fell directly."[66] But the reports from provincial France showed defi-

nitely that the two speeches had made a good impression on the public, winning more adherents to the policy of a foreshortened war. Although there were only seven procureur reports which referred specifically to the two speeches, they represented all parts of France except the southwest. Likewise they have a convincing ring despite the complimentary language always used for words or deeds of the ruler. Here are some of the significant passages:

(Rennes): The speech . . . . and the few words to the diplomatic corps caused . . . ., among the upper and more intelligent classes, a deep and salutary impression. (Angers) The emperor's two speeches . . . . have contributed a great deal to [a] change in sentiment. The effect . . . . was excellent. (Besançon) The impression caused by His Majesty's speech . . . . has been profound. . . . . The public expression of joy and admiration appears on every hand. (Nîmes) The conclusion of peace . . . . for a moment irritated opinion. . . . . But the feeling soon passed under the influence of the emperor's . . . . words. . . . .The political feeling of the people [is] excellent. (Metz) A grateful people admired . . . . the emperor's conduct as explained in his speech. (Colmar) The clarifying speech . . . . has obtained unanimous support.

Again this may be an instance where the emperor knew when to say the right thing, however harsh, to enhance his popular support.[67]

The emperor's resentment toward the appearance of Prussian threats, which contributed to the sudden armistice, was shared by large segments of the public. On the first announcement of the armistice, Thile (in the Prussian embassy) reported home that on the news of the Prussian mobilization of its Army of the Rhine "French animosity toward Prussia increased unmistakably in both army and the general public." Ten days later Reuss, the Prussian ambassador, wrote: "The same people, even among the emperor's intimates, who were urging war against Austria last winter, now show a similar disposition toward Prussia. Many, who only a short time ago called Prussia's attitude a wise one, now after peace has been concluded, use a different and scarcely friendly designation."

This hostility noted by the Prussians themselves in the upper circles of Paris was also found in eastern France, where nearness to Germany and memories of Prussian excesses during the occupation of 1815 to 1818, made the people especially ill-disposed. Three reports from Nancy reiterate this resentful attitude in Lorraine. The one on the eve of the armistice affirmed that "all shades of opinion are united in viewing a war with Germany without alarm, a war which less than a month ago would have undoubtedly caused serious apprehensions." Alsatians reacted as violently as did the Lorrainers. The prefect of Haut-Rhin declared: "Germany's attitude has excited the strongest resentment on the part of the rural population. . . . . We have had to . . . . take action to prevent reprisals on foreign employees in France. . . . . The least indications of an invasion would cause the whole population to fly to arms." And in Franche-Comté, just to the south of Alsace, the procureur general noted: "Prussia is quite unpopular in these regions. . . . . An ultimatum directed at France would, I do not doubt, cause the wildest outburst among the common people." In Lyons still farther south the procureur general wrote that a war against Germany "would be more popular than any other," and in eastern Normandy the procureur general indicated that the working classes looked upon impending wars with Prussia and England as likely and logical until all the coalition against France in 1814 had been duly punished.

While this angry and defiant attitude was appearing in the east and north, reports from nine other regions scattered all over France, showed at least concern and apprehension over the growing Prussian menace. These reports came from Rennes, Amiens, Paris, Metz, Dijon, Riom, Aix, Pau, and Bordeaux. An attitude of concern, of course, was not as militant as those noted along the eastern borders, but from the nature of the reports there was no indication of any greater love for the Germans.

Cowley summed up the situation just before the armistice when he said:

> The present war is not popular. . . . . But change the tune to Germany, and every Frenchman who can carry a musket will lend himself and she [France] will have a million of soldiers under arms within a month. I think then that unless Prussia intends under certain contingencies to go to the assistance of Austria her arming has been a great error. Surely, with a man of the Emperor's character, anything like menace does more harm than good, unless he is afraid of the power that menaces. And the only one I know capable of inspiring that sentiment in H. M.'s mind is England.[68]

Indeed, at the close of the war England *was* on the mind of the emperor and the French public, and in none too friendly a way. British opinion, not influenced greatly by any Roman Catholic element, was much more pro-Italian than the average French opinion. Consequently it showed, as did the Palmerston cabinet, considerable irritation at the apparent concessions made to Austria in the armistice. Furthermore, the British were somewhat apprehensive over the signs of Franco-Russian friendship during the war. But real alarm broke out as they saw the emperor's attempt to increase his navy as a part of his general war effort. While it seemed to be directed against Austria, it was bound to be interpreted in London as a covert attempt to sneak in an increase in seapower to England's disadvantage.

The naval question led to proposals in parliament for an increase in British naval construction and a rise in taxes to support it. During the debates in the middle of July Lord Lyndhurst, in defense of the proposals, uttered rather frank and uncomplimentary words about France and her emperor:

> If I am asked [he said] whether I cannot place reliance in Emperor Napoleon, I reply with confidence that I cannot, because he is in a position in which he cannot place reliance on himself. He is in a situation in which he must be governed by circumstances, and I will not consent that the safety of this country should be

placed on such contingencies. . . . . The question of money expense sinks into insignificance. It is the price we must pay for our insurance, and it is a moderate price for so important an insurance.

Others picked up the theme in further debating, and several leading newspapers were outspoken in criticizing the Italian policy and naval program of France.

On the French side of the Channel there were even signs of anti-British sentiment during the war. The procureur general in Nancy remarked that the people looked upon Russia as a potential ally, but "as to England, her general reputation for cunning and perfidy is so prominent in the French mind that there exists an irresistible mistrust of her everywhere." In Normandy (Rouen) people were hoping that after defeating Russia (in 1854) and Austria (in 1859), France might have the chance to do the same to England.

But when the British parliamentary and press attack came in mid-July, the French reaction was more violent. The report from Rouen stated that "England [wrote the procureur general] had aroused against herself the patriotic susceptibilities of all classes." The procureur general at Angers wrote: "In the field of foreign policy I note one feeling growing rapidly: the old national prejudice against England. The injustices and the insolence of the English press and parliament are bitterly resented by all classes in this region, and they revive the hatreds of the common people." From Brittany came the report that "the aggressive speeches in the last few days in the House of Lords, the persistent and hostile insinuations directed against the increase of our navy, represented as a permanent menace to England, have, I believe I can say, deeply affected public sentiment." In Nancy (Lorraine) it was "against England and Prussia that opinion [was] particularly irritated." In Besançon (Franche-Comté) "only the attitude of England in the [Italian] peninsula [aroused] some easily excited people." "The policy of the English cabinet had completely alienated opinion before and during the war" in Douai; and the "systematic hostility of England . . . . left in its wake a certain uneasiness" in the district of Aix, which included Marseilles.

This wave of anti-British feeling became serious enough to require government action. On 26 July a semiofficial article was put in the *Moniteur* asserting that France was not the cause of England's new naval expenditures but rather England's wild imagination about French designs. Finally on 6 August at his Chantilly palace Napoleon III had a long argumentative conversation on the matter with Lord Cowley, who reported: "More than once, in the course of the evening His Majesty reverted to the state of public opinion in England with regard to himself." After both men had exhausted the arguments on both sides, the emperor closed the discussion by remarking that "if he had spoken on the subject, it was because he was afraid that the feelings of the British people would arouse corresponding sentiments in France, and this was not desirable."

Of course by that time the epidemic of Anglophobia was already raging in many parts of France. It seemed to be an intermittent and endemic disease with the French public in certain periods of alleged or justified provocation. Fortunately this time, as on all such occasions since 1815, it did not lead to open hostilities.[69]

France's anger at Prussian threats and English insinuations is understandable, but her growing dislike for her erstwhile allies in Italy might seem at first sight surprising. Yet on closer examination such a trend appears almost natural. After all, the great block of Legitimist and clerical opinion was deeply hostile to the Italian national movement with its threats to the little absolute monarchs and the pope. While some Orleanists, like Thiers, were not averse to the expulsion of Austria from the Italian peninsula on grounds of French international interests, for the same reason they did not want to see this Italian national movement lead to the erection of a powerful national state on France's borders. Likewise, as we have seen, the great mass of the French people had been opposed to the idea of a war for Sardinia and Italy before its outbreak. This background of dislike and unconcern was bound, then, to become fertile soil for anti-Italian feeling as developments during and after the war increased the incidence of petty irritations.

Colonel Claremont, the British military observer in the theater of war, was constantly reporting the bad feeling existing between the French and Sardinian officers in the field. In mid-June Prince Albert remarked in a letter to the Prussian prince regent "that the feeling between the French and Sardinian armies is not good"; and just before the armistice Cowley wrote Russell: "I enclose the copy of a letter which I have just received from Claremont and which gives some insight into the sentiments prevailing at the Imperial Headquarters. With respect to what he says about the Italians I may add that the letters recd. from the [French] army all concur in stating that they are not worth fighting for."

This attitude in the French army infected the people while hostilities were still going on. On another occasion Cowley observed that the people "have no real sympathy for Italy." At least two procureur reports from two widely separated areas in France seem to confirm Cowley's remarks. The procureur general in Rouen wrote that "the sympathies for the Italians have none-the-less remained, it must be admitted, rare and weak," while from Agen in the far south came the report that "the Italians, from which I must naturally distinguish the brave Piedmontese army, have not made much progress in public sympathies."

After the armistice the occasions for friction became even more frequent. The coolness and even insulting attitude shown toward the emperor in northern Italy on his return journey is well-known. The empress told Cowley that two of the reasons for the armistice was the emperor's disgust at Italian apathy for the common cause and his distrust of the intentions of Victor Emmanuel and Cavour in central Italy. Even Mérimée, a friend of the Italian cause, admitted (18 July) to Panizzi that the lack of co-operation of the liberated Italians was one of the causes for the quick peace. And the emperor frankly told the Italian patriot, Arese, that French "interests made it an imperious duty for him [the emperor] to put an end to sacrifices which he had made for a people who did not seem to show him any gratitude for them."

The emperor's resentment was easily reflected in the army as a whole. Prince Reuss, the Prussian embassador, reported that "the emperor himself had mentioned the coolness with which he was received by the Italians after the peace" and that this might not be unrelated to the "apparent disappearance of the emperor's and his staff's enthusiasm for Italy and the Italians." And the changed attitude of the army in turn soured the French public toward their southern neighbors. In another letter to Panizzi (20 July) Mérimée noted: "Our people are coming back furious at the Italians. They say that the common people are completely *Austrian*." The prefect of Ain department, in discussing the return of the troops, remarked: "Our soldiers appear disgruntled with the Italian people and even with the Piedmontese army. Their accounts and their views are changing opinion on the Italian cause and diminishing the sympathy and interest which it inspired." From the procureur general in Grenoble came the same story: "The Piedmontese [he wrote] is well known in our upper Alps, and he has won no sympathy there. They complain that he is quarrelsome, vain, and unreliable. What our officers tell of their relations with our allies had not helped to change these impressions." From Nancy came the report that "opinion . . . . dis-associates itself from Italian affairs to withdraw into its habitual calm" and that "public opinion, satisfied by the moral conquest just won, does not mean by that to be in favor of the excesses of the Italian movement." Likewise the report from Besançon noted: "After the return of our soldiers, [opinion] has begun to judge the Italians severely and to consider them more disruptive than desirous of a safe and sane liberty." In the Limousin "Italian affairs . . . . no longer excite any one."

From the emperor, then, down through his army to the people in many parts of France spread this postwar reaction against the Italian cause. It is significant that in no reports consulted was there evidence of a continued or increased popularity for Italy. Thus on

the eve of further disturbing events in Italy the French public was
in a very unsympathetic mood toward any appeals from that quarter.[70]

One of the most important long-range results of the Austro-Sardinian War was the shift of political support for the imperial government from the right to the left. The clerical party, except for some
ultramontane Legitimists, had rallied to the Second Empire before
the Austro-Sardinian War. Maurain declared that "the alliance between the government of Napoleon III and the church appeared
[in 1856] to be at its zenith."[71] But the opposition of the pope to
the Italian nationalist movement and the revolution in his Romagna
states, which the war had brought about, both, combined to alienate
many of the clergy and their Catholic followers from the imperial
government in spite of their satisfaction over the early peace. From
eighteen different districts or departments, representing all parts of
France, came in October 1859 unanimous statements of the disaffection of the clericals. The prefect of Ain noted "an ever-increasing
concern spreading among the clergy and the numerous Catholics who
would not like to see the Holy See's possessions decreased because
they were necessary to the church's independence." "There is a political angle which must be considered"; he added, "in spite of the
intentions of the government, its reiterated statements, and the well-
known sentiments of the emperor, the clergy may well take an unfortunate, even hostile, attitude if the present state of things continues." In a like vein the procureur general in Rennes reported:

> For the clergy and for the ardent Catholics, very numerous in Brittany, the
> question of the temporal power of the pope is identified with religion itself. In
> their eyes, to disturb or weaken the one is to disturb or weaken the other; and it
> would be very difficult to convince them that a necessary administrative reform is
> not a threat to papal supremacy, to the legitimate authority of the Holy See. From
> this comes a profound emotion, a new agitation which must be taken into account,
> a real danger which need not be exaggerated but which it would be unwise to
> ignore and which must not be allowed to get worse.

Similar reports and warnings of a growing Catholic opposition also
were sent in from sixteen other judicial districts representing all parts
of France. Nowhere was there evidence by October 1859 of an increased Catholic support of the government.[72]

But the losses of the government on the clerical right were at
least in part compensated by gains on the left from the liberal bourgeoisie and the Republican working class. This more radical left had
supported the war policy with enthusiasm but had been somewhat
disgruntled over the early peace and its partial settlement of the
Italian question. Conscious of the fact that it might lose these new
gains because of the postwar disappointment, the government tried
to conciliate the radicals by a general amnesty (16 August) and by
a cancellation of all existing press warnings. These two generous
gestures together with the dulling of the disappointment by the pros-

pects of more Italian gains than Villafranca specifically provided for tended to mollify the left and retain its support.

From fourteen different districts or departments in all parts of France came reports of leftist or Republican adherence. Here are passages from some of the more significant ones:

(Nancy) The Italian campaign has had this other effect of attracting to the government by the prestige of glory a large number of Republicans who are carried along by national feelings. (Besançon) The former demagogues, today rallied to the government, have stopped serving as pawns [to the old paarties]. (Poitiers) Almost everywhere . . . . the war and its successes have . . . . produced new [Republican] adherents. (Grenoble) This generous war has brought to the support of the government the more honest segment of this [Republican] party, and outstanding conversions can be cited. (Aix) The emperor's policy . . . . has more or less openly attracted to the support of the empire . . . . a good number of Republicans. (Nîmes) Information . . . . shows the political attitude of the people to be excellent. . . . . An appreciable transformation has taken place in the attitude of the old parties. (Toulouse) A certain number of honest and conscientious Republicans have seen fit to rally to the emperor's government. (Bordeaux) In general, Republicans are applauding the emperor's present policy and the Italian war. Such is also without exception the attitude of the working class.

And in the seven other areas of Vendée, Angers, Orleans, Metz, Lyons, Allier, and Riom the same conversions from the Republican to the Imperial party were reported. Only in the districts of Dijon was Republican and socialist opposition reported as remaining sullen and silent because of the early and incomplete peace.[73]

The experience of the Austro-Sardinian War tightened the strait jacket of peace opinion about the free movement of the French government in foreign policy. Before the war, opinion was constantly consulted, and just as regularly it showed a prevailing antiwar sentiment. While Napoleon III was obviously plotting the outbreak of the war and was indicating to the Italians his need to prepare French opinion, the antiwar attitude of his advisors and international circumstances seemed to make it impossible for him to whip up a war spirit in the public mind. Only Austria's rash ultimatum could cause an early and momentary war fever in France. This was enough to get the hostilities under way but not enough to give sustaining support to the Italian crusade. The desire for an early peace revealed the return of strong peace sentiments to the three major segments of French society: the Catholic clericals, the peasants, and the bourgeoisie. Their opposition to any general war and their insistence on a quick finish to even the local war were an open book to the French government and to foreign observers. To those who were adept at reading the signs of the times it was clear that, barring a direct attack on French soil, the French government would not be permitted by her public to take effective action against Prussia or against any future adverse moves on the diplomatic chessboard. The realization of this deep-seated peace obsession of the French people was to haunt the Tuileries and the Quai d'Orsay from this time forth and weaken their grip on the rudder of the French ship of state.

CHAPTER V

SARDINIAN AND FRENCH
ANNEXATIONS

It was easy enough for two emperors to draw up the preliminary peace terms at Villafranca, but it was quite a different matter to carry them out in the face of Sardinian objections and the widespread disappointment of the Italian people in Parma, Modena, Tuscany, and the Romagna. During the next nine months the inhabitants of north Italy and their revolutionary leaders were to counter Napoleon III's surprise solution of the Italian question with a surprise solution of their own. In August and early September the revolutionary governments in Tuscany, Parma, Modena, and the Romagna held elections for representative assemblies in which annexation to Sardinia became the major issue. So overwhelming was the victory for annexation that these assemblies quickly voted the dethronement of their former princes, including the pope in the Romagna, and their annexation to Sardinia.

Napoleon III was in a doubly embarrassing position as a result of these developments: He had promised Austria the peaceful return of the Austrian princes to the central states, and he feared the hostility of the French Catholics if the pope lost the Romagna permanently. As these resolutions were being passed in the newly elected assemblies, he had a warning published in the *Moniteur* (9 September 1859) in which he implied that the provision for making Austrian Venetia an Italian state in the Italian confederation was contingent upon the return of the Austrian archdukes to the central states. Rejection of the archdukes would mean the loss of Venetia to a future Italian union. "We doubt very much that a congress can obtain any better conditions for Italy." Then toward the end came the veiled threat: "Would it be just to ask a great power for important concessions without offering him equivalent compensations in return? The only other way out would be war; but Italy should not delude herself, there is only one power in Europe which will fight for an idea: that one is France, and France has accomplished her task."

Victor Emmanuel II had already learned of the emperor's objection to annexation. Thus, when the delegations came to Turin to lay their annexation request at his feet, he welcomed them warmly but deferred to a future congress the decision as to annexation. To the Romagna delegation he also added that "he would always have a profound and unalterable respect for the supreme head of the Church."[1]

The Duchies: Reactions to Annexation Proposals

La Gorce, in speaking of the annexation movements in the duchies (Parma, Modena, Tuscany), believed that "this piecemeal demolition of all that previous public law had established provoked surprise bordering on stupefaction."[2] But La Gorce again must have been judging general opinion by his own reaction and that of his circle of friends because the procureur reports indicated rather a prevailing lack of concern about the fate of the duchies. Again and again in the October reports appear the remarks of little interest in the fate of the duchies. "The information coming to me from all parts of the district [eastern Normandy]," wrote the procureur general, ". . . . all agree that there is very little interest in the future destiny of the duchies." In the Limousin, Italian affairs "no longer excite anyone, especially among the common people." "The question of the duchies . . . . has ceased to worry opinion [in Provence]." It "no longer had the privilege of exciting opinion" in Franche-Comté. In western Normandy Italian complications "caused rather lively concern for well-informed people," but "the lower classes of society . . . . hardly think of the Italian question." And in Lyons the public "was quite uninterested" in the duchies. So it was too in Brittany and in Burgundy.

While this lack of interest seemed to prevail, there were only two instances reported of actual sympathy for the duchies in their rejection of the archdukes. The procureur general in Douai wrote at some length:

What they [the Legitimists] want, although they do not dare say so, is the re-establishment of the situation changed by our arms, that is, the restoration of the dukes and archdukes.

These impressions are not those of the great majority of the inhabitants in the departments of Nord and Pas-de-Calais. On the contrary we find in all ranks of society, especially among the masses, a strong sympathy for the people in the duchies. . . . .

In Allier the prefect reported that the Republicans "attack the idea of the restoration of the former dukes."

Indeed, there was more evidence of lack of sympathy for the duchies than sympathy. In the reports—to balance the two produchy instances in Douai and in Allier department—there were seven other districts showing hostility toward the aims of the duchies. The procureur general of Nancy discussed at length the antiduchy and anti-Sardinian sentiment in his district:

In the educated classes [he said], prudent men with no partisan prejudice, and I am happy to say they constitute here the vast majority, are not without some concern. . . . . They fear that the counsels of moderation given to the populations of central Italy may not be heeded. After the movement which has occurred in the duchies, the restoration of the former sovereigns seems to them very difficult, and these sovereigns so completely devoted to Austria do not seem to them to offer France sufficient guarantees. On the other hand, a too extended expansion of Piedmont [Sardinia] appears to them to be dangerous for the future, for as long as they control the Alpine passes, they possess the keys of our country. . . . . The federative form promised by the Villafranca agreements would suit their preferences, but the votes cast by the people, who have come out in favor of annexation to Piedmont, appeared to them to be a difficult obstacle to surmount.

People in eastern Normandy went so far as to doubt the genuineness of the popular vote. Similar sentiments were shown in five other districts. The Ultramontanes and Legitimists in Allier department were "extremely irritated at the king of Piedmont." Opinion in Besançon was sure that "the emperor did not want the immoderate enlargement of Piedmont." Likewise in Nîmes people were "alarmed by the ambition of His Sardinian Majesty and by the revolutionary and antireligious spirit of the men in Italy who then directed public opinion and the provisional governments in the duchies"; while the Legitimists and Orleanists in Grenoble "hoped for the restoration of the princes." Some people in Marseilles were also disturbed by "the complications arising in the duchies." Quite often, however, these anti-Italian sentiments concerning the duchies were limited to the conservative monarchist and clerical factions.

At least it can be seen from the above descriptions of opinion that there was enough general disinterest and produchy sentiment to blunt La Gorce's claim of surprise and stupefaction at the annexation movement.[3]

The Romagna and Papal Temporal Power

French indifference may have predominated in the question of the duchies, but such was not the case with regard to the Romagna. In these Legations of the pope there had been the same overwhelming election results for annexation to Sardinia, and on 24 September the Romagna delegates had presented their petitions to Victor Emmanuel, receiving the same temporary rejection coupled with promises of support in a European congress.[4] The clergy and the clericals, who had at first seemed pleased with the Villafranca armistice, now took alarm at the prospect of the pope's loss of the Romagna. Pius IX himself gave them the signal for a campaign of protest. On 26 September he issued an allocution in which he defied the revolutionary Romagnols, claimed that a majority still supported him in the Legations, and stubbornly defended the type of government he had given them. Bishop Parisis in his charge to his faithful remarked that the growing alarm over the pope's temporal power was regretfully connected with France's recent victories. The *Univers* published it on its front page on 25 September. Three days later Bishop Pie of Poitiers also issued a pastoral letter defending the papal government and showing its superiority to modern governments generally.

More virulent, Bishop Dupanloup of Orleans attacked the Italian nationalists and Sardinia in his *Protestation* of 30 September. "In your dreams of Italian unity," he asked, "why should the cities you leave to him [the pope] have any different fate than Bologna and Ferrara [in the Romagna]; why, if you are revolutionary and anti-Catholic do you stop, trembling, in applying your principle of spoliation, or if you are Catholic, why do you proclaim it [such a principle]?" Fifteen other bishops publicly endorsed Dupanloup's *Protestation.*[5]

The cardinal-archbishop of Bordeaux, while more circumspect, had a much more dramatic occasion to publicize the papal cause. On 11 October the emperor and empress stopped at Bordeaux on their return to Paris from a vacation in the Pyrenees. His Eminence, in welcoming the imperial couple to the city, craftily wove in references to the Romagna question to publicize the issue.

Sire [he said] eight years ago when the city of Bordeaux gave you such a rousing welcome . . . . my priests and I . . . . prayed for him who had stopped the ever-rising flood of revolutions, who had set again on the brow of the church and its clergy the halo of honor which others had tried to remove, who had started on his road to a great destiny by restoring the Vicar of Jesus Christ to his city, to his people, and to the fullness of his temporal power.

Today we pray again, Sire, with more fervor, if it is possible, that God furnish you with the means, as he has given you the will, to remain faithful to that Christian policy which blesses your name. . . . .

The emperor, somewhat surprised by this oblique attack, rose to the occasion and used the publicity to present a defense of his policy.

I thank Your Eminence [he replied] for the sentiments just expressed. You do justice to my intentions without overlooking, nevertheless, the difficulties in the way, and you seem to understand so well your high calling in trying to strengthen confidence instead of spreading useless alarms.

. . . . The government which restored the Holy Father to his throne can only give him advice inspired by a respectful and sincere devotion to his interests; but it is rightly worried about the day, which cannot be far off, when Rome will be evacuated by our troops, because Europe will not permit that a ten-year occupation last indefinitely. And when our army retires, what will it leave behind—anarchy, terror, or peace? Those are questions whose importance everybody acknowledges. But you can be quite sure, in the times in which we live, to succeed in solving them, we must, instead of appealing to enflamed passions, search for truth calmly and pray that Providence will enlighten peoples and kings on the wise exercise of their rights as well as on the extent of their duties.[6]

The clerical newspapers, especially the *Univers, Ami de la Religion,* and the *Correspondant,* became very active in publishing these pastoral letters and the Bordeaux speech of Cardinal Donnet and in commenting on them.[7]

Forcade, however, in the Orleanist *Revue des deux mondes* was forthright in his criticism of the clergy and the pope. The clergy should have spoken out before instead of after the war. Especially they should have urged the pope to inaugurate liberal reforms. He turned on Dupanloup's *Protestation,* calling it clerical hyperbole and charging the bishop with disregard for realities. Forcade said that he favored the government's program of some temporal power along with genuine papal reforms. He asserted that it was absurd to insist that the pope cannot relinquish the Romagna when one of his recent predecessors had been able to approve the loss of Avignon. Besides, the Romagna were originally seized by force by earlier popes, were later surrendered by treaty and received back by treaty. Presumably still a third treaty could transfer them to Sardinia.[8]

The reaction of opinion to the clerical manifestoes and the newspaper controversies seemed in general to be favorable to the papal cause. The strong religious feeling in Brittany made this province particularly concerned with events in the Romagna.

> For the clergy and for the very numerous ardent Catholics in Brittany [wrote the procureur general at Rennes] the question of the temporal power of the pope is associated with religion itself. In their eyes to disturb or weaken the former is to do the same to the latter; and it will be very difficult to convince them that an urgently needed administrative reform is not a move against papal supremacy and the rightful authority of the Holy See. From all this arises a profound uneasiness, a growing agitation which it is important to take into consideration, a real danger which should not be exaggerated but which should not be ignored or allowed to get worse.

The neighboring province of Normandy showed a similar concern for the pope in the report of the procureur general in Rouen:

> . . . . Information coming to me from all parts of the district is unanimous [in reflecting apprehension over France's involvement in central Italy]. These reports are also in agreement on three points: First, that opinion bothers very little about the destinies of the duchies, while it takes to heart anything concerning the fate of the Papal States; secondly, in general it considers as just and necessary, on the one hand, the full maintenance of the temporal domain of the Holy See and, on the other hand, the introduction of administrative and political reforms in its states; and thirdly, that this concern is concentrated in the middle and upper classes and has not seeped down to the masses. . . . . The lower classes without distinction have appeared up to now in this district to be completely indifferent to all these debates on foreign policy.

The prefect of Ain, writing to the minister of interior, pointed out "the ever-growing concern spreading among the clergy and large numbers of Catholics, who would not like to see the possessions of the Holy See reduced because they consider them necessary to the independence of the church." A particularly detailed analysis of opinion on the Romagna question was given by the procureur general of Nancy.

> The declaration of the Bologna assembly [he wrote] which proclaimed the downfall of the pope's temporal power in the Legations has especially stirred the Catholic party. . . . . It is certain that all the clergy and their supporters are carrying on a great deal of agitation. While calling upon the government of the emperor to support the cause of the Holy Father, they seem to impute to him a partial complicity with the most advanced reformers.
>
> . . . . The enlightened classes . . . . and I am happy to say they form the great majority here, are also not without some concern. . . . . The proclamation of independence by the Legations did not surprise them, but they are grieved by it. The distaste of the people subject to the Holy See for the administration governing them has been in fact known for a long time. They have known that if the temporal power of the pope is only maintained in Rome with the support of French troops,

it only continued in the Legations in the presence of Austrian troops. After the departure of the latter they could not be astonished by almost foreseen events. But these events were none-the-less considered as a very regrettable incident. They would like the lofty views which dictated the emperor's reply to the Archbishop of Bordeaux to be finally understood in Rome.

Likewise the report of the prefect in Marseilles not only echoed these sentiments but also showed a preference for the temporal power.

Nine other districts or departments of France (making fifteen in all) reflected a pro-Catholic reaction to the Romagna question. The Romagna revolt "disturbed the clergy and the profoundly Catholic peoples" of Languedoc; while in Allier department clericals, Legitimists, and Orleanists opposed Sardinian annexation, some Liberals, however, were against the papal administration. The agitation of the bishops had stirred up the clergy in Franche-Comté where they had much influence on the people. General sentiment in the Nîmes district was that the emperor should very energetically use his influence with Sardinia to get it to respect "the legitimate rights of the pope as temporal sovereign" and put a stop to the ambitious expansion of Piedmont. The procureur general in Bordeaux confirmed the report of the prefect in describing the Romagna question as "a serious subject of profound affliction and grave concern for those believing in law and order and for Christians." Other judicial districts where anti-Sardinian or anti-Romagnol sentiment prevailed were those of Orleans, Riom, Metz, Lyons, and Grenoble.

There was, however, some hostility to the campaign of the bishops, particularly in Poitiers where the procureur general, discussing the charge of Bishop Pie, declared: "This work may have pleased some men in the royalist and ultramontane parties. Liberal opinion, devoted to the government of the emperor, considered it an act of aggression against modern ideas and against the power founded on the national will. I have been assured that the general impression has been unfavorable to the charge and that in public gatherings, cafes, and [social] circles, it has been greeted in a far different way than that expected by its author." He confirmed this again three weeks later when he wrote that "opinion seems disposed to judge severely the decisions of the Holy See, if, while remaining deaf to the legitimate complaints of the people and to the wise counsels of the [French] government . . . ., it persists in keeping intact its outmoded institutions, which are a permanent cause of irritation and disorders." In the district of Douai, too, a great deal of sympathy was found for the people of the Romagna "in all classes of society, especially among the masses"; "they would deplore the unconditional re-establishment of the authority of the pope." Similar attitudes were reported from Bordeaux, Nancy, Moulin, and even from the Vendée. But such reactions were quite the exception in contrast to the prevailing tendency to side with the pope and his temporal power in the Romagna.[9]

The campaign of the bishops and the effect it had on opinion did not go unnoticed by the emperor and his government circles. On 4 October he told Arese, "I am the only one here who is devoted to the Italian cause."[10] On the same day "he informed me [Cowley] .... that his lukewarmness in the Pope's interest was already exciting the anger of the French Bishops and that he must not push matters too far."[11] But the government's concern over the developing hostile public opinion emboldened it to push matters further with the clerical newspapers and the bishops. Rouland, minister of interior, sent one of his agents to Veuillot to warn him gently against publishing in the *Univers* the letters of the bishops "which could compromise the interests of religion." "They beg us respectfully," was Veuillot's rueful remark, "but on pain of death."[12] When he persisted in publishing and agitating, he was sent an official warning on 11 October. Then three days later all papers were officially prohibited from publishing the bishops' letters. The clerical papers protested angrily and tried to evade the prohibition by just listing the letters of bishops as more and more of them appeared. The government countered this with even more vigor. It replaced the clerical Duke of Padua at the ministry of interior with Billault, much less sympathetic toward the papal cause. The new minister put a stop to all evasion. A general warning was published in the *Moniteur* of 18 November. From this general warning the new minister proceeded to give individual warnings on specific counts to the *Correspondant*, the *Ami de la Religion*, the *Union de l'Ouest*, the *Indépendant de l'Ouest*, and the *France Centrale*. Even the progovernment *Opinion Nationale* was warned because it denounced too vehemently the temporal power. Finally when the *Ami de la Religion* and several provincial papers published an apocryphal letter attributed to Victor Emmanuel, the ministry subjected them to punitive fines.[13]

After an examination of the procureur and prefect reports, which show a general and predominant concern for the pope's retention of the Romagna, we are somewhat surprised to come upon statements by Maurain that "these charges [of the bishops] caused no disturbance," that "there was a great deal of talk about the Romagna question in the drawing rooms, but the masses were indifferent."[14] Especially is this conclusion astonishing in the light of the government's alarm at the decided public reaction and the severe measures it took against the press, measures which are treated at length by Maurain himself. Maurain to the contrary notwithstanding, there was a widespread disturbance of opinion way beyond the narrow confines of the drawing rooms. Although some reporters on opinion noted an indifference among the lower classes, such observations were not general. Only five districts showed a pro-Romagnol sentiment; while in fourteen others the clergy, clerical Catholics, Legitimists, Orleanists, as well as conservative business and professional classes, under the influence of episcopal agitation, evinced a definite concern for the fate of the pope's temporal power as the Romagna slipped out of his grasp.

Le Pape et le Congrès

One possible solution of the problems of central Italy and the pope's temporal power in the Romagna was to call a European congress. The Congress of Vienna had decreed one settlement, which later had been enforced by the concert of Europe at Laibach. Now that Italy was in turmoil and the Vienna solution partly dissolved, what could be more natural than to have another congress formulate a new organization of Italy? Indeed, such an idea was uppermost in the minds of the negotiators. At Villafranca it was agreed that a congress would determine the final and more detailed arrangements. The inspired article in the *Moniteur* of 9 September mentioned the congress idea again. It warned the Italians that a congress demanded sacrifices in return for gains, that the archdukes would have to return if Venetia was to become independent of Austria in an Italian confederation. Also the public was reminded of the proposed congress in Victor Emmanuel's replies to the delegations, wherein he promised to plead their cause before the congress. Indeed, Napoleon III had made the same promise to Cavour a few days after the Villafranca armistice.[15] Then in November, when the final peace terms were drawn up at Zurich, a congress was again indicated for the solution of questions beyond the treaty terms.

Strangely enough, although the congress idea had been in public circulation during July, August, and September, very little attention was given to it in France. The Italians, of course, were discussing it a great deal, but only a few French papers mentioned it. However, the procureur reports of October, covering opinion for the previous three months, contained no reference to public attention on the congress idea; nor did any of the fourteen prefect reports, consulted for the same period, allude to it.

Seeing that the people of the Romagna and the duchies were successfully resisting the return of their prewar sovereigns and that the people of France did not seem greatly interested in a congress to restore or dethrone those sovereigns, Napoleon III evidently decided that it was not politically profitable for France to resist the inevitable union of Italy around Sardinia. That a congress would settle the Romagna question or bring about any solution satisfactory to France was out of the question. Therefore it behooved France to change her policy abruptly, approve the separation of the Romagna from the

Papal States, and reap whatever side benefits might accrue, such as
the annexation of Nice and Savoy and a cordial alliance with the
Italians.

But the emperor likewise recognized what a fund of sympathy
for the papal cause had been shown in the October reports and earlier.
To make an abrupt change of policy in the light of that propapal
opinion would require considerable effort at conditioning opinion
to the unpalatable change. A letter from Pius IX of 2 December 1859
seemed to precipitate the move: the pope made an official appeal
to the emperor to help him regain possession of the Romagna.[16]
Instead of replying immediately, Napoleon III began his campaign to
condition home opinion to just the opposite solution from that proposed by the pope. And the first salvo in this attack was made, as
so often before, by the issuance of a pamphlet, the famous pamphlet
Le Pape et le Congrès. La Guéronnière worked hard on it during the
month of December, and issued it anonymously on 22 December.

The pamphlet began by espousing the golden mean between two
extremes. On the one hand the temporal power was absolutely necessary to the pope; on the other hand it was very difficult to combine
a religious leader with political power. The solution should be found
in leaving him a small restricted area. "Not only is it not necessary
for his territory to be very extensive, but we believe it is even essential that it be restricted. The smaller his territory is, the greater will
be the sovereign." Rome, of course, should be a part of his territory
but with its own municipal government and separate membership in
the Italian federation. A federal army would protect it, thus eliminat-
ing the incongruity of a papal army. The expenses of this little state
should be borne by annual contributions by the Catholic powers.
While the brochure was vague on what other territories in addition
to Rome would belong to the pope, it was forthright in its belief
that the Romagna should retain its independence—annexation to
Sardinia was not mentioned. France will not intervene to force the
Romagnols back under papal sovereignty, she will not permit Austria's intervention, and Naples should not intervene and cause inter-
Italian dissensions. Only a congress could give final sanction to a
solution. The Congress of Vienna gave the pope the Romagna; another can take it away. The pope's territory is not inalienable. One
of his predecessors had agreed to the loss of Avignon, and Pius IX
did not still claim the department of Vaucluse. "May [Napoleon III]
be the one to have the honor to reconcile the pope, as temporal
sovereign, with his people and with his times! That is what all sincerely
Catholic hearts should ask of God."[17]

The appearance of the pamphlet was not as much of a surprise
as was its contents, for the Times correspondent in Paris had obtained
advance word and announced it in his column. He even predicted

that the author would be La Guéronnière, causing the reading public
to expect a sensational revelation. Again the bookstores were stormed
by an eager public as copies appeared on the afternoon of 22 December. By evening everyone in Paris interested in politics seemed to be
reading it. The next day the leading Paris papers summarized it, thus
spreading the news to their provincial subscribers.[18] "All of Paris
is in emotion over the pamphlet; the general feeling is that of alarm,"
wrote the British ambassador.[19] In Brittany its arrival stirred lively
discussion, particularly in clubs and drawing rooms. It caused a
veritable "explosion" in Normandy and a "profound sensation" in
Lorraine. "I had not seen for a long time the outbreak of such agitation
around me," wrote the procureur general of Alsace. In Franche-Comté
it was "an event all by itself," arousing "the keenest interest." To the
procureur general in Provence it seemed as if everybody had a copy.
The appearance of the pamphlet in Languedoc had such a "disastrous"
effect that the procureur general hastened to send in a special report.
In Guyenne the procureur general felt that "never in the memory
of man had such a stir been aroused over a book." Whether in Paris
or in the provinces it can be said without much exaggeration that the
pamphlet was a bombshell. Opinion could not and would not ignore
it. From the excitement, it was hoped, would come recognition of
the fact that the pope's loss of the Romagna was inevitable. At least
it would evoke some sort of expression of opinion by which future
Italian policy could be guided.[20]

While there was a great deal of discussion over the authorship
of *Le Pape et le Congrès*, there was unanimity as to its source. The
Morning Post attributed it to La Guéronnière as a matter of course;
the *Times* called it a statement of the French government. Prince
Richard Metternich, the new Austrian ambassador, was assured that
it was "drawn up by the emperor himself or by the unofficial author
of most writings published to sound out opinion [*tâter le terrain*]."
"*Le Pape et le Congrès* . . . . was published with the approval of the
emperor," Rogier flatly stated to the Belgian foreign office. "Then
everybody became anxious to know," said the procureur general of
Rouen, "from whom came such a valuable statement, and I must
say that after a moment's hesitation there is scarcely a person who
does not admit that if the emperor's hand did not write these pages,
at least they were conceived with his inspiration and published at his
command." In Besançon it was "regarded as the expression of the
emperor's thoughts," and in Nancy "the high origin attributed to
this writing gave it an extreme importance." The fact that the semiofficial press gave it such spontaneous support and favorable publicity
was enough to convince any doubters. The day after its issuance some
of his people at court actually asked the emperor whether he was
the author. "No," he replied, carefully choosing his words, "I am

not the one who wrote *Le Pape et le Congrès*, but I approve all its ideas." La Guéronnière's style was readily recognized and his connections with the emperor were not overlooked. Indeed, in Paris, in the provinces, in all Europe no one doubted for a minute that the voice was Napoleon's voice, though the hands might be the hands of La Guéronnière.[21]

The reaction of the clergy and the clerical press was, as might be expected, violent and bitter. The anonymity of authorship gave them supposed license to attack the pamphlet without restraint. The Ultramontane *Univers* gave it a blistering greeting the day after its appearance: "Whoever may be the author, he will have no influence on Catholics. All our bishops, save two or three, have spoken, and the Holy Father has answered them. We know the sentiments of Pius IX as to the *faits accomplis* which they invoke against his sacred rights. The kiss they give him today will deceive neither him nor anyone else. *Dixitque illi Jesus: Amice, ad quid venisti!*"[22] On the 25th it called upon the faithful to sign addresses of protest to the pope and received an official warning from the government for organizing political agitation. Several other clerical or Legitimist papers, who reproduced Veuillot's appeal, were likewise warned. Antonelli, the cardinal secretary of state in Rome, complained to the French ambassador that the government was unfair in giving full rein to the enemies of the pope and in repressing those who would defend him. "The pamphlet in question," he added with pretended innocence, "is no more nor less than a direct incitation to revolt against his authority."[23] Bishop Dupanloup of Orleans published a counter-pamphlet[24] on 27 December in which he defended the pope particularly on the grounds of public law. He ended his tirade, however, with a protest against anonymity. "We must have a face here, some eyes whose glance is recognizable, in fact a man from whom we can demand an accounting of his words."

Already in the intimate circle of his court Napoleon III had acknowledged his sympathy with the ideas in *Le Pape et le Congrès*. Now, after this challenge to come out in the open, he tore off his mask and wrote a letter directly to the pope. In this communication he complained because the pope had not followed his advice after the war and instituted political reforms in his states. Such a refusal had made it impossible to obtain the return of the Romagnols to him. Now the only way would be by force and occupation, to which France would not be a party. "What else is there to do? . . . . What appears to me to be the most consonant with the real interests of the Holy See would be the sacrifice of the revolted provinces."[25]

Even before receiving this letter, Pius IX took the occasion of a New Year's reception to denounce the pamphlet openly. When he greeted General Goyon, commander of the French occupation troops, he closed his allocution with the prayer that the Most High "would let his light fall upon the chief of this army and this nation [France] so that he can walk steadfastly in his difficult way and recognize the falsity of certain principles which have been offered in recent days in a work which must be called a notorious monument of hypocrisy and an ignoble tissue of contradictions." On 11 January Napoleon finally allowed the *Moniteur* to publish the allocution but along with it also the emperor's letter to the pope of 31 December. Then, as if in reply to the letter, the pope ordered out his heavy artillery in the form of an encyclical on 19 January in which he flatly stated that he could not give up any territory belonging to the church. He would face torture and death rather than submit. Finally he exhorted the bishops to "inflame every day more and more the faithful entrusted to your care so that under your leadership they may never cease to employ all their efforts, their zeal, and the application of their minds to the defence of the Catholic church and the Holy See as well as to the maintenance of the civil power of this same see and of the patrimony of St. Peter." Thus the gage of battle was thrown down. It would be a cold war between church and state, to be fought out on the field of public opinion.

The first casualty of this cold war was Walewski, the foreign minister. He had always evinced clerical sympathies in dealing with the pope and was constantly warning the emperor of the danger of alienating Catholic opinion. The pamphlet was issued without his knowledge, as many other things had been done in the field of foreign relations. Time and again he had complained to the emperor of being kept in the dark on matters pertaining to his office, but he had never before had the courage to resign. He was financially in need of his office. To several members of the diplomatic corps he had asserted emphatically that the views of the pamphlet were not those of the government. In the council, it was said, he proposed that the government disavow the pamphlet by a note in the *Moniteur*. Instead, the note was sent to the pope repeating the proposal that he relinquish his claim to the Romagna. After learning of the pope's New Year's allocution, he offered his resignation, which was accepted. Edouard Thouvenel, ambassador to Constantinople, was appointed in his place, with Jules Baroche performing the functions of that office until the arrival of Thouvenel.[26]

The next important victim was the Catholic paper, the *Univers*. On 28 January it published the pope's encyclical without governmental permission. This was in violation of the law and came on the heels of two previous warnings. The following day an order was issued suppressing the *Univers*, declaring that it had violated Article XXXII of the organic decree of 17 February 1852.[27] In his explanation in the *Moniteur*, however, Billault, the minister of interior, did not mention the publication of the encyclical but implied subversive activity as the cause in a war between two conflicting authorities.[28]

Salvo was answering salvo in this bitter struggle. And now the serried ranks of the French clericals began to move up into the line. Dupanloup wrote a *Second letter to a Catholic;* Pie forbade the teaching of the ideas contained in the pamphlet; Bishops Parisis and Gerbet issued counterpamphlets of their own. Even the Orleanists, Thiers, Guizot, and Cousin, sided with the pope.[29] This was particularly unusual in the case of Guizot, who was a Protestant. Three members of the legislative body, Cuverville, Keller, and Lemercier, asked for an audience with Napoleon III to remonstrate against the new policy. Having been denied the audience, they promptly wrote a letter of protest (9 January). *La Bretagne* published this letter on 11 February and was just as promptly suppressed on the ground that the deputies had violated their oaths. In reply they wrote a *Letter to our constituents* in which they asked: "Does the deputy's oath have the effect of forcing him to approve all measures, good or bad, taken by the government? In that case why have a legislature? The deputy is not a civil servant; he does not just perform a job. He fulfills a mission, and one of the highest and freest." In February these men also joined with other leaders in encouraging people to sign petitions to the senate, petitions in favor of the pope, though carefully phrased so as not to denounce the French government. But this move was quite inconspicuous. There were only 42 petitions containing in all 6,342 signatures.

The higher clergy became more circumspect as the fight waxed hotter. Some bishops made no public protest. It was more definitely the lower clergy who took up the cudgels for the pope. Their sermons became violent, even threatening, toward the emperor. They tried to stir up the people to active and open support of the pope. They even omitted frequently from the service the *Domine salvum,* or prayer for the ruler. But the government also took action on this front. Rouland, in charge of religious affairs in the ministry of interior, sent a circular to the bishops ordering them to keep the lower clergy out of political activity; while Billault, the minister of interior, instructed his prefects and Delangle, the minister of justice, instructed his procureurs general to apprehend and prosecute higher or lower clergy whenever they violate the laws. "In a few weeks," concluded Maurain, "the administrative and judicial repression, the bishops' instructions, and also the indifference of the people brought an end to the agitation."[30]

After the tumult and shouting had died, the question remained as to who had won the battle for opinion. Maurain seemed to indicate a government victory when he concluded that the people remained indifferent to the incitations of the clergy. "The clerical agitation . . . . failed," he affirmed, "in the sense that nowhere were the people aroused by it: either because they were hostile or indifferent to religious interests, or because, with public worship undisturbed, they did not think of the church as threatened, or because even in the regions where the clergy's influence was strong, it was counterbalanced by that of the administration."[31] And, as far as clerical influence is concerned, Maurain is amply confirmed by the procureur reports of January and April. Out of twenty-one districts reporting on the influence of the clergy seventeen indicated little or no influence and only two showed considerable influence. Franche-Comté was one of the latter where the procureur general wrote:

If the political influence of the clergy in this province has diminished a great deal in the last ten years, it is not the same with its religious influence. Catholicism has lost none of its power in the country, and all the clergy has to tell people, not too well informed on the present complications, is that some one wants to destroy the pope and change religion and they would rise up in the most violent of protests.

In the district of Nîmes the clergy was also reported to be influential on country folk and Legitimists.

On the other hand the procureur general of Orleans declared: "In the departments of this district there is very little piety and therefore an absolute indifference toward the temporal interests of the head of the church. The wine grower seldom frequents the churches; he does not like priests, and, if he takes part in the controversy, he would certainly be against the clergy and against anything which might increase or preserve its influence." Likewise from Pau in the far southwest came a similar report: "They [the clergy] do not exercise any ascendancy over the people among whom they have not been able, in spite of all their efforts, to infuse their concern about the pope's position." The same sort of commentaries—some longer, some more brief—came in from fifteen other districts scattered all over France.[32] The verdict was overwhelming if not precise. If the pope had support among the French people, it would be largely in spite of the clergy's campaign rather than because of it.[33]

So far the evidence shows that the controversy stimulated by *Le Pape et le Congrès* aroused the clergy but that the clergy was unable to stir up opinion. The question remains as to how the public reacted to the pamphlet independently of the clergy's encouragement. And reaction to the pamphlet would mean reaction to the prospect of the pope's loss of the Romagna. A survey of the reports of the procureurs general and prefects seems to indicate an interested and divided opinion. And, in spite of all the activity of the clergy, the balance of opinion seemed generally in favor of the ideas expressed in the pamphlet, that the pope should recognize his loss of the revolted Legations. From twenty-one districts reporting on the pamphlet there were eighteen instances given of support and fourteen (outside the clergy) of opposition. Ten other instances of indifference were also cited.

The report from eastern Normandy showed a clear preponderance of opinion for the pamphlet:

> The effect of the brochure on the lay population is not as the priests might have wished.[34] Its publication seems to have been ignored in rural areas. The questions treated therein interest in the cities the more skilled workers and their friends, but for them it is only going half way not to make the pope just a plain bishop of Rome. The democratic bourgeois support the indicated solution, although they consider it incomplete and temporary, and they reserve for the future the destruction of the last vestige of the temporal papacy. The Legitimists, nobles or commoners, join their protests to those of the clergy and share the irritation of the most discontented of them.[34] Almost all the Orleanists by the nature of their political and religious opinions preferred the liberation of the Romagna to its restoration to the pope, and the secularization of the government of Rome to the continuance of the clerical administration; but, seeing in all this an issue for opposition to the empire, most of them criticize what at heart they approve and defend by word what they would rather have more completely abolished. And these men supporting law and order, who have never belonged to the old parties, ... have generally adopted the anonymous proposal; but their support is more complete and open in the department of Eure than in Seine-Inférieure.

The procureur general in Poitou gives us a sample of the reaction not only to the pamphlet but also to one of the counterpamphlets, to the emperor's letter, and to the encyclical.

> In general [he said] opinion is very favorable to the idea in the pamphlet *Le Pape et le Congrés*, and the emperor's letter was greeted by an unequivocal approbation. The decree of condemnation was therefore badly received. Sober people criticize this act as excessive. The faithful see in it a harmful schism in the church itself, since the opposite opinion has its supporters. The liberals are all strongly aroused. The young people are ablaze. The working class itself, which Mgr. Pie has not conciliated, criticizes his enterprise. Some disrespectful words were uttered which betray a popular sentiment of a regrettable nature. They go to church just to see the show put on by the monsignor when he's angry. . . . . It also appears that since his letter of condemnation the pamphlet *Le Pape et le Congrés* has only increased in sales: the bookstores have had to put in repeat orders to Paris several times. This is not just out of mere curiosity; it is a genuine interest aroused by the question generally solved along the lines of the wise views of the emperor. The rural people do not share in these reactions. On the question of the pope's rights, as on all the rest, I am assured from all parts [of my district] that they rely on the emperor's prudence.

Likewise in sixteen other districts favorable support was shown for the pamphlet's solution.[35]

Then on the other side of the controversy came the report from Franche-Comté:

> In this country [wrote the procureur general] the religious question as it touches Italy now overshadows the political question, and what complicates it is the profound ignorance generally prevailing on the conditions in the Roman States, the dangers menacing the papacy, the needs for sweeping reforms to avoid terrible catastrophies. Public opinion was scarcely prepared for the revelations found in the pamphlet, and it resigned itself with difficulty to the territorial restrictions which seemed, alas, necessary in the states of the Holy Father. If there are men, calmly considering the facts and taking into account all the incidents of the present situation, who highly approve the pamphlet's solutions as being the only possible ones today, there are others, and many more of them, some honestly and others spitefully against the government, who predict the early and inevitable ruin of the pope's temporal power and a serious threat to Catholicism.

The procureur general of Nîmes found opinion so aroused against the pamphlet that he felt impelled to hurry in a special report on 9 January. Then in his regular report a week later he confirmed his earlier impression.

In addition to the judicial districts of Besançon and Nîmes twelve other districts had lay groups opposing the pamphlet.[36] There were only eight which reported indifference on the part of peasants or city workers.[37] Yet, out of all the evidence apparently interest prevailed over disinterest, and the pamphlet's pro-Romagna views gained more support than the pope's temporal power, though by a close score of 18 to 14.[38]

Such a result in assaying opinion is so close that as much confirmation as possible should be sought. Maurain seemed to verify this trend by his thorough analysis of the attitude of the country, province by province. Only Normady, Alsace, and the Lyonnais, according to him, showed any predominance of propapal opinion among lay groups; all the rest were more or less favorable to the pamphlet ideas.[39]

Likewise the press leaned heavily on the side of the pamphlet. Lord Cowley claimed that "all the French press is favorable [to the pamphlet] except the Ultramontane papers."[40] A survey of the press comment shows that the British ambassador was not far wrong. Of course the clerical press[41] was very hostile, and on the other hand the semiofficial press[42] could be counted on to support the imperial views in the brochure. The significant element of the press would be those between the two extremes. Here we find that two of the principal Orleanist organs gave grudging adherence to the pamphlet program. The *Journal des Débats* noted that the Romagna were treated on the same basis as were the other central Italian states and closed by saying that France must follow the pamphlet's policy to outstrip England's bid for Italian favor. Forcade in the Orleanist *Revue des deux mondes* was less wholehearted in his approval. His attitude had been consistently favorable to the separation of the Romagna; but he criticized the pamphlet on secondary points, such as the inconsistency between concern for the pope and willingness to deprive him of his territory; and also the ill-disguised anonymity of authorship. Naturally the leading democratic paper, the *Siècle*, applauded the pamphlet by declaring that "never had a more clearcut and striking statement been put to use for such definite ideas."[43]

Apparently the cold war of words on the Romagna question had resulted in a slight victory for the opponents of the pope's cause as shown by procureur reports, the press, and the estimates of Maurain and Cowley. If the emperor wanted to follow through with the pamphlet's policy, he could feel that he would have more support than opposition as well as a great element of indifference, which at least he would not have to fear.

Annexation of Savoy and Nice

It was now obvious that the majority of public opinion would not insist on the pope's retention of the Romagna. This being true, there would be even less public objection to Sardinia's acquisition of Parma, Modena, and Tuscany. The way seemed cleared, therefore, for France to let nature take its course in Italy and thereby retain the goodwill of the Italians for later use. What Napoleon III wanted to avoid particularly was to see England replace France as the best friend of the Italian cause. As a sign of England's efforts in this direction, Lord John Russell, foreign secretary, had already proposed a solution on 16 January which provided for Sardinian annexation of the Romagna and the three duchies if another favorable vote were taken and that the French should withdraw their troops from Rome. France, being Catholic and concerned over the growth of a strong power in Italy could not be as generous as England, but Napoleon III tried to make every possible concession to Cavour, who had returned as prime minister of Sardinia when he saw events moving toward his ultimate goals. The French proposals acquiesced in the annexation of Parma and Modena after another vote, suggested that Victor Emmanuel be vicar over the Romagna for the pope, who would remain the sovereign, and insisted that Tuscany remain independent with a relative of Victor Emmanuel as ruler.

When both Sardinia and the pope rejected the vicariat plan for the Romagna, there was no other destiny than annexation after another vote. The main demand of the French, then, remained the acceptance of their plan for an independent Tuscany. This too Cavour rejected because he knew that he would have the Tuscans and England on his side. It was with the prospect of a surrender on this point that moved Napoleon III to strike a bargain which would give him and France the duchy of Savoy and the city of Nice in return for the annexation of Tuscany by Sardinia.

The idea of French annexation of these two areas was not a new one. Savoy had belonged to France until the Second Peace of Paris had given it back to Sardinia in 1815. At Plombières in 1858 Napoleon had made its cession and that of Nice a part of the alliance arrangement, but he had not insisted on them when he obtained only Lombardy for Sardinia at Villafranca. However, the emperor was not unmindful of the keen dissatisfaction with the peace terms among the bourgeoisie, the workers, and the army. The clergy and some devout Catholics were now also hostile because of the Romagna question. The annexation of Savoy and Nice might be just the trick to recoup public favor. Indeed, during the last three months of 1859 a considerable agitation for these areas appeared in southeastern France. The procureur general in Grenoble wrote as follows on the sentiment in the previous months of October, November, and December:

There would be a big gap in this report on foreign policy if I did not give some attention to what is going on in my district . . . . on the subject of the eventual annexation of that province [Savoy] to France. . . . . The thought of annexation is shared with extreme intensity by the departments in old Dauphiné and the Lyonnais. . . . . Today when a new extension of Piedmont in central Italy seems to have become possible, the wishes of the people located on the left bank of the Rhone are reviving much more emphatically because of their concern at seeing in the Isère valley at the gates of Grenoble this military power enlarged by new international transactions; and in case these transfers in Italy take place, they rail against France's abnegation in acquiescing in the offensive frontier set up by the treaties of 1815. In addition to this interest of national security, I hardly need mention the considerable advantages that the departments in Dauphiné and the Lyonnais expect from the annexation of Savoy to France.[44]

Two factions in Savoy itself also kept the question alive. The pro-French group, with its fear of being engulfed in a large sea of Italian nationalism, campaigned against the pro-Piedmont group, which wanted to retain Savoy's historic ties with the king of Sardinia.[45]

The French government, therefore, moved right along with opinion, if not ahead of it, on the question of Savoy and Nice. As early as September, when the duchies began to ask for annexation to Sardinia, Walewski suggested confidentially to Cowley that France might then have some demands of her own to make.[46] Two months later the emperor himself told the Austrian ambassador that "the day that I obtain Nice and Savoy in the south and sufficient fortresses in the north, my mission will be accomplished."[47] By the turn of the year he was stating categorically to the army that he was sure to get Savoy. The Prince de Joinville told Prince Albert: "The Emperor felt the danger of this [clerical hostility], and the necessity of compensating the nation, and particularly the army, which felt that it had made war for nothing. The Emperor had therefore given out in the army, that *he had obtained* the acquisition of Savoy as the *frontière naturelle de la France vers les Alpes*,—which, by all the Prince heard from France, has given great satisfaction."[48] By 10 January the Sardinian minister in Paris noted that "according to the general tenor of things being said around here, it appears that the dominant ideas of the moment may be to consent to the annexation of central Italy in return for the cession of Savoy and Nice."[49]

Then toward the end of the month the semiofficial *Patrie* began a series of articles on the annexation of Savoy, the tenor of which stressed the French characteristics of the people, their own desire for annexation, and the justification for France's acquisition. One reason, of course, was the increase in size and power of Sardinia.[50] The general discussion stemming from this obvious trial balloon seemed to indicate a public demand for annexation. Thouvenel declared that "the Emperor could not answer the French nation" if he could not have compensation for the enlargement of Sardinia.[51] And Cowley acknowledged this situation when he observed that Savoy could not be withheld, "such was the state of public feeling here."[52] Even Arese, the Sardinian special emissary, stressed the opinion angle when he wrote back to Cavour that "it is precisely . . . . to stir the national fibre and calm the effervescence of the parties at home that the emperor would like to obtain the annexation of Savoy and Nice."[53]

The negotiations which were going on in Paris were now supplemented by those in Turin. Thouvenel told Talleyrand to demand Nice and Savoy "as a geographic necessity for the safety of our frontiers." "He could only consider it [the press campaign] as the expression of an ever-growing opinion which must be recognized."[54] Cavour, realist diplomat that he was, held out as long as he could, but he knew that the concession would eventually have to be made.

In the meantime the emperor precipitated demonstrations of public opinion by his speech to the two houses on 1 March. In this he took up the duchies and the Romagna as well as Savoy and Nice. After having mentioned the failure of the plans for the return of the archdukes, the emperor declared:

> I advised him [Victor Emmanuel] to answer favorably the wish of the provinces which offered themselves to him, but to maintain the autonomy of Tuscany and respect in principle the rights of the Holy See. If this arrangement does not satisfy everybody, it has the advantage of reserving principles and calming apprehensions, and it makes Piedmont a kingdom of more than nine million souls.
>
> In the face of this transformation of northern Italy, which gives to one powerful state all the passages through the Alps, it was my duty for the safety of my frontiers to demand the French slopes of the mountains. [Applause.] This demand for so limited a territory has nothing in it which should alarm Europe or conflict with a policy of disinterestedness that I have more than once affirmed, for France wants to proceed with such an enlargement, however small it may be, neither by military occupation, nor by provoking revolutions, nor by underhanded methods, but by frankly explaining the question to the great powers. No doubt they will understand in all fairness, as France would certainly understand it for each of them in similar circumstances, that the big territorial change which is about to take place gives us a right to a guarantee indicated by nature herself. [Repeated shouts of Vive l'Empereur!]

Then the emperor proceeded to chide the French clericals for their hostile agitations. He said he had tried to get reforms in the Papal States and a reconciliation of the Romagnols with the pope—all to no avail. Now at least he still hoped to preserve the principle of temporal power.[55] Two days later Thouvenel's earlier instructions to Talleyrand were published in the Moniteur.

Nearly all observers in Paris agreed that the legislative and public reaction to the speech was two-fold. It was hostile on the part concerning the Catholics and the Romagna but enthusiastic about the prospective annexation of Savoy and Nice. Nigra admitted on 3 March that the annexation of the Romagna "continued to be judged severely."[56] Pourtalès, the Prussian, asserted that the part on the papal question was received "with marked coolness," but he was struck by the unanimity of the general approval which greeted the proposals on Savoy and Nice.[57] Likewise Cowley reported that the speech "was but coldly received," but "there was immense cheering at the allusion to Savoy."[58]

Five judicial districts, which specifically mentioned the speech, reported favorable reactions. In Brittany hostile sentiment had quieted down after the speech. In eastern Normandy "the annexation of the duchies to the Sardinian monarchy no longer caused displeasure as soon as it was known that it would be followed by the reunion of Savoy and Nice to the Empire." Likewise in Nîmes and Lyons the speech seemed to calm opinion. But in the region of Riom, while the speech had the same soothing effect on the public in general, one clergyman, Abbé Fage, had to be arrested because his anger at the abandonment of the pope led him to tear up the speech in public. The rest of the clergy kept quiet. Five districts give only a limited view, but the uniformly favorable response described by each of their reports would seem to confirm the belief that the joy at the prospects of receiving Savoy was making more palatable the pope's loss of the Romagna.[59]

After the publicity of the speech and Talleyrand's instructions Cavour could see that there was no choice but to cede the border territories, but he still hesitated, probably waiting for pressure to give him a good pretext for capitulation. Napoleon obliged with the pressure on 20 March by sending Benedetti to Turin on a special mission to stay until he obtained a cession treaty. Hard on the heels of Benedetti went a written warning to Cavour from his good friend, Bixio, back in Paris.

I think I know how to feel the pulse of this country [Bixio asserted]. They do not want to see their 50,000 men and their 500,000,000 [francs] sacrificed for Italy without some return [*stérilement*]. In exchange for these sacrifices, in exchange for Lombardy and the duchies, in exchange for the reconstitution of Italy, they want the fun of tearing up the treaties of 1815 and of breaking the ring drawn around France by the victorious European coalition.
. . . . If you resist on constitutional grounds the cession of Savoy, the nation here will not understand you, they will cry out that Italian policy is always of such bad faith, that that shows us how little we can rely on your alliance, etc.[60]

On this occasion Benedetti, like Caesar, came, and saw, and conquered. Cavour argued but signed the Treaty of Turin on 24 March, which provided for Sardinia's cession of Savoy and Nice and plebiscites to determine the will of the people. These were held in the last half of April, and the results were overwhelming majorities for transfer to France. On 14 June 1860 the official transfer of the areas took place. By this bargain the French people had made themselves accomplices in the Sardinian annexation of the Romagna and the duchies.[61]

The emperor was always saying that he knew France better than the French knew it themselves,[62] and in the case of the trade of the Romagna and duchies for Savoy and Nice he was eminently right. So overjoyed were Frenchmen about the acquisitions that they scarcely realized how they were implicated in the two-way bargain. In thirty-one reports from eighteen judicial districts was found almost unanimous rejoicing at the news of the French annexations. Only in Flanders and Brittany were there small minorities disgruntled by the arrangement. The procureur general at Rennes reported that "in the eyes of a very small minority, the annexation of Savoy was the price paid for the cession of the Romagna; henceforth this precious acquisition seemed [to them] sullied at its very source."

However, the tendency of the vast majority of Frenchmen in all parts of France[63] was not thus to look a gift-horse in the mouth but rather to give themselves over to rejoicing and exultation. The report from Besançon stressed particularly the exultation over the reversal of the treaties of 1815:

> The definitive annexation of Nice and Savoy [wrote the procureur general] has been welcomed by unanimous favor, less for the expansion given to France than for the satisfaction demanded by national pride. Everywhere you hear that, in extending our frontiers to the Alps, the emperor has torn out one of the painful pages from the treaties of 1815; he has regained for us a people who are French at heart not by right of conquest but by benefit of an equitable policy. The general enthusiasm, which a few days ago accompanied the religious consecration of our peaceful acquisitions, is sufficient proof of the strong public feeling and the gratitude of the country.

If such was the reaction in Franche-Comté, it can be imagined what was the rejoicing in the Dauphiné, adjoining the annexed areas:

> At Grenoble [wrote the procureur general] on that day [of annexation] all the public buildings were illuminated. The excitement here was easily foreseen. For the rest of France it was less a rectification of borders than an increase in power and the legitimate reward for a campaign which will still not lose thereby its chivalrous renown. For the departments of the former Dauphiné, besides the national interest, it means security for the Isère valley down which the Austrians were able to come unopposed in 1815. And I could see at the beginning of the Italian War how the recollection of this caused resentment and patriotic concern.[64]

Of course, Paris, the capital city, had the greatest celebration of all: salvos of guns at six A.M. on 14 June, a *Te Deum* at Notre Dame at ten, and a great military review on the Champ de Mars on the 15th. As usual M. Dabot was in the midst of it all: "Oh, with all my heart, Hurrah for Savoy! Hurrah for Nice! All the houses on my rue de Beaux-Arts are decorated with flags. Unfortunately since my windows are on the court, I cannot thus affirm my patriotism." In the evening the boulevards and the Champs Elysée were crowded with people to see the brilliant illuminations.[65]

On the crest of this wave of seeming popularity Napoleon III thought it might be a good time during August 1860 to make a tour of southeastern France. It gave another opportunity to gauge the mood of the public at this juncture. And from appearances it would seem that he had recouped much of his losses caused by the conflict with the clergy and their Catholic supporters. At Lyons the Belgian consul gave the following disinterested report of the visit:

> Their Majesties were greeted by a very big turnout of all classes. The enthusiasm increased gradually with each visit by Their Majesties to some new establishment. The densely populated sections (La Croix Rousse—Saint Juste) and all those inhabited by workers have given the warmest acclamations.
>
> Apparently it had been feared that the welcome might be generally less favorable, but this was far from the mark. It should be recognized, it is true, that the presence of the empress contributed a great deal to the spontaneity of the greeting.
>
> . . . . They have to admit, and it is the opinion of people who are in the opposition by interests or affections, that the attitude of the people is favorable to the emperor.[66]

This impartial report was confirmed by Lord Cowley's account of the imperial visit to Marseilles. "The Emperor's progress has been one of complete triumph," he wrote. "I am told by eyewitnesses not over well disposed to him that there never was such an ovation as was given him at Marseilles."[67]

Thus Napoleon III had at least for the moment overcome his unpopularity after Villafranca and after his abandonment of the pope's claims to the Romagna. By his victories in the war, by his political amnesty after the war,[68] and finally by his rectification of the southeastern border he had again endeared himself to the major portions of his public. But Italy would give him no rest. No sooner had he apparently calmed the French public after Cavour's annexation of central Italy than Garibaldi stirred it up all over again by his filibustering expedition to Sicily.

Garibaldi's Expedition to Sicily

Garibaldi had been very angry at the cession of his native city of Nice to the French. He even threatened to raise a force to go in and take it back. Fortunately for the Piedmontese, revolts began to break out in Sicily against the Bourbon king, and Garibaldi's friends could turn his attention away from Nice to wider fields of conquest. During the month of April 1860 he recruited over a thousand followers and obtained supplies, arms, and transportation, not without the connivance of local and royal authorities. Their successful landing was made at Marsala on the west coast of Sicily on 11 May, while a British naval vessel shielded the operation.

The news of Garibaldi's landing was received in France on about 13 May and set in motion a whole new train of opinion reactions. The press was the first to react, with the semiofficial *Constitutionnel* taking a strong, hostile stand. In it Grandguillot wrote:

> It is an act against the principles of international law and the real interest of Italy; and, if there is anything in such audacity which may justifiably strike and attract the imagination, reason and conscience must nevertheless reprove its serious violation of all international obligations.

> We do not know whether it was in Count Cavour's power to lay his hand on Garibaldi; but according to us, this act of extreme energy might well do more harm than good, it could stir up in Italy a dangerous reaction which it might be more politic not to provoke.[69]

But the official *Moniteur* a little later seemed to defend the Sardinian government by repeating the latter's lame explanations for Garibaldi's get-away.[70] Finally with the fall of Naples the *Constitutionnel* was no longer protesting against the expedition, but on the contrary acquiesced in Sardinia's annexation of the Two Sicilies and merely advised her to set up a federation instead of a centralized state.[71] Of course the clerical and Legitimist papers detested Garibaldi and sympathized with the Neapolitan Bourbons. With similar consistency such radical papers as the *Siècle* and the *Opinion Nationale* went all out in support of Garibaldi, even undertaking a campaign to raise funds for his expedition.[72] What was more significant was that the Orleanist organs, *Revue des deux mondes* and the *Journal des Débats*, both showed favor toward Garibaldi's enterprise. Forcade in the *Revue des deux mondes* considered the movement to be a logical continuation, perhaps a little more rapid than anticipated, of the general trend toward Italian unification. "If we [editorial] consult our personal feelings more than public instinct," he added, "we would not be frightened by the perspective of France having a united Italy next to her." Again in August he wrote: "Everybody knows that our sympathies have been for a long time on Italy's side, and we have no antipathy toward any of the men who have distinguished themselves in the cause of Italian independence."[73] On 25 July the *Débats* had an article showing a sympathetic understanding of Garibaldi's enterprise. A letter from Nigra gives some background to its publication. "Bixio," he boasted, "was the one who inspired the article; we work together in trying to influence public opinion." On the occasion of Garibaldi's deliverance of Sicily and the Neapolitan provinces to Victor Emmanuel, Weiss commented in the *Débats* on "the grave and dignified tone" of the letter.[74] Even the Orleanist leader, the Duke of Broglie, exclaimed: "It is impossible not to admire his courage and self-devotion. . . . . Garibaldi's wild attempt aims at nothing beyond the overthrow of a despot and the dismemberment of an ancient monarchy, without a notion as to what may be its consequences."[75] Here was no sympathy for the King of the Two Sicilies, but merely a fear of the eventual spread of Garibaldi's expedition into a general revolutionary movement. Thus most of the major segments of the press—radical, Orleanist, and eventually the imperialist—either favored, or showed little opposition to, the conquest of the Two Sicilies.

When the reports of July 1860 arrived, the government also began to see how provincial opinion reacted. Here the results were indecisive. There was much less indifference than in the case of the Romagna because of the romantic heroics of the Garibaldian campaign, but the opinions expressed were almost equally for and against the Italian leader. Out of twenty-one districts reporting on the question there were eighteen groups favoring and eighteen opposing the campaign. One report after another commented on the divided opinion in their districts:

(Montpellier): Terrifies the conservatives and delights the demagogues. (Dijon): Viewed differently according to opinions and tendencies. (Riom): Differently appreciated. (Toulouse): Various sincere opinions and others that are not. (Agen): If feeling runs high, it is also very diverse; and unanimity . . . . is no longer to be found. . . . . Some applaud the success of the insurrection, while others are dismayed by it. (Pau): Greeted with joy by the supporters of advanced ideas . . . . men favoring law and order see [it] only with apprehension. (Rouen): Praised by some, cursed by others. (Grenoble): Sympathy among the masses . . . . in the educated portions of the population serious concern.

The elements making up the two sides of opinion were shown particularly well by the report from Toulouse. This passage was carefully penciled in the margin in the ministry of justice:

The Garibaldian enterprise . . . . today dominates all thinking. . . . . Those who like order, quiet, and authority above all else consider Garibaldi to be a detestable adventurer, and so they ardently hope for his ruin. On the other hand the friends of liberty, the democrats, the real republicans exalt him as a hero. The men who are devoted to law and order but who are not insensible to the suffering of the people nor indifferent to the rights of nationalities, hope that Garibaldi will triumph to a certain extent, but that he will stop or be stopped in the course of his success.

Then there are those who connect it with the government of the emperor, either in the name of conservatism or under the colors of liberty. The former use Garibaldi's ghost to create a scare, the latter secretly look forward to a general upheaval on the heels of his triumph.

Significantly enough many of the conservatives were already fearing for the pope while Garibaldi was moving up from Sicily, as several July reports show:

(Besançon): The upper classes are worried more than ever over the pope's position. (Montpellier): They fear that, once victorious at Naples, the revolutionary spirit may invade the rest of the peninsula, even the States of the Church. (Riom): Feared by some as just one more step forward by the revolutionaries whose eventual goal would be the papacy and Rome. (Agen): The Catholics are seen to be worried. (Lyons): And then a great many people are frightened over the pope's position, between a revolution surging toward his borders and a tottering state, whose fall may also bring him down. (Rennes): The Roman question is so close to that of Naples that in reality it seems hard to disassociate them.[76]

Umbria and the Marches

And they were eminently justified in their fears, because Garibaldi had every intention of invading the Papal States and even of taking the city of Rome. He was urging Bertani to come down from the north into Umbria and the Marches with detachments of new volunteers.[77] Cavour's reaction to such schemes was hostile for three reasons: first, he was afraid Garibaldi's success would make him so powerful and influential that he could no longer be kept under control; secondly, he feared that the more radical revolutionary elements might insist on attacking the Austrians in Venetia; and thirdly, and

most important of all, he knew that an attack on the city of Rome
would start hostilities with France. With Austria, France, and the
remnants of the Neapolitan army all converging against the Italians,
all the progress toward Italian liberation and unity might be destroyed.

At this moment Cavour learned that Napoleon III was making
a visit to Chambéry in France's new territory of Savoy. Diplomatic
courtesy required that he send an emissary with official greetings
from the Sardinian government; the emergency required also that the
emissary should present Cavour's desperate plan for taking the initiative from Garibaldi. The initiative Cavour had in mind was one that
would not only head off Garibaldi from Rome but would also put
Sardinia in possession of two-thirds of the pope's remaining territory,
the provinces of Umbria and the Marches. Thus on 28 August 1860
the two Sardinian emissaries, Farini and Cialdini, had a long interview with the emperor in which they stressed the dangers of revolutions
in the Marches and Umbria and a Garibaldian encounter with French
troops in Rome. What Cavour proposed was that France permit
Sardinian troops to go into Umbria and the Marches at the first signs
of insurrection, whence they would proceed toward Naples to head
off Garibaldi from Rome.

Again the Emperor of the French faced a dilemma. Either he
should oppose the scheme and see revolution run wild in the peninsula
and war break out with France, thus ruining all his schemes of building Italy up as a part of the French diplomatic bloc; or he should
approve the scheme and become still more an accomplice in depriving
the pope of other areas of his temporal possessions. If Napoleon reflected at all on home opinion, he remembered that it did not want
war, but also that it had not been generally opposed to the pope's
loss of the Romagna, had responded with some favor to his pamphlet
Le Pape et le Congrès, and had been about evenly divided on Garibaldi's expedition. Furthermore, he was even more disgruntled over
the attitude of the pope. Pius IX had refused all French advice on
reforms, had been stirring up the French clergy against the government, and had appointed French Legitimists to the main posts in the
papal army. With these considerations in mind he appeared to ac-
quiesce in Cavour's scheme, adding some reservations, however: revolts should first actually break out in Umbria and the Marches, the
Italians should await a decision of a congress before taking over the
two provinces permanently, and Cavour would have to expect strong
protests by the French government. Thinking particularly of the danger from Garibaldi, he may have said, "Act quickly"; as a friendly
farewell remark he may also have said, "Good Luck." At least Cialdini
reported his last remark to have been *"Bonne chance et faites vite."*[78]

Cavour, in acting quickly, did not even wait for the insurrections to break out. Having sent an ultimatum to the pope to remove

all foreigners from his fighting forces, he ordered troops to invade the provinces as soon as the pope rejected the demand. The invasion took place on 10 September, and by the end of the month the two provinces were overrun after two serious engagements with papal troops at Castelfidardo and Ancona. The Sardinians proceeded towards Naples, capturing Capua on 2 November, and Victor Emmanuel entered Naples with Garibaldi on the 7th. On the following day he took over Garibaldi's army, while the renowned hero retired in a pique to his estate on Caprera.

Napoleon III's public reaction was immediately one of protest. He recalled his minister from Turin and sent reinforcements to Rome. But he telegraphed Thouvenel from Toulon, "I fear from your dispatches that you are taking things in Turin too seriously, I mean to threaten but not to act."[79] Cavour understood this well enough and took the French rebukes philosophically. To Nigra in Paris he wrote: "It is clear to me that France must not seem to be our accomplice in this expedition. . . . . We might be scolded by the emperor without being disapproved."[80]

The first reaction to the Piedmontese invasion came in the Paris press, which in general took a hostile view. The semiofficial *Constitutionnel* of course took the government's protesting line. In its columns Grandguillot said that the bad governments in central and southern Italy had compelled France not to interfere in the liberation movement up to now. But when the pope's temporal power was involved "our honor also required that France be removed from any solidarity with such enterprises." While France wanted the independence of Italy, she also wanted the same for the pope.[81] Of course the clerical *Union* was one of the most violent in its expressions: "There is a universal cry against the aggression of Piedmont on the Holy See. The shameful complicity of the Sardinian cabinet in all the movements of revolutionary brigandage was bad enough. . . . . But now the scene changes; it is a government which calls itself regular, a ministry of a monarchy recognized by Europe which substitutes itself for Garibaldi and which will do the work of that filibusterer with all the forces of an organized nation."[82] The *Siècle*, to be sure, favored Sardinia's action.

What would be more significant would be the attitudes of the two important Orleanist organs. Weiss in the *Débats* called the invasion "one of the most serious events in contemporary history if by chance it leads to an Austrian intervention and will be one of the most serious in all history if it brings about . . . . the destruction of the temporal power." However, about a week later he was opposing French intervention.[83] Likewise Forcade in the *Revue des deux mondes* qualified his opposition. There is a suggestion of implicating the French government in the invasion by the forced innocence of his remarks on the Chambéry interview. "In their visit to Chambéry," wrote Forcade, perhaps with tongue in cheek, "M. Farini and General Cialdini said nothing to him [the emperor] about the scheme. Perhaps the Piedmontese emissaries knew nothing of it themselves,[84] perhaps the Piedmontese government had not yet made up its mind." Then he proceeded to criticize the invasion: "What is to be blamed from the point of view of accepted ideas in international law is all too obvious. The pretexts for the invasion of the Papal States, if they be taken literally, violate the principles of sovereignty and international law." However, he continued, "From the point of view of Italy's new needs and the tendencies of the unification movement, it is no less than a necessity shrewdly recognized and boldly accepted by Piedmont."[85] Two weeks later he showed the same sympathy for Piedmont when he declared, "As far as we're concerned, we have always been convinced that . . . . Piedmont is destined to expand still further and to furnish Italy gradually the framework of her political and military institutions." But he spoke approvingly of the increased French forces sent to Rome and of the withdrawal of France's minister.[86] The Orleanist papers were therefore greeting the event with mixed feelings, and looking at the press as a whole, one would seem to gain the same impression as to general press reaction.

In all the French agitation which the new Italian upheavals were causing, one new mood was noticed, the desire for an early and definitive solution of the whole problem. Bixio's report to Cavour is particularly emphatic on this point:

> You should realize that with the exception of the clergy, who are relatively few in number, the great mass of conservatives, rich people, merchants, financiers, business men of all degrees want an immediate solution. Whether Italy is unified or federated, whether the pope, dukes, and King of Naples be restored or expelled, all of that is secondary to the big majority of the country. What they want is to be rid of it, what they wish is a solution without war which will bring up stock and bond quotations as well as the values on farms and houses, etc.[87]

The next day, Gropello was telling Cavour the same story. "Almost everybody here," he wrote, "is now agreed on the necessity for us to go right ahead and make an end once and for all to what is left of the old order in Italy, except Rome and Venice."[88] And in the same week Thouvenel expressed the same idea to Lord Cowley: "This crisis . . . . cannot be continued. The Emperor must take a resolution one way or the other, and either identify himself with revolution in Italy or step in and put it down. France will no longer bear this expectant state."[89] However impatient the French public may have been, the question of outlying papal territory was soon to merge into the question of Rome itself. And the Roman question was to vex French politics and diplomacy for another half-century. As Cesare Cantù[90] once said, "The Roman question is one of those which one century poses, but only another resolves."

By October the provincial reports were coming in, showing again a divided opinion, but not as evenly divided as in the case of Garibaldi's expedition. In this new instance of the Marches and Umbria there was not as much romanticism and the pope's temporal power was more directly involved. Consequently, a slight preponderance opposed Sardinia's invasions of Umbria and the Marches. Twenty-five of the twenty-eight districts[91] gave expressions of opinions on the invasion. Twenty identifiable groups seemed opposed, fourteen sympathetic, and eleven indifferent.

Most of those groups favoring Sardinia's bold move were Republican (eight out of fourteen), and it is difficult to estimate Republican strength in 1860. Most procureurs general and prefects minimized their importance. They probably did represent only a small minority at this time. But the six other instances of sympathy showed that many other groups were also involved. In Aix, according to the procureur general, this sympathy "emanates from all Republicans, from a goodly number of Orleanists, and . . . . from the major part of the Imperialists." Likewise the procureur general at Douai declared: "This bold [and sympathetic] view of so grave a question could . . . . seem to Your Excellency to be the expression of [my] individual opinion. But I do not doubt that this feeling is abroad among the masses and shared by a great majority of the educated classes. Indeed, it would be almost unanimous except for the Ultramontanes and Legitimists."[92] Even in the supposedly strongly Catholic Vendée, observed the procureur general at Poitiers, "Italian liberty has a large number of supporters, and [my subordinate] quotes this significant remark from a Vendean peasant in his conversation with others on the temporal power: 'He wants to be pope and king; two such jobs at one time are too many.' "[93]

Eleven other groups[94] were reported indifferent as to what happened to Umbria and the Marches. For example in Picardy the procureur general remarked that the question "would be a source of serious danger if it had penetrated to the masses; but . . . . it stops at the surface of society and only stirs the uppermost stratum." In the Limousin "the events in Italy leave the masses indifferent," and the wealthy classes "no longer consider the successive invasions by Piedmont as anything more than a subject of conversation." If the indifferent elements were joined to the pro-Sardinian, as they might very well be for Napoleon III's purposes, it left a preponderance against the pope's cause (25 groups out of 45).

The remainder were strongly anti-Sardinian.[95] In the arrondissement of Nay, department of Basses-Pyrénées, "there is but one cry of disapprobation of the entrance of his [Victor Emmanuel's] troops in the states of the pope, and it was with satisfaction that they saw our government join the general sentiment by withdrawing its ambassador from Turin."[96] The procureur general in Rouen said: "The invasion of the Piedmontese troops in the states of the pope has . . . . aroused from the beginning serious fears. . . . . The recall of the French ambassador from Turin and the sending of additional troops to Rome have satisfied public opinion."

However, even greater than the fear of what would happen to the pope was the fear of the development and spread of a general revolution. In eight of the twenty groups this nightmare was reiterated again and again. The report from the procureur general in Metz is typical:

Also what worries the men of law and order, and therefore devoted to the imperial government, are, in fact, the examples crowned with success and the excitement given by the Italian revolutionaries to the revolutionary emotions in France and all Europe. If this torrent encounters no dike beyond the Alps, will it not spread thence to our own country where it will grow with the addition of numerous supporters?

But this same concern over possible spread of the revolutionary movement was expressed in reports from Bordeaux, Agen, Pau, Montpellier, and Rennes.[97]

Again, as with Garibaldi's invasion of the Two Sicilies, the French emperor could find in the reaction to Sardinia's invasion of Umbria and the Marches no protest strong enough to be insistent or prevalent. His cautious nod to Cavour could stand; perhaps even further acquiescence in the Italian movement would be tolerated by the French public.

The revolutionary process continued during the months of October and November with the holding of plebiscites in the former kingdom of the Two Sicilies and in the Marches and Umbria. France and England could not very well challenge this new principle of popular self-determination, since their own governments were based on it. But the old continental monarchies and the French Legitimists refused to recognize this principle in public law. They not only protested the principle of plebiscites but also criticized the procedures of these particular votes because they were open and public, putting the voter under great pressure to vote for annexation. However obtained, the annexationist majorities were overwhelming: in the Two Sicilies 1,732,117 for and 10,979 against; in the Marches and Umbria 231,023 for and 1,520 against. Now all Italy, save Rome and Venice, was united under the aegis of Sardinia.[98]

Strangely enough, as these final events unrolled, there was very little reaction in France. Of course the clergy was angry and alarmed but in general kept discreetly quiet. However, the procureur reports of January 1861 covering the previous quarter showed that, out of 24 groups identified in 17 districts, 14 were indifferent, 1 more fearful than ever, 6 opposed to the new Italy, and 3 sympathetic toward it. The prevailing indifference is revealed by the following typical report from Orleans:

> At the beginning people were extremely concerned over the aggression committed by Piedmont against the States of the Church; but there has happened with this question what happens with everything, time dulls the intensity of the first reactions and today this serious question no longer troubles anyone except the clergy and the handful of laymen who form what is called the Catholic party. They have come to that point of indifference that Mgr. the Bishop of Orleans himself is reduced to silence because he feels that the interest in this question is exhausted and his words can no longer revive it.

Similar attitudes of indifference and disinterest were found in the reports from Lyons, Douai, Bordeaux, Pau, Besançon, Rouen, Nancy, Bourges, Rennes, Dijon, and Aix. Indifference had been a frequent reaction during all the events of 1860; now it seemed to be not only on the increase but also predominant.

Added to these attitudes of indifference were a few instances of positive favor for the new Italy. "I believe I sum up rather accurately the attitude of mind in Brittany," wrote the procureur general from Rennes, "by saying that the great majority of moderate and intelligent men look with favor on the consolidation and development of the principle of independence in northern Italy and would be opposed to the return of Austrian domination in Italy in any form, but . . . . they would prefer the separate sovereignty of the states to an [integral] unity. . . . ." Such views were also found in certain groups in Flanders and Provence.

On the other hand, in addition to the clergy there were areas still opposed to the Italian movement. In the district of Toulouse, for example, the procureur general noted: "It can not be ignored that the Italian cause has lost a great deal of the sympathy that it had at first inspired, and the demagogues are now the only ones who applaud the upheavals in the peninsula. . . . . There are some who deplore the frequent sham plebiscites in the revolted provinces, which could, by unfair comparison, only diminish respect for the great manifestations which served to found the Empire." In summarizing his report, the procureur general of Agen also declared that "it seems to me that the vast majority are hostile to the annexationist policy of Piedmont."[99] The reports, taken as a whole, however, showed that the causes of the pope and the King of the Two Sicilies were on the decline, whether a new united Italy was popular or not.[100] As Thouvenel warned the pope at this time, "the wind is no longer blowing toward crusades."[101]

A Stormy Parliamentary Debate

But the controversies over Sardinia's annexations and the pope's temporal power stirred up stormy winds in the legislative halls in Paris. Since 1852 the senate and the legislative body had not been very loud sounding boards for public opinion. Packed by means of authoritarian procedures, they had been largely rubber-stamp chambers. Furthermore, they had had little chance to discuss general policy, since they had been compelled to consider only fully elaborated measures presented to them by the council of state; and then their debates had not been published. Suddenly on 24 November 1860 decrees were issued which increased considerably the role of the two houses. They provided that the two legislative chambers could deliberate upon an address in reply to the emperor's opening speech, that the full debates would be published, and that the government would designate certain ministers without portfolio to explain and defend government policy in such debates.[102] It meant that general policy could henceforth be discussed independently of specific legislation and that speeches would now be given with an eye to public reaction and support.[103]

Considerable speculation arose as to Napoleon III's reasons for such an innovation. No doubt agitation in the country had something to do with it—both the clergy's campaign for the pope's temporal power and the journalists' endeavors to obtain more freedom of the press. The Duke of Morny, president of the legislative body, believed that now was the time to liberalize a little the repressive regime of the empire, and he was convinced that it would be better to start with the legislature than with the press. The legislature would be much less likely to abuse its new freedom.[104] The emperor's own explanation to Cowley was that "he had thought it necessary . . . . to do something to meet public opinion, which was not satisfied with the manner in which the Senate and Corps Législatif fulfilled the functions assigned to them."[105] But the representatives of Great Britain, Prussia, and Sardinia—Cowley, Pourtalès, and Gropello—all three felt certain that the emperor's main motive was to use the legislature as reinforced support for future policies in Italy, either in abandoning an aggressive Sardinia or in encouraging the nationalist movement further by abandoning a recalcitrant pope.[106]

As usual the sessions were opened by a speech from the throne in which Napoleon III tried to be both conciliatory and noncommital.

> Some extreme opinions [he declared] would prefer to have France make common cause with every revolution, others would have her take the lead in a general reaction. I shall not allow them to divert me from my path by any of these contradictory agitations.
> . . . . If France had sympathies with all that is great and noble, she did not hesitate to condemn all that violates the law of nations and justice. . . . . In Italy . . . . my government in accord with its allies felt that the best way to avoid greater dangers was to have recourse to the principle of nonintervention, which leaves each country master of its own destinies, localizes questions, and prevents them from degenerating into European conflicts.
> . . . . It suffices for the country's greatness to maintain its rights where they are unquestioned, to defend its honor where it is attacked, to lend assistance where it is implored in the name of a just cause.

There was a veiled censure of Sardinia for "violating the law of nations and justice," but on the other hand there was little comfort for

Francis II, the King of Naples, for whom only a weak sympathy was expressed as one who "so nobly supported royal misfortune."[107]

From two eyewitnesses came conflicting reports as to the reception of the speech by the legislators. Thouvenel, a member of the government, said that the speech "obtained the universal and loud approval of the senate and the legislative body." But, Cowley, a more disinterested observer, remarked that he "had never seen the Emperor so coldly received, and no notice was taken of the Empress or the little Prince Imperial."[108] In spite of this disagreement on the legislative reception the reports of the procureurs general seem to show uniform satisfaction with the speech. All seven reports which specifically mentioned the speech indicated favorable reactions. The one from Lyons stated: "In foreign affairs [his] principle of non-intervention admits and proclaims our responsibility withdrawn from Italian complications [and] a calm, liberal, and moderate attitude toward other powers. For all sensible men it is a promise of European peace unless some unforeseen incident occurs. This program is definitely accepted by the immense majority with warm gratitude. The disdain with which the emperor seemed to reply to some rash threats flattered the patriotism of the masses." A similar report came from Alsace: "It is with happiness that it [the region] greets the assurance of it [peace] from the very mouth of the head of the state in his speech from the throne. . . . . It resounded far down the industrial valleys of the Haut-Rhin. . . . . Alsace is at this moment entirely devoted to peaceful enterprises." The same reactions were found in Brittany, Poitou, Lorraine, Orléanais, and Paris, most of them stressing the peace implications of the speech.[109]

In spite of the favorable reaction to the speech among the people and their peaceful interpretation the recently ungagged legislative houses made the phrasing of their address the occasion for a propapal demonstration of opinion. In the senate Rochejacquelein, Heeckereen, and Gabriac urged the cause of the pope. Piétri and Prince Napoleon defended the government. Indeed, the prince carried the fight into the opposite camp with one of the most violent speeches heard by the senate. He denounced Rochejacquelein for accepting an appointment to the senate and then misrepresenting the empire with medieval ideas, for the empire denoted the spirit of modern times. He ridiculed the sympathy shown for the Neapolitan Bourbon dynasty and then lashed out into an intemperate attack on the French Bourbons, accusing them of disloyalty to each other and boasting of Bonapartist solidarity. Then turning to the papacy, he not only demanded Rome for Italy and the end of the temporal power, but he actually attacked the institution of the papacy as a "crystallization of the middle ages." Yet, after all this denunciation, he ended by proposing that the pope be allowed to retain his temporal sovereignty in the Vatican area west of the Tiber River, while Italy takes over the rest of the city.

While the prince received applause here and there at passages in his speech which seemed especially pro-Bonapartist, the senate showed more opposition to the government than had ever before been shown on the question of the pope's temporal power. A passage in the proposed address read: "We shall continue to place our confidence in the monarch who covers the papacy with the French flag." This passage was acceptable to the government because it showed sympathy for the pope without committing the government to continue the occupation of Rome indefinitely or to support the temporal power. But the clerical senators offered an amendment which added the words: "And maintains in Rome the temporal sovereignty of the Holy See on which rests the independence of his spiritual authority." Baroche, the government spokesman, combatted this amendment, which was then voted down, but by a close vote of 78 to 61. Never had such independence and opposition been shown before among the emperor's hand-picked senators. The final version of the senate's address read: "Your filial devotion to a holy cause . . . . has been evinced unceasingly in the defense and maintenance of the temporal power of the sovereign pontiff, and the senate does not hesitate to give its most entire approval to all the acts of your loyal, moderate, and persevering policy."[110]

The emperor's reaction to his cousin's speech seemed rather favorable. "Although I do not agree with all your opinions," he wrote, "I wish to congratulate you, however, on the immense success you obtained yesterday in the senate."[111] Shrewdly he did not specify with what opinions he disagreed, but he evidently did consider this as a possible weather vane to indicate which way the public wind was blowing. Not only did the *Moniteur* publish the speech as a part of the debates, but also the *Moniteur des Communes* gave it special publicity in the provinces.

The reports from the provinces indicated an almost evenly divided opinion on the prince's speech. From ten districts there were fourteen groups of opinion noted, seven favorable and seven opposed to the speech. The tendency seemed to be that the workers and the lower bourgeoisie favored the views of the prince, while the upper classes inclined to the opposition. Thus in Lyons, the procureur general said: "The speech of Prince Napoleon achieved a veritable success among the masses. In the upper classes they were pleased with, and proud of, the oratorical talent so strikingly manifested, but they regretted the violence of his attacks as well as the severity of his solution." Likewise from Limoges came the report that the workers "take their stand for Italy and against the pope, and they could not have enjoyed more the speech of Prince Napoleon." The report from Paris, however, in dealing with the prince's speech distinguished between the upper and lower bourgeoisie. "The lower bourgeoisie [wrote the procureur general], who furnish the subscribers and readers of the *Siècle,* concern themselves very little with the temporal power of the head of Catholicism and give unreserved approbation to the policy of nonintervention regardless of consequences. . . . . The upper class . . . . would not like to see consummated what it considers a flagrant usurpation and asks that, come what may, the Sovereign Pontiff be maintained in the capital of his states." The procureur general in Pau remarked that the Bonapartists in his district liked the speech but the clergy and their followers protested strongly. From Aix came the interesting remark that the speech had revealed a recent displacement of the center of government support from the right to the left. In addition to these reports of divided opinion came unfavorable reports from Toulouse, Agen, and Bordeaux and favorable ones from Amiens and Nîmes.[112] Thus the prince's speech had revealed to the emperor again a divided opinion with considerable reiterated support from the left and from the masses.

Just as the speech of Prince Napoleon in the senate served as a trial balloon for the emperor, so the clericals hoped to use the debates and votes in the legislative body to the same purpose, to convince the emperor that there was a strong body of opinion favoring the pope. After an exchange of mediocre speeches by David and Koenigswarter (favoring Italy) and by Kolb-Bernard and Plichon (favoring the pope), there arose an inconspicuous member, Keller from Alsace, who made one of the most eloquent and forthright speeches of the clerical opposition.

Piedmont could be stopped [he cried], but you must want to do it. . . . . France has changed her policy, France has retreated, not before little Piedmont, not before England, but before a power whose program, drawn up in a famous letter, was on one occasion inserted in the *Moniteur.* [The speaker then read Orsini's letter.] . . . . The revolution embodied in Orsini, that's what has made France back down. . . . . Let's not evoke the shades of former parties. We are not soldiers of some sort of Austrian country hiding under the cloak of religion. The fight is, as in 1848, between the Catholic faith, which is both French and Roman, and the revolutionary faith; it is between men who, on both sides, openly fly their flags and who, if need be, set the seal of their blood upon their ideas. . . . . You who had the imprudence to reopen this arena without considering its vastness, who are you and what do you want to be? Are you revolutionary? Are you conservative? Or are you simply sitting on the sidelines of the contest? Up to now you are none of these, because you back down before Garibaldi at the same time that you say you are his worst enemy, because here you send effective aid to Piedmont and there you send lint [bandages] to the King of Naples, because you have them write on the same page the inviolability of the pope and the dethronement of the Holy Father. Come out and tell us then just what you are! . . . . You have asked for our complete thought, I am about to finish giving you mine. It is time to look revolution right in the eye and tell it: 'No farther shall you go!'[113]

On went the sessions with government and opposition speakers countering each other. But the showdown came on an innocent amendment to the committee's version of the address in which the clericals asked for the removal of the words: "his [the pope's] rejection of good advice." This proposal was bitterly combatted by Baroche, the government spokesman, and the chamber did vote to continue the passage in the text. However, the clericals mustered 91 votes as against 126 for the government. As in the senate, this sign of a large courageous opposition, it was hoped by the clericals, would so impress the emperor that he would not dare to go any further toward abandoning the pope.[114]

After two such trial balloons as the prince's speech and the debates of the clericals both sides naturally turned to see what was the public reaction. La Gorce, witnessing the reaction of the educated classes in Paris, felt that "the public had definitely revived its taste for parliamentary debates." He spoke of an "unusual attendance," of large numbers of students walking toward the Bourbon Palace, seat of the legislative body.[115] Likewise Pourtalès, the Prussian ambassador, moving in the same circles, said he had heard that "Emperor Napoleon [was] much impressed by the effect on France and Europe by the debates in the senate and legislative body on the Roman question."[116] Actually, it would seem to be inaccurate in this case to judge the country by the attitudes of the elite in Paris, because, except for the attention given to the speech of Prince Napoleon (already discussed above), scarcely any interest in the debates themselves was noted. In only eight reports out of twenty-eight from the judicial districts were there direct mentions of public attention to the debates, and four of the eight registered a lack of public interest. In Alsace, it was said, "the discussion of the address in the chambers has not aroused . . . . excitement." Keller's speech "portrays very inexactly the attitude of the region he represents." In the Orléanais "the immense majority of the inhabitants in the country . . . . did not even seem to know the debates were going on." In southwestern France, around Pau, "the parliamentary fights . . . . went almost unnoticed by the farming and working classes." Among the bourgeoisie they received only "a very limited reaction [echo fort restreint]." Likewise, in and around Paris, the city workers and the nearby peasants were definitely indifferent to the debates, whatever others may have said about the interest of the upper classes within the city. Of the four reporting attention to the debates two (Amiens and Nancy) showed sympathy with the government,[117] one other (Nîmes) tended to be in favor of the Catholic cause, while the fourth (Rennes) showed antigovernment sentiment during the early debates and a prevailing progovernment sentiment towards the end.[118]

The granting of fuller and more open debate seemed in this first session to have benefited the government in two ways. It gave the opposing political leaders a chance to blow off steam, while at the same time it aroused little interest or reaction in the country at large. The tendency in the country and the legislature during the sessions was not so much to look back to the annexations with recrimination as to look ahead with apprehension to the future fate of papal Rome. What sentiment had appeared had been about evenly divided during the debates. In most instances the Catholic clergy, the core of the opposition, had felt constrained to remain silent.

The Shift of the Center of Political Gravity

It is difficult to compute the aggregate attitudes of opinion during the period of the annexations because of the variety of issues involved and the lapse of time (at least a year) during which the events took place. If, however, there be any validity in the rough computations from the provincial reports of the procureurs general, perhaps an approximate view of public attitudes may be discerned from a composite picture of the reactions on the main issues. The procureurs general endeavored to distinguish opinion by both political and social groups,[119] although we have no way of knowing how many people composed the groups. Yet, if we take these groups as units and let the numbers of the "masses" be balanced by the influence and public concern of the "educated classes," we may be able to discern the preponderance of influence exerted on the imperial government.

Re-examining the reactions of the identified groups to the controversial question of the annexations as well as the trial balloons of *Le Pape et le Congrès*, the emperor's speech, the prince's speech, the clergy's propaganda, and the legislative debates, we will find the following totals for all groups in all the districts:

Sympathetic to the Italian cause: 92 groups[120]
Indifferent to Italy and the pope: 69 groups
Sympathetic to the papal cause: 68 groups

This computation, however rough it may be, seems to indicate a preponderance of favor or tolerance toward the unification of the Italian areas, especially if the "indifferent" totals are added to the pro-Italian ones. At least the papal cause shows up clearly as the weaker. This also confirms Maurain's conclusions on the indifference toward the clergy's campaign. At any rate it could, and did, give the emperor and his advisors the impression that they need not defend the extreme claims of the papacy nor assume an unfriendly attitude toward the newly constituted Italian state.

Such a reassuring estimate of the popular attitude toward the government's policy seems also to have been supported by several reports of a continuation in 1860 of the shift of the center of gravity in French opinion since the Austro-Sardinian War from a loss of rightist support to a gain of leftist support. One of the clearest ex-

pressions of this most significant development came from the procureur general of Aix:

> The line of conduct of the government [he wrote] between these extreme
> theories, its expectant attitude, and especially the speech given by H.I.H. Prince
> Napoleon have simply resulted in shifting, shall I say, the center of support for
> the imperial institutions. Hence the Legitimists and religious elements, who in the South
> had accepted the empire without entirely giving up their distant hopes, manifested
> their impatience and felt a keen irritation. But the ground lost on that side has
> been amply compensated for by that gained in the Orleanist, liberal, skeptic, and
> Voltairian bourgeoisie and in the moderate faction of the Republican party.
>   It would be very difficult to find by a clear and precise formula just how
> much the government has lost or won by these fluctuations of opinion. However,
> there are some sure indications which seem to give some idea of the inability of
> the Legitimists and clergy to excite serious agitations among the people.[121]

But Aix was not the only district noting the shift. From at least eight
other districts (those of Toulouse, Montpellier, Bordeaux, Riom,
Lyons, Besançon, Metz, and Orleans) came similar reports of this
significant swing of sentiment in 1860 and 1861.

In contrast to these nine areas showing in 1860 a continuing
general shift favorable to the government, only two reports indicated
no such shift. The district of Agen revealed no rallying to the government. "Unfortunately," declared the procureur general, "there's nothing of the sort going on [here]." The corresponding official in Nancy
saw no significant shift in his district. "The parties," he asserted,
"have gone back to their opposition role and have sought every occasion to attack the government and cause it embarrassment." The
favorable shift was not, therefore, unanimous, but it was preponderant.
The emperor and his government could then take heart from the
evidence of pro-Italian sentiment and indifference, from the lack of
influence of the new clerical opposition, and from the reiterated statements from most parts of France that in the new political realignments
the imperial government was not the loser.[122]

Thus the aftermath of the Austro-Sardinian War had brought
the unification of most of Italy and the pope's loss of most of his
territory without any great loss of support to the government of Napoleon III. The clergy had definitely been alienated, but their political allies, the Legitimists, had always been the emperor's opponents. The renewed parliamentary debates had seemed to indicate
a great new ground swell of opposition in the country. La Gorce himself was impressed by it. "For the first time since the establishment
of the Empire," he observed, "an opposition imposing in numbers
asserted itself, not on an economic but on a political question."[123] But
the emperor had shrewdly countered both the clerical and legislative
attacks. The pamphlet, *Le Pape et le Congrès*, had marshaled the arguments against the pope's extreme stand; the emperor's letter to the
pope had pushed the argument further; and finally the annexation
of Savoy and Nice rallied most elements in the country to renewed
expressions of loyalty. The imperial journey gave an occasion for a

public demonstration of this new popularity, and the procureur reports furnished a secret confirmation of it, contradicting the shift of sentiment in the unrepresentative legislature. There were to be rough days ahead, when the Roman question—as distinguished from the questions of the other parts of the Papal States—was to become acute. Again Napoleon III was to experience embarrassment, but he could feel somewhat reassured that he would not be abandoned by opinion in the future as he had not been in the past, provided he took a reasonable middle course and continued to influence opinion along the way.

CHAPTER VI

THE ROMAN QUESTION

The temporal sovereignty of the pope over the States of the Church had been a controversial subject in French politics ever since 1849 when French troops, dispatched to Rome, had overthrown the anticlerical Roman Republic and restored Pius IX to his papal throne. It troubled French opinion as well as the French government all during the Second Empire because of the continued occupation of Rome and its environs by French troops to protect the pope after his restoration. Catholic clerical support had been given to the establishment of Napoleon III's Second Empire not only because it would combat democratic revolutionary movements in France but also because it was hoped it would also prevent the nationalist revolution in Italy from seizing again the States of the Church and dethroning the pope as in 1849. These hopes were dashed in 1860 when the imperial government acquiesced in Italy's annexations of the papal territories of the Romagna, Marches, and Umbria. Then it was that the clergy and their clerical lay followers turned against the regime, while the democratic "revolutionaries" on the other hand became more sympathetic to Napoleon III. The loss of clerical support was shown particularly in the legislative debates and votes in 1861. But, strangely enough, these debates, instead of emphasizing the Italian annexations of papal territory of the previous year, looked forward toward the future in combatting any suggestion of Italian annexation of Rome and its surrounding area of the Patrimony of St. Peter. This was the last

small remnant of the pope's temporal power and was also the precise
territory occupied by French troops.

Thus what had previously been a more general Italian question
was now narrowed down to the Roman question:[1] the question of
whether the pope should retain Rome and his temporal power or
whether Italy should also annex the last remnant of the Papal States,
make Rome its capital, and impose its political rule over the pope,
leaving him only his religious leadership. The Roman question also
involved, in the case of France, the problem of withdrawing their
troops of occupation from Rome, obtaining a more enlightened papal
government, and retaining friendly relations with the Kingdom of
Italy in order to keep it within France's diplomatic orbit. The Roman
question was therefore not a simple one. It caused no end of soul
searching and heartache for both French opinion and the French government. Indeed, this thorny question was in 1870 an important contributing factor to the downfall of the Second Empire and to the
French defeat in the Franco-Prussian War.

Diplomatic Recognition of the Italian Kingdom

While the French legislators were having their debates over the
Roman question in the Spring of 1861, the Italian chamber was also
having its own debates on the same question, debates which could
only aggravate the situation in France. After Cavour's secret negotiations with the Vatican for a complete settlement of all outstanding
differences had definitely fallen through,[2] the Italian prime minister
found it necessary to retain his popularity with Italian nationalists
by reaffirming his demand for Rome as Italy's capital, while at the
same time he reassured France against any rash Italian move contrary to French interests. Cavour hoped now to find some settlement
by a Franco-Italian agreement involving the withdrawal of the French
occupation of Rome. With this new approach in mind he arranged
to have his friend, Audinot, interrogate him in the Italian chamber
and thus give him an opportunity to state his new policy in the form
of a reply. Cavour's declaration on 25 March 1861 therefore injected
a new element into the controversy in France. Answering Audinot,
he stated: "Without Rome as capital of Italy, Italy cannot be constituted. . . . . We must go to Rome, but with two conditions, we
must go there in accord with France, and . . . . without lessening the
independence of the Papacy . . . . without the power of the civil authority being extended to control that of the spiritual."[3] Two days
later the Italian chamber of deputies passed a motion in line with
Cavour's views.[4]

So absorbed was French opinion with its own parliamentary debates that it seems to have given little attention to those going on in
Turin. Only eight procureurs general noticed them or reported what

little opinion was developed by them in France. Most of the reactions were adverse. From Besançon came the report that "a large number of government supporters show very acute apprehension over Piedmont's plans concerning Rome and express the hope, even from a purely political point of view, of seeing France preserve for the Holy Father his last remnant of his former power." Reports from Metz, Riom, Limoges, and Nîmes showed similar tendencies. The lower classes in the districts of Metz and Riom, however, seemed indifferent to Italy's designs. On the other hand "a very considerable section of opinion in Corsica" favored Rome as Italy's capital; the urban and rural workers around Limoges sided with Italy against the Pope; while in the district of Nancy opinion seemed reassured by "Cavour's public promises that Italy would not aggravate the difficulties she had caused her benefactor." In spite of the reserves Cavour had made, the majority of the sparse reactions were not sympathetic to Italy.[5]

Then suddenly on 6 June, Cavour died from the effects of strain and overwork. Napoleon III was very much disturbed by this tragic turn of events because he counted on Cavour to restrain the violence of Italian nationalism. In the last few weeks before Cavour's death the two had been negotiating a treaty for the withdrawal of French troops from Rome based largely on guarantees which only Cavour could be trusted to fulfill. This treaty also would have included France's recognition of the new kingdom of Italy and a renewal of normal diplomatic relations. In the new critical situation resulting from Cavour's death the French emperor decided to divide the benefits of his previous plans by recognizing the Italian government without concluding the treaty on French withdrawal from Rome. In granting this recognition, however, the French government made two reservations which were publicized at the time of the recognition: that recognition did not imply approval of Italy's previous acquisitions of papal territory and that France would not withdraw from Rome until a reconciliation with the Holy See or Italian guarantees were forthcoming.[6]

Italian parliamentary debates may not have aroused much interest in the general public in France, but Cavour's death did stir at least the upper levels. Both the British chargé and the Belgian minister observed that it caused a sensation in Paris. The latter, Baron Beyens, reported a considerable slump on the stock market and added that "the loss of this statesman . . . . is considered a disaster by everybody, even by his political enemies."[7] The death of the Italian count may have caused a sensation in the upper circles of Paris, but it hardly caused a ripple in the provinces. Probably the recognition of Italy, which followed so closely upon the news of Cavour's death, diverted the attention of opinion and the observers of opinion from the earlier event. At any rate only three procureur reports mention popular reaction to the death itself, and these reactions were mixed.

The procureur general in Aix remarked that "in Legitimist and ultra-religious circles, they looked upon it as a sort of providential punishment, but men of good faith and all the parties deplored the loss of this great man." In like manner the procureur general in Riom noted that "liberal people . . . fear the complications and bad consequences that so sudden and unforeseen a disappearance of such a great statesman from the political scene can have on [Italian] independence." "The clergy and all the Ultramontane party prefer to see in it a decree of Providence and a just punishment from Heaven inflicted on the one who dared think of getting Rome as the capital of the Kingdom of Italy."[8] The report from Nîmes indicated that "the death of Count Cavour grieved the men of law and order and elated the Mazzinians." Cavour's death may have been greeted with mixed emotions, but the mixture was very thin for want of content.[9]

Slight attention was not the case, however, when it came to French recognition of Italy. While the death of Cavour may have caused a sensation among certain circles in Paris, the recognition of Italy was notable for causing no surprise at all. Indeed the progovernment *Patrie* published a forewarning of what might come several days before the council had decided on recognition. "They tell us," it asserted, "that negotiations may be under way to attain the re-establishment of diplomatic relations between France and the court of Turin." Even the reservations were suggested by the article. What was more significant was that the *Moniteur* reproduced the article.[10] Thus tipped off in advance, opinion was generally not surprised at the news when it was published during the last week of June. Seven procureur reports,[11] out of sixteen specifically mentioning the recognition question, commented particularly on the lack of surprise. The general tone of most of these sixteen reports was favorable to recognition, especially as circumscribed by the reservations.[12] The report from Nancy was typical of most of them:

> At this particular moment [wrote the procureur general] the *de facto* recognition of the Kingdom of Italy by the government of the Emperor does not astonish most of our people. The uninformed classes were even of the belief that this *de facto* recognition had been given long before. . . . . Thus public opinion looked upon the renewal of international relations with the court of Turin with no surprise, relations which the majority had not even realized were interrupted. . . . . Conceived in the most measured terms, with the duty and obligation of Piedmont to respect the sovereign authority of the Holy Father and the maintenance of our troops in Rome so long as the religious interests of the Catholic world are not sufficiently guaranteed, the recognition of the new kingdom within the limits of established facts seems to give satisfaction to public sentiment. This step will become even more popular in no time at all, if it can be thought of, if not as a setback, at least as a counterweight to English policy.[13]

In only three districts was any opposition (mostly clerical) noted; these were in Bourges, Besançon, and Nîmes. In three others (Bordeaux, Rennes, and Pau) there was an appearance of indifference. The procureur general in Bordeaux thought that the lack of interest, at

least in his own district, was due to the belief that the recognition
was inevitable and to the growing weariness over the whole Italian
question.[14] The favorable attitude in the district of Riom seems to
be borne out by the observations of the British military attaché,
Claremont, who accompanied the Imperial Court while it was making
its summer sojourn at Vichy. "I have a letter from him," wrote Cowley,
"stating that the Emperor's popularity is immense, crowds coming
from the neighboring country only to see him."[15]

Interval of General Indifference

The general interest in the Roman question, which was aroused
by the death of Cavour and the French recognition of Italy, quickly
subsided during the last half of 1861 for want of any sensational
development in that field. Out of twenty reports in October mentioning the question, seventeen indicated either indifference or a decline
in interest. The procureur general in Orleans declared:

> The masses still remain indifferent to the difficulties of the Roman question.
> Some priests from their pulpits are trying to stir up alarm by recounting the dangers
> and misfortunes of the papacy; [but] they themselves are forced to recognize
> that these are not today issues over which the working people of town and country
> are getting excited.

Similar reports also came from the sixteen judicial districts of Rennes,
Caen, Rouen, Douai, Amiens, Paris, Nancy, Metz, Besançon, Dijon,
Lyons, Riom, Aix, Nîmes, Toulouse, and Agen. Only from Montpellier, Bordeaux, and Corsica came evidence of continuing general
concern, although a persisting interest by small minority groups
was also noted in the districts of Agen, Douai, and Besançon.[16]

This indifference toward the Roman question persisted through
the last quarter of 1861; but the lack of interest was not as widespread
as during the summer. The growth of brigandage in southern Italy,
a little flurry over an insult offered to the French general in Rome,
and renewed activity of the Legitimists, particularly against the restrictions placed upon the Society of St. Vincent de Paul, stirred a
few districts out of their lethargy. Nancy, Rennes, and Nîmes reported a change from indifference to interest since the summer; Colmar and Limoges also showed continued interest; but a much longer
list of districts— Caen, Douai, Besançon, Dijon, Riom, Toulouse, Agen,
Bordeaux, and Pau—still reported profound indifference to the whole
question.[17]

The spring of 1862 saw a revival of activity in the legislative
houses, but even this did not stir up much interest in the general
public. The emperor's reference to Italy in his opening speech was
very brief and casual: "I recognized the Kingdom of Italy with the
firm intention of contributing by sympathetic and disinterested advice,
to conciliate two causes whose antagonisms trouble minds and consciences everywhere."[18] It looked as if the emperor by gliding briefly

over the question, was trying to preserve the indifference which had prevailed in the country during the last six months. But the senators would not leave the Roman question alone to that extent. Bonjean made a temperate defense of the temporal power, while he regretted the papal *non-possumus*. On the other hand Prince Napoleon made another provocative speech in which he did not even concede to the pope the Leonine (Vatican) City.[19] This forced Billault, the spokesman for the government, to elaborate the emperor's policy more fully.

> *I* am the one who expresses the emperor's views [he asserted], I have special authority to declare them before you. These views are still the same as before: to insist firmly at the same time on the independence of Italy and on the independence of the Holy See, to admit neither reaction in Italy, nor revolution in Rome, nor the submission of the revolted provinces which they would like to turn back, tied hand and foot, to the Holy Father, nor the abandonment of Rome which would fall immediately into the hands of Piedmont. The emperor had undertaken the war for the liberation of Italy, not for its unity; that unity was constituted in spite of his advice; he would have preferred a confederation under the honorary presidency of the pope; now unity being an accomplished fact, he would not disturb it and would not permit it to be disturbed, but he will not sacrifice the papacy to it.

Billault then obtained the passage of a clause in the address which expressed regret at the intransigent attitude of the pope.[20] The minister defended this policy also in the legislative body where he obtained unanimous passage of a similar clause.

Yet, even these heated debates in the chambers did not cause much excitement in the country beyond the clubs and drawing rooms in Paris. Only five procureur reports out of twenty-eight noted any specific reaction. The one from Bordeaux was typical:

> The discussions relative to the religious question and more particularly to those which deal with the Roman question have been followed with a lively interest. I believe I can say that here public opinion seems very satisfied with the unanimous vote on the paragraph relative to the affairs of Rome. The question posed in the terms defined by the government appears to correspond with the general feeling. The very clear, precise, and elevated explanations presented by M. Billault in support of the policy pursued by the government has produced a most favorable reaction. If I have been able to ascertain exactly what public opinion is, I would say that here they do not want to recreate a past which is henceforth impossible, nor do they want to see Rome abandoned by our soldiers.

Three other reports, from Nancy, Lyons, and Toulouse, expressed similar views in favor of Billault's declarations. One other, from Amiens, merely noted that the debates had received attention.[21]

Such relative indifference to what were supposed to be exciting debates would seem to indicate a persistence of indifference on into the first half of 1862. This also seems to be borne out by the reports of early 1862. Only eight mention interest or disinterest; and of them five[22] reported indifference, three[23] some interest by certain small groups such as Legitimists, clergy, and Republicans. The great mass of the people, however, were indifferent to the issues involved.[24] Maurain, who studied public attitudes toward domestic religious affairs, gained the same impression. "They [the debates] did not cause any agitation in the country," he affirmed. "They had lost the attraction of novelty, and the monotony of the discussions on the Roman question began to weary the public."[25]

Such popular indifference did not mean, however, that there was not lively discussions at court over the Italian issue. Two opposite factions fought each other in the open and under cover. The pro-Italian faction was much the stronger and more active because the pope's refusal to compromise or negotiate made it difficult to support him in the long run. This pro-Italian group consisted of members of Napoleon's own family, Prince Napoleon, Princess Mathilda, and his illegitimate half-brother, the Duke of Morny; of two generals, Fleury and Montebello; of his private secretary, Mocquard; and of several close friends and ministers such as Thouvenel, Fould, Persigny, Rouher, Baroche, Billault, La Valette, Benedetti, and Conneau. The propapal faction had Empress Eugénie on its side but otherwise counted only Walewski, Magne, Rouland, and Marshal Randon. A great deal was done to counter each other's influence, but it was obvious that the pro-Italian group was more numerous and had an easier job in selling its ideas to the emperor. And the emperor, knowing the general public's lack of interest over the issues, was able to keep more calm and balanced in spite of court pressures and legislative debates.[26] Baron Beyens, the shrewd Belgian diplomat, was able to keep his judgment sufficiently free from the current gossip and intrigues surrounding him[27] to see the situation as it is now revealed by the secret reports.

In spite of the apparent causes of alarm [he wrote home] one should not believe that there are serious dangers inside [France]; the support of the people and the army will not be lacking, the emperor knows it. He remains calm and imperturbable in the knowledge of his popularity and strength. No doubt they may reply that he exaggerates them, but I think they may find themselves mistaken.[28]

The public's lack of interest may have reassured Napoleon III, but it worried no end the French clericals and the papal court. In an effort to stir the French people from their lethargy and to show the whole world that the Catholic church had general support in its intransigent stand against Italy, Pius IX convoked an assembly of bishops in Rome in June 1862, supposedly for the canonization of the Japanese martyrs. The departure of the bishops, the proceedings in Rome, and the return of the bishops were all to be occasions for demonstrations and propaganda in a psychological war against Italy and the French government. Only fifty of France's eighty-three bishops left for the assembly, and they were able to elicit very few farewell demonstrations, indeed only two as far as they were observed by government officials. Plantier, Bishop of Nîmes, was not only given an ovation as he left the city, but these were also repeated by bands of the faithful at several stations on his trip to Marseilles. At Marseilles,

too, his embarkation and that of several other bishops was the occasion
for an organized demonstration. Hymns were sung at the pier; and
at a signal given by a rocket from a small boat in the harbor the
crowd shouted in unison, "Long live the Pope-King!" But the effect
of this ovation was marred by a counterdemonstration organized by
anticlericals, among whom were many Italian workers, who replied
with shouts of "Down with the Pope-King," "Down with priests
[la pretraille]!" "Long live the Emperor!"[29]

In Rome the canonization of the Japanese martyrs was hardly
more than a side show, leaving as the main event the papal allocution
and the bishops' address in reply. In his allocution of 9 June, Pius IX
denounced the Italian government, ignored the French government,
which was protecting him by its troops, deplored the revolutionary
errors of the times, and violently attacked all modern ideas being
elaborated outside the church in the fields of philosophy, morals,
and politics.[30] The reply of the bishops of the same day, which had
been carefully and deliberately composed under pressure from the
papal court, omitted mention of modern ideas as well as any com-
mendation for France's protection, but concentrated on a defense
of the temporal power. The address insisted that the divinely established temporal power was indispensable to the church, denounced
those who would end it, praised the pope for his uncompromising
defense of it, and vowed that the bishops would be at his side in this
fight even if it meant imprisonment or death.[31]

Then the return of the bishops to their dioceses, especially to
those in France, it was hoped would be an occasion for popular
ratification of the pronunciamentos in Rome and would crown all
these efforts to rout indifference. But the response must have been
very disappointing: in only five cities were there noticeable demonstrations. The French government's definite efforts to discourage
demonstrations and forbid the papal flag may have had some effect
on this poor showing. In Nîmes, Bishop Plantier was given a rousing
popular welcome, but, the procureur general reported, there were no
disorders, no shouts or emblems of a political nature. In Rennes the
clericals and Legitimists organized a big welcome for the returning
archbishop, but the occasion was marred by an equally energetic
counterdemonstration including even moderate people who were dis-
gusted by the declarations in Rome. They shouted "Long live the
Emperor!," "Down with the skullcaps!," "Long live Italy!" The archbishop was so impressed by this storm of protest that he limited
himself to a very moderate sermon. The procureur general, after
describing this scene, added: "The noise over the Roman question
is continuing to subside. . . . . There is astonishment that the pope
and the bishops proffered not a word of thanks to the government

whose flag maintains the Sovereign Pontiff in Rome."[32] The welcoming
demonstration in Angers also backfired. A procession of priests, seminarians, and church women went to meet Bishop Angebault on his
return. But, when it passed the barracks, the soldiers greeted it with
shouts of "Long live the Emperor!" The crowd took up the cry and,
swelled by unemployed workers suffering from the effects of the
American Civil War, who resented the sending of 150,000 francs as
a Peter's Pence to the pope, it followed the procession to the cathedral, shouting over and over again, "Long live the Emperor!"[33] The
procureur general in Agen gave this description of the receptions in
his district:

> The archbishops and bishops of my district in Auch, Agen, and Cahors went
> to Rome with some of their clergy. Their return to their dioceses has excited some
> emotion, but it all passed off well without any untoward incident, either because
> of the good sense of the people or because of the moderation of such men as the
> Messeigneurs of Auch and Agen. . . . . The people here look on but hardly bestir
> themselves. Even the Monseigneur [of Cahors] has noticed how . . . . the collection
> of the Peter's Pence has produced only 601 francs 80 centimes in his whole
> diocese between 21 February and 12 May.[34]

The archbishop of Besançon also was received by a welcoming committee, but, wrote the procureur, the affair was cold, restrained, and
without enthusiasm.[35] While two of the five welcoming demonstrations
had counterdemonstrations, it must be realized that the government,
as easily as the church, was capable of organizing synthetic crowds,
especially among the soldiers and the unemployed.

But in contrast to the five proclerical ceremonies of welcome,
and in addition to the two counterdemonstrations, there were eight
other districts where general disapprobation of the whole affair was
noted. One report from Rouen in eastern Normandy is particularly
interesting.

> The two documents [the allocution and the address] have produced in Nor-
> mandy an entirely opposite effect from what was expected in Rome [wrote the
> procureur general]. The reports of my assistants are almost unanimous in remarking
> an ever more obvious alienation of moderate people from the temporal power.
> French feeling is deeply wounded by these anathemas hurled against ideas and
> principles on which repose our modern civilization and by those solemn declara-
> tions which go so far as to raise the maintenance of the temporal power of the
> pope to the status of a dogma. Behind it all are seen the old theories of the
> supremacy of the spiritual over the civil authorities and the defense of the principle
> of legitimacy. Everywhere they repeat that the pope in showing his insistence on
> eternal opposition has made impossible any conciliatory solution. Especially national
> susceptibilities have been justly hurt by the failure to note the services rendered by
> the emperor and by France to religion and to the Sovereign Pontiff. I have heard
> fervent Catholics express themselves very positively in condemning in the very
> name of religious interests the attitude just taken by the pope and bishops. . . . .
>
> To sum it all up, the cause of the temporal power during the last quarter
> seems to have lost, if not the support of its declared advocates, at least the sympathies
> of a rather large number of moderate men who up to that time had believed a
> compromise to be possible between the demands of the pope and those of the
> Italian people.

Similar reactions were reported in briefer form from the seven districts of Rennes, Nancy, Besançon, Lyons, Aix, Toulouse, and Bordeaux.

What was almost as bad as this rise of resentment against the clergy was the great lumps of indifference which remained unleavened by all this fermentation. From eight other districts[36] came reports that the church's psychological warfare had left opinion untouched. What was more, these same July reports from another seven districts[37] told that independently of the bishop affair the majorities in their districts continued to remain indifferent to the whole Roman question. Maurain, after his account of the Roman assembly, concluded that although it caused lively press discussions, it did not arouse the public and that the lower clergy's public adherence to the address "left opinion indifferent."[38] Just as in the previous question of annexations, a drive by the church and the clericals to elicit popular support had not only failed to reduce appreciably the lethargy of opinion but in a few cases had merely transformed it into hostility. It is no wonder that a goodly number of sincere clerics, both high and low, had opposed such public demonstrations and preferred to remain quiet on political issues.[39]

Aspromonte

This continuing public indifference was evidently having its effect on the debates in the inner circles. The expense and embarrassments of the unappreciated occupation could not go on forever. The British seemed on the point of weaning Italy away from France; there was even a fear that England, Austria, and Italy might join in isolating France just at a time when Prussia was taking steps to build up her army. The Italians were also constantly pressing for the evacuation of Rome. Now the clergy and the church had revealed themselves powerless to dent the public indifference in France. It was under the impact of such considerations that the emperor and Thouvenel, his minister of foreign affairs, began to explore again, unbeknown to the French public, the possibility of a reconciliation between Rome and Turin. And, when Pius IX still interposed his *non-possumus*, they turned once more to a project of a Franco-Italian bilateral agreement.[40]

All these fine plans of mice and men were rudely interrupted by another filibustering expedition by Garibaldi. As early as July 1862 the old venerated hero was again recruiting volunteers for an expedition against Rome. In Sicily he was winning followers with the cry of "Rome or Death." The Italian government, unable to obtain a last-minute agreement with France, in desperation turned to the only other alternative of stopping Garibaldi, in the hope his suppression would bring the desired reward from an appreciative French public. Garibaldi and his band crossed the Straits of Messina on 25 August with Cialdini and his Italian troops hot on his trail. And five days later, high on a mountain plateau near Aspromonte, Italian hero faced Italian hero, a brief clash ensued, and Garibaldi's venture came to an inglorious end.

The Italian government now found itself in an embarrassing position before an aroused Italian public. It would never be forgiven for defeating and wounding Garibaldi unless immediate concessions could be obtained from France. To the Italian cabinet it seemed like a case of produce the goods or go out of business. In the face of this challenge the inexpert minister of foreign affairs, General Durando, issued a circular note placing France publicly on the spot in terms which could not possibly win the desired result. By the Aspromonte affair, he asserted, Italy had shown she was strong and determined enough to validate any guarantees undertaken. But instead of demanding the French evacuation of Rome in return for guarantees, he demanded Rome itself.

> But the watchword of the volunteers was this time, one must admit, the expression of a more imperious need than ever. The whole nation opposed Garibaldi's incautious move only because it was convinced that the king's government would be able to fulfill the mandate which it received from parliament in regard to Rome. . . . . The European powers will understand how irresistible is the movement which draws the entire nation toward Rome.[41]

To make matters worse, Durando inserted a statement in the official journal that "the monarchy cannot but affirm openly that its existence is not complete, that the exercise of its rights is not unimpaired, and that its efforts are not entirely efficacious, without Rome as Italy's capital."[42]

The reaction of the French government to the circular was most unfavorable. Since Italy had proclaimed to all the world her demand for nothing less than the city of Rome, Thouvenel, himself sympathetic to Italy, declared that France could not now negotiate even on evacuation.[43] Napoleon III, Thouvenel told Cowley, "looked upon [it] in the light of a summons to himself to order the evacuation of Rome, and consequently as a gross affront."[44]

Inspired by this resentment the emperor countered the public circular with the publication in the *Moniteur* of three documents involved in the latest negotiations which had taken place between Paris and Rome just prior to Garibaldi's most recent escapade. In the first document the emperor had explained to Thouvenel that he hoped for a Papal-Italian reconciliation based upon a mutual recognition of the *status quo* and upon liberal local self-government for the people remaining under the rule of the pope. In the second Thouvenel instructed La Valette in Rome to urge the pope to accept the *status quo* and liberal self-government for his people or to face the prospects of a withdrawal of French troops. The third was a reply from LaValette reporting the pope's continued intransigeance in the face of France's advice and threats.[45]

Under the stimulus of Aspromonte, the Durando circular, and the French published documents the French public did seem to emerge from its indifference. At least the press gave great prominence to the events, since they savored of the sensational in which newspapers revel. The semiofficial press, such as the *Constitutionnel*, as well as the *Opinion Nationale*, the *Siècle*, and the *Journal des Débats* praised Italy for her firm repression of the Garibaldian undertaking. The clerical papers, such as the *Monde* and the *Union*, gave Italy little credit. In the midst of it all La Guéronnière came out on his own this time in an article in *La France Politique, Scientifique et Littéraire* with the proposal that a congress set up an Italian federation of four states. This gave all other papers of all differing shades of opinion the opportunity to denounce and ridicule both La Guéronnière and *La France Politique*.[46]

While the newspapermen were having their fun over Aspromonte and La Guéronnière, the people of the country roused themselves sufficiently to express almost universal approval of Italy's action against Garibaldi. Only some groups of Legitimists, clericals, and Republicans seemed to regret the successful action of the Italian troops: the Legitimists and clericals because it enhanced Italy's position;[47] the Republicans, because it checked their hero, Garibaldi, and prevented the pope's loss of his remaining territory. All other groups, including the great majority of the French people, hailed the outcome, whether from the French, papal, or Italian point of view. The report from Riom is rather typical of the rest:

> The audacious and criminal attempt by Garibaldi . . . . received universal reprobation, and the news of the defeat and capture of the famous partisan was acclaimed by the people with unequivocal satisfaction. . . . .
> Truly though, it must nevertheless be recognized that this bold challenge had encountered in the Legitimist and clerical faction an indignation more apparent than real. . . . .
> Besides, their regrets are augmented by the stronger position won by the government of Turin by performing an act of loyalty, virility, and constancy in the frightful crisis it has just gone through.[48]

It seems evident now that the Durando circular caused more disturbance in the councils of the emperor and in the press than among the French people. Or, indeed, as so often happened, it was eclipsed two weeks later by the publication of the three French diplomatic documents to the extent that most opinion reports dealt with the later incident rather than the earlier. The newspapers took what could be expected to be their traditional positions: the clerical papers were hostile, the liberal papers favorable, and the semiofficial papers were cautiously noncommittal.[49] But in all the procureur reports there were only two appreciable instances of reaction to the Italian ill-advised circular: the reports from Nancy and Dijon, both hostile.[50]

The first French reply to the Durando circular was as oblique as it was inscrutable: the publication of the three letters. The emperor ordered it while on vacation at Biarritz, as much to the surprise of Thouvenel as to that of the public. There has been much speculation on why these were published and why later Thouvenel was dismissed. The most plausible theory seems to be concern over the coming national elections of 1863. The empress and Walewski in particular were constantly pressing Napoleon to get right with the clergy and the clericals by continuing the Roman occupation indefinitely. Knowing the emperor's political shrewdness, they no doubt linked the situation with the coming elections. The whole firm foundation of the Empire could be shaken if the clericals and devout peasants could be led to join forces with the Legitimists; there was even defection among the most progressive industrialists over the Cobden-Chevalier Treaty. Fences must be built, and pre-election reconciliations consummated. It was not the first or last time that foreign policy was to become a political football. Down in Biarritz the empress and Walewski may have been able to make more headway in the absence of most of the "Italianissimes" of the court, as the pro-Italian faction was dubbed. From our vantage point of ninety years of hindsight, putting together all that occurred in the last half of 1862, one could almost imagine Napoleon III trying to think out how he could hold the support of the pro-Italians and at the same time regain the favor of the clericals before 1863. The Durando circular may have been the deciding factor in getting the election ball rolling. In the first place it made a Franco-Italian treaty on the evacuation of Rome impossible for some time to come. Therefore, the documents preserved for that occasion to prove the recalcitrance of the pope could now be used for another purpose to prove the government's pro-Italian attitude at a time when the government could do nothing for Italy after the Durando circular. This move would keep the pro-Italians in line on the eve of selling them out to the clericals, which would be the next move beyond.

If these were the purposes of the emperor, he must have been highly gratified by the effects on public opinion because the documents not only elated the pro-Italians with hopes but even won some favor from the clericals, who no doubt leaned heavily on Thouvenel's promise *never* to let Italy have Rome. The semiofficial papers of course praised them slavishly. But the pro-Italian papers, such as the *Siècle*, the *Opinion Nationale*, the *Temps,* and the *Esprit Publique*, responded in the hoped-for fashion by interpreting them as a step toward evacuation. Some clerical papers such as the *Monde* and the *Gazette de France* criticized the documents as being antipapal, but the clerical *Union* and the Orleanist *Journal des Débats* were puzzled as to just what their publication really did mean.[51]

So far the press reaction was what could be expected. Yet, the procureur reports from the provinces were beyond all expectations, for pro-Italians and clericals alike hailed the documents as harbingers of success for their respective causes. Napoleon was already beginning to win the clericals even with what was supposed to be his consolation award to the pro-Italian faction. All the eleven procureur reports stressing the public reaction to the documents in their respective districts indicated favorable responses—eight instances of clerical support and seven of pro-Italian support, but no real antagonism. The report from Lyons illustrated the two-way favorable reaction to the documents:

> The recent publication in the *Moniteur* of the documents concerning the Roman question have been interpreted by the various parties according to their respective points of view. Those opposed to the temporal power of the pope saw in this publication a sort of respectful ultimatum and seem convinced of the early downfall of that power. The opposite party finds in the same documents the promise of the status quo.

Those from Metz and Corsica also showed contrary interpretations prevailing. On the other hand the districts of Amiens, Nancy, Montpellier, and Bordeaux hailed the documents as being favorable to Italy; while on the other hand the districts of Paris, Orleans, Bourges, and Nîmes welcomed them for being favorable to the pope. Again Baron Beyens seemed to have astutely observed these contrary interpretations when he wrote: "Was this [publication] to prepare opinion for a withdrawal from Rome? That is what is impossible to conclude from the documents themselves, which may have been equally well received by the papers of every shade and which justified the arguments of every party."[52]

What is even more interesting is that two of the procureurs general appeared to be thinking along the lines of the emperor in linking the documents with the coming elections. The procureur general in Amiens wrote that "a solution of Roman affairs . . . . especially after the recent publications in the *Moniteur*, ... would have only a very weak influence on the forthcoming elections"; while the procureur general in Nîmes declared that he had no doubt but "that these measures [publication and dismissal of Thouvenel], reassuring to all men of law and order and especially hailed by the sincere friends of the emperor, will exercise on the results of the coming elections a most favorable influence for his government."[53]

The perplexities of some of the opposition press and the conflicting interpretations over the documents were suddenly set straight by the cabinet crisis which came to a head early in October 1862. The emperor returned to Saint-Cloud (near Paris) on 9 October, fully determined on the second step, which would be an open bid to the clericals. He would ask the entire cabinet to resign, appoint the propapal Walewski as foreign minister and build around him a sympathetic cabinet. After the bombshell had struck the council of ministers, Thouvenel wrote to Flahault in London:

> We are certainly on the eve of a crisis which I foresaw. The emperor, without taking up with his ministers the examination of the serious pending questions, seems determined to invite them all to hand in their resignations and then to reconstruct the cabinet under the influence which Count Walewski represents. Prince de la Tour d'Auvergne or Mr. Drouyn de Lhuys may be my successor.[54]

Whatever may have been the emperor's motives in making a clean sweep, by the 13th he had modified his plan to the extent of removing only Thouvenel and Persigny, the latter being the minister of interior. The main "Italianissimes"—Fould, Rouher, Baroche, Morny, and Flahault—men who had been the closest associates of Napoleon III before and after his rise to power, now presented a united front and asserted their intentions of resigning in a body unless Thouvenel were retained and his policy followed. The emperor protested that he was not changing his policy but merely making a change of certain men by which the same ends might be achieved by a new approach. There were many conferences back and forth and much plain talking,[55] and the emperor and Walewski countered with persuasion and threats. It all ended in a further compromise on 15 October: Thouvenel had to go, but all the rest stayed, even Persigny. Benedetti and La Valette were also recalled from Turin and Rome. In the place of the ousted three, Drouyn de Lhuys became foreign minister, while Sartiges and La Tour d'Auvergne went to Turin and Rome.[56] The news of the change in foreign ministers came out on the 16th,[57] and on the 18th Drouyn de Lhuys announced by a circular dispatch that the policy of the French government concerning Rome had not changed from that expounded in the emperor's letter of 20 May. France was going to continue the policy of hoping for a reconciliation between Rome and Turin. It will be noted that the new statement of policy did not refer to Thouvenel's published dispatch elaborating the emperor's letter in a manner less sympathetic and more threatening toward the pope.[58]

The emperor's change of ministers may have been a bombshell in governmental circles, but in the country at large it was a "dud." Of course the newspapers seized upon it for sensational copy: the clerical papers naturally hailed it, the governmental papers approved it with soothing explanations, and, as might be expected, the *Siècle* and the *Journal des Débats* regretted it.[59] The procureur reports from the provinces also noted some transitory interest in the change of personnel. Fifteen reports noted an interest; thirteen hardly referred to it. All fifteen districts reporting seemed to give a rather automatic and casual approval. In only three of these areas was there indicated a little opposition by small groups of radicals.[60]

In spite of the "life-or-death" arguments put up by both sides in governmental circles concerning the fate of the Empire over the issue, nothing could be further from reality. With all the hullabaloo of the politicians and the press eleven procureur reports out of seventeen discussing the Roman question in January 1863 still indicated deep indifference, especially among the masses and in the rural areas. The procureur general in Toulouse declared:

> The question has been pending for so long, they [the liberals] have been so often wrong in their predictions, that they are tired of it and fear they will be mistaken again. As to the masses, they just wait, willing to accept any solution which will not hurt their interests or way of living; they just want to be left in peace. The result of it all is a very real let-down, at least for the moment.

Again from Aix came this general comment: "This insoluble Roman question is not one to exercise a decisive influence on the country. The ineffectualness of the clerical agitations is proof enough that the destinies of France are not at stake on that issue."[61] Napoleon III, in making his brusque decisions, was interested in winning an election[62] and was not particularly perturbed by dire warnings of the Empire's downfall. Turning to Persigny during the heated discussions, he had boasted: "I also, Gentlemen, feel the pulse of France twice a day; I know her sentiments, and I shall not abandon the pope."[63] If he did feel her pulse twice a day by reference to the procureur reports, he knew of this persistent indifference. Indifference would not shake his throne, but it would permit him to stand by the pope by appointing Drouyn de Lhuys and thereby win the clericals for the election. Apparently many in the country would not care one way or the other. Cowley came to the same conclusion without seeing the procureur reports when he wrote: "The country seems apathetic. The masses care little whether their foreign policy is guided by Drouyn de Lhuys or by Thouvenel, but the clergy are delighted." The Austrian, Count Mulinen, and Maurain concurred in this view.[64]

But how "delighted" really were the clericals, clergy and laymen, by the appointment of Drouyn de Lhuys? Their reactions would be the real payoff for most of the changes of the past three months. Twenty of the twenty-eight procureur reports of January 1863 dealt specifically with the clericals and their allies, the Legitimists. Fifteen of these twenty showed a more favorable clerical attitude toward the government: they were not all "delighted," but they did seem to be more favorably inclined. For example, from the district of Dijon came this report:

> His Majesty's decision [change of foreign ministers] has had another excellent effect, enormous in its present consequences, when the legislative body is rounding out its last year, it is bringing around to the government's side the opinion of the clergy and of those who share its aspirations. . . . . [It] removes from the vicinity of the ballot box one of the banners, papal independence, which they contemplated raising at the risk of dividing the men of law and order and good government.
>
> My various assistants, in the three dioceses of this district, are unanimous in

pointing out the pacifying effect that the appointment of Mr. Drouyn de Lhuys and the statements accompanying it have had on the clergy. . . . . In my preceding reports I had said that the attitude of the ecclesiastics was more reserved than at the beginning of the Roman question; today they seem to me to have taken a step forward and to have become trustful and even affectionate.

There were similar, if not as detailed, accounts of clerical rapprochements from Caen, Douai, Paris, Metz, Colmar, Besançon, Orleans, Riom, Aix, Montpellier, Toulouse, and Bordeaux.

But there were five districts which seemed to indicate the continuance of clerical hostility. These were Rennes, Rouen, Nancy, Grenoble, and Agen. But these irreconcilable attitudes were rare and certainly not representative. From the evidence at hand it appears that Napoleon's wooing of the clergy was showing good results. The election campaign and the final returns, of course, would be the real test.[65]

The Elections of 1863

Of the four general legislative elections held during the Second Empire the third, that of 1863, was the first one to offer any real contests between the government and its opposition groups. The elections of 1852 and 1857 were held under the stern hand of the authoritarian dictatorship and its instrument of official candidates. Thanks to the revived political activity accompanying the freer legislative debates since 1860, the public was able for the first time to emerge to some degree from behind the iron curtain of Caesarism to express a slightly more independent opinion at the polls.

The election campaign was a vigorous one on the part of both the government and the opposition. Persigny, as minister of interior, directed the government's campaign. The system of official candidates was still preserved in his instructions to the prefects: "So that the good faith of the people may not be led astray by clever language or equivocal promises."

The newspapers were supposed to be free to list the opposition candidates and to support them, but there was always the danger that what they would say would make them subject to warnings or even to suppression. Consequently, the opposition could not take full advantage of press publicity. Likewise, if the opposition resorted to handbills their candidates ran the risk of being prosecuted for violations of the complicated rules against peddling (le colportage). Furthermore, fourteen legislative districts seemed to have been gerrymandered in order to swamp city Republican majorities with large numbers of neighboring rural votes.

Next there was the question of the government's support of 91 of its previous governmental deputies who had voted for an anti-government amendment on the Roman question in 1861. "We'll meet again at the polls," Persigny had threatened ominously after the exciting session. Now again in his circular to the prefects he declared: "The government in fact can support before the electorate only those men who are devoted to the imperial dynasty and our institutions without qualifications or mental reservations." But the government's withdrawal of support was not as sweeping as Persigny's earlier threat had indicated. On the heels of the partial reconciliation of the clericals it only excluded 24 of the 91 from government patronage; among these were some of the more critical deputies, such as Keller, Plichon, Lemercier, Cuverville, Ancel, d'Andelarre, and Flavigny. However, the administration took pains to explain that this exclusion from the ranks of official candidates was not because of their stand on the religious question but because of their attempt to use that question merely as a weapon to attack the government in general.

The clericals were hard put to know how to approach this new type of election. In the face of Drouyn de Lhuys' appointment they did not want to antagonize a more favorable administration. On the other hand they wanted to take advantage of the greater freedom to strengthen their position in the legislative body. Particularly they wanted to support the 24 who were losing the government's sponsorship because of the religious question, and they wanted to defeat the anticlerical Republicans wherever they appeared. In the face of this perplexity seven of the more liberal Catholic bishops issued a letter, called the Letter of the Seven Bishops,[66] in which they urged every good Catholic to vote. Catholic voters should perform their duty with respect for the government, but in a spirit of critical examination; they should vote without bringing in question existing institutions and without distinction of party, whether Imperialist, Legitimist, Orleanist, or Republican. What should then be the criteria for Catholic voters? They should judge all candidates on three issues: the temporal independence of the pope, religious freedom, and general liberty. While the bishops based their approach on imperial institutions, Napoleon III was angered because nowhere did they mention him or loyalty to him. Significant, too, is the fact that they seemed to favor a further liberalization of the Empire. The liberal program of the clericals was particularly disliked by the pope himself.

The elections took place on 30 and 31 May. In the cities the voting was quite free, but in the country, where the voters were well-known and closely watched, there was more restraint. Besides in rural precincts the progovernment mayor selected the poll-watchers and kept the ballot boxes during the intervening night between the two election days. There was considerable rumor of dishonesty and tampering with the ballot boxes.[67]

When the returns were all in, it was found that the government

had won in the rural areas of the provinces but had lost in the big
cities. Of the nine deputies in Paris eight were Republicans and one
was Thiers, an opposition Orleanist. Similar victories were won by
Republicans or other liberals in Lyons, Marseilles, Bordeaux, Nantes,
Toulouse, Le Havre, Brest, Nîmes, Lille, Saint-Etienne, Toulon, Metz,
Mulhouse, Nancy, and Limoges. The government received 5,300,000
votes to 1,954,000 for the opposition, a gain for the latter since
1857 of 1,290,000 votes. The government won 250 seats; the opposition, 32, a gain of 27. What was surprising about the results of
this election was not the victory of the victors but rather the urban
victories of the vanquished. A sizable opposition was developing.

But how did the clericals fare in the results? Of the 24 clerical
deputies abandoned by the government, 6 dropped out of the race
before election day, 12 were defeated, and 6 won. There were seven
others of the original 91 who declined even to run. Nine other new
clerical candidates won, making 15 in all out of 282, but few of them
cared to stress their clericalism in the campaign. The leading outspoken clericals—Montalembert, Cochin, de Meaux, Keller, Lemercier,
and Cuverville—all lost. But these figures do not reveal the total
clerical vote. In many districts where there was not a clear-cut choice
on the issue a considerable number of anticlericals voted for clerical
candidates, and likewise many clericals had to vote for Imperialists
or Republicans.

In spite of the confusion over the scattering of the clerical vote,
the general consensus of observers was that it was a clerical defeat.
Maurain, who made a most thorough analysis of the vote on religious
issues, concluded that "the elections of 1863 showed that even in
the most clerical regions, [the clergy] did not deliver a majority
of the votes."[68] Ollivier, anticlerical and Republican, remarked:

> Another salient character of the election is the complete rout in Paris, as
> well as in the departments, of the party of the episcopal agitators. They represented
> France as a prey to a violent religious upheaval, alarmed over the dangers to the
> papacy, indignant over the favors to Italy, ready to rise up for the defense of a
> threatened faith; the answer was the almost total defeat of the defenders of the
> papacy and of the enemies of Italy.[69]

Even the clericals themselves acknowledged defeat. Cochin, who obtained only 6,000 votes in Paris, exclaimed: "Help me to declericalize
myself!"[70] And Bishop Dupanloup, one of the signers of the Letter
of the Seven Bishops, remarked ruefully that "the elections, in general,
went against the church."[71]

The real victors in the opposition were the anticlerical Republicans and the monarchist liberals, who won 17 seats. The Duke of
Morny admitted this to Ollivier:

> The elections [he remarked] have left only two forces facing each other, the
> Empire and democracy. . . . . It is time now to concede, if not complete political
> liberty immediately, at least civil liberty, and to study social problems. It is urgent

that the emperor, instead of proceeding by surprises, should no longer leave his councillors in complete ignorance of his foreign policy.[72]

The procureurs general had had considerable correspondence concerning the campaign and infractions of regulations during and after the elections,[73] but their regular reports do not deal very fully with the election returns, since these results were all public. One report from Besançon is of some interest because it pointed out the resentment against the system of official candidates.

> The times of imposed candidates has passed. The liberal spirit has awakened, the people want no more constraint, they consider themselves free to express their own wishes, and represent their own ideas and interests. . . . . It will be necessary to abstain from that immoderate pressure, from that clumsy brokerage which is exercised by the lower agents of government. These practices do not frighten anybody and alienate everybody. . . . . It is because it did not take sufficiently into account these natural susceptibilities that the administration suffered its worst setback in the Haute-Saône. Not only did the official candidate lose in Vesoul, but this first disaster was followed by a completely unexpected and very regrettable second one in Gray. . . . . The people, feeling their dignity and independence insulted, exasperated by petty measures and haughty demands, reacted by one supreme effort and gave an overwhelming majority to the candidate of their choice.[74]

What was most noticeable in the procureur reports for the periods before, during, and after the elections was the uniform lack of interest in the Roman question. This, more than anything else, cut the ground from under the clerical campaign. And this indifference can be attributed largely to the wise replacement of Thouvenel by Drouyn de Lhuys to lull the electorate on election eve. The procureur general in Nancy wrote a significant report on this point: "Although the voters have evidently condemned the exaggerations of the clerical party and the aroused defenders of the temporal power have taken a bad beating, it [the Italian question] has not emerged from the state of immobility which calm and moderation has little by little woven about it." All the reports, without exception, which mentioned the Roman question in April, July, and October of 1863 reported continued and widespread indifference.[75]

Napoleon III by his pre-election maneuver had laid the clerical ghost only to find himself haunted by the Republican and liberal bogy. Again he readjusted his administration to meet the new trend. First, he dismissed Persigny, who, although pro-Italian, was disliked because of his arbitrary handling of the campaign. His dismissal would appear to be motivated by the increase in the opposition's strength. Then the emperor set up a new office of minister of state to which Rouher was appointed after Billault, the original designee, had died. The minister of state and his staff would represent the government in legislative debates.

Whatever may have been the motive, perhaps as a countercheck on the clerical poor election showing, the emperor also requested an examination of the procureur reports of January 1863 for the clerical reaction on his appointment of Drouyn de Lhuys. Some one in the ministry of justice took extracts from only eight of the twenty reports dealing with the clericals. Only one of these showed the clericals to be still hostile. Eight others were inaccurately summed up by the brief general statement that in these districts "the clergy is calm and expectant." In fact the actual reports from these latter districts showed the clergy and clericals as increasingly progovernment. This little step in the process of rechecking thus also revealed how sometimes the material gathered on opinion can be inadequately evaluated for higher authorities.[76] Yet the accompanying summary by the new minister of justice, Baroche, more nearly approximated the true picture of the situation in January 1863. He wrote:

> The new policy of the emperor [on the Roman question] is a marked progress toward conciliation. . . . . It has already produced the conciliatory attitude of the clergy. . . . .
> When it is a question of abandoning the temporal power of the pope, many liberals, sincere supporters of the imperial government, hesitate and do not desire that the emperor take the responsibility for that catastrophe. . . . . The preoccupations of the clergy have almost disappeared.[77]

Thus by the election results, by a recheck on the favorable clerical attitude in January 1863, and by the remaining reports of 1863 the emperor could not help but become convinced that the Roman question no longer endangered his government, at least as far as a threat from the clericals was concerned, so long as he did not deliberately abandon the pope to Italy. If the situation continued to remain quiet over a sufficient period of time, it would probably be safe to make a guarantee treaty with Italy which would permit the withdrawal of troops without the sacrifice of the pope.[78]

The September Convention

The first half of the year 1864 was a worrisome one for Napoleon III. Three crises had developed in foreign affairs which were turning out unfavorably for France. The emperor's lame attempt to intervene diplomatically on the side of the insurgent Poles in 1863 had failed to accomplish anything except to arouse the antagonism of Russia. Again when he tried to organize an Anglo-French intervention in favor of Denmark in 1864, the movement had succeeded only in antagonizing England, Prussia, and Austria and in disturbing French opinion by the setback. In Mexico French troops were meeting with stubborn resistance and American ill-will, while opinion at home was generally hostile to this overseas adventure. Italy and Great Britain were continuing to oppose the French occupation of Rome. Wherever France looked, whether to Russia, Prussia, Austria, Italy, Great Britain, or the United States, she found disgruntled neighbors instead of allies and friends. The emperor's policy seemed to be creating a self-imposed isolation for France, and isolation of any sort at any time was dangerous for a continental power.[79]

The reaction of French opinion to all these developments was very disconcerting. From 1861 when the expedition began in Mexico to its end in 1867, the great bulk of the procureur reports had shown opinion generally hostile to the enterprise.[80] One report from Colmar is typical of the majority of the reports during those years.

> This expedition [wrote the procureur], judged with so much hate and disparagement in foreign countries, continues besides to be the subject of rather severe criticism. I would not try to judge it myself, I merely limit myself to adding . . . . the impressions which I receive. . . . . Now that the occupation of that country appears to require an extension of time, general concern is reviving and it is that much stronger in industrial circles because they are apprehensive lest that occupation may end sooner or later in a war with the United States.[81]

After Russia's suppression of the Polish insurrection Grey (British chargé in Paris) wrote home concerning rumors of Drouyn de Lhuys' possible retirement:

> The reason for his [supposed] retirement would, according to the public, have been the course adopted under his advice in the Polish question, a course which has resulted in a conclusion highly distasteful to the sensitive feelings of the French nation. . . . . I hear from all sides the opinion expressed that the Emperor *must* do something for the dignity of France. . . . . My own feeling is that Mr. Drouyn de Lhuys shares in this feeling.[82]

Drouyn de Lhuys was not forced into retirement at this time, indeed he was to remain in office for another three years, but there was little doubt that in the first half of 1864 French opinion became more restive and critical. In March 1864 Carnot and Garnier-Pagès, Republican candidates, were elected to fill two legislative vacancies in Paris. In the procureur reports of January, April, and July 1864 there was considerable discussion of the rise of opposition sentiment and activity in other parts of the country. A January report from Bordeaux had this passage penciled in the margin by some one in the ministry of justice: "Among the educated classes and the working people of the cities one cannot deny that political activity is reviving and that a spirit of criticism and discussion is taking on proportions that it had not attained up to now." Again from Lyons: "In the large cities of this district the election campaigns [local], the legislative debates, the candidates' platforms seem to have reawakened everywhere democratic aspirations and hostile instincts." A similar report came from Aix in July, and in the local elections of Bordeaux and Orleans the governmental candidates barely won a majority, so strong was the opposition.[83]

With all this discontent over foreign policy and this internal disaffection one feature of public opinion continued unchanged. Over and over again in one report after another the indifference of public opinion to the Roman question was reiterated *ad nauseam*.[84]

If the emperor and Drouyn de Lhuys felt that "something must be done for the dignity of France," that France must not allow herself to become isolated among the great powers,[85] what would be more natural for them than to turn to the question about which the public showed the greatest indifference. The Roman question, dormant since the aftermath of Aspromonte, appeared chosen for further operations. A bilateral agreement with Italy would have several advantages: it would please the restive liberal groups in France; it would tend to bring Italy and England to France's side in the power lineup in Europe; it would prepare the way for future joint Franco-Italian action concerning the election of a new pope in case of the anticipated death of Pius IX; and it would relieve France of the military burden of occupation at a time when she had new military burdens in Mexico and along the Rhine.

The occasion for reopening the question came in April 1864. Italy, which had remained discreetly silent on the question since the appointment of Drouyn de Lhuys, now sensed the opportune moment to reopen negotiations. Minghetti, then Italian prime minister, engaged Vimercati, a close friend of Napoleon III living in Paris, to approach Rouher rather than Drouyn de Lhuys. Right away Rouher, one of the "Italianissimes," showed interest and promised to "provoke the appreciations of the emperor and . . . . try to smooth out the obstacles to a lasting settlement."[86] The negotiations, thus begun, were continued by Pepoli and Nigra with the emperor and Drouyn de Lhuys. They used the old Thouvenel-Cavour proposed treaty as a basis of discussion and added a new Italian proposal to transfer the capital from Turin to Florence as the guarantee to reassure French Catholics. Five months of difficult discussions intervened until finally on 15 September 1864 the convention was signed by Drouyn de Lhuys, Nigra, and Pepoli. For Italy it provided that Italy would not attack and would assure against attack the present territory of the pope; that Italy would agree to negotiate the assumption of part of the papal debt; and that Italy would allow the pope to raise a small defensive force. For France it provided only that she would withdraw her troops from Rome within two years. In a protocol it was stipulated that the convention would go into effect when Italy had officially transferred her capital to a new location (understood to be Florence).[87]

Although the negotiators had hoped to keep the Convention secret until the ratifications had been exchanged and the capital transfer decreed, the news leaked out through a subordinate of the Italian foreign office and was published in the *Opinione* of Turin on 17 September 1864. This gave the terms of the Convention without the capital transfer protocol. Thus the first news France received was from abroad and did not contain the main guarantee destined to satisfy French opinion.[88] Drouyn de Lhuys counteracted the effect of the leak by having the semiofficial *Constitutionnel* publish a statement in which it summarized the Convention, stressed Italian restraint

for the past two years, and hinted at the capital transfer.[89] Also on
2 October the French foreign minister had the *Moniteur* publish a
note sent to the Holy See in which the reasons for the Convention
were explained. They included French disappointment at the pope's
refusal to make liberal administrative and judicial reforms and Italy's
reasonableness on the questions of her capital and the papal debt.[90]

The reactions of French opinion to the September Convention
have to be found almost entirely in the procureur and prefect reports.
The press divided about evenly between supporters and opponents
according to the traditional views of the individual newspapers.
What was immediately obvious in the reports was that the reassuring
indifference was gone. Interest was so keen on the sensational new
development that only Agen and Montpellier reported indifference.
But even in October certain groups in Montpellier showed some interest,
and later in January and April 1865 indifference had mostly disappeared. Public opinion on the Roman question had therefore come to
life all over France, and the reaction would be watched carefully by the
government.

There were only six districts where the public reactions were
so scanty or confused that no evaluation of them could be made;
these were Angers, Rouen, Poitiers, Pau, Nîmes, and Corsica. From
all the other twenty-two districts, covering every major part of France,
the procureur and prefect reports between October 1864 and April
1865 gave a fairly good picture of the general public reaction. Some
procureurs general—those in Amiens, Besançon, Limoges, and Lyons
—found that it was too early to estimate opinion in their October
reports. However, by the end of six months after the first news of
the Convention, it became apparent that there was overwhelming
approval of the treaty. Eighteen districts showed general satisfaction
with the arrangement.[91] In the district of Metz the department of
Ardennes was favorable but that of Moselle was hostile, while the
opinion of Bordeaux was reported as favorable by the prefect and
unfavorable by the procureur general. Eighteen and a half approving
districts, out of twenty-two reporting, reveal the widespread support
given to the Convention.

Broken down in more detail the revived expressions of opinion
also revealed other tendencies. The Legitimists, clericals, and the
clergy itself generally disapproved the arrangement, although the
clergy tended to keep quiet. The Republicans and liberals on the
other hand were inclined to give their approval, while a few of the
more extreme wing regretted that obstacles still remained to prevent
Italy from taking over Rome. The most striking revelation of opinion
on Rome was that sentiment in at least sixteen districts, except in
Republican circles, was clearly for the preservation of the pope's

temporal power.[92] The October report from Colmar showed this attitude particularly:

Public opinion, with which I am concerned [wrote the procureur general], believes that . . . . the temporal independence of the pope is, even in the eyes of the most lukewarm, indissolubly linked with his spiritual independence, and consequently also with the reassurance of Catholic consciences as well as with regular relations between governments. Those who share this view, in principle, are far from thinking in fact that the present government of the Holy Father is a model government; they do not even hesitate to declare that, to become a model government, it would have to be completely changed.

Even some of the orthodox Protestants in Alsace shared this view; and in radical Lyons the procureur general stated that "the immense majority ask that the pope not be abandoned." Only the newly acquired district of Chambéry seemed opposed to the temporal power.[93]

The French government had learned then, from this reopening of the Roman question, that while public opinion would follow it as far as the terms of the Convention, it would go no further. The predominant sentiment inclined toward guaranteeing the pope his temporal power within his present restricted boundaries. It was on this remaining question that the Legitimists and clericals could really cause trouble for the government. But the government, by making the Convention, was trying to get out of trouble; it was not looking for more.

However, while the French government was particularly anxious to avoid having anything said in Italy about eventually getting Rome as capital, the Italian government had the corresponding concern not to imply the surrender of their Roman aspirations as they presented the proposed capital transfer to the Italian parliament. The two delicate problems of approaching two conflicting public opinions led to further publications of documents. On the eve of convening the Italian parliament the Italian government published Nigra's report of the negotiations in which he claimed that the present convention was similar to the Cavour-Thouvenel project and that the transfer of the capital did not preclude Italian "moral" means to achieve conciliation with the papacy on the basis of a free church in a free state.[94] This interpretation of the Convention was embarrassing to Drouyn de Lhuys on two counts: it made him look as antipapal as Thouvenel, and the program of "a free church in a free state" suggested the abolition of the pope's temporal power. Consequently, the French foreign minister insisted upon further consultations with Nigra on proper interpretations of the treaty. Out of these conversations came agreement that the Convention differed from the Cavour-Thouvenel project, that "moral means" did not imply excitation of the Romans to insurrection, and that the capital transfer was "neither a provisional expedient nor a step toward Rome." Then on 5 November Drouyn de Lhuys published the correspondence in the *Moniteur*.

Since this French publicity on interpretations came at the time of the convening of the Italian parliament, General La Marmora, the new Italian prime minister, felt it was necessary to defend his government by publishing a note he had sent to Nigra wherein he explained that Italy had no ulterior motives in the words "moral means," that Italy did not intend to make her national aspirations the subject of a treaty, that Italy, however, would not achieve her national aspirations by violating the Convention, and finally that Italy, like France, reserved her own liberty of action concerning future eventualities in Rome.[95]

Of course the French public was sitting on the sidelines during this exchange of publications, and the net effect was reassurance and increased acceptance of the Convention. The report from the Paris area, after describing the concern caused by Nigra's account of the negotiations, went on to say:

> However, the language held by the papers which seem to interpret the ideas of the [French] government most faithfully and the publication of documents by the foreign minister himself have reassured those who, in this grave question, consider above all else the interests of Catholicism or of French influence. The great majority therefore look forward to the future with absolute confidence in the wisdom and loyalty of the emperor.

Reports from Douai, Nancy, Besançon, and Montpellier expressed similar sentiments.[96]

Quanta Cura and Syllabus

Since the later middle ages and the pontificates of Innocent III and Boniface VIII, the Roman Catholic Church had been intensely perturbed by the increased authority of lay princes and their secular states over the lives and religious practices of their subjects. The nineteenth century had intensified this papal anxiety with the rise of anticlericalism and nationalism. The former insisted on the supremacy of the state over the church in many fields, such as education, where the church claimed supremacy for itself. The latter, nationalism, was introducing almost a competitive religion, the worship of the sovereign national state, the placing, as the church saw it, of Caesar above God. The Roman question brought these hostile forces right up to the doorstep of the Holy See. The waves of Italian nationalism swept over three-fourths of the Papal States and threatened the last remnants of the pope's temporal power. When Pius IX resisted this with stubborn firmness, he was lectured by the Caesar of the Tuileries for resisting modern progress and modern thought. After the September Convention had been concluded between two such national sovereign states to the discomforture of the church, the pope finally on 8 December 1864 hurled a ringing defiance at secular states and modern ideas in the form of an encyclical letter, Quanta Cura, and an accompanying Syllabus of Errors.

In the encyclical the pope condemned vehemently all modern liberties and all principles which limit the authority of the church over civil society. Particularly did he assail freedom of conscience, freedom of worship, freedom of the press, the secularization of civil law and education, and the right of peoples to self-determination.

The encyclical itself was couched in such special theological and legalistic terminology that it might not have touched general opinion very much, but the *Syllabus* was designed to penetrate down to the very grass roots of public opinion, for it listed in a brief catalogue of eighty concise propositions the major errors of the times. In designating the errors in modern thought the *Syllabus* required acceptance of the following propositions:

15. No free choice of religion in the light of reason.
16. Salvation not to be found in every religion.
18. Protestantism, not just another form of the same true Christian religion.
20. No civil government's permission required for the exercise of ecclesiastical authority.
21. The only true religion, that of the Roman Catholic Church.
24. The church's right to temporal power.
45. No exclusive civil authority over public schools.
55. No separation of the state from the church.
77. The continuance of the Roman Catholic religion as the state religion.
80. "The Roman Pontiff can [not] and should [not] reconcile and align himself with progress, liberalism, and modern civilization."

The encyclical *Quanta Cura* and the *Syllabus* struck so at the root of the authority of the French state that the government forbade the French bishops to publish them as official religious instructions and protested vigorously to the Holy See. Since, however, some bishops had already read them in their cathedrals, the contents were common knowledge. Therefore the government allowed the secular press to publish them because in that form they would not have the force of religious injunction. Besides the government sensed that the two "historical" documents would do more harm than good to the cause of the church.

This last calculation of the French government was only too correct. Every one of the eighteen separate judicial districts reporting on the encyclical described public opinion as predominantly hostile to it. The report from Besançon will suffice as graphic illustration of the resultant public antagonism toward the church:

The encyclical caused no less a stir [than the Convention], but it produced no controversy because everybody joined spontaneously against it. In the minds of those most devoted to the cause of the church it is a deplorable anachronism! The clergy itself shrinks from the consequences of such a declaration, and, not daring to contradict it, claims that the text is misunderstood.

And similar reports came from the procureurs general of Rennes, Caen, Orleans, Metz, Paris, Bourges, Riom, Chambéry, Limoges, Aix, Montpellier, and Toulouse.[97] Maurain confirms these reactions when he says that opinion "came out so strongly against the encyclical and the *Syllabus* that the clergy and the clerical newspapers were very much embarrassed by it."[98]

Speeches and Resolutions

The favorable public reaction to the September Convention and the contrary reaction to the encyclical were already known. The reaction of the legislative chambers would be shown by the debates and resolutions in the spring session of 1865. The emperor's opening speech touched on both questions:

In the south of Europe [the emperor declared] France's action was to be exercised more resolutely. I wanted to make possible the solution of a difficult problem. The Convention of 15 September, disengaged from extreme interpretations, consecrates two great principles, the liberation of the new Kingdom of Italy and the independence[99] of the Holy See. We no longer have here scattered parts of an Italian nation trying by feeble ties to join themselves to a little state situated at the foot of the Alps; what we have here is a great country, which rising above local prejudices and scorning rash incitements, boldly removes its capital to the center of the peninsula in the midst of the Appenines as if into an unassailable fortress. By that act of patriotism Italy is definitively established and at the same time reconciled with Catholicism. She promises to respect the independence of the Holy See, to protect the frontier of the Roman States, and thus permits us to retire our troops. The papal territory, having been satisfactorily guaranteed, is found now placed under the safeguard of a treaty solemnly binding two governments. The Convention is therefore not a weapon of war but a work of peace and conciliation.

. . . . [Concerning the prohibition on the publication of the encyclical, he remarked rather gently] The more we surround the clergy with consideration and deference, the more we count on its respecting the fundamental laws of the state. It is my duty to preserve intact the rights of the civil authority, which since the time of Saint Louis[100] no sovereign of France has ever abandoned.

From this speech stemmed the debates in both houses. Rouland, no longer an official member of the government, openly attacked Ultramontanism and defended Gallicanism. The bishops in the senate were moderate in their speeches, but all speakers urged the preservation of the temporal power in the execution of the September Convention. Rouher, speaking for the government, underlined France's desire to reconcile the pope to Italy and to modern civilization. In the end an address, approved almost unanimously, put the senate on record in favor of the Convention.

In the lower house the violent debate swirled around the encyclical and the September Convention. The clericals bemoaned the fact that there had been no clear-cut declaration that the government would return troops to Rome if the treaty were violated or that the government would uphold the temporal power. Thiers made a powerful speech against the whole pro-Italian policy on the basis of pure power politics and urged the preservation of the temporal power. Rouher insisted that the government-approved address would satisfy the demands on papal "sovereignty." Nevertheless, the clericals tried to insert more explicit passages, which were voted down 166 to 84. This tell-tale division showed that the recently elected chamber had almost as many clericals as the previous body, even though clericalism was not an important issue in most of the individual districts. The final form of the section of the address dealing with the Roman question was phrased thus: "We count resolutely on the exact and loyal execution of the engagements which reciprocally bind Italy and France. There are, no doubt, Sire, events which human prudence could not always foresee, or avoid, but full of confidence in your wisdom, we approve your having reserved for yourself your full freedom of action in this regard."[101]

Ten district reports indicated opinion reactions to the debates, and every one without exception showed popular approval of the emperor's speech, of Rouher's declarations, and of the final phraseology of the addresses on the September Convention. The report from Rennes stated: "The discussion of the address in the senate and legislative body has happily combined to reassure opinion. The government's decisions on the encyclical and the Convention of 15 September appear today for the great majority clearly explained and justified." These sentiments were echoed in all the other nine reports, from Douai, Nancy, Metz, Orleans, Paris, Besançon, Riom, Montpellier, and Pau.[102]

While both public and legislative opinion seemed to have quieted down in a somewhat favorable frame of mind on the September Convention, Prince Napoleon suddenly stirred it up again by a speech unveiling a monument to Napoleon I at Ajaccio in Corsica on 15 May. At this moment Napoleon III was on a tour of Algeria, having left the government in the hands of the empress as regent. In reviewing the life and principles of the first Napoleon, the prince declared:

Napoleon was religious in a general and lofty way, but it is difficult to find in his convictions a formulated religion. . . . . He found it necessary to suppress the temporal power of the popes. Have not subsequent events sufficiently justified his foresight? Do you not sense in these disputes arising from the temporal power of the popes that all the supporters of liberty and modern thought must today remove this last fortress of the middle ages? Rome in the hands of the pope is a center of reaction against France, Italy, and our society.[103]

The emperor, angered by this unnecessary revival of discussion and uneasiness, gave the prince a thorough dressing down in a public letter published in the *Moniteur*:

I cannot refrain from letting you know what a painful impression your Ajaccio speech caused me. In leaving you during my absence by the side of the empress and my son as vice-president of the privy council, I wanted to give you a proof of my friendship and confidence, and I hoped that your presence, your conduct, and your speeches would bear witness to the solidarity existing in our family. . . . . The political program which you place under the aegis of the emperor can be of use only to the enemies of my government. To ideas that I would not admit you add hate and rancor which are out of place today. . . . . But what is clear to everybody is that to prevent anarchy of thought, the redoubtable enemy of true liberty, the emperor [Napoleon I] established in his own family first, and subsequently in his government, that severe discipline which allows but one will and one action. Henceforth, I shall be unable to depart from the same rule of conduct.[104]

Upon receipt of the letter the prince promptly resigned and retired to his Villa of Prangins in Switzerland.

No such family quarrel on the highest level over such a live issue could possibly be ignored by the general public. Indeed there was sufficient public reaction to this petty affair to give a basis for analyses in ten of the July procureur reports. Every one of the ten reports showed opinion condemning the speech and justifying the letter. The account of the reaction in Franche-Comté was particularly full:

The Ajaccio speech [wrote the procureur general] made a very distasteful diversion from the interest aroused by the sovereign's voyage and the empress-regent's activities. The radicalism in that speech . . . . and notably its death sentence for the temporal power, especially at a time when such declarations are so painfully different from the generous efforts toward appeasement, has caused an astonishment amounting almost to stupefaction. It made people wonder whether there was something official in such a change of policy. The significant silence already revealed by the *Moniteur* was not enough to relieve such an impression. Nothing less than the firm and severe voice of the emperor was sufficient to mark the great distance existing between that revolutionary manifesto and the imperial program. So the letter of 27 May was greeted with marked satisfaction. They were especially struck by the tartness pervading the document, so obviously different from the usual circumspection of the writer. But this astonishment, far from being a criticism, was on the contrary an approval. The party of law and order, if it can be so designated, loudly applauded this action and also felt elated at the resignation of the prince as vice-president of the council. It hopes to see him out of political affairs for a long time, since he can only compromise them with such capricious sallies.

Of like nature were the observations from Rennes, Caen, Douai, Orleans, Lyons, Riom, Aix, Toulouse, and Paris.[105] The reaction to the Ajaccio speech was just another proof that, while public opinion would go along with the emperor on the September Convention, it would stop short of favoring the abolition of the temporal power.

Withdrawal and Return: Mentana

The main development of the years 1865 and 1866 was France's withdrawal of her expeditionary force from Rome. Article II of the September Convention had provided that "France will withdraw her troops from the papal states gradually . . . . within two years." The anticipation of this evacuation and the various stages of its accomplishments, beginning in December 1865, gave continuous opportunities for the expression of opinion of France's main obligation in the Convention. Out of sixteen districts heard from on the occasion of the first installment of evacuation in December 1865 in the reports of October 1865 and January 1866 eight were favorable, two were opposed, and one showed a lack of concern. Those favorable to the withdrawal contained the following remarks: (Amiens) "greeted with general assent"; (Riom) "seen with satisfaction"; (Montpellier) "almost universally applauded"; (Bordeaux) "looked upon with more equanimity [*plus froidement*] and without suspicion"; (Limoges) "produced no emotion"; (Poitiers) "no uneasiness, no regret"; (Besançon) "has in no way weakened general confidence"; (Paris) "hopes for . . . . the end of an expedition . . . . which would be onerous." The unfavorable reports on evacuation were not very strong in opposition: (Rennes) "at first aroused rather acute concern in Brittany, no longer appears so redoubtable"; (Pau) "[Roman] question is now dormant . . . . but will revive apparently when the time comes for the final withdrawal of our soldiers." Of the three showing anxiety two (Besançon and Toulouse) became favorable and reassured according to later reports.[106]

However, accompanying these opinions on evacuation were two other elaborations just as significant for the government. One of these had to do with the temporal power. In the sixteen reports of October and January there was no majority opinion against the temporal power, and five of them came out strongly and positively for it. The procureur general in Nancy declared: "I have no fear in affirming that nothing would antagonize public opinion more acutely, nothing would give occasion for the most bitter recriminations than enterprises whose results would undermine the independence of the Holy See."

The districts of Rennes, Paris, Besançon, and Riom held similar views in the early reports. This tendency of opinion continued almost unanimous, except for some of the Republicans and some of the extreme liberals, through the years 1866 and 1867. In these latter two years seventeen districts were heard from on the issue of the temporal power; fifteen were definitely in its favor, the other two were merely indifferent.[107] From this evidence the French government could have no doubt that public opinion was generally favorable to the maintenance of the temporal power. The French people might favor the September Convention, and the clergy might have little influence in arousing the public over the annexation (up to Rome) and the Convention; but if the temporal power were threatened in its last remnant of territory, a major uprising of opinion might take place under the prodding of the now somnolent clergy.[108]

Napoleon III took notice of this concern of opinion and tried to reassure it as to the temporal power in his opening speech to the legislature in January 1866. "We have reason to count on the scrupulous fulfillment of the treaty of 15 September," he declared, "and on the indispensable maintenance of the authority of the Holy Father.[109]

Although he continued to avoid the term "temporal" authority, the clericals in the legislature insisted that was what he meant; and Rouher, speaking for the government, confirmed this view when he said, "The speech from the throne could speak of, and meant only to speak of, temporal sovereignty."[110]

The second elaboration of opinion, beside that on the temporal power, was one more ominous in its connotations. Between October 1865 and October 1867 thirty-five separate reports from nineteen different districts of France asserted repeatedly that they would hold Napoleon III accountable for the safety of Rome and the pope. For example, the procureur general in Besançon wrote: "Every one here remains convinced that the deep concern stirred up [a while ago] will be avoided by the unshaken determination of the great prince governing us and that, as has been said, France, in leaving Rome, will leave there a guarantee as valid as her sword: her honor!" The same sort of remarks, perhaps less elaborate, are to be found in the reports from Rennes, Douai, Paris, Metz, Nancy, Lyons, Bourges, Poitiers, Grenoble, Chambéry, Nîmes, Montpellier, Toulouse, Agen, Bordeaux, Pau, and Corsica.[111] As the months wore on, Napoleon III could not help but become convinced that the bulk of the French nation considered that he and he alone stood between the pope and imminent disaster. Woe to him, should he, like the priest and Levite, "pass by on the other side" while "a certain man" was stripped of his remaining possessions on the last dangerous mile of his journey between Jerusalem and Jericho. In this sorry predicament the emperor confided to Cowley:

> The fact is, my position is detestable. For fifteen years I have been the pope's mainstay and now I have all the appearance of abandoning him. If anything was to go wrong, I should be obliged to go to his assistance, 'quitte à m'en aller le lendemain' [even though I'd be out the next day].[112]

These words were spoken just at the time of the withdrawal of France's last soldiers from Rome in December 1866, and already by the summer of 1867 something began "to go wrong." Garibaldi was crusading again. The Romans had not risen when left alone with the pope, as had been hoped by the extreme Italian nationalists. These extremists, to whose ranks were now added the more conservative Turinese, bitter over the loss of the capital, turned their attention to Rome in 1867, since Venetia had already been obtained in 1866 during the Austro-Prussian War. If the Romans would not free themselves, patriotic Italians must liberate them. While presiding at a "peace congress" of European republicans at Geneva in September 1867, Garibaldi denounced the temporal power of the pope and called upon his listeners and all Italians to join in a final effort to strike down this "monster" of theocracy. Returning to Italy a few days later he began to recruit volunteers. Under French pressure the Italian authorities arrested him. However, when his recruits continued on their march toward Rome, Garibaldi escaped from his guarded island of Caprera and assumed leadership of the invasion of papal territory.

It can be imagined with what consternation and embarrassment Napoleon III received the news. He warned Italy of its duty and called a council of ministers at Saint-Cloud on 16 October. Here some of his most important advisors—Moustier, Rouher, and Forcade—insisted on military intervention if Italy did not break up the expedition.[113] Baroche and La Valette, on the other hand, reminded the council of all the difficulties that a renewed occupation would involve.[114] The emperor decided to warn Italy that French troops would come back if they did not repress the movement. Troops were embarked, then held back in port when Italy seemed to be taking action, and then finally dispatched when Rattazzi resigned the Italian premiership and claimed he had no further authority to act. During a visit to France Clarendon was told by Napoleon: "I have had to make this expedition against my will, but I couldn't do otherwise because every French pulpit would have become a rostrum attacking me."[115]

Ten thousand French and papal troops, the former armed with the new Chassepot rifle, crushed the Garibaldian forces at Mentana on 3 November. "The Chassepots had performed marvelously," wrote General de Failly; but French troops had returned to Rome, this time to stay, at least in nearby Civitavecchia, until the downfall of the Second Empire.

It is not surprising that French opinion, which had been so strong for the defense of the pope's temporal power, should have been much aroused over Garibaldi's preparations for invasion. Nineteen districts[116] sent in a total of twenty-two reports, nearly all of them heavily underlined with pencil in Paris, which almost unanimously condemned Garibaldi's speech in Geneva and his recruiting activities in Italy. Among them may be found some of these characteristic remarks: (Chambéry) "Garibaldi's arrest . . . . viewed everywhere here with the greatest favor"; (Limoges) "strongly aroused by Garibaldi's expedition . . . . news of arrest provoked an almost general reaction . . . . of relief"; (Lyons) "people are indignant"; (Dijon) "everyone approves the attitude taken by the emperor's government"; (Riom) "arrest of Garibaldi . . . . greeted with unmixed satisfaction"; (Bordeaux) "arrest . . . . has had the best sort of effect"; (Rouen) "all people . . . . unanimous in condemning the adventurous spirit again taking hold of Garibaldi"; (Metz) "energetic measures taken [arrest] . . . . have general approval"; (Montpellier) "the energetic attitude of the government . . . . has increased still more the emperor's popularity"; (Nancy) "profound emotion seized the people"; (Pau) "indignation caused by the audacity of the Garibaldians and by the disloyalty of the Italian government." The earlier reports praised

Italy for arresting Garibaldi, but the later ones condemned the inaction or complicity of the Italian government.[117]

As the forces became engaged in battle on the fields near Mentana, opinion in France appeared, on the surface, to be divided. When Emperor Francis Joseph arrived in Paris on a state visit, he and Napoleon III were greeted at the station by Republican cries of "Long live Italy! Long live Garibaldi!"[118] At the news of Mentana, known a week later, the press reception was mixed: the government and clerical papers welcoming the news, the liberal and Republican papers regretting it. Those disliking the expedition and the embarrassing victory were the *Journal des Débats*, the *Siècle*, the *Opinion Nationale*, the *Temps*, and the *Liberté*. The first four of these, because of their large circulation or their reputed independence, made a considerable impression.[119] Baron Beyens declared that "the unanimous sentiment of the political world is that they [the French] have come to the point where they have to open fire on Italy or suffer the most complete humiliation."[120]

Beyens, along with Napoleon III, read the signs aright, for French opinion in all parts of the nation seemed overwhelmingly favorable to the expedition and delighted with the victory. A clear-cut opinion was obtained in twenty-five of the twenty-eight districts, and in all of them without exception sentiment supported the action and its results. Never before had so many districts reported unmistakable attitudes, and never before had they been so nearly unanimous.[121] Here are some typical passages from the reports: (Lyons) "in all ranks of society the impression is of the very best, and right now the intervention is understood and approved"; (Agen) "assistants are unanimous . . . . on the good impression produced by the energetic action of the emperor's government"; (Bordeaux) "all my assistants report . . . . general approbation"; (Bourges) "a feeling of almost general approbation"; (Rennes) "the most genuine assent . . . . the government of the emperor has regained in Brittany the support and devotion of better days"; (Paris) "reports unanimous in noting sympathetic confidence . . . . the nation as a whole has ratified the expedition." And so the accounts came in all during the months from October 1867 to February 1868, an unvarying ratification by the people of all the provinces of the emperor's distasteful decision to renew the occupation.[122]

Such unanimous opinion was bound to be reflected in the debates in the legislature late in 1867. The legislature now began its sessions in November rather than in February, and, after the reforms of 1867, had the right to interpellate the government on specific questions. The senate, too, now had the right of a suspensive veto on all bills and not just the authority to reject bills on constitutional grounds.

The emperor in his opening speech explained the necessity of sending troops to Rome but softened his remarks concerning Italy by saying: "Calm is today almost entirely re-established in the states of the pope, and we can anticipate the early return of our troops. For us the Convention of 15 September exists so long as it is not replaced by a new international act."[123] These words, reassuring for Italy, merely caused uneasiness among the clericals in both houses. The bishops in the senate were careful not to embarrass the government, but Thiers in the legislative body received strong approbation from most of his colleagues when he denounced Italian nationalism and insisted on the maintenance of the pope's temporal power. Rouher, the government's spokesman, feeling the necessity of drawing away the popularity Thiers had gained by his assertions, took a firmer stand against Italy than had the emperor. It was on this occasion that he uttered his famous "Never" speech:

There is here a dilemma [he argued]: the pope needs Rome for his independence; Italy aspires to Rome, which she considers an imperious necessity for her unity. Well, we declare it in the name of the French government, Italy will never take Rome! [After loud applause from all over the chamber, he went on.] Never will France endure such a violent act committed against her honor and against Catholicism! . . . . Is that clear?[124]

Nothing could be clearer than that unequivocal assertion, but it was too clear for Napoleon III, who had always carefully avoided the word "temporal" in his statements and who at this very time was hoping Italy could be brought into an alliance against the Prussian threat. At the council meeting the next day the emperor needled Rouher in one of his most delightful sallies. He began by congratulating Rouher "on his fine speech of yesterday." Then he added, as if by afterthought, "You know, in politics, one should never say: Never." At this point silence fell over the council, whereupon the emperor continued his musing: "Suppose one day the pope and Victor Emmanuel came to an agreement, what would then become of the eloquent word of the minister of state?" Rouher had also been somewhat opposed to any great concessions to parliament or the press. He preferred to retain some vestiges of the old authoritarian regime. Napoleon could not forego the opportunity of teasing Rouher on this score: "Why it looks as if we're re-establishing the parliamentary regime." Poor Rouher, squirming under the sly jabs of his sovereign and disconcerted at the suppressed amusement of his jealous colleagues, blurted out: "Sire, there wasn't anything else I could do."[125]

For once, though, the public, parliament, and Rouher were in agreement. The loud applause of the legislative body echoed throughout the land. Twenty reports in December 1867 and January 1868, representing eighteen different districts in France, showed majorities in seventeen of them[126] favoring Rouher's "Never" speech. In only one district, Dijon, did there seem to be a majority against it. Typical comments on the speech were such as these: (Marseilles) "this opinion [favorable] represents the great majority"; (Lyons) "the attitude of the people on the Roman question has been greeted with general satisfaction"; (Chambéry) "Savoy applauded with all her strength .... the categorical declarations"; (Colmar) "greeted with enthusiasm especially by the people in the country"; (Rouen) "speech .... swelled the ranks of the immense majority .... and rallied .... a good number of people to the policy of protecting the temporal power"; (Moulins) "the speech .... has produced the most favorable impression .... the mass of the population viewed [it] with strong satisfaction"; (Quimper) "the speech .... was completely welcomed and produced a very good effect"; (Grenoble) ".... viewed [speech] with satisfaction"; (Nîmes) "disapproved by the Protestants but highly praised by the Catholics"; (Orleans) "applauded the declarations"; (Agen) "fine impression produced .... by the solemn declarations"; (Metz) "the best sort of influence on the attitude of the clergy"; (Riom) "eloquent echo of the wishes of this region"; (Pau) "radical party .... disappointment .... but the mass of citizens .... applauded this language"; (Rennes) "genuine assent .... greeted .... the formulated assurances"; (Toulouse) "excited a veritable enthusiasm"; (Besançon) "enthusiasm .... greeted .... the solemn declarations." Dijon alone noted that the bourgeois majority preferred the moderate language of Moustier to the extreme pronouncement of Rouher.[127]

If opinion were to be judged by the newspapers, it would have appeared to be just the opposite from the universal approval in the procureur and prefect reports. The government papers said very little about the Rouher speech or glossed over it with suspected embarrassment. They evidently learned very soon that the emperor was none too pleased. The only other papers to praise his stand were the clerical *Univers* and *Union,* but even these wanted a promise that the pope's lost territory would be returned. Most of the other papers, liberal or Republican, denounced the "Never" speech.[128] The *Journal des Débats* said that Thiers' policy had won and that he should therefore become premier; the *France* observed that now an international conference in Rome was useless. The *Siècle* was particularly caustic. On 7 December Jourdan, commenting on Rouher's denunciation of revolution, inquired: "But where did you come from, my fine ministers, if not from a triumphant revolution?" On the next day he cited other instances of famous but fallible "nevers": Thiers had said that long-distance railroads would never be built; Pliny had prophesied that Christianity would never supplant the old pagan sects. He closed by recalling an old troubadour song:

> Ni jamais, ni toujours
> C'est la devise des amours.

Brisson in the *Temps* entitled his article "The Clerical Empire," denounced this trend toward political clericalism, and ended with indignation: "Is that clear? Yes, it's clear, very clear, too clear."[129]

Clear it was, how these liberal and radical journals felt, but it was equally clear that they did not represent the majority of the country at all on the questions of the pope's temporal power and the inviolability of papal Rome.

However, the events connected with the Roman question were not happening in a vacuum. A much greater threat was looming up before the eyes of Frenchmen in the direction of Prussia,[130] a state which by military might had defeated Austria and the south German states in 1866, had united north Germany into a powerful federation in 1867, and now stood poised ready, the Frenchmen thought, to pounce on France at the most favorable moment. Therefore, the new expedition to Rome and the battle of Mentana could not be considered without reference to the new danger along the Rhine. Italy had been Prussia's ally in the war of 1866. That fact alone tended to make Italy less popular in the eyes of the French. The nationalism in Germany, now so obviously menacing to France, tended to make Italian nationalism disliked. Indeed, nationalism, a war cry of revolutionary France and of the Napoleonic legend, was now being lumped with revolution in general. Hence there was a greater trend toward sympathy for the papal cause and his temporal power as an uncompromising bulwark against these nationalistic revolutions. The *Journal des Débats* accused Prussia of financing Garibaldi's expedition in 1867 to keep French troops tied down in Italy and to prevent France from getting Italy as an ally.[131] Some looked upon the new expedition to Rome as a good way to show Prussia that France would stand her ground. The concern to have the new French Chassepot rifle become a match for the new Prussian needle gun is shown by General de Failly's inept boast that "the Chassepots had performed marvelously" at Mentana. And yet there were others who regretted that France had to scatter her military strength by a new occupation and who now distrusted Italy as a country which would start more revolutions as soon as Prussia attacked France, if not actually stab France in the back on such an occasion.

From October 1867 to January 1868 twelve reports from eleven different districts linked the Roman situation with the German danger. Opinion around Paris thought Mentana was a good warning to Prussia. In Dijon they thought Prussia was instigating the trouble in Italy. Opinion in the districts of Rennes, Caen, Nancy, Poitiers, and Montpellier suspected Prussia would start something either on the Rhine or in south Germany as soon as France got involved in Italy. In Lyons, Nîmes, Montpellier, and Agen people felt that Italy would ally with Prussia in any future war. One passage in the procureur report from Nancy is particularly illustrative:

Behind Italy who had never been popular and who has just put the finishing touches on alienating public sympathy, they saw Prussia ready to profit from the embarrassments into which a new war could plunge France. The fear of seeing arise from these events some unknown complications disturbed opinion: the phantom of a war with Germany haunted again their troubled imaginations. So a great many men . . . . did not conceal their apprehensions and obviously inclined toward a policy of abstention.[132]

French opinion had been at times very shortsighted, if not almost blind, but the severe lesson of Prussia's victory over Austria at Sadowa in 1866 had opened many eyes even low down on the social scale. While looking at Rome and Mentana, they cast repeated nervous glances at the Rhine. Indeed, the Rhine was already commanding the main attention of peoples all over Europe. Once Mentana had been won and Rouher had pronounced "Never," Rome sank from view as a major consideration. Out of fifty-six procureur reports in April and July 1868 only three mentioned the Roman question, and even these three mentioned that opinion had lost interest in Rome. Two others reported no interest in any foreign affairs.[133]

The excitement accompanying the elections of 1869 involved the Roman question very little. Internal religious matters, such as education and the danger of revolutionary movements and the rise of republicanism in France, were the main concerns of the clericals. The Chambrun circular, backed by the *Univers,* did stress the temporal power as one of the issues, and over half of the official candidates gave lip service to that cause; but Boullier, writing in the clerical *Correspondant,*[134] admitted that the temporal power "is only secondary," that "the Roman question is not today a direct issue" but rather subsidiary to the question of maintaining peace. And Maurain summarized the results thus: "In most parts of France the elections showed, as did those of 1863, that its [the clergy's] influence was weak. . . . . The elections of 1869 confirmed then that the clergy dominated the majority of voters in only a very small number of regions."[135] The Roman question had hardly re-emerged from the subconscious mind of the French public, where it had lain dormant since Rouher's "Never."

The years 1868 and 1869 constituted a lull before the storm, a storm which was to break in Germany rather than in Italy. And when that storm did break in 1870, instead of Prussia taking advantage of an Italian conflict to advance her own interests, it was Italy which took advantage of a Franco-Prussian war to seize Rome. The papal temporal power in Rome fell less than three weeks after the fall of the Second Empire, but Frenchmen of all groups and parties were then too absorbed with the war and possible foreign subjugation to formulate much opinion on a catastrophe which seemed so much smaller and more remote than their own.

With the establishment of Rome as Italy's capital in 1871 the Roman question was still not solved. It was to rise again to plague French politics and diplomacy, under a new regime, until the beginning of the twentieth century.

CHAPTER VII

THE POLISH INSURRECTION AND THE DANISH WAR

The resentment toward Prussia expressed by French opinion in connection with the Mentana episode in Italy was only one phase of a continuing attitude going back at least to the treaties of 1814 and 1815. Prussia was one of the powers responsible for the defeat of France in 1814. Her attempt at the Congress of Vienna to acquire all of Saxony, a protégé of France, had led the French delegate, Talleyrand, to join in an Anglo-Austrian-French alliance against Prussia and Russia in January 1815. After Napoleon I's return from Elba it was German troops under Blücher which had turned the tide against France at Waterloo, and it was Prussia's vindictiveness which demanded the taking of large areas of eastern France when the Second Peace of Paris was being considered. By the Vienna settlement and the Second Peace of Paris, Prussia received the Rhineland areas as a bulwark against any French expansion toward the Rhine, and the French people could never forget the abominable conduct of the Prussian troops during the postwar occupation of northeastern France, a conduct which even made Wellington, the allied commander, ponder the possibility of withdrawing the Prussian element from the allied occupational force.

But in the period after 1815 there were many other occasions when Prussia aroused French hostility. During the Crimean War the French were more resentful toward Prussia for neutrality than toward Austria, because the Prussian agreement with Austria had helped the latter to stay neutral, and, after all, Austria had finally worked with the allies to force Russia to sue for peace. Frenchmen experienced considerable satisfaction when Prussia was denied admission to the Congress of Paris in 1856 until the last days of its sessions. Again in 1859 it was the menacing attitude of Prussia which had forced the French to make peace in Italy while still short of their goal.

Just as Sardinia's annexations in 1860 whetted Italian appetites for Rome, so France's annexation of Savoy turned French eyes toward further acquisitions along the Rhine. Fear of a Prussian attack across the Rhine in 1859 intensified this feeling, and the exultation over having reversed the Second Peace of Paris in the Savoy region naturally led to thoughts of finishing the job farther north. Several of the important diplomats in Paris were reporting home the French *Drang nach Rhein*. Lord Cowley said that at the celebration for the annexation of Savoy "a few cries of *Au Rhin* were heard."[1] The Russian ambassador, Kisselev, believed France would not object to an enlarged Prussia and Austria if she could be compensated on the Rhine.[2] Count Pollone, writing to Cavour in June 1860, remarked: "The opinion of those interested in politics is that it will not be long before a new war will break out. . . . . I have heard them utter the words 'war against Prussia.' "[3] Beyens, the Belgian minister, revealed that in April 1860 Napoleon III did mention his intentions of getting the Rhine to his ambassador, Moustier, in Berlin, indicating it as a necessary sequel to Savoy but intimating that it would have to be accomplished by peaceful means.[4] William, Prince-Regent of Prussia, had received sufficient information in 1860 to suspect that Napoleon III would try to obtain the Rhineland in exchange for letting Prussia have Schleswig-Holstein.[5]

These suspicions in political circles in Paris are borne out by at least one procureur report from the provinces. The procureur general in Rouen reported in July 1860: "Peace . . . . was the definite desire of the region. . . . . Yet . . . . the least war-minded men . . . . take delight in the thought that after having retaken the line [of the Alps], France one day must recover the Rhine boundary."[6]

The Polish Insurrection

The next crisis in central Europe which disturbed European diplomacy, the Polish insurrection of 1863, caused a more hostile French public attitude toward Russia than toward Prussia, but Prussia came in for her share of French criticism.

Poland, like France, had been one of the victims of the settlements of 1815. Although the Poles had fought hopefully for their national liberation in the campaigns against Napoleon I in 1813 and 1814, the Congress of Vienna had decreed the continuance of her partition between Russia, Prussia, and Austria. Russia, however, had been given the larger share of Poland with the understanding that Czar Alexander I would make it a separate kingdom with himself as King of Poland and with the grant of liberal representative institutions. Such liberal plans for the Russian Poles, so out of harmony with the autocracy of Russia proper, were sidetracked after the Polish revolt in 1830. Thereafter the Poles were ruled as subject people of Russia.

The discontent over this oppression, simmering beneath the surface, finally came into the open in 1861 when the Poles, under the incitation of their Roman Catholic clergy, began to make peaceful, unarmed religious demonstrations. The Russian authorities fired upon the unarmed demonstrators, killing many people whose manifestations were merely by means of prayers and hymns. Even churches were profaned when services were interrupted and worshipers were dragged away by Russian police.

The sullen resentment, which the Russians now felt everywhere in Poland, led them finally late in 1862 to resort to a plan for the liquidation of potential rebels. They devised a conscription plan for men of military age and on that pretext began to round up all able-bodied Poles for transportation to Siberia or worse. The scheme seems to have been deliberately delayed until December 1862 to enlist the winter weather as a weapon against guerrillas. Yet hundreds of thousands of Poles naturally chose guerrilla resistance rather than "conscription," and the great insurrection was on. The Polish guerrillas, suffering from cold and privation, murdered and plundered and fought without quarter; the Russians retaliated with equal ruthlessness.

The reaction in Europe was a feeling of horror akin to that experienced on hearing the reports of the later twentieth-century Nazi genocidal atrocities. People were saying that the powers, responsible by their participation in the Congress of Vienna, should intervene to bring an amelioration of the situation of the Poles. While England, France, and Austria seemed to be in the process of doing something for the Poles, Prussia, under the shrewd guidance of Bismarck, decided in February 1863 to take advantage of this situation to win the friendship of Russia. Prussia negotiated the Alvensleben Convention, which permitted Russian troops to pursue fleeing insurrectionists into Prussian territory and promised the return of fugitives apprehended on Prussian soil.

Traditional French policy had always been sympathetic toward Catholic Poland situated between Protestant Prussia and Orthodox Russia. Before the late eighteenth-century partition the Polish kingdom had been considered by France as a counterweight to all three continental great powers, Russia, Austria, and Prussia. It is not therefore surprising that these three powers snuffed out this buffer state and partitioned its territory between them while France was involved in her own internal revolution. French policy as well as sympathies would then incline France to help in the re-establishment of an independent Poland, and political as well as humanitarian reasons would incline French public opinion to take a strong attitude in favor of the Poles during the insurrection.

It would therefore be a work of supererogation to detail the reaction of French opinion, month after month, to the progress and repression of the hopeless Polish revolt. French opinion was universally and unanimously sympathetic to the Polish insurrectionists all during 1863. Altogether, between April 1863 and January 1864, seventy-nine

procureur reports from all twenty-eight judicial districts of continental
France showed a continuous and uniform sympathy for the Poles and
a detestation of Russian repressive methods.[7] The report of the procureur general in Nancy would be a good example of the many from
the other districts in France:

> In fact everywhere in this district [wrote Neveu-Lemaire], where one of the
> last kings of Poland left so many monuments to his magnificence,[8] good wishes are
> expressed for the independence of that unfortunate country. A situation familiar to
> all—age-old sympathies, political traditions, battlefield comradeships—all combine
> to excite the profoundest interest. It may be asserted that there is but one voice
> in this regard, and anyone can confirm this assertion by just looking around him.
> The Catholics are touched by the community of belief and the sufferings endured
> for the faith; the liberals and democrats by the natural rights of a people and the
> principle of nationalities; they all sympathize with their unheard-of suffering so
> courageously endured. What one must especially notice in this general feeling is
> to what point it has penetrated to the lowest levels of the population. The work-
> ing classes and peasants are perhaps those who react the most strongly. Very little
> impressed by theoretical discussions, the citizens of these classes are moved by tra-
> dition and political instincts, stronger than any reasoning. Not only do they protest
> ceaselessly against the injustice of another century that the consecration of history
> could not efface, but they rise up in indignation against a measure as odious as it
> is arbitrary and against these proscriptions disguised under the name of conscrip-
> tion and aiming at the very sources of life of a nationality which refuses to perish.
> Aid is even being organized by contributions in the three departments of the district.
> In a word this cause has long been popular, like the eternal martyrdom of an
> innocent victim![9]

The testimony of the foreign diplomats was just as unanimous.
The Prussian, Goltz, recounted that Empress Eugénie declared that
"all the prefect reports bear witness to the recent general and dominant
enthusiasm for them [the Poles] and show that something must be
done for the Poles by the imperial government if it did not want the
election results to go against them."[10] Cowley observed that "feeling
in the country is warming again in favor of the Poles."[11] "The attacks of
several Parisian newspapers against the Russian government," wrote
Rogier, the Belgian minister, "at the same time that the subscriptions
are being opened for the Poles, have made a very painful impression
on Mr. Budberg [Russian ambassador] and will be strongly resented
in St. Petersburg."[12] Metternich found "the agitation [for the Poles]
daily taking on greater and greater proportions,"[13] and the American
minister observed that "the insurrection in Poland has driven American affairs out of view for the moment" and that "the French press
have almost universally condemned Russia and sympathized with
Poland."[14] And the little Parisian lawyer, Dabot, looks in to tell us:
"Everywhere subscriptions for Poland. The students of law and medi-
cine have together taken up collections which they sent to the *Siècle*
subscriptions."[15] Thus there is enough evidence from every side to
show how thoroughly France was aroused by the tragic events in
Poland. La Gorce gives us an excellent line on the agreement between
the opposite extremes of French opinion: "The *Siècle* spoke the same
language as the *Monde,* the clergy as that of the University, the

Academy as that of the Faubourg Saint-Antoine [working district],
and strangest of all, unbelievable, unprecedented since the beginning
of the reign, on the Polish question the empress and Prince Napoleon
saw eye to eye."[16]

If Napoleon III ever wanted a war to change the map of Europe,
now, it would seem, would be the propitious moment, when the people
were unanimously for the Polish cause and England and Austria might
have become his allies. But this time the emperor did not want war,
and for a very definite reason: the same people who were shouting
for Poland were no less insistent on peace. In effect they were saying
to the Poles, we will cry for you, but we will not fight and die for
you. Seventy-eight of the seventy-nine reports cited above[17] accompanied their expressions of sympathy for Poland with demands for
a peaceful solution. The report from the procureur general in Paris
is a particularly good example of sentiment:

> Her [France's] sympathies [for Poland] are warm and intense . . . .; but how-
> ever much she may be stirred by emotion, if the word 'war' is pronounced, she re-
> strains the indignation she feels, she keeps control over it, and her sympathies
> for Poland diminish not at all her aversion for a new war.
>
> 'The whole interest of the moment is on that question,' one of my assistants
> in the largest arrondissement of the district tells me, 'opinion here is tense and
> perplexed, it fears that the future and the welfare of France is at stake, and it does
> not want to subject them to the chances of battles, and the uncertainties of war.'
> And in this evaluation he expresses with only a little more emphasis the language
> of all his colleagues.[18]

And in just the same vein was the sentiment of twenty-five other
districts of the twenty-eight.[19]

Public opinion, not fully cognizant of all the implications in
international relations, was suggesting a policy which was very difficult
for the emperor to follow. It was asking in effect that he do something
for poor Poland but that he should not back up his deeds by the
ultimate deed of going to war if he was not given satisfaction. Since
force is the final arbiter in the state system, one should not take
measures against another state unless one is prepared to back them
by forceful action. In this case the people were telling him: "Hang
your clothes on a hickory limb but don't go near the water."

The proceedings in the senate in March finally brought this
contradictory situation to a head and elicited a statement from the
government. The senate had received about four thousand petitions,
some of them signed by members of the French Academy, by former
ministers and deputies, and by bishops, asking that something be
done for Poland. Such an unusual popular demonstration could not
be ignored, and the petitions were therefore submitted to a committee
for consideration. Senator Larabit reported back the government-
sponsored resolution that the petitions be returned to the committee,
that the senate have confidence that the emperor would do what was
possible, and that the senate pass to the order of the day. The pro-

Polish opposition wanted to have the petitions sent to the minister of foreign affairs. Around this committee recommendation centered the debates on the issue. Prince Napoleon made such a violent speech against the government's position that it elicited a full-length reply from Billault, the minister of state. In his speech Billault expressed sympathy for the Poles and gently chided Alexander II, but he also chided his opponents and indirectly public opinion when he declared: "You will not succeed in re-establishing ancient Poland by many words and little action." Yet at the close of his speech he indicated that the government itself was going to do just that by joining with other powers through moral pressure to persuade the czar to find a generous solution. Particularly did he criticize those who gave vain encouragement to a revolutionary movement. On 20 March the senate approved the committee's report by a vote of 109 to 17 and shelved the petitions.

The emperor gave added emphasis to Billault's words by publishing a letter to him in the *Moniteur* of 22 March. "Your words," wrote the emperor, "were at every point in entire conformity with my ideas, and I reject any other interpretation of my sentiments." The last passage was also a public rebuke to Prince Napoleon. The government also had published on 16 March the first of its "many words," a letter of admonition to Russia.

The communication was followed a month later by simultaneous protests to Russia from France, England, and Austria. Gorchakov, the Russian foreign minister, made a disdainful reply on 26 April in which he denied that the present Polish question came under the terms of the treaties of 1815 and insisted that it was a purely domestic question for Russia. Since none of the three protesting powers would intervene by force, as Gorchakov well knew, the Poles were left to the gentle mercies of their masters and were cruelly repressed by the advent of autumn. Napoleon III, pushed by public opinion, had committed the serious plunder in statesmanship of alienating a Russian ally without gaining allies elsewhere and without accomplishing the purpose of his protests. Reuss, the Prussian, recorded an interesting conversation he had with the emperor on the question:

He [the emperor] had found sympathy with Poland already established in France, and it had been impossible for him to ignore it completely. So, rather than follow in the footsteps of Louis Philippe, he had been obliged to take a side, and that necessarily at the expense of his friendship with Russia. . . . .

As regards French sympathy, the emperor was well aware that, though everyone desired Polish independence, no one was prepared to go to war about it.

I suggested that this was a very cheap form of sympathy, to which he had little to answer.[20]

The emperor no doubt refrained from much comment because he knew the sympathy had been costly and not cheap at all, as far as France was concerned. This was to be only one of several occasions when the new element of irresponsible public opinion was to force unwise action in situations too complicated for it to be a helpful initiator of policy.

But French opinion was consistent at least in its pacific inclinations by its wholehearted approval of Billaut's speech in the senate. From twelve different procureur reports of April 1863 came information that the people concurred in the minister of state's declarations. There were no reports condemning him. Two of these twelve (from Agen and Dijon) also praised the emperor's supporting letter.[21]

Also French opinion was consistent in its sympathy for Poland by showing its disappointment over Russia's rejection of the overtures of the Western powers. The October report from Nancy in particular showed anger toward Russia: "Among men belonging to the educated classes," wrote the procureur, "the reprobation against the kingdom of the Russians [for] the cruelties and spoilations perpetrated by their armies is not less universal than in the more excitable classes. The very notes by which Russia declared that she no longer intended to continue diplomatic discussions deeply wounded national sentiment." The same opinions were voiced in the reports from Rouen, Douai, and Agen.[22]

Balked by England and Austria as well as by his own public opinion from following up his peaceful protests by forceful threats, Napoleon III consulted Morny, Billault, Baroche, and Boudet at Saint-Cloud in the first days of August 1863, where they "decided on peace."[23] In the place of war the emperor resorted to one of his favorite and most statesmanlike expedients: on 4 November 1863 he invited all the powers to attend a European congress in Paris where all the difficulties arising from national aspirations would be met and solved by a concerted agreement. This was publicly announced the following day in his opening speech to the legislature. Like all other such proposals which he made on many occasions during his reign, this invitation was turned down, this time by all the sovereigns except the King of Prussia. The emperor was thwarted again in his efforts to redraw the boundaries of Europe by peaceful means.

The congress proposal was quite in line with public opinion, which wanted something done without resorting to war. Rogier of Belgium wrote: "If I may judge by the way this speech was received, I must say that it made a favorable impression on the entire assembly. That passage—'the treaties of 1815 no longer exist'—was especially acclaimed with rapture and enthusiasm."[24] "The speech was greeted with great enthusiasm," Goltz confirmed in a telegram to Bismarck.[25] From thirteen different districts, representing all parts of France except the southern tier, came reports hailing the congress idea with favor. There were no adverse comments. Napoleon had squared him-

self with his people, but he had not accomplished a thing diplomatically.[26]

With the repression of the Polish insurrection, with the rumblings
of trouble between the German states and Denmark, and with the increasing economic suffering caused by the American Civil War, public
sympathy for, and interest in, the Polish cause began to wane. Twenty-
two reports, representing nineteen districts in all parts of France except the very center, showed a decline in expressed sympathy for Poland after October 1863. By July 1864 much of the decreased sympathy
changed to indifference.[27] As early as 5 August 1863 the Prussian
ambassador noted "that the concern over the Polish insurrection was
actually losing ground in public opinion and very soon would be
buried."[28]

In spite of the decline of French interest for Poland by the
end of 1863 the Polish affair did bring out some other aspects of
opinion. One such aspect was the increasing unpopularity of England.
Her failure to give support to forceful intervention or to accept the
congress bid revived all the latent Anglophobia so prevalent among
the French. In seventeen reports from thirteen different districts over
most of France came stories of bitterness toward England. Again from
Nancy came this account:

> In the face of all these dangers [wrote the procureur general] it is not on
> England that public opinion could be expected to count. In all my reports I have
> had to point out to Your Excellency the deep distrust existing in this region against
> the English alliance. Too many circumstances have brought about this distrust:
> their abandonment of us in Mexico, their attitude when we took Puebla and Mexico
> City, the intrigues of their agents in Athens, Constantinople, and Alexandria. Also
> even though by the speeches of her statesmen England may not have declared that
> the support she was giving Poland would be only moral, one was convinced that
> in case of war she would not follow us. Once our relations were violently broken,
> the usual aim of her policy would be attained, and if war broke out against Ger-
> many, we wonder if she would continue her neutrality but rather turn against
> us in fear of seeing us by victories expand toward the Rhine.[29]

On the contrary friendliness toward Russia in the two anti-English
areas of Rouen and Bordeaux was beginning to appear. "There does
not even exist a hatred toward Russia," asserted the procureur general
in Rouen, "whom the greater number persist in considering as being
able to be one day the most profitable ally for France." His colleague
from Bordeaux declared: "No one in France forgets the respective
attitudes of Russia and England at the time of our annexations of
Savoy. These memories, still very much alive, explain why the Russian
alliance has good reason to count on such warm advocates." While
these opinions represent only the Rouen and Bordeaux areas, these
people at least should have remembered all these things sooner, before
they had pressed the emperor to antagonize Russia the year before.[30]

And what about Prussia, who had made the friendly Alvensleben
Convention with Russia during the Polish insurrection? Did French
opinion like or dislike her? At least the newspapers immediately raised

a chorus of protest on hearing of the Alvensleben Convention. The Prussian ambassador confessed to the strong press attack:

The convention between Prussia and Russia [he wrote] helps the latter. The press here is united in condemning it; the revolutionary papers do not hesitate to brand Prussia as the hanger of Polish patriots; the liberal journals are less sharp, but just as unanimous in the expression of their disapprobation, which the inspired papers themselves do not conceal.

This same report was repeated at least three times in his correspondence and can be confirmed in the columns of the papers themselves.[31] Strangely enough, however, the procureur reports do not indicate any notice taken by the general public of the Alvensleben Convention nor any particular attitude toward Prussia at this time. Only Alsace, on the German border, showed any hostility toward Prussia, but even here the conservatives were not inclined to share this attitude for the very reason that the radical papers were so loud in their anti-Prussian protests.[32]

This is just another example, but an important one, of Goltz's reliance on the press for his judgment of French opinion and of the disparity between press opinion and general public opinion. Some radical and clerical papers had not been averse to war, an attitude belied by all provincial reports. So great was the discrepancy between press and people that a spate of procureur reports went out of the way to discuss it. The procureur general in Rouen declared: "The orators and journalists who urge the government to throw itself into that dangerous adventure [war for Poland] do not understand either the interests or the real sentiments of the country." The procureur general in Rennes, Paris, Orleans, Colmar, Limoges, and Pau made similar observations. Thus ten reports from eight different districts scattered throughout France (except in the southeast) insisted that opinion was just the opposite of the most vocative newspapers on the question of going to war for Poland.[33] The voice of the press may have been loud and raucous, but the still small voice of the man in the street and in the field made itself heard above the din, and the emperor, when he "felt the pulse of France twice a day," discerned the heartbeat of the nation and not just that of the editorial rooms.

But woe to him who held the stethoscope! The heart to which he turned his ear was a faithless heart. For when it commanded "Speak but do not act!" and was obeyed and when obedience brought frustration and humiliation, then was the servant blamed for the master's whims. "The people have a heavy weight upon their hearts [declared the procureur general of Amiens]. . . . After having raised our voice in vain, are we going to draw the sword alone? No one seriously asks for that, no one really desires it. Each one vaguely senses that suddenly the imperial policy has experienced an inevitable setback and a few are glad of it."[34] Baron Beyens was amazed at the abrupt change of attitude in all walks of life:

I do not have to dwell on internal difficulties. They become more obvious every day in the press and the legislative debates. But what is not so easily discerned except at close range is the rapid decline in the prestige of the government and the growing disaffection. . . . . Especially, besides, in official circles and in the lower ranks of the administration, they discuss, with unheard-of freedom, with bitterness and discouragement, the very person of the sovereign, his entourage, his expenditures, his arbitrary actions, the election scandals, the daily uncertainty which depends on one impenetrable will. This concern for the morrow—ever-present for over ten years—a vague feeling of fear, an extreme let-down feeling pervade the situation. Almost by instinct they sense that they are on the threshold of great unknown events, and on every side I hear repeated: 'If we are not at 1847,[35] we are at least at 1845.'[36]

A familiar American expression says you should either put up or shut up. At the urging of his people Napoleon III did neither, and a serious loss of prestige for France ensued. Since the sovereign people could do no wrong, however ill-advised their conflicting sentiments may have been, on the shoulders of their emperor fell all the blame. Like a nemesis this same fate was to haunt the ailing emperor time and time again until at last Louis Philippe's 1848 arrived for Louis Napoleon in the tragic year of 1870.

The Danish War

By the army bills of 1861 and 1862 Prussia had almost doubled the size of its army, and Bismarck had proclaimed his policy of "blood and iron." Such a brash policy included designs for Prussian territorial expansion and for the eclipse of Austria as leading state in the Germanic Confederation. Bismarck's friendly gesture to Russia during the Polish insurrection turned out to be but the first step in achieving his objectives because he could thereby neutralize Russia at a future time when Prussia would be involved with struggles in the German area.

Indeed, trouble had already been brewing for some time between Denmark and the Germanic Confederation over the duchies of Schleswig and Holstein. It was in effect a dispute between the rising nationalistic movements in both Denmark and Germany. The Schleswig-Holstein question is much too complicated to be explained in full. Suffice it to say that the King of Denmark had been granted Schleswig-Holstein by the Congress of Vienna in 1815. He was to govern them separately from his Danish kingdom, and Holstein was to be a member of the Germanic Confederation. In northern Schleswig there was a preponderance of Danes. The nationalistic Danes, fearful that their brethren in northern Schleswig might be swallowed up in a future German national state, campaigned for the equally extreme solution of incorporating all of Schleswig into the Danish kingdom proper and even of tying Holstein more closely to Denmark. An attempt to carry out these Danish designs during the German revolutions of 1848 was prevented by Prussia and the other powers, who, in London in 1852, reimposed the Vienna decisions.

Now again in 1863, with the accession of Christian IX to the Danish throne, the Danes tried the same thing. Although the Germanic Confederation sent troops to occupy Holstein, Bismarck, scheming to obtain the duchies for Prussia, inveigled Austria into joining Prussia and supplanting the Confederation action with their own. With Denmark's rejection of their ultimatum, the Danish War began on 1 February 1864 between Prussia and Austria as allies and the recalcitrant Denmark.

Napoleon III then found himself in just as perplexing a position as in the case of the Polish insurrection. Frenchmen would probably be sympathetic to Denmark because that kingdom had remained more loyal to Napoleon I in 1813 than had other French satellite states. Furthermore, France not only counted on a strong Denmark as a counterweight to Prussia but also counted on Austria to be Prussia's rival rather than ally. The developing situation demanded that France join with England to go to Denmark's aid. But here the shadows of the Polish insurrection fell across the map of Europe. Russia, grateful for the Alvensleben Convention of 1863, would not join against Prussia; England, who had backed out on military assistance to the Poles, could not be trusted to go to war for Denmark; and French opinion, which had demanded peace in 1863, would probably not support war in 1864. In addition to all these considerations, Napoleon III, sympathetic to national movements in general and resigned to the prospect of some national unification in Germany, was not inclined to sweep that sea with a broom. Under these circumstances it might be wiser for him to let the war go on. As the belligerents became more bogged down with war difficulties and as the other powers became more alarmed at Prussia's aggrandisement and the union of Prussia and Austria, he could perhaps at last obtain his long-sought European congress in which he could justly ask for the Rhine territories in compensation for Prussia's gains.

The confirmation of these views came in response to a British proposal that England, France, Russia, and Sweden give "their material assistance to Denmark" in case the Germanic Confederation attempted to take Schleswig and Holstein from the king of Denmark by force.[37] This would mean going to war to defend the *status quo* set up by the powers in 1815 and 1852. The French minister of foreign affairs, in declining to join in a continental war, stated that France had much greater risks to run than England if war should ensue. England's action would be largely limited to a naval blockade and shore raids, while France would bear the brunt of land campaigns against an aroused Germany.[38] As the Austrian ambassador so aptly put it, Napoleon III preferred to play the role of "the mystery man, watching from his balcony while others run into the street to mix in the fight." Again three weeks later Prince Metternich wrote: "The emperor always comes back to expatiating on his disinterestedness, which consists in not putting himself forward in order not to have it look as if he wants the left bank of the Rhine."³⁹

But at the first class of arms between Prussian and Danish troops the French press did not take a disinterested attitude. The early Danish reports of success in holding back the Prussians were hailed with delight "even though [as the Belgian minister observed] it meant a prolongation of hostilities."⁴⁰ As days passed with more and more victories for the Prussians and Austrians, the Prussian ambassador became alarmed at the unanimity of the press in favoring Denmark and denouncing the German invaders.⁴¹ When the campaign had advanced until Schleswig-Holstein had been overrun and Jutland in Denmark proper was invaded, the press became so loud in its denunciation of Prussia that Goltz protested directly to Drouyn de Lhuys. At the same time he complained about the attitude of the French government and of Druyn de Lhuys himself. The French foreign minister impressed upon the Prussian minister that "public opinion, becoming more impatient, was taking sides more strongly every day with the little heroic people engaged in battle against forty million people, who take unfair advantage of their strength." Goltz asked, "What about France's recent conquests of the little heroic people in Mexico and Algeria?"⁴² On two other occasions during the war the Prussian ambassador acknowledged the unanimous hostility of the French press.⁴³

If on this occasion the newspapers were in harmony with French opinion in general, it does not mean that they were now more qualified as a barometer of opinion because in this very crisis there was more evidence of outside influences and pressures on the newspapers than on most previous occasions. Twenty-two different dispatches from the Prussian embassy in Paris to the Wilhelmstrasse in Berlin between December 1863 and September 1865 revealed efforts to influence the French press not only by the French government itself but also by Prussia, Austria, and Italy.⁴⁴

If all these people putting money into the French press had seen the little effect it had on general opinion throughout the country, they might have been less sanguine about their efforts. After all, the poor transportation services of the day did not distribute the Paris papers very widely into the provinces, and the majority of the people read local papers or could not read at all. This discrepancy between the procureur reports and the Paris press in the Polish affair is a striking illustration. But in the Danish affair by coincidence rather than by direct causation public opinion was in line with the press in sympathizing with Denmark and in condemning Prussia. There was this difference at the beginning that, while the press from the start seemed to understand the issues in the Schleswig-Holstein question, many common people in the provinces were completely baffled: (Chambéry) "nobody in France understands it [the war]"; (Lyons) "the Dano-German conflict is not understood"; (Metz) "the Dano-German conflict, generally not understood. . . ."; (Pau) "the Dano-German war, in spite of its importance, is in general scarcely understood."[45]

However, as the war went on, the definite pro-Danish opinion began to appear. So unanimous was it that again, as in the Polish question, it is not necessary to elaborate in detail. Between April and October 1864 twenty-five reports from seventeen districts discussed opinion on the war. Nineteen of these reports, coming from every section of France, were sympathetic to Denmark and angry at Prussia; six were indifferent; none was pro-Prussian. A report from Besançon is typical of the country:

> The Danish War [wrote the procureur general], whose causes and motives are not very clearly defined in the minds of public opinion, has however caused a rather strong reaction. It is considered a misuse of force, and the sight of a small people invaded by two big nations naturally arouses all the sympathies of a chivalrous country like ours.[46]

As with the Polish insurrection, so also with the Danish War, there was no question of a divided opinion, but there was significant evidence of opinion on accompanying issues. Again involvement in war was an ever-present preoccupation; and again opinion was unanimous in demanding a peaceful policy, however much they pitied Denmark. A procureur report from Nancy is a good illustration of this universal sentiment:

> It is also understood [wrote Neveu-Lemaire] that sympathy should not go to the lengths of rashness. Poland had aroused a stronger and deeper interest in the rural areas, and yet no sensible man dared censure the government for not having lent her our material assistance. What general sentiment did not demand three months ago in favor of Poland, it asks for even less today for Denmark, and for these same reasons it continues to give the same approval to the prudent and firm attitude assumed by the emperor in this new conflict.[47]

This same sentiment in very emphatic form appeared between January 1864 and January 1865 in thirty-six different reports from seventeen districts covering all parts of France except the extreme northwest and southeast. Nowhere was there shown a general desire for joining the fray to rescue Denmark.[48]

It was easy for Napoleon III to guess this sentiment after the Polish affair, but this time, more cautious and shrewder in his designs concerning the Rhine, he "shut up" when his people would not let him "put up." After the April 1864 procureur reports had all been received and digested, Cowley informed London that the emperor had said that "he was satisfied with what he had and did not want more; nor did France—she preferred peace and tranquillity to an increase of territory."[49] With such openly avowed French intentions of adhering to peace at almost any price, Prussia had little to fear from her western neighbor as she went ahead with her long-range plans of annexing Schleswig-Holstein. "The present situation," observed Bismarck, "does not seem urgent enough to overcome the present love of peace doubtless existing in a large part of France and, as we believe, shared by the emperor himself."[50]

But France's policy of remaining peaceful at any price, commendable as far as peace was concerned, could be at too high a price if it weakened her satellite, Denmark, and swelled the power of her most threatening neighbor, Prussia. Furthermore, it did not even gain for her the respect of the Prussian beneficiary. "It is just one of the faults of the imperial system," observed Goltz scornfully, "that it is exclusively based on the ignorant masses, whom they deceive without realizing that they thereby sacrifice at the same time the confidence of foreign cabinets and the respect of the enlightened classes of the French population."[51] Yet in this case both the "masses" and the "classes" had joined in demanding the abandonment of Denmark in her hour of trial.

The two phases of the Danish War were separated by an unsuccessful attempt by the powers to settle the dispute by a European conference, meeting in London in June. Here the English foreign secretary, Lord Russell, tried to settle the quarrel by giving all except northern Schleswig to Denmark's enemies. France countered with a proposal of a plebiscite as a basis of settlement. Since these were both rejected, Russell tried to compliment France by suggestion that Napoleon III be accepted as arbitrator. Prussia and Austria gave this proposal the kiss of death by stipulating that they should not be obliged to accept the final decision and that the armistice should be extended until late in the year—at a time when the frozen Baltic would have prevented the British fleet from aiding Denmark. Thus the conference came to an end, and hostilities began again immediately (26 June).

French opinion, so anxious to avoid involvement in the war, welcomed the English proposal of an armistice and a European conference in London. Since the idea of a conference was a traditional French policy, there was no opposition to a conference, but positive favorable opinion was rare, coming only from the border districts of Metz and Colmar.[52] Russell's proposal to enlist French opinion behind a peaceful solution by making Napoleon III an arbitrator elicited sufficient favorable opinion to be noted in the five districts of Rouen, Besançon, Lyons, Montpellier, and Agen. The Anglophobe district of Rouen was easily taken in by the arbitration proposal. "The preponderance of France in the decisions of the European cabinets," wrote Millevoye from Rouen, "has thus been demonstrable once more; and national feeling has found a new satisfaction in the choice of the emperor himself as arbitrator." Other districts, such as those of Bordeaux, Colmar, Besançon, and also Rouen were pleased that France did not finally fall into the arbitration trap, but retained its attitude of reserve at the end of the conference. Finally, the dissolution of the conference without a peaceful solution brought its crop of disappointment from such districts as Paris, Colmar, Lyons, and Riom. There was not, however, a widespread reaction to the more complicated circumstances of an international conference.[53]

During all the more dangerous and active phases of the Danish crisis, when France seemed likely to get involved in a shooting war, public opinion time and again showed itself wholeheartedly behind the government's chosen policy of "reserve," "abstention," or "neutrality"—the favorite words used to describe it. "There was not a single one of my assistants [affirmed the procureur general of Toulouse] who did not point out to me the peaceful desires of the people. . . . . The dignified, calm, and reserved attitude of the government of the emperor has fully reassured opinion and has received almost unanimous approval." Twenty-nine reports, representing twenty districts in all parts of France except the northwest, repeated the same story as that of Toulouse. *Le neutralisme* seemingly had had a strong following on the eve of France's disaster of 1870, just is it still had in the face of another threat to France in 1950; and the public wish was the supporter, if not perhaps the father, of the government's deed.[54]

Neutralism, like isolationism, may bring you immediate peace, but it may also lose you your friends, who would be useful in later troubles. The fear of a renewal of the Holy Alliance against France began to creep into the thoughts of government circles as well as of a few more discerning people in the country. The *Morning Post* early in March published articles pointing to the possibility of an anti-French alliance of the powers of the north. Although this was denied by Prussia, the three monarchs of Prussia, Russia, and Austria did meet in Kissingen during the period of the London Conference. There were again widespread rumors at that time that this was the beginning of a new Holy Alliance against France. Goltz reported to Berlin that "with some bitterness the empress repeatedly mentioned the meeting of the northern monarchs." She said that in any case it had taken a lot of courage [?] for the emperor to leave Denmark in the lurch . . . . [and] they had replied to public opinion that no essential French interest was at stake there."[55] In nine other dispatches Goltz brought these French fears to the attention of the Prussian government.[56] Only two procureur reports (from Rouen and Nancy), however, confirmed these fears. While the procureur general in Lyons said the dangers of an anti-French coalition "were not taken seriously," his colleagues in Rouen and Nancy noted real alarm. The account from Nancy is particularly detailed on this point:

From this dismemberment [of Denmark] will there not also develop for Europe in the more or less immediate future [asked the procureur general] a new Polish

question, a new Holy Alliance among the oppressors to assure each other the retention of the nationalities oppressed by them?

Such are the questions which still agitated opinion and was agitating it at the
time of the Carlsbad and Kissingen interviews. . . . . Fears had been aroused over
the possible existence of a holy alliance, not exactly like the one formed against
us at the beginning of the century, not entirely a threat to us now, but a concern
for the future.

While the concern in Nancy and Rouen was no doubt symptomatic
of similar fears among politically conscious people in other parts of
the country, especially in Paris, it evidently did not penetrate deeply
enough into the middle and lower classes of the provinces to be generally noted by the other procureurs general and their assistants.[57]

The renewed war after the London Conference was a hopeless
endeavor for Denmark. On 1 August the little country had to agree to
preliminaries of peace and on 30 October 1864 to sign the final Treaty
of Vienna by which she handed over all of Schleswig and Holstein
(including Lauenburg), not to the Germanic Confederation, but to
Prussia and Austria.

Naturally French sympathy for Denmark caused some criticism
to be expressed against the peace terms. The semiofficial and liberal
journals denounced the terms as extreme and wished that the people
of the surrendered duchies might have been given a chance to vote
on their fate.[58] In the provinces people at least in the districts of
Bourges and Bordeaux regretted the severe terms imposed on Denmark, but otherwise there was very little strong reaction noted: People
in the Douai and Colmar areas were just relieved that the war was
over without involving France, others in Nancy saw now with some
gratification a three-way split in Germany itself, while in the rest
of France a lack of reaction indicated the indifference which came
with the end of hostilities.[59]

However, the question arose almost immediately throughout Europe, and especially in Germany, of what was going to be the final
disposition of the surrendered duchies. The smaller German states
and Austria seemed inclined to favor the establishment of a new independent state of Schleswig-Holstein under the Augustenburg family
with separate membership in the Germanic Confederation. Prussia
strongly opposed this arrangement because she coveted eventual sole
possession of the provinces for herself and also because she feared
that such an independent Schleswig-Holstein would become an ally
of Austria both in the Confederation diet and in any possible future
Austro-Prussian war. As a result of Prussia's stronger military and
diplomatic position Bismarck was able to defy the other German
states and maneuver Austria into signing the Gastein Convention of
14 August 1865 by which the two German powers agreed to the outright cession of Lauenburg to Prussia in return for a monetary compensation to Austria, joint sovereignty of Prussia and Austria over
Schleswig-Holstein, and the partition of administrative responsibility

between the two—Prussia to administer Schleswig and Austria, Holstein. This impossible arrangement could only cause constant friction between the two joint-owners and pave the way for an eventual showdown between Prussia and Austria, which Bismarck was anxious to hasten before the diplomatic situation changed to Prussia's disadvantage.

The reaction in France to the Gastein Convention was immediate and hostile. The semiofficial press was suspected of having received instructions to denounce the arrangement, and the liberal papers needed no such prodding to blast it in most vituperative terms. The *Constitutionnel*, the *Patrie*, and the *Pays* joined with the *Débats*, the *Siècle*, the *Temps*, and the *Presse* in denouncing the arbitrary and selfish disposition of the duchies without regard to the desires of its inhabitants or the wishes of the other German people. Finally on 29 August, Drouyn de Lhuys sent out a circular to his diplomatic representatives abroad (published two weeks later), which added the strongest kind of official criticism to the clamor of the press. After condemning it for violating the international agreements of Vienna (1815) and of London (1852), for destroying the integrity of Denmark, and for ignoring the wishes of the Danes in northern Schleswig, the circular concluded:

On what principle, then, is this Austro-Prussian arrangement based? We regret to find in it no other basis than force, no other justification than the reciprocal convenience of the two partners. That is the sort of practice which present-day Europe has gotten away from, and one must search for precedents for it in the most baneful periods of history. Violence and conquest pervert the notion of the rights and consciences of people. As substitutes for the principles which prevail in the life of modern societies, they are an element of trouble and disintegration and can only overthrow the old order without erecting any new one on a sound foundation.[60]

From the eastern districts of France and from Bordeaux, came reports (seven in all) showing provincial dislike for the Gastein Convention. The attitude of the Bordeaux district was typical of these protests: "The Convention of Gastein [wrote the procureur general], if it has not aroused opinion, has not, however, gone unnoticed. Opinion has appeared indignant over this traffic in national groups coming at the end of a war supposedly undertaken to break a foreign yoke." Such sentiments were shared by most people in the districts of Douai, Amiens, Nancy, Besançon, Grenoble, and Chambéry. On the other hand people in the regions of Limoges and Paris seemed indifferent. "The recent success obtained by [Prussia] in the Gastein Convention," remarked the procureur general in Paris, "has hardly had any reverberations beyond the public press."[61]

The reaction to Drouyn de Lhuys' circular was equally limited; but where it did arouse attention, it received a favorable response. Of course, when one began to spin out detailed and legalistic arguments, popular interest tended to decline. Again only along the eastern borders—in the regions of Nancy, Besançon, Grenoble, and

Chambéry—as well as in the environs of Paris did this favorable opinion appear. France had not shown up too well in this dismemberment of Denmark, and some opinion was glad to hear some strongly-worded protests from the ministry of foreign affairs.[62]

But Drouyn de Lhuys had to eat his words the next month by issuing another circular, showing more friendliness and circumspection toward Prussia. The French government was now thinking of getting Rhineland compensation from Prussia in return for what appeared to be her inevitable absorption of the duchies. Treading softly became the new attitude, as the French obsequiously began to beg for their waiter's tip. The idea of compensation along the Rhine always seemed to be in the back of all Frenchmen's minds. The enlargement of Sardinia had brought the compensation of Savoy and Nice; now with Prussian acquisitions what should be more natural than to think in the traditional terms of compensation in the Rhine area? Napoleon III had implied such compensations when he answered England's suggestion of armed intervention to help Denmark. This had cooled Lord Russell's ardor, and no joint intervention materialized.[63] During the war Drouyn de Lhuys had told Goltz flatly that his colleagues and French opinion would not tolerate Prussia's annexation of the duchies without compensations for France.[64] How much such compensation ideas had emerged from the subconscious mind of the public to take an active form as early as 1865 is hard to determine. Only seven reports in 1864 and 1865 seemed to note such sentiments, and these came from three districts—Nancy, Douai, and Bordeaux. One report from Bordeaux affirmed: "People here understand very well that this event [Prussian annexations] would perhaps be less unfavorable to French interests than at first sight and could become the signal for just and legitimate compensations of a nature to protect our eastern borders so cruelly denuded by the disastrous treaties of 1814 and 1815."[65]

The fact that England always shied away from a general congress in which France could have put in a bid for Rhineland compensations and that England always opposed any change in the territorial settlements of 1815, whether in Savoy or elsewhere, intensified and perpetuated the Anglophobe feeling in French circles.[66] At the beginning of the Danish War Cowley admitted: "Irritation [against England] is evinced in no measured language by the Emperor, by the Government, and by French society in general. That the press is very violent I can myself bear witness." Then he added with surprising innocence that he did not know what France wanted. But Russell was not so naïve, for he wrote in the margin in pencil—"Rhine."[67] Cowley's description of French feeling is borne out by the procureur reports. Again, as during the Polish affair, twenty reports in 1864 from thirteen districts scattered throughout France denounced British policy on Danish affairs. The one from anti-British Bordeaux echoed the sentiments of most of the other twelve districts as far as the failure of the conference was concerned:

No one [wrote the procureur general] in Bordeaux had any illusions about the probable outcome of the London conference. Up to the last day, however, they doubted that, after such ostentatious demonstrations and haughty words, England would bring herself to admit her inability to protect Denmark whom she had unwisely allowed to get involved in a war. The serious setback, suffered by Lord Palmerston's policy, however much it was foreseen, was none-the-less greeted with expressions of a proud satisfaction by public opinion.[68]

A people which scorns or distrusts most of its neighbors begins to feel very lonely. Haunted by the phantom of a new holy alliance, it was rather unwise to spurn England's friendship. In fact as Prussia's power became more evident in 1865, some more sober groups began to advocate closer relations with Great Britain. As early as July 1864, when the possibility of a continental coalition against France began to dawn on public opinion, the procureur general in Toulouse wrote:

If, however, the powers of the north succeeded in cementing their alliance again, opinion could become so aroused that in reacting against this serious event, it would come to wonder whether it was not time to sacrifice resentments for a solidarity of interests, and, the Polish and Danish questions both being on the docket, to solve them by an agreement which would satisfy at one and the same time the differing inclinations of both great western nations.

Similar chastened sentiments were exhibited in Amiens, Paris, Nancy, and Grenoble.[69]

While some were thus advocating an Anglo-French alliance to save France from isolation and while Napoleon III himself was trying to enlist Italy on his side by making the September Convention, his government was beginning to think in terms of a straightforward deal with Prussia by means of a Franco-Prussian alliance. This seemed to be revealed by certain inspired articles in the semi-official newspapers, such as the *Patrie, Pays, France,* and *Mémorial diplomatique.*[70] Whether this was a trial balloon or not, it seemed to have had no echo in basic opinion itself. Although Napoleon III from 1864 on flirted with the idea of a Prussian agreement which would include French compensations along the Rhine, nothing definite was proposed until the ill-fated Benedetti-Bismarck conversations in 1866.

France was in a worse position after the Danish War than she had been after the Polish insurrection. The mood of the public was uneasiness, confounded by confusion as to the future direction of policy. If the main threat seemed to come from Prussia, there appeared at least the likely prospect of an Austro-Prussian quarrel, which would hold Prussia in check or make her dependent on France's good will.

CHAPTER VIII

THE AUSTRO-PRUSSIAN WAR

At the beginning of the year 1866 the French government and the French public were more and more concerned over what seemed to be an impending Austro-Prussian war over Schleswig-Holstein in particular and over rivalry for dominance in the German area in general. Ever since 1815 France had counted on this Austro-Prussian rivalry to preserve the balance of power in Europe. Austria and Prussia would not only check each other, but by their mutual suspicions they would, it was hoped in French circles, prevent the formation of a coalition against France. However, if one of these rivals should seriously defeat the other in a trial of strength, the resulting disruption of the balance of power would adversely alter France's relative position in Europe. Even more, such a victory would probably encourage the victor to compel the smaller German states to transform the loose Germanic confederation into a powerful federation dominated by that victorious power. Such an eventuality would be doubly calamitous to France. Her relative position would be still more weakened, and she would have to consecrate more and more of her wealth and manpower for military defense, especially on the most vulnerable of her borders.

Since an Austro-Prussian war seemed inevitable, Napoleon III had to consider the wisest policy for France in such a contingency. Obviously he must try to keep both sides as equal as possible so that neither could win an overwhelming victory. If they both insisted on fighting to the bitter end, they would then happily wear each other out. Prussia's military advantage was not too well known at that time because, as far as armaments were concerned, Austria was trying to keep up with the Prussians. The probability that most of the other German states would join Austria perhaps made the line-up appear to Napoleon a little too favorable to Austria. He therefore encouraged Italy to make an alliance with Prussia to counterbalance Austria's German support. This Italian alliance would promise Venetia to Italy and also make her more friendly to France in case France needed friends after a one-sided victory.[1]

But a policy also had to be evolved in case the other contingency arose—that of the complete defeat of one of the two prospective belligerents. In such a case France, in self-defense, would be compelled to intervene. This would mean mustering her forces and entering the war on the weaker side. By doing this France could prevent one dominant nation from upsetting the balance of power and could impose her will in the final settlement—a settlement which would save the weaker contestant and give France a chance to demand her border territories along the Rhine which she had lost in 1815. This territorial compensation Napoleon III had always dreamed of as one of the aims of his reign.[2]

Peace Opinion in Early 1866

To enter a war at such a psychological moment without being attacked presented, however, the difficulty of carrying public opinion with him. Napoleon knew that opinion had seemed hostile to war both in 1854 and 1859 when he had had to take up arms. Yet in both of these instances the enemy (Russia and Austria respectively) had appeared as plausible aggressors, and the French public had supported the wars. But the strong peace sentiment during the Polish and Danish crises would certainly have strengthened his misgivings about public support of an unprovoked French counterbalancing intervention into this future German conflict. The Emperor of the French, therefore, needed to know just how much the public would qualify its peace sentiment in case the second alternative materialized. Consequently it would have been surprising if he had not continued to feel the pulse of France through the administrative reports to learn what the people were thinking in the early months of 1866. These reports could give him, and do give us today, a fairly clear picture of French opinion on the eve of the Austro-Prussian War.

In the early period, before 3 May 1866, the manifestations of French opinion were again overwhelmingly opposed to war and to France's participation in one. All the procureur reports mentioning foreign affairs during the month of April, except that from Lyons (covering opinion from January to April), showed either definite opposition to France's entering the impending war or at least alarm at the prospects of war. The report from Rennes is typical of the attitudes reported:

All my information [wrote the procureur general] was in agreement in asserting that at no time has the maintenance of peace been so unanimously desired. This trend of public opinion has been so energetically expressed that the people seemed to refuse to admit that there could be any circumstances urgent enough to oblige the emperor to abandon the wise neutrality he has enunciated. This ardent and absolute desire for peace, pushed almost to the point of obsession with a large number, can be explained by various causes, the principal one of which can be found in the more threatening perils and the more general uneasiness that war would engender for private business interests in these days.

Twelve other districts, scattered throughout France, revealed similar strong pacific attitudes. There was no opinion expressed in favor of the war.[3]

But, in addition to the official reports coming into the minister of justice, evidence of antiwar sentiment was found in the observations of the foreign diplomats in Paris. Wächter from Wurttemberg told how Rothschild and Pereire, representing French financial circles, had pleaded with Napoleon III on 10 April to throw his great influence in the scales of world diplomacy to prevent war. They painted a very somber picture of what would happen to the stock market and to business in general if peace were not assured.[4] Beyens, the Belgian minister, also reported on the antiwar sentiment of the business classes: "There was a bad slump on the stock market today on receipt of the news [war crisis in Germany], although it was known only vaguely. Instinctively they still want to doubt the possibility of a war. . . . . Everybody says it is senseless. . . . ."[5] The Austrian ambassador, Richard Metternich, said he had heard that peace opinion was so strong that the government was going to have to reassure it by some statement in the legislature or in the *Moniteur*.[6] Even Count Nigra, the Italian minister, who hoped for French support of Italy's war policy, admitted the hostility of French opinion. "Businessmen, bankers, merchants, speculators of all sorts," he complained in April, "are most hostile to war" and "as a consequence the French government is still more confirmed in its attitude of neutrality and freedom of action."[7]

This decision to adhere to a peaceful neutral policy was shown by the tone of the semiofficial press. The *Constitutionnel* declared that "the French government had no intention of departing from its policy of strict neutrality which it had maintained up to now," while the *Patrie* echoed the same sentiments.[8] The *Siècle*, a democratic opposition paper having curious connections with the ruling clique, took a more vigorous stand for watchful neutrality and for intervention only if Austria endangered Italian unity or if the German conflict harmed France's position by a shift in the balance of power. These, wrote Emile de la Bédollière in the *Siècle*, were also the views of "the majority of the newspapers."[9]

Thus by the testimony of Napoleon's procureurs general, of the foreign diplomats, and of the semiofficial press French opinion strongly favored a peace policy up to the month of May.

And in the first week of May two incidents occurred which gave the emperor a chance to see how this opinion was becoming stronger and more emphatic. We have an advance warning of the first impending incident from Count Nigra who, writing to his government on Tuesday (1 May), said:

The French government is concerned about the interpellations which will take place Thursday in the legislative body. . . . . It will be asked for an explicit declaration concerning the attitude it will take relative to Italy. . . . . But in the face of the [Austro-Italian] military preparations, which the supporters of peace at any price like to present as simultaneous or almost simultaneous, the French government will have some embarrassment in making a reply.[10]

The dreaded parliamentary attack came on Thursday, 3 May, and from the most formidable member of the opposition in the lower house, Adolphe Thiers. In a long and masterful speech he underlined one guarantee which France had received in the treaties of 1815, that of a Germany only weakly united in a loose confederation. That, he said, was the basis of French policy. Germany must be warned against forming a strong federation; Prussia must be told politely but firmly that France will oppose any considerable expansion of the Prussian state. Thiers also denounced France's help in achieving Italy's unification, and he insisted that France should not enter the impending war to protect Italy. Indeed, France should insist that she withdraw from her Prussian alliance. If Italy imprudently entered the war, she should have to take full responsibility for her eventual fate.

Go [cried Thiers], go anywhere in France, go into the smallest towns and villages, and you will see whether this policy, which would tend to re-establish the ancient German empire by placing the power of Charles V in the north instead of in the south of Germany, whether that power [Prussia], supported by Italy, would be popular in France. No, there is too much common sense in France ever to welcome such a policy.

But Thiers recognized that sentiment was also opposed to war to protect France's position. "Undoubtedly we agree with the policy of neutrality," he added, "because no one here is foolish enough to insist on plunging into a war to avoid a war." Consequently France was to give Prussia a polite warning, and, if Prussia refused to heed it, to maintain an ominous silence. Thiers's policy, then, was a curious combination of "speak up" and "shut up" with no tolerance for "putting up" a threat of force to back the protests.[11]

Thus Thiers had said all he could to discourage moral support of the Prussian-Italian cause without daring to be caught in the trap of advocating war. But the speech was an open criticism of Napoleon III's tendency to encourage various national aspirations. In a speech just preceding that of Thiers the government spokesman, Rouher, had tried to be as reassuring as possible. If Italy attacked Austria, he declared, it would be at her own risk and peril. As for France, she adhered to "a peaceful policy, a genuine neutrality and freedom of action."[12] Whether it was Thiers or Rouher, the policy—in line with prevailing opinion—was peace.

What response did this debate have in the chamber? Kern, the Swiss minister, immediately telegraphed his Federal Council, "Thiers's speech provoked strong demonstration in the interest of peace."[13] The Belgian minister likewise noted the strong approval given to the spokesman of the opposition by Napoleon's hand-picked majority. On the point which advocated leaving Italy to her own fate, he said:

"The various interruptions which greeted it are difficult to characterize."[14] Even the Italian minister admitted that "the prospect of considerable [territorial] acquisitions was not enough to persuade the emperor to enter the war against the wish of the country after the demonstration in the legislative body."[15]

Napoleon's Trial Balloon: The Auxerre Speech

But the emperor was cut to the quick by the courage of Thiers's attack, by the general approval he obtained among Napoleon's own legislators, and especially by the favorable references to the treaties of 1815, which the emperor detested. He finally decided to make an issue of the debate and at the same time send up a trial balloon to ascertain once and for all just what was the attitude of the country and whether at least it might not be lured into intervention for the sake of compensation.[16] He did it in a curious way by a public speech given in Auxerre on 6 May. Its most significant passage was:

> I have, besides, a debt of gratitude to repay to the department of Yonne. It was one of the first to vote for me in 1848 because it knew, like the great majority of the French people, that its interests were mine and that I, like it, detested the treaties of 1815 which they would like to make the sole basis of our policy.
> . . . . In your midst I breathe more easily, for it is among the working people of town and country that I rediscover the real genius of France.[17]

The general impression the emperor wanted to make was that he favored the national movements which changed the settlement of 1815, that he wanted a rectification of France's boundaries of 1815, and that he was not averse to a war in central Europe to achieve these ends. Now he could sit back and watch the public reaction, and could see whether the public, looking at the situation in this light, would be less averse to war and France's possible involvement in it.

The first returns came from the stock market. "The Auxerre speech has provoked a panic," Metternich wired to Vienna.[18] Rothschild, a guest at the Tuileries the next evening, spoke out openly among the invited company that "the Empire means slump (*l'Empire, c'est la baisse!*)."[19]

The press was the next to respond to the printed version of the Auxerre speech, and here it is noted that, in spite of control and censorship, seven of the fourteen papers consulted opposed the warlike implications of the speech. These were the *Journal des Débats, Temps, Monde, Union, Gazette de France, Phare de la Loire* (Nantes), and the *Progrès*.[20] On the other hand, seven other papers (most of them semiofficial) praised or approved the emperor's remarks. These were the *Constitutionnel, Patrie, Pays, Opinion Nationale* and *Salut Public* (Lyons)—imperialist papers; and the *Siècle* and *Presse*—democratic papers.[21] Baron Beyens, who was inclined to show sympathy for Austria, expressed disgust at the servility of the press on the Auxerre speech.

Messrs. Paulin Limayrac [*Constitutionnel*] and Dréolle [*Patrie*] [wrote Beyens] have been pleased to strum their lyres on a bellicose tone of servile chauvinism. M. La Valette is especially responsible for this zeal and, like the good courtesan he is, has pronounced the speech admirable. And the journalists, as one of them was saying, are like an electric wire which has no idea of what it's transmitting.[22]

What Beyens said about the press was nothing in comparison with the picture he painted of the adverse reaction of the public. Here are a few passages from another report:

The emperor's speech at Auxerre has naturally produced here the deepest emotion, and it has excited that much keener alarm because nobody can seem to explain the meaning of His Majesty's words. They see the augury of serious events which they cannot measure with exactitude.

. . . . In the midst of this mess, if you'll pardon the word, one point alone stands out clearly and that is the resentment of all sensible people toward the emperor. Whatever his views may be or whatever profit can be gleaned confusedly, they do not like it. They forgive him neither for the harm he is causing now nor for the eventual benefit in the future about which they have no concern. They could not believe that the sovereign is responding to the ardent desire for peace and to the general animosity of the nation, and especially of the army, toward Prussia. . . . . So discontent is appearing with extreme intensity, and with an unaccustomed liberty. Trade in Paris and industry in the provinces complain bitterly. A great many of the members of the legislature appear deeply hurt and several speak of resigning. The public, in a word, is angry and is visibly shaken in its confidence (*se désaffectionne visiblement*).[23]

On the emperor's return to Paris, Fould upbraided him for his Auxerre speech, claiming that "the confidence of the country was gone" and that his speech "was an insult to his ministers and to the chamber."[24] Goltz confirmed Beyens and Fould when he reported:

His speech at Auxerre . . . . made a bad impression on everyone: the pride of the servile majority was wounded, and they threatened a counterdemonstration which would have obliged the Emperor to dissolve the Assembly. Several of the more important Ministers (Rouher, Fould, Béhic) wished to tender their resignations.[25]

These estimates of opinion as well as the open criticism of seven newspapers would seem to indicate a very adverse response to the imperial trial balloon. But what would the procureurs general and prefects have to say in their next reports? It is significant to note that three weeks later, when the returns came in, four-fifths of these loyal appointees of the emperor felt obliged to assert that the people were opposed to his Auxerre speech and to any encouragement of war. Considering that these officials were inclined to look for favorable reactions, this high percentage of admitted unfavorable opinions is impressive. The procureur report from Orleans is typical of the vast majority:

I have to inform Your Excellency [wrote the procureur general], with a deep feeling of regret but none the less faithfully, that the Auxerre speech has not obtained the approval that the emperor's words have always before received. I must say that public opinion appears hostile and defiant. The demonstration in the chamber in the session of 3 May and the speech delivered at Auxerre were so closely connected and yet seemed so opposed to each other that it was a serious matter to

see a sort of current draw the public to the side of the chamber and just to that
extent draw it away from the emperor.

The procureur general in Amiens also noted that "an unwholesome
tendency has appeared of . . . . a desire to see parliament as a more
direct counterweight to the will of the sovereign." Out of thirteen
procureur and prefect reports from all parts of France except the
central west ten showed clear-cut opposition to the Auxerre speech,
three indicated important hostile groups, and only three (Metz, Lyons,
and Marseilles) were genuinely favorable. In this case the packed
legislature seemed closer to general opinion than the press.[26]

Napoleon III apparently had his answer: the public had definitely
and consciously supported the legislature against the emperor and
preferred a policy of peace to one of adventure. Lord Cowley, the
British ambassador, in accusing the emperor of wanting war so that
he could dictate terms in favor of France and Italy, summed up his
impression of the response to the Auxerre speech thus: "But the
country did not respond to this ill-concealed, if unavowed, policy. So
strong a desire for the maintenance of peace was manifested that the
emperor was obliged to change his tactics and propose conferences
for the settlement of the differences which were likely to lead to war."[27]

Peace Opinion during the War

A new proposal on 24 May of a European conference in col-
laboration with England and Russia was then the emperor's next step.
He did not have much hope of the success of a conference, but it
would leave the impression with the public that he preferred a peaceful
solution. Austria, however, rejected the conference in early June, and
the outbreak of war then became only a matter of time.

It is one of the ironies of history that French opinion, by being
for peace at almost any price, contributed to the outbreak of the
Austro-Prussian War. Bismarck could not have felt safe to unleash
a war if he had not been reasonably sure that the French government
would be restrained from intervening against Prussia by a strongly
pacifist public opinion. Prussian agents and army officers, entering
France from Geneva in the months just preceding the war, were seen
by the prefects themselves in all parts of the country even as far as
Marseilles, Toulouse, and Bordeaux, checking on the antiwar sentiment of the populace and on any secret war preparations by France.
As a result of their reports and those of the Prussian military attaché
in Paris, von Loe, Bismarck was able to boast to the French ambassador
in Berlin, Benedetti, at the start of the war: "Our confidence in the
emperor is so great that we are not leaving one soldier on the left bank
of the Rhine."[28]

Three days before hostilities started, in the session of 13 June,
Napoleon III had read to the legislative body a letter he had written

to his minister of foreign affairs, Drouyn de Lhuys, as the vehicle for giving to the public his views on the situation. Here under a sugar-coating of peaceful neutrality he retained a vague suggestion of French intervention in case of an unfavorable disturbance of the balance of power. The letter also suggested to the public that France would demand compensations if one side acquired enough territory to upset the balance of power, that France was assured participation in the final settlement, and that the present policy of "attentive neutrality" might require the use of "our strength."[29]

We now also have evidence of what was French opinion from the middle of May to 1 July, much of which was available to Napoleon III at the time he had to make his critical decision of 5 July. This new evidence of the public reaction to the conference proposal and to France's attitude during the early weeks of the war shows conclusively that the French people of all classes and of most shades of politics were still strongly opposed to France's engaging in a war.

After the news of the proposed conference was made public, Baron Beyens noted the "vehemence of public feeling against Prussia and Italy and its revulsion against the spirit of war and conquest."[30] Hansen reported a statement made to him by Thiers that he and his political followers (liberal Orleanists) wanted peace above all else.[31] Cowley said a "strong desire for peace was manifested" in the country;[32] and Bigelow, the American minister, confirmed this impression when he wrote to Seward that "the public of France [is] generally very much indisposed to a war in Europe at the present time." The opposition in the chamber, Bigelow said, disliked this determination of foreign policy without the chamber's participation, but the majority did not make an issue of it.[33] Even Nigra, who as an Italian would dislike this pacific trend, had to admit that "the emperor's letter . . . . has not completely reassured the peace party which is the most numerous in Paris."[34] On the letter itself Fane, the British chargé d'affaires, said the people were confused: some said that it meant peace, others that its reservations indicated possible war for France. The stock market fluctuated up and down, also reflecting this uncertainty. It was no doubt equally disturbed because there were so many holders of Italian securities. "On the whole," Fane concluded, "it may be said that the emperor's letter is more criticized than approved by those who desire to see the war, if it breaks out, confined within the narrowest limits."

As to the legislators themselves, Cowley wrote the next day that "the impression made on them is that the emperor intends war but that he is afraid to say as much."[35] The Hungarian, Kiss, in writing to Bismarck, acknowledged that "everybody here is disconcerted, Emperor Napoleon is besieged from all sides to work for *peace at any price*, he hesitates, he is shaken. . . . . "[36] Magne in a detailed letter to

the emperor, at a later date, revealed in an outspoken fashion what
was the general opinion in June:

> Would it please Your Majesty to permit me . . . . to communicate to him the
> impressions I was able to obtain from the public on two points of current policy.
> Certainly it is not for the public to decide such matters, but the tendencies of
> opinion are an element that is essential to know.
>   . . . . The great current of public opinion is above all concerned with French
> interests. At no other time perhaps has this attitude been shown with such emphasis.
> As the great mass of the people live by labor and business, it sincerely desires
> peace. . . . .[37]

Thus Belgian, Danish, English, American, Hungarian, Italian, and
French observers all concurred in the intense French desire for peace.
It will be seen later that what was known by these diplomatic observers
was known, could not help but be known, by the emperor.

The press reaction to Napoleon's policy letter was almost unanimous in interpreting it as one of peace and neutrality. The *Constitutionnel* not only stressed the peace overtones of the policy but
denounced those journals which hinted that more than one interpretation might be made. The Orleanist *Journal des Débats* thought
it answered "the necessities of the present situation." The *Siècle*,
favoring war to protect Italy or to preserve the balance of power,
used its own interpretation when it said that the letter agreed with
its own policy "except in a few details." The *Revue des deux mondes*
hoped "that France will allow the tempest to pass by persevering in
attentive neutrality." "He [the emperor] has promised peace," it
went on, "and all who earnestly desire it should have faith in his
promise."[38] In general the newspapers either wanted peace or pretended to interpret the letter as peaceful.

In the meantime the procureurs general and the prefects, along
with their advocates general, assistants, subprefects, justices of the
peace, mayors, and police officers were busily engaged (in addition
to their other prescribed work) in sounding out opinion in every
nook and corner of their districts and departments. And their returns
were coming in all during the months of May and June and early
July. Twenty-eight separate reports on opinion before the battle of
Sadowa, coming from every part of the country, touched on the feeling
for or against war, but in not one instance was there a suggestion
of a preference for war. They all joined in one harmonious chorus
for the preservation of peace. Quotations from a few of the more
significant reports will bear out this evaluation: (Caen) "Peace is
the general wish." (Quimper) "The people are worried about . . . .
war." (Paris) "The assurances of neutrality . . . . correspond to the
general desire for peace." (Orleans) "Such [peace] is the wish of all
classes of the population in my district." (Lyons) "I . . . . find only
aspirations for peace and quiet." (Grenoble) "Peace is in fact the
almost unanimous wish." (Montpellier) "One outstanding fact . . . .
the people evince an immense urge for peace and quiet." (Toulouse)

"Public opinion declares itself strongly, perhaps too strongly, in favor of peace." (Bordeaux) "Peace tendencies are indicated here more and more." And the same unequivocal antipathy for French participation in the war was shown in the reports from Amiens, Versailles, Bar-le-Duc, Metz, Colmar, Tours, Napoléon-Vendée, Bourges, Dijon, Moulins, Limoges, Riom, Chambéry, Aix, Nîmes, and Agen.[39]

Thus peace sentiment was the universal, overwhelming feeling of the French people as described by diplomats, politicians, journalists, prefects, and procureurs general. Some of the procureur reports on opinion in May and June did not come in until after 5 July, however, but they did not differ in general sentiment from those received before that date.

Yet, did the emperor know fully about the state of opinion as indicated by all the earlier or later reports? An account by Baron Beyens, fortunately preserved, gives convincing proof of the emperor's knowledge of it and of his efforts further to confirm it. On 10 June the baron wrote the following significant information to Brussels: ". . . . The emperor . . . . has been able to determine better each day how the country is opposed to war and irritated at Prussia and Italy. Although this sentiment has been affirmed in more ways than one, although the police reports from all over the empire confirm it,[40] they wanted to consult again the opinion of the common people (*classes populaires*). Prefects were ordered to Paris, secret soundings were made by the mayors in various parts of their territories, and everywhere the answer was an ardent desire for peace. His Majesty did not conceal the impression produced on him by this result."[41] Nothing shows better than this dispatch how much care the emperor took to ascertain public opinion, how well he knew that opinion in early July, and how impressed he was with its emphatic insistence on peace.[42]

Sadowa: Consternation and Confusion

Then suddenly during the night of 3-4 July came the telegraphic news of the overwhelming Prussian victory at Sadowa. The emperor, his counselors, and the discerning public were stunned by the implications of the news. The Europeon balance of power had been destroyed overnight, and France was on the light end of the balance. La Gorce, contemporary and historian of the period, exclaimed: "We felt that something on the soil of old Europe had just crumbled. . . . . Among the people uneasiness . . . . in the sovereign's official circle . . . . bitter perplexity."[43] The *Times* correspondent wrote home: "The intelligence of the Austrian defeat has produced consternation. You hear it remarked on all sides that this tremendous weapon [needle gun] makes the Prussians almost masters in Europe."[44] Even before the battle of Sadowa, Napoleon III had shown concern over Prussia's

initial minor victories. "I saw the Emperor this morning [1 July],"
wrote Cowley, ". . . . it was clear from His Majesty's tone that the
Prussian successes have taken him by surprise and that he is in some
alarm at them."[45] After Sadowa, Empress Eugénie expressed her un-
concealed alarm directly to the Prussian Prince Reuss: "You have
displayed such energy and promptitude in your operations that with
such a nation as a neighbor we run the risk one fine day of seeing you
at the gates of Paris before we scarcely realize it. I'll go to bed French
and wake up Prussian."[46] The Prussian troops, confidently removed
from the Rhine area, had helped to make these operations successful.
Thus French pacifist opinion had not only contributed to the outbreak of the war but had also unwittingly compassed the defeat of
Austria and the disruption of Europe's balance of power.

On the heels of this disconcerting news came Austria's surrender of Venetia to Emperor Napoleon, accompanied by a request
for his mediation to end the war. This new development presented
another perplexing problem—or perhaps a happy opportunity. "The
French monarch," observed La Gorce, "felt too overwhelmed by
events not to look for some way out, whatever it might be."[47] Here
was the sought-for escape. Sybel pointed up this mood with a clear
reference to opinion: "Public opinion held him firmly in its grasp.
Since Sadowa its jealousy of Prussia had been doubly aroused: the
simple refusal to accept Austria's offer would have been impossible
for the Emperor."[48]

Not only did Napoleon III accept the mediation offer, but he
also immediately made use of it for favorable publicity. Under his
own supervision a brief announcement was composed and published
in the next morning's *Moniteur*. It read:

> An important development has just occurred.
> After having safeguarded the honor of his arms in Italy, the emperor of Aus-
> tria, acceding to the ideas put forward by Emperor Napoleon in his letter to his
> minister of foreign affairs of 11 June, cedes Venetia to the Emperor of the French
> and accepts his mediation to bring about peace between the belligerents.
> Emperor Napoleon hastened to answer this appeal and immediately addressed
> himself to the kings of Prussia and Italy to effect an armistice.[49]

The emperor's knowledge of the moods of public opinion usually
seemed unerringly accurate. But on this occasion he overplayed his
hand. The change from consternation to loud rejoicing, which this
announcement inspired, bordered on the hysterical. The *Moniteur*
was hardly off the press before Paris was shouting with joy. Public
buildings and private shops and dwellings all over town were decked
out with flags. There was enthusiasm everywhere. The stock market
jumped four francs. The ubiquitous little lawyer, M. Dabot, was a
witness to the celebrating but not a participant. In his diary of 5
July he wrote: "The flags are flying from the windows. Why? From
pure national vanity! For the gift is dangerous. Naturally the em-

peror is going to give Venetia to Italy, and she angered . . . . will store up another grudge against France. Well, I'm not going to fly a flag from *my* window."[50] And then at night the streets and buildings were illuminated. The long lines of gas lights which fringed the balconies and roofs created a joyous holiday brilliance. The emperor had kept France from war, and now as the arbiter of a continent he was going to restore peace to the rest of Europe—and perhaps some lost provinces to France. Hopes were high after a previous night of dismay.[51]

And in the provinces there was the same spontaneous rejoicing as in the capital. The procureur general in Rouen described the magic transformation thus:

> The great news of the surrender of Venetia to France and of Austria's request for the emperor's mediation swallows up all the emotions of the last few weeks . . . . so violent has been the explosion of enthusiasm everywhere. The great event gives satisfaction to all patriotic feelings as well as to all [business] interests; the excitement has been as great as on the morrow of a brilliant victory. As so often happens with public emotions which take possession of a whole people, national pride silences for the moment partisan differences. . . . . This unprecedented page added to our history has caught up the timid, stiffened the irresolute, and united all the people in a unanimous sentiment of joy, gratitude, and confidence in his genius. This outcome after so much concern gives to the unexpected a providential appearance which takes violent hold on French imaginations as it has to every decisive event of this reign.[52]

It was the same story in every one of the other districts and departments which reported on the public response to the *Moniteur's* announcement—in Rennes, Colmar, Dijon, Bourg (Ain), Riom, Grenoble, Marseilles, Nîmes, Bordeaux, Pau, Bar-le-Duc, and Napoléon-Vendée.[53] In not one report consulted was a contrary reaction found. Prefects and procureurs general all agreed on what proved to be a momentary exaltation.

But the Paris press was more sober in its reception. The nongovernmental papers did not forget the Sadowa disaster and discussed the possible difficulties of getting Italy's co-operation. To the extent that they were saner in their appreciation just so were they still failing to reflect general opinion.[54] The semiofficial press, however, took the hint from the *Moniteur* insertion or from some prodding of La Valette, the minister of interior, and further emphasized the glory coming to France and her ruler. The *Constitutionnel* expressed pride that Austria would "so nobly seek out the imperial government." The *France Politique* exclaimed, "Immense victory for humanity, for civilization, and for France." The emperor was hailed as liberator of Venetia, founder of world peace, and arbiter of Europe.[55]

The Saint-Cloud Council

Yet on the same day of the flag flying, public rejoicing, and stock-market rise (5 July) the fatal council meeting at Saint-Cloud took place. Napoleon knew that his position was weak in comparison with what the public acclaimed it to be. He quickly sensed that his face-saving announcement in the *Moniteur* had worked too well and might embarrass him in some warlike decisions he might have to make. Goltz reported that he tried to have the demonstrations of rejoicing stopped, but it was too late.[56] The council meeting was initially arranged by Drouyn de Lhuys, the foreign minister, in a way to favor his forceful intervention policy. He deliberately excluded La Valette, the minister of interior. Moreover, he managed to see the emperor alone before the meeting opened. He and Randon, minister of war, brought out the seriousness of the Sadowa victory and the necessity for quick action to salvage the situation. To the eastern border 80,000 men could and should be sent at once. France still had a chance to retain Austria and the other German states as allies. Then by mobilization and legislative appropriation she could follow up the initial movement of the 80,000. The decrees for the movement of troops and the summons of the legislature and a note announcing the forceful policy should be published the next morning (6 July) in the *Moniteur*.

For a moment the tragedy at Sadowa and the urgency of the situation completely overwhelmed the emperor. They seemed to have blotted out all his consideration for the peaceful pressures of public opinion. Influenced by the insistent pleas of his two leading ministers and of the empress herself Napoleon indicated his agreement with the policy of forceful intervention.

It was at this point that La Valette, uninvited, walked into the council meeting. Since he was minister of interior, the emperor welcomed him and explained the subject under discussion. La Valette immediately jumped up and opposed vehemently the whole proposal. A mediator, he declared, cannot start out by threatening force. The one who encouraged the Prussian-Italian alliance cannot be the one to urge perjury on the Italian king. And then La Valette advanced what he hoped might be the clinching argument—public opinion. "What would Europe say [including French public opinion] if Italy, forced to justify herself, published documents to show that her treaty with Prussia of 8 April had been, not only approved, but actually promoted by the imperial government?" The emperor was visibly affected. Neither he nor Drouyn de Lhuys replied, but they and the empress deliberately withdrew from the council for a short time. When they returned, Napoleon persisted in his agreement with Drouyn de Lhuys. La Valette, however, would not let the matter rest here. He went on with further arguments about France's unpreparedness, the drain on her men and supplies by the Mexican expedition, the threat that Prussia and Italy would fight rather than submit to forceful intervention. Turning upon the foreign minister, he castigated him for his irresponsible and hazardous policy. The atmosphere became so charged with recrimination that the emperor finally closed the meeting without indicating any change in his previous resolution. By that time, however, he also knew that Rouher, his favorite advisor and minister of state, and Baroche, his minister of justice, were in entire agreement with La Valette.[57]

The night of 5-6 July must have been a sleepless one for the emperor, for he finally brought himself to abandon the war policy of Drouyn de Lhuys and the empress for the peaceful mediation policy of La Valette and Rouher. The importance of this decision in assuring Prussia's complete victory and her dominance in Europe is revealed by Bismarck's admission before the Reichstag (16 January 1874) of the bad situation in which Prussia would have found herself if Napoleon III had chosen the opposite policy of forceful intervention. "France had but few available forces [he declared], but a small contingent would have been enough, along with the large numbers of troops of southern Germany, to constitute a very respectable army. This army would have immediately forced us to cover Berlin and abandon all our successes in Austria."[58]

The reasons for Napoleon III's sudden change to a nonbelligerent policy in the face of Prussia's victory have been the subject of much historical discussion because it eventually reduced France to a second-rate power and led directly to her disaster in 1870. Sybel, Guyot, Doutenville, Vautier, Binkley, and Oncken, the principal commentators on the motivations of this policy decision, almost completely ignored the factor of public opinion. They attributed the decision to one or more of the following causes: the emperor's illness, his sympathy for Italian and German nationalism, his uncertainty about France's preparedness, the Mexican expedition's military and financial drain on France, and the influence of Prince Jerome Napoleon.[59]

Only Bourgeois, Albert Thomas, and Ollivier mention public opinion in this episode, but they judge it entirely by the legislative reaction to Thiers's speech without much confirmation of this faulty representative system by the use of other sources. Furthermore, Ollivier was always inclined to blame opinion for any unfortunate decisions made by himself or others. Consequently his views require corroboration.[60]

However, the more the developments of opinion since January 1866 are studied, the more the conviction grows that public opinion was one of the emperor's most important considerations in his debates with himself that night. He had noted the universal rejoicing at the *Moniteur*'s announcement. To threaten force would belie the favorable position the people had attributed to him. Metternich reported thus on the emperor's indecision:

A regular panic seized him at the idea of an Italian rejection [of mediation] and the sight of the illuminations glorifying the triumph of his policy made him feel doubly the weight of the engagements he has assumed and which could throw in his lap a war in two directions. From that moment he began to hesitate and vacillate.[61]

Yet it must have been more than just the celebration of 5 July. As has been shown, he had been preoccupied with opinion all during his reign. Regular reports during the Polish and Danish crises and in the months just before the outbreak of the Austro-Prussian War had clearly informed him of the almost unanimous insistence on peace. The people and the press had both openly condemned his Auxerre speech, and he had recently made further spcial inquiries of the prefects and the mayors concerning opinion. Perhaps he had forgotten his public for a moment, but in the quiet of that wakeful night the still, small voice must have again spoken loudly in his inner ear. Especially, who were those opposing the policy of force? They were La Valette who, as minister of interior, received and analyzed the prefect reports on public opinion, and Baroche, minister of justice, who received the reports of the procureurs general, and finally Rouher, minister of state, who represented the government in the legislature and who knew the legislators' hostility toward war. They were closest to opinion, they were always the ones to whom he turned for information on opinion. Rouher, to be sure, usually had great influence with Napoleon III, but both La Valette and Baroche were of secondary importance at court. That their advice prevailed over that of the empress, Drouyn de Lhuys, and Randon must be in part explained by the force of opinion they represented. Rothan affirms that "public opinion at that advanced stage of the reign was in fact the great concern of the imperial government."[62] But a more direct acknowledgment of it came from the emperor himself in a conversation he had with the Spanish ambassador, Olózaga, on July 1870 during the crisis over the Hohenzollern candidacy. On that occasion he confessed:

It cost us a great deal to recognize the state of affairs which the battle of Sadowa created in Germany. We tolerated it, although not without regret. French public opinion was at that time very emphatic in favor of peace, and I was resolved to respect that trend of thought (ce courant).[63]

On the face of it this admission might appear to be merely Napoleon III's attempt to elude the blame for the disastrous outcome of his decision and cast it upon the French people. But in this instance there is now abundant proof that opinion did unequivocally and universally demand a peace policy during the entire four-year period between 1863 and 1866, that the emperor solicited reports on this opinion and had full knowledge of it, and finally that many neutral observers (American, English, Belgian, Spanish, and Swiss) support the emperor's own assertion that he was swayed by the opinion he had ascertained.

Napoleon III, like many responsible chiefs of state in our present-day democracies, faced a perplexing dilemma of following what he thought was his own better judgment or of yielding to the less discerning public demand. He had to choose between the exigencies of the state system and the democratic dictates of opinion. Perhaps he should have been more vigorous and courageous in educating opinion to the point where it would have understood the far-reaching implications of the diplomatic situation. His one adventure in this direction, his Auxerre speech, was certainly inadequate and ineffectual. Yet, if his final decision, made in response to the popular will, brought misfortune to France, the French people themselves must bear their share of the blame.

Public Sympathies During the War

A universal desire for peace and nonintervention did not prevent the French public from cheering their favorites as they sat on the sidelines. Indeed, among some of these spectators there was difficulty in deciding which side to take. The procureur general of Toulouse exclaimed: "I must say that nothing is more contradictory than the current of public opinion. Even those who do not wish the success of the allies, because of hatred for the ideas they represent [nationalism], come around to the hope that they will not experience a complete setback, for fear that the storm they apprehend may strike [French involvement against Austria for Italy]." His colleague in Lyons thought at the beginning of the war that "Austria excites peoples' sympathies no more than does Prussia." In Colmar this contradictory opinion of Alsacians brought contradictory reports from the prefect and the procureur general. While the prefect was saying that "the majority hope for the triumph of Italy and Prussia," the procureur general was reporting that "the majority of the people are favorable to Austria."[64]

But these evidences of contradictions or indecisions, however understandable they may seem, were not characteristic of most of France during the war period. A careful study of the procureur and prefect reports during the war shows that the French definitely took sides. Out of twenty-five reports from twenty-three districts or departments, representing almost every part of France, fifteen districts were against Prussia and only six against Austria. Since Prussia was the most prominent of the three belligerents, it might be well to analyze the attitude toward her in more detail:

24 reports mentioning Prussia
18 districts or departments represented
1 favorable (Marseilles)
15 opposed[65]
2 divided (Colmar and Moulin)

A typical report came from the procureur general in Dijon, who wrote:

The efforts of a certain part of the press, trying to influence public opinion in favor of Prussia, remained unavailing. The specious quibbles used by Prussia to disguise her ambitious plans generally irritated the sense of fair play animating the masses, and their wishes, right up to the last, were not on the side of North Germany. Italy herself, although they were interested in her current national endeavor, only found opinion disgruntled by her imprudent impatience.

The prefect of Seine-et-Oise noted that "the upper classes are almost exclusively Austrian; elsewhere there is some sentiment favorable to Italy, it can be said that there is none for Prussia." Even the Italian minister to Paris observed the general anti-Prussian sentiment. Nigra admitted: "Unfortunately the tendencies of public opinion in France .... are at this moment in favor of Austria, not in Italy but in Germany. Paris would illuminate her streets if the news came of an Austrian victory over Prussia."[66] Nigra's comment does reveal that Italy was not disliked as much as Prussia. In fact there was as much sympathy for her as for Austria. Out of twenty-three districts or departments thirteen were pro-Italian, seven were anti-Italian, and three were divided in sentiment. The old animosity toward Prussia, persisting since 1814, was merely becoming sharper and more conscious. But it was to be nothing compared with the even more intense postwar hostility.[67]

Nikolsburg and Prague

After the Saint-Cloud conference France's efforts at arranging an armistice were rather pathetic. Benedetti was ordered to contact Bismarck and William I in Bohemia and urge a lenient peace on Austria. Pressure was also brought to bear on Italy to cease hostilities. Bismarck played with Benedetti like a cat would a mouse. He tried to avoid him as much as possible, and in the end negotiated a lenient armistice directly with Austria, which gave Prussia all the credit for leniency. When Bismarck did see Benedetti, he pretended he was listening to France's advice. In Paris, however, he had Goltz dangle compensation hints before Drouyn de Lhuys and Napoleon III. But the French emperor avoided any appearance of asking for territorial compensation while the armistice negotiations were in progress, lest France's motives be impugned or her designs might be used by Bismarck as clubs over the heads of the small German states. Such caution in one way was well advised, but it also gave Bismarck the green light to proceed with plans to take Hanover, Nassau, Hesse-Cassel, and Frankfort. He wrung from Napoleon his consent to these acquisitions in return for a promise to leave Saxony intact, to have Prussia and her new confederation stay north of the Main River, and to hold a plebiscite in North Schleswig.

The preliminaries of peace signed at Nikolsburg on 26 July 1866, and the final peace terms of the Treaty of Prague of 23 August 1866 were practically the same in providing for Prussia's free hand to make a North German confederation north of the Main River, for the independence of Saxony within that confederation, for Austria's withdrawal from any German union, for Austria's relinquishment of her half-interest in Schleswig and Holstein, for a plebiscite in North

Schleswig, for the transfer of Venetia to Italy, and for the payment of about $7,000,000 as indemnity to Prussia. The lenient aspect of these terms was that the indemnity was so small and that Austria lost none of her traditional territory. Austria had always favored relinquishing her rights in Schleswig-Holstein, and she had previously transferred Venetia to France.

The sensational aspects of this peace settlement were that Prussia had doubled her power in northern Europe and completely upset the balance of power as established by the treaties of 1815. Also as a part of the enlargement of her weighted side of the balance Prussia took over the states of Hanover, Nassau, Hesse-Cassel, and Frankfort. These revolutionary transformations were of serious concern to the other powers, especially to France.

It would not be surprising, then, to find that the French people with essential unanimity denounced the outcome of the war in Germany. During the last six months of 1866 fifty procureur and prefect reports analyzed public reactions to the peace terms. These reports came from twenty-nine different districts and departments covering all of France. Twenty-eight of these areas showed definite hostility to Prussia's terms and acquisitions. The one remaining area (department of Indre-et-Loire) indicated only satisfaction that peace had been restored. The procureur report from Toulouse contained almost all the elements of opinion found in the other twenty-seven:

If the rapid and irreparable defeat of Austria [wrote the procureur general] disconcerted those who had been on her side (and they were rather numerous in our departments), the suddenness of Prussia's victory was hardly less a surprise to most of those who prophesied the best of success for her arms.

. . . . When silence had fallen over the battlefield and opinion could put its first impressions to the test of reflection and try to measure the importance of the political transformation in Germany in terms of French interests, after passing through several intermediate phases, it came forward with a general reaction, one might say a unanimous reaction [unanimous underlined with pencil in Paris] which should be noticed here and whose significance will be only imperfectly realized unless one recalls the [peaceful] tendencies evident at the beginning of the war.

. . . . The territorial expansion of Prussia, raising her in the space of a few days to the rank of a first-rate power, as a result of forceful annexations, has not only been considered an abuse of force but a menace to France. . . . . Prussia as a Protestant power is looked askance at by Catholics and Legitimists. Those whose regrets or desires are attached to parliamentary institutions do not pardon her sovereign, and especially the statesman who made her so large, their disdain for these institutions. The Republican party is no more favorable to her. Indeed she [Prussia] finds no sympathy in any fraction of the opposition. Finally the memories of the last half-century have not effaced, rather have combined, in regard to Prussia, animosities and mistrusts strongly revived in the circumstances which we have just traversed [most of this paragraph underlined and marked in the margin with pencil in Paris].[68]

No better confirmation of this reintensification of anti-Prussian feeling can be found than in the liberal papers which previously had been so sympathetic to the nationalist role they attributed to Prussia. By August the *Opinion Nationale*, *Siècle*, *Temps*, and *Presse* were regretting the great increase in Prussian power; while the semiofficial papers, such as the *Constitutionnel* and the *Patrie* were momentarily trying to reassure the public because they had to admit that Napoleon III had planned it that way by his approval of the Nikolsburg terms.[69] But Rouher himself, after noting that "public opinion . . . . is day after day directed, stirred, and led astray by the cleverness of party men," acknowledged that "the press favorable to the government cannot moderate this feeling because it dares not share in it to any degree whatsoever."[70] But share in it or not, the strong feeling was there, a feeling which did not need clever men for its creation, and a feeling which was to have strong repercussions on many important subsequent issues.

No doubt Napoleon III saw in advance the possible necessity for France to intervene in the impending Austro-Prussian war. Having still a semiauthoritarian regime, he could not avoid considerable responsibility for France's unpreparedness. Also, still having much control over the press, he was not absolved from the criticism of not having thoroughly prepared public opinion in advance for support of a countervailing intervention at the moment when he would have had Austria and her German allies to back the moderate French forces available. He bungled both his diplomacy and his public relations. The Auxerre speech was no more than an isolated clumsy effort to rally opinion at the last moment. There is no doubt, too, that his illness paralyzed his will right at the time when a strong will was needed to match that of Bismarck. But there is little evidence to show that anything the emperor might have done could have modified French public opinion appreciably, so strong and universal was it for peace and nonintervention. This much can be said, however, that he did not make the effort. Perhaps he was hampered in making such an attempt by the divergence of opinions among his most important advisors. La Valette, hostile to Drouyn de Lhuys's forceful policy, controlled the press as minister of interior. An all-powerful ruler probably needs differing opinions among his counsellors so that he can be aware of all aspects of questions. What he also must have to complement that authority is the ability to make final decisions and deliberate preparations, and the will to carry them to conclusion. These qualities Napoleon III seemed to have lost just at the most critical moment of his career.

On the other hand public opinion, if it prefers to be spontaneous and not manufactured and if it insists on being the crucial factor in decisions, then must inform itself well and be prepared to make the sacrifices to obtain its long-range desires. If it is to be respected, it too must have a sense of responsibility. To be sure, it is hard to achieve that sense in a dictatorship where the public is tempted to leave matters to its "adored" chief and where a throttled press cannot inform it properly. Yet, in the case of the Austro-Prussian War the French people had gotten what they wanted—peace and nonintervention. But, like thoughtless and pampered children who insist on eating green apples, they did not relish the consequences. Sadowa and the peace terms were as disagreeable as the stomach-ache and as bitter as the inevitable dose of castor oil, bitter especially after the momentary exhilaration of 5 July. Prussia had become bigger and more powerful and more menacing, and France by remaining the same as before had actually grown smaller and weaker. Jacques, the Frenchman, emerged from this trying experience, a poorer but a wiser man. Would his hard-bought wisdom guide him in the treacherous years ahead?

<hr>

CHAPTER IX

COMPENSATIONS AND ARMAMENTS

The Great Reversal

"In our country," Magne warned Napoleon, "where emotions hold sway over reason, opinion has a way of suddenly reversing itself, which must be anticipated."[1] Indeed, Magne was on the threshold of one of French opinion's greatest reversals, in the months of July and August of 1866. The emperor's popularity, which had declined badly during the Polish and Danish crises and the Mexican fiasco, had momentarily experienced a strong recovery during the ill-advised celebration of 5 July. Napoleon III, perhaps, was also deluding himself on that occasion because the empress had noted on the evening of 4 July that it was the last time he had had a sparkle in his eyes, and that was at "the thought of the immense effect his note, destined for the morrow's *Moniteur*, would have on the world."[2] Then came the cold light of subsequent days: the decision after the Saint-Cloud council to pursue peaceful mediation, Prussia's vast acquisitions of territory with apparent French approval. The public evidently expected momentarily another startling announcement of French territorial compensations, which, it thought, must have been arranged beforehand or at the time of the armistice negotiations. Great was its disillusionment, then, when the days and weeks passed with no such news forthcoming. Within nine days after the hysterical celebrations of 5 July, Beyens wrote: "Public opinion becomes more and more clear-cut—

not by the press, which is everywhere bought up and has no reliability whatever—but a remarkable movement of honest indignation is developing among all classes, in the army and even around the emperor: His Majesty cannot help but be struck by it."[3] And the sensitive emperor was noticing it. Cowley, after checking his sources of information, wrote home: "There is no doubt that the Emperor is seriously alarmed at the information he has received from the country. The Empress told Goltz that she looked upon the present state of things as *le commencement de la fin de la dynastie*."[4]

Whatever may have been his sources of intelligence at that moment, they were amply confirmed by subsequent reports from the procureurs general and the prefects, which indicated widespread dissatisfaction with the peaceful mediation method and the way it was managed. A few extracts here will leave no doubt on this point: (Rennes) "People have not forgotten that . . . . the emperor . . . . reserved the possibility of intervention . . . . and yet he has not budged." (Saint-Lô) "[They are saying] it would have been better to attack Prussia when she was at grips with Austria." (Rouen) "After the battle of Sadowa . . . . the most prompt and energetic measures should have been taken to put us in position to combat the formidable power emerging." (Paris) "People . . . . wondered whether it would not be to the interest of France to put an end to [Prussian] victories by armed intervention." (Dijon) "They experienced bitter disappointment . . . . when they compared the growth of Prussia beside a France with static borders." (Riom) "People had generally expected territorial changes for France . . . . and a pained feeling began to be evident when . . . . France made no demands." (Montpellier) "They had hoped for territorial concessions to France in exchange for . . . . the successful mediation of the emperor." (Toulouse) "People say we played the game badly." These reports, plus six others from Grenoble, Poitiers, Agen, Bourg, and Orleans, thus representing every major section of France, bore testimony to the violent criticism of a fickle public, which should have more properly been beating its breast in a mood of contrition and remorse.[5]

The story of the about-face of public opinion, however, is only half told, for the extent to which this reversal went can be measured by the way the universal and unanimous peace-at-any-price opinion of June turned to the other extreme of demanding war against Prussia. One could hardly believe that France was the same country in August. Magne told the emperor in the same letter of 20 July: "The country, which up to now had agitated for peace, would show itself in favor of extreme measures. It would not take long before they could be demanding war, which would be a terrible misfortune."[6] Again Magne's estimate was right in line with the mass of reports from the provinces, extracts from a few of which will confirm his impressions: (Colmar)

"I heard an industrialist say: '. . . . If Prussia forces France to go to war . . . . I would applaud it.' " (Colmar) "They would not be far from wishing to come to grip with her [Prussia]." (Grenoble) "Peaceful aspirations seem less ardent." (Chambéry) "They anticipate it [war] . . . . without regret." (Agen) "Public opinion . . . . would appear today to accept . . . . war if it would bring . . . . the Rhine frontiers." (Toulouse) "It seems today that the eventuality of a war would be accepted." (Metz) "The masses . . . . would like to have an immediate war with Prussia." (Nancy) "The masses . . . . appear to want it [war] as an opportunity to even old scores." Among those quoted are the eastern border provinces of Alsace, Lorraine, Dauphiné, and Savoy, those most likely to suffer invasion if war should come. Yet they are crying for war, and eleven other districts in the southern and central parts of France stoutly support their warlike inclinations. Only Rennes, Rouen, Orleans, and Corsica sent in reports still opposing war.[7]

This willingness, even desire, to have war, existing over so large an area of France, so different from the attitudes shown before the Crimean, Austro-Sardinian, and Austro-Prussian wars and during the Mexican, Polish, and Danish troubles, only reveals more emphatically how stirred the French people were over Prussia's conquests. All of a sudden they realized the implications of power politics and the balance of power. They had had to learn this in the school of "hard knocks," and the lesson was not to be forgotten during the rest of the period of the Second Empire.

The Frantic Quest for Compensations

There seemed to be but one way to stem this flood of war sentiments, to satisfy it by territorial concessions from Prussia. For one month after Sadowa the channels of French opinion were not at all backward about making these demands. Magne in his famous straightforward letter to the emperor also pointed out the demands for compensations: "National sentiment would be deeply wounded, let there be no doubt about it, if in the end France should obtain by her intervention only two nations attached to her flanks who had become dangerous by their exorbitantly increased power. Everybody says that greatness is a relative thing and that a country can be reduced while remaining the same when new forces increase around it."[8] Four newspapers were quick to raise the cry of territorial concessions: the *France*, *Siècle*, *Opinion Nationale*, and even the semiofficial *Patrie*. On the other hand the *Temps* and the *Journal des Débats* discouraged the idea.[9] Although this month (July) was too early to obtain much evidence of the new mood, four judicial districts and one department not too far from Paris were heard from on the subject. The procureur general in Colmar declared: "I know many people who . . . . began to recognize that it would be good to retake the Bavarian Palatinate and who today would be angry if France did not recover her Rhine provinces." The prefect in Colmar confirmed his observations: "They are coming around to the idea that Prussia cannot increase in size without ceding the Rhine frontiers to France." "I need not add," wrote the procureur general in Lyons, "that compensations, even modest ones, would flatter national amour-propre." It was the same insistent story from Douai, Nancy, and Tours.[10]

And during this month of mediation efforts the emperor's soul was in torment. He had made the fatal decision to pursue the peaceful mediation policy against his own inclinations. Italy was balking at making an armistice, and Prussia was holding out until Italy would comply. France, he felt, could not put forward compensation demands until she could set aside her mediatory role, and he sensed that that eventual day would be too late to obtain satisfaction. By that time Prussia, freed from the threat of her Austrian and South German enemies, could face France alone with a firmer refusal of all concessions. His only hope rested on Bismarck's good will, and he already knew the Prussian statesman too well to expect any voluntary sacrifices on his part. In the meantime there were coming in to him the reports of the reversal of opinion. They were already blaming him for his peaceful mediation policy, they were crying for war instead of peace, they were demanding fulsome compensations. Now the sparkle had gone from his eyes, and his old sickness returned to paralyze his thought and will. The correspondence of Metternich, the Austrian ambassador, who saw Napoleon III every few days in this period, make almost a continuous log book of the course of the emperor's physical and moral decline. On 7 July he wrote: "Never, since I have known the emperor, have I seen him in such a state of complete prostration." On 26 July the empress, returning from a five-day trip in the provinces, confided to Metternich: "On my return I found the emperor weaker than ever and completely at the mercy of the one he has made first minister [Rouher], who is the cause of our moral decline and who, if we let him go on, will have us dethroned. I had come back indignant at what I had learned en route, so much more indignant because I had witnessed the detestable effect on the public and the army caused by the incredible attitude of the government. . . . . He [the emperor] cannot walk any more, nor sleep, nor hardly eat." Metternich added his own comments to this account: "He is very pale, very wan, with the appearance of a man whose will power has been forced to succumb to a general exhaustion." The causes, according to the Austrian ambassador, were the politics and events of the day. The emperor was going to leave on Saturday (28 July) for a long rest at Vichy until 14 August.[11]

Thus it was while he was at Vichy that the armistice was made and France's mediation ended. Now France could begin to look out for her own interests and request compensations. Drouyn de Lhuys was particularly anxious about this because, although overruled on the policy of forceful intervention, he wanted to see what could be salvaged from Rouher's peaceful mediation policy as soon as possible. The empress was fully in accord; indeed she insisted on extreme demands including the demilitarization of Luxemburg and the ceding of Rhine territory up to and including Mainz because, she thought, while you are asking, you might as well go the whole way. You have a better chance at bargaining. The emperor, prostrate with pain, was persuaded to approve such instructions to Benedetti in Berlin. Thus on 29 July the instructions went to Benedetti; and the very first sentence stressed public opinion: "In the state of opinion, the acquisitions planned by Prussia, without safeguards for France, would lead to grave and inevitable difficulties for France."[12]

In Benedetti's interview with Bismarck on 5 August the latter refused to consider the transfer of any Germans to France because it would cause such a violent storm in German opinion. Benedetti replied by referring to French public opinion: "For myself, I could not advise my government not to take into consideration at all the feeling which is appearing in all classes of our population and of alienating thus their devotion; I could not think of a more serious mistake, and you yourself [Bismarck] must not want it to be committed."[13]

In the end this attempt to obtain compensations from Prussia failed. But what was worse, Bismarck saw to it that the French public should know about it. Although he had asked Benedetti to keep the negotiations secret, he himself had them revealed to the Berlin correspondent of the *Siècle,* whose report was published in Paris on 10 August. This not only aroused French opinion but also antagonized Russia, who was trying to have a European congress and would resent France's lone-wolf policy, and frightened the South German states into an alliance with Prussia when they saw France asking for their own territory west of the Rhine.[14]

This publicity not only disturbed French public opinion more than ever, but it made impossible the continuation of this particular negotiation. It also spelled the end of Drouyn de Lhuys's tenure of the foreign ministry. He remained for another two weeks, attending to routine matters; but the emperor was already employing Rouher in the more important negotiations with Prussia. It was one of those ironies of history that Drouyn de Lhuys was failing to salvage the situation brought about by the emperor's having chosen Rouher's policy on 6 July and that he was being set aside in favor of Rouher, the initiator of the unsuccessful policy. At least now there would be more unanimity in the government, and Rouher would have the responsibility for making his own policy work.

The new team began to function at once, upon the return of the emperor from Vichy. Probably on the evening of 15 August the emperor and Rouher had "a long conference" which established "on all points our common views." An unsigned, undated note found among the emperor's papers probably indicated some of the views they discussed. France would no longer demand German territory as a necessity; her new position could be based firmly on the rights of nationality; French acquisition of Luxemburg and Belgium would be entirely in line with the orientation toward nationalism. "It is well not to ignore," one passage of this note ran, "that the recent diplomatic incidents, as well as the present dispositions of public opinion in France, should strengthen them [William and Bismarck] in the belief that we have not renounced our demands for the Rhine frontier." France should stress Belgium rather than the Rhine to reassure Prussia.[15] That the present mood of public opinion was ugly is confirmed by Cowley on that same day: "There cannot be two opinions as to the state of the public mind as well as of the sentiments of the Army. If Prussia does not make some sort of concession, the Emperor will find it difficult to keep the one and the other in order."[16]

Therefore at the conclusion of the long conference Rouher, very secretly and without the knowledge of Drouyn de Lhuys, opened negotiations through Benedetti for a treaty of alliance with Prussia, providing for the immediate French acquisition of Luxemburg and the eventual seizure of Belgium. France and Prussia were to support each other as allies in any war resulting from these changes.[17] Bismarck suggested a modification that would give Prussia the right to include the South German states in the North German Confederation in return for France's eventual annexation of Belgium.[18] Rouher had no objection, but he wanted to have a later separate treaty on Luxemburg for publication, keeping the terms on Belgium secret. "This combination," he added, "conciliates everybody." "It eases public opinion in France by obtaining an immediate satisfaction and the resulting orientation of opinion toward Belgium."[19]

Meanwhile Benedetti took a vacation at Carlsbad while Bismarck was supposed to be persuading William to accept the alliance treaty, and Napoleon III accepted Drouyn de Lhuys's resignation and published the acceptance on 2 September. This change, it was hoped, would facilitate the Prussian alliance because it was known that Drouyn de Lhuys was and had been anti-Prussian and more apprehensive of the nationalistic threats to the balance of power. Moustier was to succeed Drouyn de Lhuys, but since it would take him some time to arrange his affairs in Constantinople, La Valette, the minister of interior, was also to be minister of foreign affairs ad interim.

The La Valette Circular

But progress was slowing down on the alliance negotiations, and a delay would no doubt intervene before the good news of the acquisition of Luxemburg would ease the tension of impatient public opinion. "For my part," La Valette telegraphed to Moustier on the 3rd, "I regret so much the more that you cannot arrive before the 20th because there will probably have to be a circular made and you would be much better suited than I to do it."[20] The circular would not only explain the new policy after Drouyn de Lhuys' retirement, but it would, it was hoped, calm opinion and gain its support for the new type of approach. That opinion was still waiting hungrily for news of some compensations was evident enough. The emperor told the Duke of Leuchtenberg that "he could not disguise from himself that public opinion in France was very much excited, that his position had therefore become very difficult."[21] To Goltz he said much the same thing:

Public opinion in France was uneasy over the aggrandizement of Prussia. He had the intention to publish a circular to be sent to all French agents, which would counteract these fears through a statement that a strong Prussia was no dangerous neighbor for France but a welcome ally. However, before Your Majesty [William I] has signed the proposed secret treaty, he could not establish such a program for French foreign policy. On the other hand it would be difficult, if not dangerous, for him to remain silent any longer. The country demanded of his regime a statement on its attitude toward the changes which had taken place in Germany. Any further hesitation would arouse passions.[22]

The circular had been on Napoleon III's mind for some time, perhaps since the middle of August when it was clear that Drouyn de Lhuys would have to go. Rouher was its main author, writing it in consultation with the emperor and Michel Chevalier.[23] Moustier's approval was given from a distance, but the professional diplomatic staff of the ministry of foreign affairs knew little if anything about it. La Valette merely lent his signature to the document and, it is said, issued it from his interior ministry. The final text, then, consisted of Napoleon's ideas and Rouher's composition, with La Valette's signature at the end.[24]

Not only was a great deal of thought given to its composition, but much effort was expended to prepare the public through the press during the weeks preceding the publication. Ideas that France was the natural champion of national causes and that the friendship or alliance of France and the new Germany was the inescapable basis of European alignments were stressed. Bigelow, the American minister, in his first mention of the circular added, ". . . . for which the public press has been trying to prepare the popular mind for more than a week past."[25]

Finally on 17 September 1866[26] the circular appeared on the front page of the *Moniteur* and represented a full-dress and direct attempt by the government to stem the tide of rising criticism. After describing briefly the recent changes in Europe, it came straightway to the attitude of French opinion, probably for the benefit of the Prussians, who were deliberating on the treaty proposals concerning Luxemburg and Belgium.

> Public opinion in France is aroused. It drifts, uncertain, between the joy of seeing the treaties of 1815 destroyed and the fear that the power of Prussia may not take on excessive proportions, between the desire to maintain peace and the hope of obtaining territorial aggrandizements by war.

This frank appraisal, it has already been shown, was very close to the truth.

Then the text went on to show how after 1815 France was surrounded and isolated by the Holy Alliance, including the Germanic Confederation and a buffer zone of armed small states. For a long time France had to face "the coalition of the three Courts of the North"—Prussia, Austria, and Russia.

Here the circular passed to the more reassuring picture of the present situation and tried to persuade the doubting public that the changes in Germany and Europe were all to the good.

> The coalition of the three Courts of the North is broken. The new principle prevailing in Europe is the freedom of alliances. All the great powers have handed back to each other the plenitude of their independence, the regular development of their own destinies.
>
> The enlarged Prussia, henceforth free of all ties [solidarité], assures the independence of Germany. France should take no umbrage at this. Proud of her own admirable unity, of her indestructible nationality, she cannot combat nor regret the work of assimilation just accomplished, nor subordinate to jealous sentiments the principles of nationality which she represents and professes in regard to peoples. The national sentiment of Germany once satisfied, her uneasiness is dissipated, her animosities are extinguished. By imitating France, she takes a step toward and not away from us.

To embellish this comforting picture, the circular went on to point out that Italy was now united and free with the help of France, the "interests of the Papal Throne" were guaranteed by the September Convention, the growing small navies of the Baltic were re-enforcing the principle of the freedom of the seas, and finally Austria, no longer entangled in Italian and German affairs, could look more freely toward the East.

> By what strange reaction of the past on the future [the circular then asks] would public opinion then see not allies but enemies of France in these nations liberated from a past hostile to us, called to a new life, directed by principles that are our own, animated by those sentiments of progress forming the peaceful bond between modern societies?

At this point the writers of the circular become statistical, perhaps with the aid of Chevalier. France and Algeria had together more than forty million inhabitants; the new North German Confederation, twenty-nine million; the Confederation of South Germany, eight; Austria, thirty-five; Italy, twenty-six; Spain, eighteen. "What is there to worry about in this distribution of European forces?"

But what about the great Russian empire, which up to this point had not yet been mentioned? Here the circular tried to raise the eyes of the public to a higher horizon, to a broader outlook. This would take their minds off the smaller and more immediate threats. In doing this, the authors also elevated themselves into a realm of inspired prophesy which bridged with uncanny prescience eighty years to 1946 and gave their state paper in retrospect the aura of a divine oracle.

An irresistible force, regrettable as it may be, is impelling peoples to unite into great agglomerations by causing secondary states to disappear. This tendency comes from the desire to insure more efficacious guarantees to wider [*généraux*] interests. Perhaps it is inspired by a sort of providential foreknowledge of the destinies of the world. While the ancient peoples of the continent, in their restricted territories, are increasing only slowly, Russia and the United States of America may each by another century have a hundred million men." Although the growth of these two great empires may not be for us a matter of concern—on the contrary we applaud their generous efforts to help oppressed races—it is to the provident interest of the European center not to be split up into so many different states without strength or public spirit.

Here then was France's role for the future: to encourage greater agglomerations of national peoples in the European center, perhaps even the gathering of some small secondary states to herself, in order to form a large block between Russia and the United States.

For a moment the circular turns to a vigorous defense of France's policy of peaceful mediation.

If these considerations are just and true, the emperor was right in accepting that not inglorious role of mediator, to halt useless and grievous bloodshed, to moderate the victor by his friendly intervention, to attenuate the consequences of reverses, to persist against so many obstacles in re-establishing peace. Indeed, he would have betrayed his high responsibility if, violating his promised and proclaimed neutrality, he had rushed without warning into all the hazards of a great war, of one of those wars which re-evoke hatred between races and in which whole nations are hurled at each other.

But soon the text returns to the question of territorial compensations for France, slyly hinted at in an earlier passage. The policy is somewhat reminiscent of that of Maria Theresa in the eighteenth century who "wept but kept on taking."

But the imperial government has for a long time been applying its principles concerning territorial expansion. It recognizes, and has recognized annexations commanded by absolute necessity, reuniting to our country people having the same customs, the same national spirit as ours, and it asked for the re-establishment of our natural frontiers by the free consent of Savoy and the County of Nice. France can want only those territorial enlargements which would not alter her powerful cohesion. . . . .

Everybody who had been waiting and hoping for so long, who had heard all the rumors and had made some speculations of his own, saw immediately through this thin veil of suggestion that the government would not reject Luxemburg, Belgium, and some of Switzerland as a part of this national assimilation movement in Europe, provided a plebiscite could be managed to give the transactions the appearance of voluntary union.

Then the circular switched suddenly from calm optimism to one of restrained alarm and the need for military reform. "The results of the last war . . . . indicate that we need to improve without further delay our military organization for the defense of our territory. The nation will not fail to perform this duty, which cannot be taken as a threat to anyone." The emperor and most of his advisors knew that France's military establishment urgently needed enlarging and improving. They did not want all these reassurances to lull the public to sleep on the defense problem.

The weakest part of the circular came at the end where it did violence to even the lowest grade of common sense by returning to the optimistic theme for the last time: "As to France, in whatever direction she turns her gaze, she sees nothing that will impede her progress or trouble her prosperity." It would be a very gullible public indeed which could swallow the last paragraph.[28]

The readers had no sooner read and digested the circular than they began to look around to see what the rest of the country thought about it. The first impression of O'Meagher, the *Times* correspondent, was that "nearly all this evening's [17 September] journals express approval."[29] But a survey of the Paris papers in the next few days showed that six were generally favorable and six others mainly critical. Among the six favorable journals were the three semiofficial papers, the *Constitutionnel*, the *Patrie*, and the *Pays*, which would naturally fall into line, and the liberal or radical sheets, the *Journal des Débats*, the *Liberté*, and the *Temps*. The critical papers were the *Opinion Nationale*, the *Siècle*, the *Gazette de France*, the *Union*, the *Avenir National*, and the *France Politique*. The press, therefore, was almost evenly divided.[30] The Belgian chargé thought the public showed satisfaction, but it could not be sure the rosy aspects would last. Cowley also noted a satisfactory reception but sensed that many would object to the pacific policy contained therein. Neither diplomat believed, then, that the circular had been greeted with unqualified approbation.[31]

Within two weeks the procureur and prefect reports began to pour in to give the reaction in the provinces. How anxious the government was to study these returns is attested by the fact that the procureur reports of October 1866 were literally streaked with penciled underlinings and marginal pencilings made in the feverish offices of the ministry of justice. And at a first superficial glance the government people might have felt well satisfied. Out of the thirty-six reports discussing the circular, twenty-nine judicial districts and departments were represented: 16 of these were favorable, 9 critical, and 4 divided, a relatively satisfactory result.

But the first superficial tally must be seriously reconsidered in the light of several other circumstances. In the first place the people of the provinces had been high-pressured by a servile press *after* the publication of the circular as had Parisians *before* its publication. The government evidently was taking no chances on leaving opinion to fate. It already had regular offices set up to write government-inspired syndicated articles for the controlled press of the provinces. These offices had prepared such an article in advance strongly supporting the La Valette Circular, and now hastily distributed lithographed copies of it to all parts of the country. Suddenly toward the end of the week this syndicated article appeared almost simultaneously in innumerable provincial papers. What is amusing about the syndicated system is the fact that this particular article was signed by Alph. Malteste in the *Journal de Chartres*, by C. Lenormand in the *Echo de la Mayenne*, by Mounier in the *Union Bretonne*, by Dufau in the *Messager de la Sarthe*, and by J. Moreau in the *Journal d'Alençon*, etc. etc. The *Journal d'Indre-et-Loire* began the article rather artlessly with the direct and truthful statement—"They write to us from Paris . . . ."— leaving the puzzled reader wondering just whose editorial opinion it was. If newspapers influence opinion, as they no doubt do in some cases, then those gratifying returns were already loaded.[32]

But La Valette's ministry of interior not only controlled and influenced the press, it had direct authority over the prefects in the departments. It may not be mere coincidence that the reports of the politically-minded prefects, subservient to La Valette, had a preponderance of favorable analyses. If all the prefects had had the courage of some of their more frank colleagues, the combined score of procureurs and prefects might have been more adverse than favorable to the circular.

Then, too, on further examination of all the penciled passages it would also be found that ten of the sixteen favorable procureur and prefect reports acknowledged that, in spite of the favorable reactions, the people generally still hated Prussia and continued willy-nilly to demand territorial compensations. If these ten were counted, as well they might, as basically unfavorable in their over-all attitudes, then the combined score in this case would be at least: 6 favorable, 19 critical, and 4 divided.

While, from all these qualifying circumstances, it would be difficult to be sure of the exact provincial reactions, one does gain the impression that the circular was not a success, either in Paris or in the provinces.[33]

Finally it is interesting to see how much the public was affected by the more imaginative perspective of the future bracketing of Europe between Russia and the United States. Only three of the newspapers, the *Journal des Débats*, the *Temps*, and the *Liberté*, seemed intrigued by the idea, and they concurred.[34] Nor in the provinces did the new global possibilities of power alignments strike much fire. Only two procureur reports seem to reflect much attention to that subject. The generally unfavorable reports from Nancy added that, as far as the enlightened classes were concerned, "the symptoms of *rapproche-*

ment, appearing every day between Russia and the United States, have also given added emphasis to the considerations developed in that document"; while the slightly more favorable report from Rouen contained these remarks:

> To complete this picture of the movements of opinion, I must bring to your attention a new group [he does not say how large] which is especially interested in the alliance of Russia and the United States. They would prefer to have old rivalries and border disputes forgotten and to have France, England, Germany, and Italy closely bound to present a united front against the expansionist aims of Russia.[35]

This new idea of an alliance with England, coming from Anglophobe Rouen, is perhaps a significant footnote to the general confusion of thought during the period of the great reversal of opinion.

The Luxemburg Question

A confirmation of the fact that the La Valette Circular could not have made a very favorable impression on opinion is found in the procureur reports of January 1867 where prevailing opinion in eleven important districts, in most parts of France, was still not reconciled to the unification of Germany and was still demanding compensations to counterbalance Prussia's new power.[36] The procureur general in Dijon wrote:

> The [La Valette] circular . . . . has not consoled them and has been without influence on public opinion, which persists in believing that the treaties of 1815 have, it is true, persisted, but to the detriment and not to the advantage of France.
>
> Criticism of the acts of the government is more bitter and intense, and I would lack sincerity if I did not say that the faith in the star and good luck of the emperor has weakened. The prestige which the sovereign formerly exercised has diminished, and we are far from the days of self-satisfied pride following the Italian campaigns and the annexation of the Savoy provinces and the county of Nice.

A similar report from Metz warned: "Nor should I conceal from Your Excellency that the irritation against Prussia is still very intense in my district and that the feeling of the masses is that France must take her revenge." The other area of Lorraine, around Nancy, revealed the same opinion: "It was hoped that she [Prussia] would hasten to consent to the rectification of our [frontiers] and that we would obtain in the north what we had gotten in the south after the Italian war. Nothing of the sort has happened, and I consider this sad disappointment as one of the most important causes of irritation." In two later April reports the regions of Caen and Rennes showed the same irreconcilability: "The broad conception of agglomeration and confederation," wrote the procureur general in Caen, "is not found among us." The report from Rennes showed that the effect of the La Valette Circular had been spoiled by subsequent Prussian statements.[37]

Pietri, the prefect of police in Paris, also wrote the emperor, showing public dissatisfaction with his policy and with his policy-makers:

Wherever we look, we encounter sincere disquiet or distrust inspired by strong hostility. The active part of society accentuates more than ever its systematic and radical opposition. It openly approves party men, it shows agreement with the press attacks, it goes around repeating that the empire has suffered a blow in its prestige abroad, in the very guarantees that it had given to the social order. The masses are not yet won over to this disaffection; but is it not to be feared that, impressionable and easily swayed, they may not follow at a given moment the direction of the upper classes and may not give their concurrence to some revolutionary endeavor? They are asking what does the emperor want, what action is he taking, what is the plan being followed by his government? They complain that they see the ideas of the chief of state paralyzed by intermediaries as they pass from conception to realization. The calmness in which the ministers live reduces the good to be gotten from their abilities. The reassurance attached to the security of their positions extinguishes their spirit of initiative, their industriousness in the direction of ther departments.[38]

The emperor knew, then, from one of his most loyal supporters, that opinion was still running strongly against him, and from the penciled underlinings on the procureur reports of this period we know that his justice ministry was scrutinizing closely these hostile sentiments all over France. Vautier tells us that "several of these [procureur] reports were sent over to the minister of foreign affairs and other warnings coming in from Alsace were sent directly to the emperor."[39]

This ominous mood stirred the government to renewed activity on the question of completing at least the proposed Luxemburg treaty. Parliament was soon to meet, and the going there would no doubt be rough unless the government had something to offer by that time. Later in exile Napoleon III reminisced: "It seemed to me that the annexation to France of the Grand Duchy of Luxemburg would soothe the growing agitation in our country and lead the way to a real conciliation [with Prussia]. I knew that the Duchy was quite willing to become French, and thus aid in putting an end to the general uneasiness then prevailing."[40] Rouher, the minister of state, who had to bear the brunt of parliamentary debate, was particularly concerned. Bismarck had not made the situation much easier when he kept absolutely silent and never followed up the French alliance proposals of late August.

Rouher, himself, with no objection from Moustier, broached the question to Goltz. He did not want to seem to be putting on pressure, but he wanted to hear something before the legislature met.[41] Moustier also sent Benedetti instructions to reopen negotiations. First, Moustier complained of Bismarck's silence:

Certainly M. de Bismarck is free to reject our alliance, after having offered us his, or to keep Luxemburg after having promised it to us. But to do all that without giving us any reason for it, without explaining [colorer] it in any way—a procedure which must surprise us to say the least—is a really strange thing, upsetting every diplomatic usage and calculation.

But Moustier left no doubt about his reasons for reopening negotiations:

Anyway, we must, as I said, give reply soon to the legitimate preoccupation of the country and to the great legislative bodies. This is such an imposing requirement that it practically makes such a step necessary, which the emperor wants you to undertake without delay.[42]

But this renewal of negotiations went no further than the earlier conversations. Bismarck pleaded the difficulty of convincing the king, particularly on the question of withdrawing the Prussian garrison. The king would want to know how it would affect the defense of Prussia. Still more time was spent on getting a military evaluation from Moltke, who finally advised against withdrawing the garrison. Further time was dragged out on the questions of dismantling the fortresses, of an alliance or neutrality treaty, of a fabricated local demonstration in favor of France, of a proposed direct negotiation with the King of the Netherlands with Prussia looking on benevolently. But nothing was concluded. In the meantime a marriage was maneuvered between a younger son of the King of the Belgians with Marie of Hohenzollern, princess of the Hohenzollern-Sigmaringen family, closely related to the Prussian ruler. This put another obstacle in the way of France's acquiring Belgium.

Finally the French, after an approach from the King of the Netherlands, began negotiations with him in February 1867 for the purchase of his rights to Luxemburg, this supposedly with the acquiescence of Bismarck. But by this time the French legislative houses had met. The dreaded debates would begin, and Rouher would not yet have Luxemburg to present as the prize to satisfy public and legislative opinion.

Before the meeting of the legislature Napoleon III was forced to mollify the rising discontent in the country by introducing some liberal parliamentary reforms. By a decree of 19 January 1867 he substituted for the legislative address to the emperor the right of the legislature to interpellate the ministers; he also provided that all ministers, and not just the ministers of state, should defend their policies in the two houses and reply to interpellations. While these half-measures approached the parliamentary system, they did not institute parliamentary responsibility. The emperor still appointed, retained, or dismissed his ministers at his own pleasure. A *senatus-consultum* of 14 March 1867 gave the senate a suspensive veto on all legislation in addition to its former power to declare laws unconstitutional.

The dreaded session was opened by a speech from the throne in which the emperor in person repeated what La Valette had issued as a circular. He justified Germany's unification on the basis of the inevitable consolidation of peoples along national lines, basing these views on the Saint Helena ideas of Napoleon I. France, a national entity, could not deny the same trend to other national groups. As to the war and the peace in 1866, he put the responsibility partly on public opinion for the policy followed:

We watched with impartiality the fight going on on the other side of the Rhine. Faced with this conflict, the country resolutely indicated its desire to stay out; not only did I defer to this wish, but I did everything in my power to hasten the conclusion of peace. I did not arm an additional soldier; I did not have a single regiment moved forward, and yet the voice of France was sufficient to stop the victor.[43]

The emperor's embarrassment over the developments of the past year and the rising criticism was evident in his manner of speaking.

For the first time [wrote Beyens] . . . . the emperor read poorly, frequently hesitating and repeating words. Besides he did not make pauses in his reading, as if he understood that you could not expect a quick expression of opinion from listeners disconcerted by recent events and anxious about new measures.[44]

There was no doubt about the cool reception his remarks on Germany received from the legislators: (Beyens) "For the first time, the emperor's speech was not the object of continuous manifestations." (Goltz) "The reception of the entire speech had been icy." (Vaillant) "His Majesty's speech is applauded very little." (Ollivier) "The emperor complained about the cool reception of the day before."[45] However, there was little expression of provincial opinion specifically on the imperial speech, mainly because Rouher's speech caused so much more of a sensation a little later.

The anticipated legislative attack, in the absence of any announcement of the annexation of Luxemburg, came in a devastating speech by Thiers. Again, as on previous occasions, he denounced the principle of national unification and affirmed as the only basis of international relations the principle of the balance of power. With this as a premise he denounced the government's acquiescence in the Prussian formation of a strong North German Confederation to which might be easily attached a militarily strengthened South German Confederation.

This lamentable situation [he cried] was the work of the government. It would have only had to utter one word to stop the war; the chamber asked it to do it; it did not do it; it hesitated as between all [possible] policies, hoping that a favorable turn of events would emerge from the unknown; it was the greatness of Prussia which emerged.

Forgetting that on 3 May 1866 he had advised the government, if Prussia disregarded a French warning, not to say a word but to remain silent, he advised now that Prussia be told not to go any further. The French army, the first in Europe, would be the force to command respect. But then he continued that this policy could succeed by peace, by all the powers joining with France to impose a balance of power on Prussia. In his final appeal to adopt this policy he closed with the famous words: "They have made every mistake that there is to be made."[46]

On the following day, 16 March 1867, the anticipated reply of

Rouher was delivered. He met the challenge by declaring that "not one mistake has been made." France could not have discouraged Italy from allying with Prussia, because France had no other way of assuring the acquisition of Venetia. Austria had refused to negotiate on the question and had rejected the congress. He tried to show that Germany was weaker than before. Up to 1866 all Germany was united, a hundred million people, in a Germanic Confederation; now they were "divided into three segments": the North German Confederation with twenty-two million, South Germany with fifteen, and Austria with thirty-three. Thiers had said France had no allies. "She has more than that, she has universal good-will. Nowhere has she any ill-feeling towards her, any hostile interests. . . . . It matters little whether France grows in width so long as she grows in stature."[47]

The disappointment in the legislature and in the country can well be imagined. Nothing on compensations, nothing on Luxemburg; not even any indication that France was trying to obtain compensations. But a greater chagrin was to come a few days later. Rouher with his warm air of self-assurance had inflated a balloon labeled "The Three Segments." Bismarck proceeded to burst the balloon by announcing publicly the existence of an offensive-defensive alliance between North and South Germany, both organized now on the Prussian military system. If Napoleon's hand had trembled as he spoke, if Rouher had put on a bold front to hide his embarrassments, now the government's position was thoroughly deflated.[48] The Prussian ambassador acknowledged: "The publication of our defensive-offensive alliance with Bavaria and Baden has had a shattering effect on public opinion here. . . . . The people openly blame the political impotence of the emperor." A few months later Goltz gave additional evidence of this feeling:

> Minister of State Rouher . . . . is attacked by the reactionary majority almost as strongly as by the revolutionary minority. . . . . On all sides one hears that his policy of the three segments has received a definite contradiction as a result of the most recent successes of Prussian politics, thus making the program enunciated by the La Valette Circular lose all basis.[49]

Goltz's impressions were confirmed by the procureur and prefect reports. Bismarck's alliance announcement came so soon after the speech that the reports seem to combine the reaction to Rouher's speech and Bismarck's announcement. Twenty-two reports mentioned one or the other or both, representing sixteen districts and departments in almost every section of France. Every report showed hostility toward either Rouher's speech or the German alliances. For example: (Rennes) "Let's admit it frankly, the country does not appear sufficiently convinced that we have lost nothing of its security and greatness during the last year." (Nancy) "The discussions in the legislative body have not appeased public feeling." The same angry reactions were reported from Rouen, Orleans, Bar-le-Duc, Metz, Colmar, Besançon, Dijon, Moulins, Lyons, Chambéry, Toulouse, Agen, Bordeaux, and Pau.[50]

Meanwhile the secret negotiations with the King of the Netherlands, who was also Grand Duke of Luxemburg, were progressing. A treaty of purchase and transfer had finally been drawn up on France's assurance that Prussia was agreeable to the idea. Yet, the grand duke was hesitant without some outward sign from Bismarck. After all, Prussia had garrison troops in Luxemburg, her own territory bordered on the whole east side of the Netherlands, she had a dispute with the Netherlands over Limburg, and ominous whispers of Prussian opposition to the deal began to reach the king-grand duke. It was at the moment of hesitation that Bismarck struck another blow at France, who was already down at least to the count of five. He had his friend Bennigsen interpellate him in the new Reichstag on 1 April. In reply, while couching his words in a mild tone of courtesy, he let it be known that Prussia would not favor any such arrangement without the approval of the powers, the German states, and the German people. This April-Fool prank ruined the treaty; the king-grand duke immediately refused to sign.

The French government had been so sure of the treaty that it had let rumors leak out, and now Bismarck's statement brought the whole affair into the open. Napoleon told Cowley that "the susceptibility of the nation, however, had been excited by the course which events had taken, and therein lay the danger."[51] Consequently the government had to clarify its position before France and Europe in the light of the revelations by putting as good a face as possible on the matter. Moustier declared before the legislative chambers:

The uncertain position of Limburg and Luxemburg led to a communication from the cabinet of The Hague to the French government. The two sovereigns, then, were called upon to exchange views on the possession of Luxemburg.

But these conversations had not yet taken on any official character when consulted by the King of the Netherlands as to its attitude, the cabinet of Berlin invoked the stipulations of the treaty of 1839.

Faithful to the principles which have constantly directed our policy, we have never considered the possibility of this acquisition of territory except under three conditions: the free consent of the Grand Duke of Luxemburg,—the loyal examination of the interests of the great powers,—the wishes of the people as manifested by universal suffrage.

We are therefore disposed to examine, in concert with the other cabinets of Europe, the clauses of the treaty of 1839. We will bring to this examination the most complete spirit of conciliation, and we firmly believe that the peace of Europe cannot be troubled by this incident.[52]

The French government was now in a difficult spot. It was evident that its compensation plans had again been blocked by Prussia, this time concerning even non-German territory. Some face-saving device was necessary or its stock would be the lowest it had ever been. Therefore Moustier demanded at least the withdrawal of the Prussian garrison from the grand duchy. The powers sensed that France would

be forced to go to war unless this modicum of satisfaction was forthcoming. Consequently England invited the powers to a London
conference (28 April to 7 May 1867); and Prussia, after putting on
a show of resistance, agreed to withdraw her garrison if Luxemburg
was neutralized in somewhat the same way as Switzerland and Belgium.
Thus ended the London Conference and France's last hopes of territorial compensations.

French opinion appeared to be pleased with the results of the
London Conference. No doubt there was an element of desire to put
a good face upon a bad matter in the response. In fact in all the
twenty-nine reports on the Luxemburg question from April 1867 to
January 1868 there had been only three (Rennes, Rouen, and Versailles) which had specifically demanded annexation. Most of them
had been as evasive on just what they wanted in Luxemburg as the
government had been, although they all indicated they wanted something. Indeed, a few had specifically limited their desires to the
withdrawal of the Prussian garrison (Meuse) or neutralization (Colmar). Most of them had preferred a peaceful solution. Therefore,
the appearance of approval is not surprising. Out of thirty-two reports
mentioning the London Treaty, representing twenty-seven districts
or departments, nineteen of these subdivisions seemed favorable, five
opposed, and three divided in sentiment. "The peaceful outcome of
the London Conference," wrote the procureur general in Metz, "un-
hoped-for up to the last minute has been welcomed with satisfaction,
without enthusiasm however, for they generally see in it only a
temporary solution." This is typical of the grudging approval given
it. Some, however, were openly critical like those in the Agen district
whose procureur general wrote:

   The peace [at London] so gravely compromised has been signed. . . . . Peace
is on their [the people's] lips, but war is in their hearts. . . . . Our national pride
. . . . evidently could not accept as sufficient satisfactions the evacuation and neutralization of Luxemburg.[53]

This top-heavy majority in all parts of France in favor of the
London settlement seems also confirmed by the Paris press where
nine papers,[54] government and opposition alike, favored the agreement
and only two[55] opposed it.[56]

When one considers the widespread demand for territorial
compensations existing in France before the London Conference,
one has difficulty in taking the above representation of opinion as
accurate. An explosion of hostile opinion could well have been anticipated when France was seen to be still left empty-handed. A suspicion
arises that French pride may have inclined those expressing opinion
to show favor for the withdrawal of the Prussian garrison as a victory
while in the secret of their hearts, as with the people of Agen, they
were still deeply disappointed and dissatisfied. Also all during 1867
sentiment was wholeheartedly against war as a means of getting com-

pensations from Prussia. The favorable reaction may have reflected merely a feeling of relief that peace had been maintained by the London Conference.[57]

O'Meagher of the *Times*, on the other hand, said that the legislative houses received the news in silence.[58] Chaudordy, speaking to Hansen, also exclaimed in despair: "For France the game is lost, and lost for a long time. The patched-up agreement on the Luxemburg affair has pleased no one. It is for France what the Gastein Convention was for Germany."[59] If there is any truth in these isolated observations, confirmation will have to be sought where the sampling will be more extensive and representative. And there are three strong indications that opinion seemed favorable to the London agreement because it brought peace and not because the French people were satisfied with its terms. In the first place twenty-two judicial districts and departments showed unanimity during the rest of the year in still being hostile to Prussia. There were no reports indicating an easing of the tension. Genuine satisfaction with the terms should have brought more Franco-Prussian good feeling. Furthermore, twenty-seven districts and departments evinced a continued belief that a war with Prussia was inevitable. No report indicated a contrary optimism. If Frenchmen were satisfied with the Luxemburg settlement, they could not have persisted in seeing the necessity for a war. A third indication of basic dissatisfaction was the fact that ten out of twelve reports (June to December 1867) still faithfully reported general sentiment to be in opposition to the emperor's foreign policy. If the Luxemburg arrangement had finally met the public's major demands, there should have been a widespread return to the support of the government. The only conclusion that can be reached is that the country did not openly complain about the London Treaty because it would intensify the conviction abroad that France had been outplayed again and also because the people were relieved that war had been avoided. But that they still disliked the settlement and felt that it did not solve the long-range problem of balance of power is brought to light by their persisting hatred of Prussia, their continued conviction that war was inevitable, and their unrelieved criticism of the emperor and his government.[60]

Aux Armes, Citoyens! Formez Vos Bataillons![61]

When a given arrangement of the balance of power in the state system has been disrupted, there are several ways by which a state adversely affected may try to preserve its relative weight. One is by obtaining by common consent territorial compensations which will increase the dissatisfied state's population, resources, and strategic frontiers sufficiently to give it again a feeling of relative security. Such an assurance France had received in the annexation of Savoy and Nice when the small Italian states had become united into the large Italian kingdom on France's southeast border. In 1866 and 1867 France had tried to obtain the same compensatory assurances from Prussia, to no avail.

Another more distasteful and disturbing method of re-establishing the balance is for the dissatisfied state to increase the size of its trained army to offset the new power on its borders. Having failed to obtain any territorial compensation from Prussia, France now had to turn to this other alternative. The very fact that Prussia had a larger, better-organized, better-trained fighting machine equipped with new factory-made weapons, such as the needle gun, would have directed France's attention to her army in any case. But with the evident necessity of remodelling the army, the government tried to use the occasion greatly to increase its size.

From Sadowa on, many elements of the French public were as conscious as the government of the need for improvement in the French military establishment. With the first news of Sadowa the *Times* correspondent heard "it remarked on all sides that this tre-mendous weapon [the needle gun] makes the Prussians almost masters in Europe."[62] After the signing of the Peace of Prague both the British and Prussian ambassadors noted signs of interest in French military countermeasures. Goltz remarked to Bismarck: "Under the fresh impression of the surprising display of power of the Prussian military organization several newspapers are now beginning to draw parallels on the one hand between the respective populations of Germany and France, on the other hand between the army organization of Prussia and France and to keep in mind in this connection the eventual necessity of the reorganization of the latter." Claremont, the British military attaché, likewise noted agitation for revision and enlargement of the army.[63] The government-inspired press led the way particularly with an article in the *Patrie* urging changes in the army.[64]

But the first official notice of the question was the passage in the La Valette Circular of 16 September which, after a section reassuring the French people that all was well in Europe, urged the need for an increased and improved military establishment. But just this vague and somewhat incidental reference to military reform stirred an interest among sensitive readers, especially among the bourgeoisie and the peasantry. Eleven of the October reports of the procureurs general showed general reactions from the public. Seven of these eleven were favorable to reform, two just concerned, two hostile (from Orleans and Bourges).[65] However, most of the prefect reports indicated apprehension or dislike for La Valette's suggestion.[66] While this may illustrate a disparity between the observations of prefects and procureurs general, it was none too encouraging for a government anxious to persuade the public to become more defense-minded.

The next step in the government's cautious approach was to announce on 31 October the appointment of a special commission to study the necessary changes in the military establishment. For a month and a half it worked on the problem and on 12 December 1866 published its report. To the amazement of the waiting public the commission proposed to increase the armed forces from 400,000 to 800,000 men. While they would retain the system of drawing lots, the "good numbers" would still be liable for training and service in the reserves. Service in the regular army was reduced from seven to six years, which would also be the same term for those in the reserves. Then both ex-soldiers ("bad numbers") and ex-reservists ("good numbers") would have to serve three more years in a mobile national guard, resembling very much the Prussian *Landwehr*. It was estimated that the permanent army would then have 800,000 men with 400,000 more in the mobile national guard.[67]

It was evident that this plan was considered more as a basis of discussion than as the unalterable minimum for the army. Indeed, it appeared to be merely another trial balloon to see how much punishment the public would take. If the people still felt as belligerent as they had in July and August, the army might be able to get an approval of a large share of these recommendations. On the same day as the publication of the report the minister of interior asked all prefects for immediate information on the public response.[68]

It did not take long for the government to obtain the returns. The prefect reports in December and January showed profound dissatisfaction throughout France. The prefect of Loire-Inférieure exclaimed: "It delivers the most serious blow to the emperor's popularity."[69] Shortly thereafter came in the more cumbersome but fuller procureur reports. Twelve districts gave careful analyses of opinion on the commission recommendations. Only three of these showed any favor at all for the proposals (from Colmar, Lyons, and Grenoble), but these in each case were qualified with many "ifs," "ands," and "buts": (Colmar) "It is the means of execution which alone divides opinion." (Lyons) "The means are discussed and criticized." (Grenoble) "It is in its application that we shall see difficulties."

If the government could distill the least essence of satisfaction from such quibbling reports, it had finally to face the bitter truth that nine of the twelve districts were unequivocally opposed to the plan. Passages from two of them will suffice to show the rather ugly mood of the country: (Metz) "The farmers are shown to be hostile to the proposed law because it would result in taking a lot of hands from agriculture." (Riom) "My assistants all say that in general the people are very unsympathetic to the proposed reform."[70] The government learned to its great chagrin that the very provinces which had been shouting "war" in the July period of shock, were now not only reluctant to fight but even opposed to training for defense.

The government, half defeated already, had to meet opposition on another front: the legislature convened in February 1867. In the same hesitant speech in which the emperor defended his German policy he also had to plead for his new military plan. Napoleon III gave the nation a sober lecture on power politics, which sounds strange to ears hearkening back to his Bordeaux speech of 1852 that declared "the empire means peace."

> France is respected abroad [began the none-too-sure sovereign], her army has proven its worth; but the conditions of warfare having changed, they require the augmentation of our defensive forces, and we must organize ourselves in such a way as to be invulnerable. The proposed law, which has been studied with the greatest care, eases the burden of conscription in time of peace, offers considerable resources in time of war while distributing the burden evenly. It satisfies the principle of equality; it has all the importance of an institution and will be, I am convinced, accepted with patriotism. *A nation's influence depends on the number of men she can put under arms.*[71] Do not forget that neighboring states accept much heavier sacrifices for the good constitution of their armies, and their eyes are fixed on you to see whether by your decisions the influence of France should increase or diminish in the world. Let us keep our national banner flying high up where it has always been, that is the surest way of keeping peace. And that peace must be made fruitful by easing miseries and increasing the general welfare.[72]

But the legislature was being pressed from another quarter. For the first time since the Polish affair people were circulating and signing petitions against the bill. Imperialists as well as Republicans, Legitimists, and clericals joined in the endeavor, so wrought-up were they over the measure. On 22 March the minister of interior finally telegraphed his prefects as follows: "Use your influence quietly to prevent petitioning on the subject of the army law project. If a desire is shown to organize such a campaign, prevent the distribution of petitions."[73] Following out these instructions, the prefects were able to deter the Imperialists and prevent the circulation of petitions in public places. But the antigovernment parties persisted by house to house canvasses, and in spite of the prefects' vigilance they were able to send up to the legislature a hundred petitions. These were most numerous from western and central France and least frequent from the south. Now that the legislature had been given the appearance of more authority, some people were also getting the idea of writing directly to their deputies. Several dozen individual letters were among the petitions. One of them warned the legislative recipient: "If you love the emperor, oppose the project. If the project is adopted, the emperor is lost."[74] The deputies, however, hardly needed these petitions to turn them against the proposal. They knew that their constituents consisted mainly of bourgeois and peasants and that these classes were opposed to increased expenditures, anxious to preserve their sons from six years of service, and suspicious of the army, which had earlier been an instrument in the destruction of their liberties. Besides, the elections of 1869 were only two years away.

It was clear to the emperor and to his new minister of war, General Niel, that a compromise would have to be effected. After long and arduous sessions in the council of state[75] a revised bill was published on 8 March 1867. The regular contingent would still be chosen by lot for a five- instead of a six-year term, with four more years in the reserves. The "good numbers" would spend four years in the reserves and five in the mobile national guard. Those who obtained full exemption or replacement would also have to serve five years in the mobile national guard.

With the publication of this compromise proposal the nation and the legislature entered into a long period of debate and discussion lasting over the last three quarters of 1867. The government went all-out in its propaganda effort. Syndicated articles were written and sent broadcast to all inspired Paris and provincial papers. They pleaded for the bill and stressed the danger of an attack on France. A veritable rumor machine got under way to spread the feeling of alarm and urgency.[76] Later in exile the emperor admitted all this activity:

> I left no means untried to enlighten public opinion on the dangers of the situation and to convince all minds of the crying need of army reform. Official notes, articles inserted in the journals friendly to the government, statistics inserted in the imperial bulletins, speeches delivered by the most prominent ministers, everything, in short, was tried.[77]

But all of this effort failed to convert the antimilitary sentiment of the nation. Opposition leaders and papers countered the government campaign with speeches, articles, and rumors. France does not need this new measure, they argued, unless the government wants to start a war. If France were attacked, Frenchmen would rise as one man, as in 1793, seize their guns, and drive the enemy from their sacred soil. One does not need to spend nine years in the service to learn to be a good soldier. Why not adopt the American system of voluntary enlistments in wartime?[78]—They forgot that the draft had had to be used in the Civil War a few years before by both North and South. They also did not realize that the industrial revolution had brought in its wake a military revolution, which required much more skill and training in mobilization, war production, supply, and use of ingenious weapons. The days of Valmy were over; these were the days of Gettysburg, Atlanta, and Sadowa.

The revised army bill was discussed fully in twenty-five procureur reports from nineteen different districts between April 1867 and January 1868. And the most optimistic score that the minister of justice would have been able to tally would have been 13 districts opposed, 3 favorable, 2 divided, 1 noncommittal. Those in the last three categories were mainly along the eastern border: divided, Metz and Colmar; noncommittal, Besançon; favorable, Grenoble, along with Orleans and Corsica. All the rest of the country was opposed to the army reform.[79] Most of the prefect reports confirmed the prevalence of hostile sentiment.[80] The procureur general in Limoges wrote a typical report on the opposition majority:

> The discussion on the military law has preoccupied and still preoccupies all classes of the population. Anxiety has been especially strong in the country. Public opinion, aroused by the opposition parties at first greeted with disfavor the extension of the service by two years. It only noticed this one aspect and did not realize the full extent of the advantage in the restriction of active duty to five years in peacetime. The creation of the mobile national guard has frightened the bourgeoisie especially. Feelings of apprehension have not yet entirely subsided. However, public opinion . . . . ends by accepting [the final version of] the new law, if not with joy at least with patriotic resignation.[81]

In Basses-Pyrénées, when the Basques heard of plans for additional military service, they began to emigrate to Argentina in ever greater numbers. The prefect was alarmed at the prospect that his department might be virtually depopulated in a few years.[82] Then just as the government was whipping together a hesitant majority in favor of a watered-down version of the compromise proposal, two special elections took place for vacancies in two usually safe Imperialist districts in Somme and Indre-et-Loire. The army bill was naturally one big question in the campaigns, although other issues were also involved. All sides watched anxiously for the returns, and again the government received a setback by losing both elections. These results were generally interpreted as a public repudiation of the army bill.[83]

In the legislative body debate and discussion had been proceeding both in committee and on the floor. In the face of clearly recognized public opposition the government had retreated step by step by accepting legislative modifications of even the compromise proposal. The final version of the bill continued the system of 1832 with slight and ineffective changes. The legislature was to determine the size of the active army each year. Annually, then, enough "bad numbers" would be drawn to fill the contingent determined by the legislature. These men would serve for five years in the active army and four in the reserves. Those drawing the "good numbers" would serve for only five years in the mobile national guard. The wealthy were still permitted the opportunity to furnish substitutes for their sons who drew "bad numbers." Marriage was now permitted during the last three years in the reserves. The mobile national guard, however, was a farce as far as being an effective addition to the armed services. Only fifteen days of training during the year were required; and the training was not to exceed twelve hours a day nor to be far enough away to make it impossible for the trainee to return home at the end of each day. This law was finally approved on 14 January 1868 by a vote of 199 to 60, but its weak and ineffective features bore mute testimony to an all-pervasive, persistent hostile public opinion.[84]

Considering all the concessions granted by the goverment and the fact that the active service had really been reduced from seven to five years, it was not surprising to find that the final version of the law received universal approval. From January 1868 to January 1869 twenty-six different reports from sixteen different judicial districts scattered in every section of France showed all sixteen of these districts to be favorable to the army bill as passed.[85]

Expressions of opinion were not ended, however, with the passage of the Army Law. When the enrollment days came in the month of March 1868, there were almost violent demonstrations of protest in as many as twenty towns and cities throughout the country. These were provoked to a great degree by the fact that the law was made retroactive to the classes from 1864 to 1867, including many men who had previously thought they had been completely exempted from any form of military service by their "good numbers." In Toulouse the enrollment office and the prefecture were invaded by hostile mobs. In Bordeaux a big parade of protest marched with a red flag to the tune of the "Marseillaise" and with cries for the republic. At Montauban the Protestant seminarians made a noisy demonstration against the army.[86] However, after the demonstrations had been quelled and arrests made, it was found that few enrollees were involved and that most of the leaders and demonstrators were Republicans who were using the occasion for political purposes. In almost all other parts of the country the enrollments went off without incidents; and, when the enrollment of the current class of 1868 took place, there was scarcely any open resistance.[87] On the contrary, there were a few instances reported where young men actually tried to go beyond the requirement to serve or to obtain training. In the district of Poitiers one enrollee tried to overcome his stammering by practising the words "qui vive" until he could say them without hesitation so that he would not be rejected. In Grenoble some young men went voluntarily to the garrison authorities seeking and receiving training for two months during the summer.[88]

In the end it seems as if all the effort to pass the Army Bill and the fuss stirred up to oppose it had been for naught. The main innovation, the mobile national guard, remained merely a list of names until the outbreak of the war in 1870. It must be remembered that 1869 was an election year, and the government did not want to do anything upon which the opposition could capitalize. Only in Paris was the mobile national guard called out for training in July 1869, but there was so much antagonism to the move that it was not tried elsewhere.[89]

Thus the responsibility for the dilution of the army bill to a weak shadow of itself and for the lack of enforcement even of the ineffective law falls directly upon French public opinion and its legislative representatives. This responsibility is all the heavier because at the same time that opinion was opposing the bill, it showed evidence of a universal belief in the inevitability of a war with Prussia. From the time of the appointment of the original commission in October 1866 until the passage of the law in January 1868 there were more than seventy-five different reports from all the judicial districts in France, except Pau, which repeated over and over again that Frenchmen of every class and area were predicting or fearful of a war with Prussia, especially after the Exposition should be terminated.[90] The two procureurs general in Normandy noted this fatal inconsistency in public opinion:

(Caen): Public opinion remained convinced that war was in the bowels of the situation and that it would break out sooner or later, propelled by Prussian arrogance and the susceptibility of our national dignity. . . . .

But by a strange inconsistency the army reorganization bill, inspired precisely because of the conviction of the eventuality of a conflict with [Prussia] . . . . , has encountered almost a general opposition.

(Rouen): They fear, and seem to believe inevitable, the occurrence of some unforeseen event which will hurl France into a struggle with Germany.

. . . . And yet, the measures designed to augment our military forces in peacetime continue to be welcomed with little favor by public opinion.[91]

Frenchmen are often considered by themselves and by foreigners to be a very logical people. On this vital issue concerning their national safety, their logic deserted them in their greatest hour of need. And yet, Frenchmen did share with the rest of humanity the inclination to get something for nothing. They saw the handwriting on the wall, they worried about it, but they did not want to accept the sacrifices and the inconveniences required to avert the danger. In the face of immediate attack Frenchmen are particularly fearless and self-sacrificing, they are capable of great acts of courage; but again and again in 1867 as in 1938 they were unwilling to face fairly and squarely the issue of effective self-defense. At the first attack by Germany there always arose from every throat the shrill cry of *"Aux armes, citoyens! Formez vos bataillons!"*; but in peacetime, when the very threat of attack was obvious, no one wanted to take up arms, no one cared to join his battalion. The road to Sedan, unlike that to Hell, was not even paved with good intentions. And when the tragedy of defeat finally broke upon the land, the unrepentant people loaded all the blame upon the one man who, accepting captivity to save the lives of his handicapped soldiers, had long before exerted himself more than all others to spare them that evil day.

CHAPTER X

THE LAST STRAW

Living in the ruthless world of power politics, military leaders are prone to warn us that unpreparedness leads inevitably to war, that weakness invites attack. It was exactly two years and a half from the passage of France's weak and ineffective Army Law to Prussia's invasion of France. One might be led to wonder whether these two events had a causal connection, whether France's poor military establishment invited Bismarck to stage a preventive war before Frenchmen should revert to real preparedness. With the many revelations of the intervening eighty years, especially those of the American, Robert Lord,[1] an almost unbroken chain of developments seems to link the two.

Bismarck, of course, was widely known as the past master of power politics. He, of all men, knew the advantages of strength in the face of even temporary weakness. It was he who ostentatiously coined the maxim of "blood and iron," who, following with even surer step after such disciples of Machiavelli as Richelieu, Frederick the Great, Napoleon I, and Cavour, brought into the diplomatic vocabulary the term *Realpolitik*. In line with his aptitude for *Realpolitik* Bismarck as early as 1866 foresaw an inevitble war with France. As he wrote in his reminiscences:

> I took it as assured that war with France would necessarily have to be waged on the road to our national development. . . . . I did not doubt that a Franco-German war must take place before the construction of a United Germany could be realized. I was at that time preoccupied with the idea of delaying the outbreak of this war until our fighting strength could be increased by the application of the Prussian military legislation not only to Hanover, Hesse, and Holstein, but, as I could hope even at that time from the observation I had made, to the South Germans.[2]

His very wording of his thoughts here might imply that after the rearming of North and South Germany, he would not be preoccupied with delaying the war. The French public, which felt the same about the inevitability of the war,[3] should have raced him on armaments, especially after they saw he had allied with South Germany. On the contrary, it forced Napoleon's government to whittle down the Army Law and then, by its threatening attitude, to postpone even the institution of the only real innovation, the ineffective mobile national guard, until after the elections of 1869. A month after the law was passed,

Moltke, the Prussian chief of staff, belittled its effectiveness.[4] And all during this time Prussia was succeeding in arming herself and her satellites.

With the perspective of eighty years it is difficult to believe that it was mere coincidence that, less than a year after the passage of the French Army Law, the Prussians were beginning their contacts with the Spanish regency to suggest the choice of Prince Leopold of Hohenzollern-Sigmaringen for the Spanish throne.[5] Leopold was a distant relative of King William I of Prussia. Although his father, Prince Anthony, ruled over a small South German enclave, he had been minister-president of Prussia for a time, and Leopold was an officer in the Prussian army. Leopold's selection would have really meant that Prussian Hohenzollerns would have ruled on both sides of France, a situation which the *Realpolitiker*, Bismarck, must have known France would have prevented by war if necessary. It would have been such a gratuitous last straw to the accumulated grievances of France against Prussia since 1866[6] that the inevitable war, no longer in need of delay, would have broken out immediately.

Although Bismarck in his reminiscences claims that he saw no reason for France to take offense and that, on the contrary, Leopold might have been a means of bringing France and Spain closer together, one page further on he admits that "the fact that Spanish diplomacy [would have been] friendly toward us might have been useful to us in time of peace."[7] Indeed, the further fact that Leopold and his father rejected the Spanish offer twice, in 1869 and early 1870, because of apprehension over France's hostility showed that they did not share Bismarck's supposed optimism. Leopold once told Bismarck to his face that he would not have had French sympathies as a king of Spain.[8]

Just before Leopold's rejection early in 1870, an unofficial crown council was held in Berlin where William I, Anthony, Leopold, Bismarck, Roon, Moltke, and a few other ministers discussed the problem. All the Prussian advisors favored acceptance, William I demurred, and then Leopold later declined the offer. Bismarck began to put pressure on Leopold by suggesting his brother, Frederick, instead. At the same time he encouraged the Spanish through his emissary, Dr. Lothar Bucher, to invite Leopold again. Bucher himself boasted later that the scheme was "a trap set for Napoleon III."[9] In spite of the irrefutable implication of the Prussian government in the affair, Bismarck tried deliberately to conceal it. He wrote a "Doctor" [probably Bucher]:

Would it be advisable to introduce my name into a public account of these negotiations? I think not, and, on the contrary, my personality ought to be completely left out of everything. In truth I am not officially involved. Whether or not he [Leopold] has had reason to seek the consent of his father and of the head of the family [William I], is a question of a private nature, not an affair of state. . . . .

I . . . . have aided him with my advice, not in my quality of president of the
council of ministers . . . . , but as a man in his confidence. . . . . Undoubtedly
they [the French] will cry 'intrigue,' they will be furious against me, but without
finding any point of attack.[10]

After the evidence produced by Lord there is no doubt that Prussia
and Bismarck were implicated, that Bismarck knew it would cause
trouble with France, and that at the council meeting Roon and Moltke,
the two highest military officials, favored the candidacy, i.e., thought
the military situation was favorable to Prussia if war should come.
Lord concludes:

Bismarck deliberately embarked on a project which, whatever its primary aim
may have been, did involve placing Napoleon in a position where he might either
have to fight or to accept another grave defeat that might involve the downfall of
his tottering dynasty.[11]

The third offer Leopold accepted on 23 June 1870, and on 3 July
the news broke on Paris and over the entire French nation.

The Hohenzollern Candidacy

The first episode in which public opinion played a part was the
receipt of the news of Leopold's acceptance on 4-5 July. An earlier
study, in questioning Ollivier's stress on the violent reaction of the press
to the news, asserts that "there is no indication, of course, that the
press was pleased" but little evidence that it favored war.[12] Ollivier,
however, in defense of his point of view, quotes many Paris papers
and by their passages reveals that the French press was so wrought
up that recourse to war seemed implicit in its reaction.[13] He also gives
a much wider sampling of the Paris press. Only John Lemoine of the
Journal des Débats did not share in this public feeling, wrote Ollivier.

His impression of a warlike reaction of press and public, rather
than a mild dislike, is borne out by ambassadors and foreign observers: (Werther of Prussia): "It may be more than current public
opinion can endure." (Beyens of Belgium): "Wild emotion caused
by the news." (Kern of Switzerland): "This news . . . . aroused all
the national susceptibilities of Frenchmen against Prussia." (Metternich of Austria): "The news . . . . aroused a very strong and sudden
emotion."[14] The London *Times* correspondent summarized press
opinion of the 4th and 5th, showing that the *Constitutionnel, Liberté,
Opinion Nationale, Temps,* and *Patrie* were all aroused and inclined
to blame Prussia. The *Journal des Débats* alone thought war inconceivable, he said, confirming Ollivier's statement.[15] There seems to
be little doubt that there was a noticeably strong reaction in Paris
against the Hohenzollern candidacy during these first two days. Some
of the newspaper comments hinted obliquely of war; Beyens' account
actually mentions the desire for it. Nine important Paris papers of
various political shades, a *Times* correspondent, and four diplomats
all attest to a violently hostile reaction, at least in Paris. The diplo-

mats often obtained evidence of opinion from other sources than the press.

On the face of it, a strongly hostile reaction could have been expected. To prove that it did occur does not establish anything sensational. Yet, many contemporary commentators outside France, and many historians since that time, could not see why Frenchmen should object so strongly to the Hohenzollern candidacy or go to war over the Ems telegram. Frenchmen, they felt, were trying to dictate to Spain on the choice of her king; they were trying to blame Prussia without proof of her direct connection with the affair. This point of view was similar to the "innocence" plea put out by Prussia. Thus for some writers it was hard to believe that the public should have resented it very much. If some papers exploded at the news, they must have been "inspired by the government."[16]

Yet a careful study of history and international practice will show that the selection of a man to be ruler of a European state was the business of the whole European community because it often involved that state in new dynastic alliances affecting the balance of power. Any disturbance of the balance of power was a matter of serious concern to all the powers. At least three times previously Spain had been the cause of such crises with Charles V (1516), Philip V (1700), and the Spanish marriages (1846). There had been three wars of "succession" over Spain, Poland, and Austria respectively. Thus in the nineteenth century it became the custom for the powers to consult each other, come to a joint agreement on a prospective monarch for a key state, and impose their decision on that state for the sake of the peace of Europe, whether the people of the state liked that choice or not. Such were the cases of rulers for Belgium, Greece, Rumania, Bulgaria, and Schleswig-Holstein (1852). In most of these instances they decided against a prince closely connected with the dynasty of a great power in order to prevent a great power from extending its influence to a small key state. From this the attitude had grown that a great power, if it wanted a certain prince on a vacant throne and if it wanted to act in an aboveboard fashion, would take the other powers into its confidence and prepare for the accession by European consultations.

In the case of the Hohenzollern candidacy Prussia did no such thing. Leopold was related to William I, was an officer in the Prussian army; his father had been Prussian minister-president. He would have been the sort of choice that Europe, by custom, would have rejected for the strategically located Spain. Yet the Prussian government, especially Bismarck, had worked under cover to get Spain's invitation and Leopold's acceptance and to present them as *faits-accomplis* to Europe. This scheme would have suddenly placed Hohenzollerns to the east and to the south of France. When it is realized that this was only the latest in a series of irritating frustrations experienced by the French people—Sadowa, North German Confederation, South German alliances, refusal of compensations in Germany and Luxemburg—it is understandable that all the cumulative animosity of the French should break forth. Even the London *Times* remarked: "None of the representatives of foreign powers received the least overture on the subject, and that conduct, we do not hesitate to say, is contrary to all the laws of usual courtesy. The whole transaction has the character of a vulgar and impudent *coup d'état*, of one of those enterprises which should not be allowed to succeed."[17] The anger of the French press would therefore have been a natural reaction. It would not have required government prodding to get it under way. The presence of French press hostility to the candidacy is less difficult to explain than would have been its absence.

The Gramont Declaration

All of these broader considerations are connected with the next episode, Gramont's parliamentary declaration of 6 July. Gramont had tried on 4 July to engage Prussia in discussions on the matter, discussions which Prussia should have initiated long before. But the answer of Thile in Berlin and of Werther in Paris were that "for Prussia the affair did not exist." The only resort then for Gramont was to go over the heads of the Prussian cabinet and appeal to the powers and the peoples of Europe. By firm, yet somewhat provocative words, he had also to meet the rising public and legislative protests and marshal this opinion to give Prussia pause. If he had said openly that Prussia refused to discuss the question, he would have transformed the legislature and the nation into howling mobs demanding retaliation. Thus it was that his answer to the interpellation contained in part these words:

But we do not believe that the respect for the rights of a neighboring people [Spanish] obliges us to submit that a foreign power, by putting one of its princes on the throne of Charles V, can derange to our detriment the balance of forces in Europe and imperil the interests and honor of France.

This eventuality, we sincerely hope, will not come to pass. To prevent it, we count on the wisdom of the German people and the friendship of the Spanish people. If it is otherwise, fortified by your support, Gentlemen, and of that of the nation, we will know how to fulfill our duty without hesitation or weakness.[18]

This was a clear affirmation that Prussia was implicated and that France would fight if Prussia did not get Leopold's acceptance withdrawn.

Many have criticized Gramont because he implicated Prussia. But Prussia was involved by the very circumstances, even if Bismarck had not conspired to bring about the antecedent events. Frenchmen took it for granted, so did the rest of Europe. Gramont has also been criticized for his threat of war. That is more vulnerable to attack and can be thought of as stirring up the war spirit in

France. This is one of the proofs used for the charge that Gramont was plotting war. In justice to him we must also listen to his and Ollivier's defense that the threat was mainly to frighten the powers into coming to France's aid diplomatically and to sober the arrogance of Prussia.

The reaction of the French press to the Gramont declaration was divided: eleven seemed to favor it and nine were opposed.[19] But the reports of ambassadors and representatives from foreign countries, observing the people directly as well as the newspapers, were unanimous in their belief that Frenchmen were solidly behind the Gramont statement: (Solms of Prussia): "Public opinion in France becomes stronger day by day in favor of war."[20] (Lyons of England) "The [Gramont] declaration, however, forceable as it was, did not go at all beyond the feeling of the country."[21] (Kern of Switzerland) "Every divergence of opinion ceases . . . . when the national honor has been engaged, as the Duke of Gramont has done it."[22] (Beyens of Belgium) "Only the personal renunciation of the prince can avert the danger. That is the unanimous view; peace is at that price."[23] (Vitzthum of Austria) "The speech made by the Duke of Gramont . . . . stirred up the whole country into a war fever."[24]

Then, too, from the police reports of that time the government learned of popular enthusiasm for the Gramont declaration:

> The language used by the government in the chamber . . . . has the approbation of the country and corresponded exactly to what general opinion expected. . . . . So forceful and yet so careful a declaration as has just been read in the chamber by M. de Gramont has been acclaimed with an enthusiasm undiminished by the consequences that it may bring on.[25]

But the newspapers, the diplomats, and the police reports revealed only the reactions of the people in Paris and its environs. It was of even greater importance to know how the people in the rest of the country felt. And for this purpose the government utilized the Gramont declaration as a clear-cut statement of policy on which to test opinion in the provinces. On the day after Gramont's declaration the minister of interior sent telegraphic instructions to the prefects of all departments calling for special reports on the reaction of provincial opinion to the declaration and to the Spanish throne affair.[26] Between 8 and 19 July, 87 of the 88 prefects in the departments outside Paris responded with special reports.[27] All but six of these replies were in the hands of the minister of interior by 12 July. Thus the government had asked for soundings of public opinion and had received most of the reports before the next important event, the withdrawal of Leopold's acceptance by his father, Prince Anthony.

At this point something should be said about this unique collection of the July special prefect reports. In the first place the originals have disappeared. Neither Carroll nor the present author found them in the prefect reports of the Archives Nationales.[28] They were probably mislaid during the siege or destroyed in the fires of the Commune. But before their loss they were brought together by the minister of interior of the Republican regime after the downfall of the Empire, and extracts were published in the *Journal Officiel* on 2 October 1870. These extracts seem to be all that remain of the collection. From the wording of the official introduction to their publication it could be inferred that they were published to disprove the Imperialist claim that public opinion pushed Napoleon III to declare war. The fact that they are extracts would make one wonder what the full reports might have revealed, or whether the originals may have been deliberately destroyed to conceal what the rest of the reports contained.

However, a careful evaluation even of the extracts would lead an impartial outsider to conclude that they tended to prove just the opposite from what the Republican regime intended. On the question of Gramont's declaration, for example, 31 departments approved it and 7 disapproved. Although the reports of 49 departments made no mention of Gramont's declaration, they did express opinions on whether France should go to war, if necessary, to prevent Leopold's accession in Spain. A prowar sentiment in any of these 49 reports should, then, be interpreted as favorable to Gramont's defiant speech, and inversely any definitely antiwar reports among the 49 should be counted as against Gramont. There were 21 prowar and 17 antiwar reports among the 49. Revising the initial tally, we would therefore have 52 approving the declaration, 24 disapproving, and 11 noncommittal. Such a large majority approving the belligerent declaration, coupled with the favorable press reaction in Paris (confirmed by the foreign observers), could have left little doubt in the minds of Gramont and Napoleon III that the people in general backed them in this initial stand against Prussia.[29]

Of course, behind this request for the reaction to the Gramont declaration was a search for evidence on whether opinion would be willing to go to war to prevent the enthronement of a Prussian in Spain. On the eve of all previous wars involving the Second Empire French opinion had been opposed to war. Yet this prospect of Leopold's accession was the worst threat France had faced since 1815. After all the uncompromising attitudes of Prussia since 1866 would public opinion be more favorable to war as a last resort in this serious crisis? Since 1859 Napoleon III had avoided war in the Polish, Danish, and German affairs partly in deference to antiwar opinion in France. Even now it was Bismarck, and not Napoleon III, who was conspiring for war. Would the French people by a belligerent attitude strengthen their emperor's hand in this crisis in his dealings with a man who judged situations largely in terms of "blood and iron"?

The answer which these special prefect reports give to the larger question raises a serious problem of the interpretation of original sources on opinion. The Republican Government of National Defense, in its introduction to the publication of the extracts, implied that opinion did not cause Napoleon III to resort to war. It cited the alleged remark of Napoleon III to his German captors that "he had been pushed into [the war] by public opinion" and then remarked cryptically that it "released the following documents without commentary for the appreciation of the public."[30] Jules Pointu, a former Republican subprefect, wrote a book in 1874 in which he used these reports as "irrefutable documents" to prove that "France [the French people] did not want the war and that the emperor and his ministers knew it."[31] He quotes fourteen reports from frontier departments and from urban centers (more strongly Republican), but even two of these are prowar (Bouches-du-Rhône and Bas-Rhin). Yet in his final tally he omits these two in his list of prowar departments. He says that 15 were prowar, 63 antiwar, and 8 were "evasive."[32] Thus the impression of Republican contemporaries and some historical scholars was that the overwhelming sentiment of the people was for peace in July 1870 in spite of the danger to France of the developing situation and that the French government had blundered into war in full knowledge of the contrary sentiment of the country.

These estimates of a very predominant peace sentiment in the special July reports are so contrary to the evidence of Paris opinion in the press and in the diplomatic reports and so at variance with the reaction to the Gramont declaration that they immediately suggest the need for a close re-examination of the reports themselves. A thorough scrutiny of the published texts, however, leaves room for a belief that there has been so serious a misreading of the texts that a more accurate evaluation would lead to an entirely opposite tally.

One reason for this important discrepancy in interpretation revolves around the appearance of a phrase in a report indicating that in general the people prefer peace. Such a phrase was evidently taken by Pointu to mean the public wanted peace in this particular crisis. The report from Eure-et-Loire begins: "There is no warlike enthusiasm." Pointu immediately tags Eure-et-Loire as an antiwar department. But the full text of the extract reads as follows:

There is no warlike enthusiasm; there is something better than that because enthusiasm dies down [easily]. There is a sentiment of reasoned and reflective patriotism boldly asserting itself [s'accentuant très résolument] and expressing itself thus: Prussian policy is tending toward a state of things that France must not allow to be constituted in Europe; only force can turn Prussia from her objective, so war with her is fatally inevitable; the occasion is good, the moment propitious, better now than later.

All of this report is prowar except the first line.[33] Again Pointu quotes the last line of the report from Gironde: "I believe that at heart they dread [*redoute*] war." Therefore Gironde, according to Pointu, is antiwar.[34] Yet the whole extract preceding this last sentence reads as follows:

> Commercial affairs are not going well right now, and the merchants, whose opinion is ordinarily for peace, appear to believe that an event like war, whether with Prussia or with Spain, would bring a change in the situation.
>
> Yesterday they had a festival in the public park in Bordeaux, and this opinion I consign in this report, however strange it may appear, was frequently expressed to me. May I add that the central commissioner, whom I consulted this morning, reported to me the same tendencies among the people with whom he has contacts.
>
> I believe that at heart they dread war.

All the report except the last line was prowar, and the last line seemed to reflect the difficulty of the prefect to believe his own ears.[35]

Now, that is the sort of revision which Pointu's tallies need. In general the present author has interpreted the extracts as prowar when an introductory sentence spoke of the normal desire for peace, followed by a "but" and the bulk of the report indicated a welcoming of war in this particular instance. However, where the bulk of the report seemed pro-peace and only indicated a willingness to accept war if it was forced upon France, he had classed it as antiwar. Even on this basis there are still others that are "evasive" enough to be classed as noncommittal. Fifteen reports defied all attempts to classify them as prowar or antiwar. Judged on a careful rereading of all the extracts, the reports would seem to indicate *on their face value* this revised tally: 40 prowar, 32 antiwar, 15 noncommittal. In this case the count is close but definitely with a majority of eight departments for war.[36]

Yet, it is necessary to take into consideration certain other typical passages in the antiwar and noncommittal reports. Some of these demanded war if France's honor or interests in the balance of power were not satisfied. In Paris these would have to be transferred to the prowar column as the subsequent days revealed Prussian uncompromising and provocative attitudes. For example, the antiwar report from the department of Rhône declared:

> If the question could be decided by a congress, that is, without war, they would be particularly satisfied. [This sentence alone justifies an initial classification of antiwar.] But they do not want things to remain as they are today. They are tired and humiliated by being exposed to the consequences of Prussia's activities [*agissements*]. They hope that the government will take advantage of a dispute [*conflit*], which it certainly has not provoked, to redeem the situation. And, if war alone must bring an end to a state of things considered compromising to our national dignity and our interests, I affirm that they will frankly and resolutely accept war. I may add that even those that dread it or pretend to dread it at present would be the first to denounce the government if it did not persist in the firm and resolute attitude it has adopted.[37]

Likewise the noncommittal report from Charente bears the same warning:

I summarize public opinion in these words: No one wants a Prussian prince in Spain; they hail war patriotically; they prefer peace with a moral victory; they would not forgive the government if it showed weakness or even timidity.[38]

Such reports, and there were twenty-three of them, contained a clear warning that they wanted a definite diplomatic victory over Prussia, or war. Looked at in the long range of the subsequent period (10-16 July), these twenty-three would have to be interpreted as demanding war in the contingencies which were to lie ahead. If these twenty-three are subtracted from the antiwar and noncommittal columns and added to that of the prowar, the score would be: prowar 63, antiwar 17, and uncertain 7.

Disagreement over the exact words of a document can be resolved with relative ease; disagreement over the meaning of these words, however, leads into the realm of semantics and personal judgments. Re-examination by the present author of the extracts of the prefects' special July reports has led him by an honest effort toward re-evaluation to put 19 of Pointu's antiwar departments in the prowar column, 11 of his noncommittal departments in the prowar column, and in the case of Var to transfer it from prowar to antiwar. The following is another example of a department classified by Pointu as antiwar which would seem to require reclassification as prowar.

(Haute-Loire): The idea of a war with Prussia is very popular. People do not go as far as to desire it, but they would be very sorry to see it avoided at the price of any sacrifice which would hurt or compromise our dignity and patriotism.[39]

Such reports as this, then, were reclassified as prowar.

Of course most of the reports had at least some passing remark about peace, but one must not seize upon that alone as the indication of antiwar sentiment. The whole context of the report must be considered before final classification. Most of them were not as clear-cut as that from the Pyrénées-Orientales, which said: "The immense majority applaud [Gramont's declaration], and, if it has to go to war, the government will not only be supported, but will be pushed into it by public opinion."[40] The government had asked for a quick report on public opinion. To be sure there was not time for the usually leisurely survey of public opinion by the prefects and their subordinates. But within five days the Paris authorities had in hand 78 of the possible 88 reports. Any one of the Paris officials having a prowar prejudice might have interpreted them as indicating more than 63 prowar reports. The present author's attempt at impartial evaluation stands on 63, which is a far cry from Pointu's count of 18 prowar departments.[41] Indeed the tone of the reports is so general and all-pervasive in demanding war unless a very favorable diplomatic victory were won that the government could not have gained any other conviction than that the people supported a firm policy backed by the threat of war.[42]

We have already seen, then, that even before the Gramont declaration, the public was strongly incensed against Prussia. His statement was thus not out of line with opinion, but it also seemed to have greatly intensified warlike sentiment. Although the press was divided, it leaned to the side of Gramont. But observations by five diplomats, the *Times* correspondent, and the police reporters, based on the public as well as on the press, seemed unanimous in commenting on the great increase of anti-Prussian and prowar sentiment in line with the spirit of Gramont's words. Then the special prefect reports came in with a 63 to 17 majority for war, if necessary, as a confirmation of provincial sentiment. Especially to be noted is the fact that the Paris and provincial publics both wanted satisfaction from Prussia rather than from Leopold. Therefore from a reexamination of the press, the diplomatic dispatches, and the prefect reports it seems as if the evidence swings back again in favor of Ollivier and of the view that opinion was moving the government toward a more belligerent policy and that the response to Gramont's declaration was strongly and predominantly favorable to the extent of accepting war if necessary. Call it a war sentiment or not, it was clearly angry and resolute, and certainly not "superficial," as Sorel would have had us believe.[43]

The Unsatisfactory Renunciation

By 12 July the government well knew that most eyes were on Prussia, expecting her to give the final peaceful solution to the affair, or else war. Spain and Sigmaringen seemed forgotten. Solms had said they were awaiting "a reply from Ems." The French may pick a quarrel with the form of the renunciation, predicted Lyons, as early as the 10th. Revenge for Sadowa was the attitude reported by Kern on the 7th. Prussia must back down (*que la Prusse cane*), they say, reported the *Times* correspondent on the 9th. From the start it had been, and still was, *Prussia* in the minds of most Frenchmen.

Then at about 2:00 P.M. of 12 July came the great news. Prince Anthony had telegraphed that in Leopold's name he withdrew his acceptance. This was not from Prussia, not even from Leopold, merely from Leopold's father. Ollivier was jubilant. Even the emperor was inclined to accept it halfheartedly as a termination of the dispute. An hour later he told Nigra:

Yes, it's peace. . . . . I know very well that public opinion in France, excited as it is, would have preferred another solution, war. But I recognize that the renunciation of the Prince of Hohenzollern removes every pretext for war, at least for the time being.[44]

The emperor, then, within an hour of the news, had already begun to have qualms about how opinion would accept that kind of a renunciation. But, Gramont, as minister of foreign affairs, was the least satisfied of the three. Prussia had violated the courtesies of international procedures at the beginning of the affair. To close the incident completely, France and Europe should have assurances from the great power which had the most control over Leopold that it would see to it that he persisted in his father's decision. Confirmation should still come from Ems. After all, Leopold might not have acquiesced in his father's decision. Indeed, it is now known that he had violently disagreed with his father. There were other ugly examples of similar situations in the past. Leopold's brother, Charles, in defiance of Prussia and the powers, had sneaked away and taken the Rumanian throne in 1866. The Duke of Augustenburg had claimed Schleswig-Holstein in 1864 after his father had renounced it for himself and his descendants. Supposing Gramont should go before the parliament and people of France, declaring the question was closed, and then Leopold should, in a month or even a year, suddenly turn up in Madrid and take the throne? Such an embarrassment would probably cause the downfall of Napoleon III himself. Only Prussia in agreement with the powers could forestall such an eventuality. Thoughts like these disturbed the French minister of foreign affairs.

> There was something to be said for this latter point of view [wrote Lord]. . . . .
> Assuming that the document was genuine, was it not suspicious that the renunciation emanated, not from the candidate, but from his father?
> . . . . Moreover, there still remained the question of the formal satisfaction that was due to France from Prussia. Regarding the candidacy (quite rightly) as an intrigue of Bismarck's against France, which had been conducted in defiance of the accepted rules of international comity and had leaked out only by accident before its consummation, the French government had, all along, desired to obtain some kind of reparation for this unfriendly proceeding. Almost any sort of courteous or conciliatory act might have been accepted, but hitherto Prussia had refused to make any such gesture.[45]

Indeed public opinion was already showing signs of dissatisfaction. Ollivier in his joy revealed the news in the rooms adjoining the legislative chamber. The first remark he heard, from one of the more peace-loving members, was: "Prussia is making fun of you." When Ollivier indicated to another that he was satisfied, he replied: "That's fine. You will perform an act of courage; but make no mistake about it, it means your downfall; the country will not be contented with this satisfaction." A group of legislators, who crowded around him, began to murmur: "That's infamous. Prussia has sought us out; we must have it out with her." The newsmen had rushed off to their papers' offices, spreading the news as they went; in no time it was the talk of the town. And one feature stood out, as the man in the street, too, is capable of seizing on the significant: *Father Anthony* had made the announcement. Everywhere people were calling in derision *"Père Antoine!"* The emperor left the Tuileries for Saint-

Cloud and was "struck by the unusual acclaim by the crowd, which [was] obviously intended as a bellicose incitation."[46]

And others were confirming the mood of public opinion:

(Nigra of Italy): The news, which spread rapidly through the city, was rather badly received by the public and by the evening press. They were denouncing the renunciation as an insufficient and almost derisory concession.[47]

(Beyens of Belgium): An expression I have picked up along the boulevards: 'The cowardly peace!'[48] 'The Sadowa of the salons.' It is probable that for the moment, out of self-pride and to disguise their setback, they [the chamber] will uphold the ministry, but will break its neck on the first occasion on some question of local roads.[49]

(Hansen of Denmark): The patriotic feeling in France was then very much overexcited, and . . . . the people envisaged war with enough confidence to oblige the government to speak up and insist on real satisfactions.[50]

(Metternich of Austria-Hungary): Here they absolutely want war, very great agitation, the cause popular, the outcome dangerous.[51]

On the emperor's arrival at Saint-Cloud he was joined by Gramont. They were both under the spell of the early evidences of opinion in the streets and in the legislative lobbies, and in the seventy-eight departments whose reports had probably been received by this time. What they had already learned seemed, on past experience,[52] to be a definite symptom of probable popular dissatisfaction with "Father Anthony's" renunciation. If Gramont and the emperor were misled by these early signs, they were misled along with Nigra, Beyens, Hansen, Metternich, and Ollivier. The latter was to oppose the next step Gramont was to take; and therefore if he reported hostile receptions to the news, he is not trying to defend his own position. What Gramont had heard or learned he described to Lyons on the same afternoon.

M. de Gramont [wrote Lyons] said that this state of things was very embarrassing to the French government. On the one hand public opinion was so much excited in France that it was doubtful whether the Ministry would not be overthrown, if it went down to the Chamber tomorrow and announced that it regarded the affair as finished without having obtained some more complete satisfaction from Prussia.[53]

That the emperor was under the same impression he recounts in his later recollections:

When we learned that the head of the family had withdrawn the candidacy of his son, we hoped that peace might be preserved. But public opinion throughout the land was in such a state that all efforts toward a conciliatory issue from the difficulty were received with disapproval by the masses.[54]

Of course these are later justificatory recollections, which are less convincing. The first sentence is confirmed by what Napoleon had told Nigra and, in the light of the ambassadors' impressions, his evaluation of opinion in Paris and the provinces was justified.

At least, late in the afternoon of 12 July, the emperor and Gramont, with these disturbing symptoms of opinion in mind, found themselves in Saint-Cloud in the midst of a court spoiling for war. In the absence of Ollivier and most of the members of the cabinet, they came to the conclusion that they must get assurance from William I not only for the present but for the future. This assurance should be obtained immediately because the legislature would have to be faced on the morrow. Consequently they drew up a telegram for Benedetti, which, because of delays in coding and dispatch, was not sent until seven that evening. The telegram read in part:

> So that the renunciation of Prince Anthony may produce its full effect, it appears necessary that the King of Prussia associate himself with it, and give us the assurance that he would not authorize this candidacy again. . . . . In spite of the renunciation, which is now known, the animation of opinion is such that we do not know whether we can control it. . . . . Reply as promptly as possible.[55]

Carroll says that "if Gramont's decision had any relation to public opinion, it was merely in anticipation of its eventual reactions, for the demand for guarantees was sent only a few hours after the arrival in Paris of Leopold's renunciation."[56] But the minister had valid grounds for his anticipations. Gramont, like many others, was aware of the early symptoms of a dissatisfied opinion on this basis, and on the basis of opinion in Paris and the provinces during the preceding days, he did then anticipate a fuller expression of opinion along the same lines. Lord gives more credit to the influence of opinion. Mentioning the diplomatic aspects, Lord says: "Some such considerations, reinforced by his knowledge of public opinion, swept the Duke de Gramont along that day."[57] Considering the fact that Napoleon III was inclined at first to accept Anthony's renunciation as a settlement, it seems now quite probable that both he and Gramont were sincerely influenced by what they saw or heard of the early signs of a dissatisfied public opinion.

Ollivier, when he learned of the instructions sent to Benedetti, disapproved of them. At the council meeting the next morning he proposed that, even if William gave no assurances for the present or the future, they should call the incident closed and rest on Anthony's withdrawal. The vote was eight to four for this decision. In the meantime they drew up a statement for the legislature which would indiacte that negotiations were continuing.

As Ollivier went into the legislative body, he felt a coolness and an aversion on every side and attributed it to the dislike of his attitude the day before when he seemed satisfied with Anthony's renunciation. Gramont rose and gave the government's statement:

> The ambassador of Spain announced to us officially[58] yesterday the renunciation of Prince Leopold[59] of Hohenzollern of his candidacy for the throne of Spain.
> Negotiations which we are pursuing with Prussia, and which have had no other purpose, are not yet closed. Therefore, it is impossible for us to speak of them and to submit a general report of the affair to the chamber and the country.[60]

Gramont had to indicate that negotiations with Prussia were under way. Probably French opinion would not have tolerated the implication that there was none. But the French foreign minister did try to ease the situation for Prussia by saying that all France wanted out of these Franco-Prussian negotiations was the renunciation of Leopold.

Immediately Jerome David rose and asked who gave the renunciation. Gramont hedged a bit by saying that he was informed by the Spanish ambassador that it was Leopold. David reminded him of the rumors in the lobbies that it was Anthony. To this Gramont remarked that he was not concerned with lobby rumors. It was Ollivier who said it, David persisted. Gramont gave no answer. Finally David offered an interpellation which asked for explanations on the reasons for his conduct on foreign policy which affected adversely general business conditions and national dignity. The discussion was put off to the 15th. His reception in the senate was even more hostile than in the legislative body.[61]

It is possible now to consider the attitude of the press both to Father Anthony's telegram and to Gramont's statement before the legislative houses. Gramont's evaluation of the press is far too extreme when he said:

> There was no longer even one paper, whatever may have been its party and its opinions, which considered the isolated act of Prince Leopold as sufficient, and the most reserved, the most pacific sheets advised the government, as the extreme limit to be contented with, the official disavowal of the Berlin cabinet or a declaration confirming the definite character of the renunciation.[62]

Carroll tells us that the prowar press was bitterly disappointed, but that the *Siècle* was correct in saying that "a large majority of the press is rejoicing because of the maintenance of the peace," although they felt the peace was precarious. Carroll then lists fifteen papers willing to accept the situation, but he does not mention any of the prowar papers by name or number. He, then, leaves the opposite impression from that of Gramont.[63]

However, an examination of the press must go further than these two opposing evaluations. In the first place Carroll lists the *Gazette de France* and the *France* among the fifteen papers on 13 and 14 July favorable to renunciation without Prussia.[64] But the Legitimist *Gazette de France*, which had been the earliest paper to suggest Prussia's implication,[65] merely ridiculed Gramont for appearing to say that just the renunciation was all that was desired. By the tone of its language it showed its readers it preferred satisfaction from Prussia:

> Peace triumphs. There will be no war. Prussia keeps her fruits of Sadowa. All of France thought that the government, having resolved to take revenge on Sadowa, believed the moment had come to engage in a serious contest with Prussia.[66]

The *France* was even more open in its demand for satisfaction from Prussia:

> The matter in dispute is an international, not a family question; and France, therefore, can only treat with the Prussian government. France demands from Prussia a protocol in which the Prussian dynasty formally engages never to accept the crown of Spain for its family or those of its allies.[67]

Furthermore, both Ollivier and Carroll state that the *Constitutionnel* and the *Patrie* were kept in line, by Ollivier's influence, in acquiescing in just Anthony's renunciation.[68] They may not, therefore, have been freely expressing their thoughts. If the *Gazette de France* and the *France* are transferred to the other side and the *Constitutionnel* and *Patrie* are not counted at all, we find that eight papers favored satisfaction from Prussia and eleven favored accepting Anthony's renunciation as a final solution, which is a much closer division.[69]

Also another factor must be considered concerning the impression these papers made on the government, on the public, and on the outside observers. Unimportant papers would have little weight with the government and the public. In the pro-Anthony list such papers would be the *Français, Réveil, Rappel, Cloche,* and *Histoire;* in the anti-Prussian list would be found only possibly the *France.* If, then, the line-up of papers omitted these, there would be seven important papers for a Prussian renunciation and six for Anthony's renunciation, which reverses the balance slightly in favor of Gramont's instructions to Benedetti.

In spite of the fact that Ollivier favored accepting Anthony's renunciation and had gotten it adopted as the official policy of the cabinet, he had to admit that opinion was rapidly going away from him. His evaluation of legislative hostility to the Gramont second statement (that of 13 July), which implied that all he wanted was renunciation, is confirmed by Beyens, Kern, and Werther.[70] As to the outside reaction, Ollivier estimated it to be increasingly against him. "Our answer to the interpellation aroused almost general reprobation."[71] Metternich wired Vienna that "public opinion begins to push the government so hard that peace appears henceforth impossible."[72] As to the newspapers, by the evening of 13 July Ollivier thought only the *Constitutionnel,* the *Temps,* and the *Journal des Débats* were on his side. The circulation of papers, he said, went up or down respectively, depending on whether they were for war or peace; the *Constitutionnel* was torn up and thrown in the gutter.[73] Ollivier may be suspected of some exaggeration because his general thesis seemed to be that he was dragged along by public opinion in spite of himself. But in all this general estimate of the situation of both 12 and 13 July he is upheld in most respects by the statements referred to above from Nigra, Beyens, Hansen, Lyons, Kern, Metternich, and Werther, as well as by the *Times* correspondent.[74]

The Ems Dispatch

While the legislature and the press were having a busy day in Paris on 13 July, Benedetti was certainly having a busy day in Ems. He saw William I in the morning, while both were taking a walk in a park, and the king refused to give any assurances for the future on the Hohenzollern candidacy. However, he did make two significant concessions: he acknowledged that he had given his personal consent to the original acceptance by Leopold; and later in the day he sent word to Benedetti that, on receiving official word of Leopold's withdrawal, he authorized him to inform Paris that he approved it. But he steadfastly refused to see Benedetti again on the subject of future guarantees.[75]

As we know now, that was more than the French cabinet had expected, and it would have accepted even less. So nothing remained to settle the entire dispute but to await the transmission of the news.

But in the meantime Bismarck came back into the picture. Knowing now how hard and long he had worked to put Leopold on the Spanish throne and how deliberately he had continued to violate proper diplomatic usages to goad France into another humiliation or war, we are not surprised to find him smarting with disappointment. He was intent on finding another pretext for war by considering France's diplomatic victory as an insult to Prussia or by meeting Gramont's challenge of 6 July by demanding satisfactory explanations for the latter's "insulting" remarks about Prussia. He threatened to resign if the king did not back him up on one or another of the plans. Bismarck said himself: "I was very much depressed, for I saw no means of repairing the corroding injury I dreaded to our national position from a timorous policy, unless by picking quarrels clumsily and seeking them artificially. I saw by that time that war was a necessity, which we could no longer avoid with honor."[76]

However, he found his "artificial" way to prolong the quarrel. William had sent a telegraphic dispatch from Ems to Bismarck in Berlin describing briefly the early interviews with Benedetti on the 13th. It omitted his final concession, because it probably had not yet occurred at the time of sending the dispatch. At the end of the telegram William had said Bismarck could decide whether to make the Ems interviews public or not. Bismarck was dining with Moltke and Roon when he received the dispatch. They were all in a glum mood because he had just told them of his intention to resign. When he had read the last sentence, he saw his chance for an artificial quarrel. By condensing an already abbreviated message he could make it appear to Germans that Benedetti had made an impudent demand and to the French that the king had curtly rejected it and had refused any audience to the French ambassador. Then he released it to the press and had an official circular concerning it sent to most capitals in Europe. In his own words he boasted: "It will be known in Paris before midnight, and not only on account of its contents, but also on account of its manner of distribution, will have the effect of a red flag upon the Gallic bull."[77] The appetites of the three men returned, and they went at their incompleted meal with a zest.

Bismarck, however, had not sprung this trap without assurances from Moltke on the comparative military strength of France and Prussian Germany. Moltke's reply is interesting in the light of the French Army Law, which had been made inadequate through the pressure of French public opinion.[78] Bismarck again recounts:

He [Moltke] answered that if there was to be a war, he expected no advantage to us by deferring its outbreak; and even if we should not be strong enough at first to protect all the territories on the left bank of the Rhine against French invasion, our preparations would nevertheless soon overtake those of the French, while at a later period this advantage would be diminished; he regarded a rapid outbreak as, on the whole, more favorable to us than delay.[79]

A sudden preventive war—it was not the first time nor the last time it was to appear in the history of the state system. If the French people could only have heard those words back in 1867!

Ollivier was calmly working at his desk on the morning of the 14th when Gramont came rushing in, livid, a yellow paper in his trembling hand. "My dear man," he shouted, "you see before you a man who has just received a slap in the face!" Ollivier was stunned as he read the news of the published Ems Dispatch. "We have no illusions now, they want to make us go to war."[80] Indeed, Bismarck had unmasked himself beyond all chance of resuming a peaceful mien.

There has also been much loose talk among historians and commentators about how foolish France and the French were to go to war over a little abbreviated telegram. But such a view overlooks all the events from Sadowa on to the Luxemburg affair and the Spanish throne incident, disregards all the provocations of French opinion from July 1866 to 13 July 1870, ignores the pride that is infused throughout a national state. Bismarck, as a master manipulator of the state system, as an artful molder of opinion in his own country, knew well how to pull the strings and strike the right notes. That the French rose up in a furious rage was not an act of idiotic susceptibility. It was the natural and human conditioned response to a cumulative series of Prussian irritations and provocations.

The French council then met for a six-hour session. First they ordered the mobilization of the reserves; then in more sober mood they decided on calling upon a European conference to extricate France from the insult. After this long session the empress remarked sharply to the emperor: "I doubt that that will correspond to the sentiments of the chambers and the country." The emperor knew what the outward aspect of Paris and provincial sentiment had been during the last week and a half; he could well imagine what it would be now. Not the empress' words so much as the prospect they evoked brought down the conference idea in the emperor's mind like a house of cards. Ollivier had been doing some thinking along the same line. Nor could it have been just the adverse reaction of his family to the conference idea that converted Ollivier. He must have realized himself, after more quiet reflection, that this straw which broke the camel's back was forcing them to grasp with unrealistic hope at another straw which would let them sink into ignominy. However they turned, they could not escape what they *anticipated* opinion would be. Napoleon and Ollivier both came back to the decision of a declaration of war. "I think the same as you do, Sire; if we took it [the conference proposal] to the chamber, they would throw mud at our carriages and hiss us."[81] Soon thereafter came the news of the insult carried in official form by a circular to foreign capitals. That astounding fact sealed the decision.[82]

Anticipated and Fragmentary Opinion

This decision for war, made before the French public was fully aware of the insult, has led some to conclude that public opinion had little to do with it.[83] Furthermore, no systematic consultation of opinion was made on this serious step such as had been made on Gramont's declaration.

The question first arises of how they could have consulted opinion overnight. But, on the other hand, could they not have given themselves time to consult opinion again? That would have hardly been possible. From Moltke's remarks we know that it was a question of who could mobilize faster. The French cabinet recognized that by his final insult Bismarck had torn off the mask and was bent on war now. They naturally assumed that the Iron Chancellor had begun full mobilization.[84] Le Boeuf, the French minister of war, was therefore frantic to have permission to call up the reserves. This they gave him before going to parliament for aproval of a declaration of war. Knowing the mood of the large majority of the two houses on previous days, the cabinet could not have expected legislative consent to postpone war for a week to consult opinion systematically, while the Prussians supposedly gained a week's advantage over France in mobilization. The die had already been cast by Bismarck at his dinner party and by the French cabinet on the night of 14 July. The Prussians would have officially declared war at the first news of French mobilization anyway. Events were moving so rapidly that it was a question of hours and minutes. Lord says that even the time taken to code and decode telegrams must be considered.[85]

Imagine, then, the consultation of opinion under such circumstances. The legislative body would have been asked to postpone action until the government consulted their constituents. The newspaper editorials of the 15th and 16th would have had to be awaited and analyzed. The prefects and procureurs general would have been instructed to conduct surveys and send in exact reports. Then the cumbrous machinery, on the style of a Gallup poll, would have begun to grind slowly: subprefects, mayors, procureur assistants, justices of the peace, surveying and reporting; prefects and procureurs general conscientiously drawing up special reports on so awful a question of war and peace. After that would have to come the painstaking analyses in the ministries of interior and justice. Working at the fastest, they could then have achieved a satisfactory consultation of opinion perhaps in a week, a week while the Prussians were supposedly arming and the French waiting. Obviously no such consultation could have been made.

Does that mean, however, that French public opinion was not a factor in the declaration of war? Possibly a phrase in Carroll's study gives us a suggestion of the answer. Speaking of the demand for reassurances for the future, he says: "If Gramont's decision had any relation to public opinion, it was merely *in anticipation of its eventual reactions.*"[86] That, perhaps, is the key to the role of opinion. A representative government, like the new parliamentary empire in France, established by plebiscite earlier in 1870, had to consider opinion even more than the autocratic Napoleon III had had to do it previously. There can, then, be no denying a constant attention to opinion. In a touch-and-go situation between 14 and 16 July, the concern for opinion had to be largely anticipatory, but that means emphatically that opinion was still an important factor.

Statesmanship is two-thirds hindsight and one-third foresight, or to put it another way, two-thirds history and one-third prophecy. Were the anticipations of opinion by Napoleon III, Ollivier, and Gramont based soundly on history, on past experience? Napoleon III remembered with much embarrassment the great reversal of opinion after Prussia's overwhelming victory in the Austro-Prussian War; he recalled the desire for war then, the unrequited demands for compensation, the unconvinced reaction to the La Valette circular, the stifled anger over the Luxemburg settlement, the uninterrupted and continuous burning hatred and fear of Prussia since 1866.[87] Between March 1867 and October 1869 there were found sixty procureur and prefect reports dealing with attitudes toward Prussia, representing every judicial district except Angers, Nîmes, and Corsica; and every one of these, save two, showed hatred or distrust of Prussia. Likewise, a great many of these passages were generously underlined in pencil by the attentive readers in the ministry of justice.[88]

Hostility toward Prussia, however, did not necessarily mean a desire for war. There was a widespread desire for war right after the Austro-Prussian War,[89] but, as we approach 1870, we see that belligerency die down. There was a gradual lull in warlike feeling. Between March 1867 and October 1869 there were ninety procureur and prefect reports, representing every judicial district in France, except Besançon, which described opinion on war and peace. A breakdown of these is as follows:

70 reports favoring peace

6 reports showing a rather even division between war and peace sentiment

14 reports favoring war against Prussia

9 pro-peace reports preferring war to the unsettled business conditions caused by uncertainty

There can be no doubt that the preponderance of opinion all over the country before 3 July 1870 was in favor of peace.[90]

However, using past experience and the special prefect reports of July as guides to anticipating opinion, the French government would have to consider the unremitting hatred of Prussia since 1866; they would have to remember the sudden reversal from peace to war sentiment caused by Sadowa, and the criticism of the government everywhere for its peaceful mediation in 1866. On this basis Gramont would have had to anticipate a violent reaction against Prussia as soon as the Hohenzollern candidacy was announced. Thus he made a restrained anti-Prussian declaration on 6 July. Soon he also had the special prefect reports to tell him that the country liked it. From this evidence as well as by that of the majority of the papers, police reports from Paris, observation of ambassadors and the *Times* correspondent—Gramont was sustained in his anticipation of opinion.[91] From that he guessed what would be opinion's reaction to "Father Anthony's" renunciation. Again he was sustained, but by evidence gleaned from less reliable and more unscientific sources of opinion—sources, however, which had to be used in the fast-moving crisis for want of any others. That is, he was sustained in his demand for future assurances and, as corroboration, *not* sustained in his contrary statement to the legislature.

Thus, when not only Gramont but the entire French nation received the slap in the face on 14 July, the trio of emperor, Ollivier, and Gramont had a good idea from long-range and immediate hindsight to guess what would be public and parliamentary reaction to the brazen provocation from Berlin. From this, war seemed the only possible outcome, even after flirting with the conference idea, and mobilization had to be ordered. Metternich, the Austrian ambassador, saw the long sweep of events clearly. To Vienna he wrote:

It must not be forgotten that in the present circumstances the least pretext would necessarily arouse all the susceptibilities of the French nation hardly quieted since 1866—that a spark falling on these smoldering embers could not avoid rekindling these fires of discontent, of bitter memories, and of jealous distrust. Such is the situation today when war seems inevitable.[92]

If an Austrian could thus connect the past with the present, was it not logical that French leaders were doing the same?

It is unfair to accuse Ollivier of reverting to the war decision just on seeing the reaction of his family and friends, or to insinuate that Napolen III succumbed to the empress' caustic reply. They all, Ollivier and family and emperor and empress, were consciously or unconsciously anticipating general public opinion in the light of the past few years and the last few days. In these hectic hours they could only know the substantial form of the opinion of the past. The opinion of the future they thought they could see, but it was like a will-o'-the-wisp, a shimmering, formless glow, ever beckoning them on into the quicksands of war.

Opinion Reactions on 14 July

Was the final fateful guess of the trio justified by the events of 14-16 July? At least five newspapers published the Ems dispatch in the evening of the 14th;[93] all the newspapers, morning and evening, had the news on the 15th. In these five early accounts there was not only the Ems dispatch with its abrupt refusal of William to see Benedetti, but below it was an additional item of news saying that the paper had heard that William may have approved the renunciation. It would have been expected that the lower item would have taken the sting out of the provocative Ems item. From mouth to mouth the news ran faster, if possible, than that of "Father Anthony's" renunciation two days before. And seemingly the Ems dispatch with its insult took the upper hand over the rumor published beneath it. La Gorce, a contemporary witness of that night, wrote: "On the 15th, from the first hours of that day, a rumor began to spread: people were speaking of an audience refused, of an ambassador dismissed [congédié], of an insult making war inevitable. They scrambled for newspapers. They repeated rumors, but without being too exact. Almost all of them [the papers] stressed the belligerent note."[94] What amazed the avid readers especially was a late postscript in the Constitutionnel—the peace paper which had insisted, on Ollivier's advice, that "Father Anthony's" renunciation was enough, the paper whose last issue they had torn up and thrown into the gutter—this paper said: "At the moment we go to press, we learn that the latest news appears to diminish the chances of peace." Then it published the provocative and shortened Ems Dispatch.[95] "Its language made a special impression," said La Gorce.[96] And La Gorce apparently did not see the most exciting demonstrations of this first night. Here are some of the accounts:

(Lyons of England): Although the news of the appearance of the article in the "North German Gazette" had not become generally known, the public excitement was so great, and so much irritation existed in the army, that it became doubtful whether the Government could withstand the cry for war, even if it were able to announce a decided diplomatic success. It was felt that when the Prussian article appeared in the Paris evening papers it would be very difficult to restrain the anger of the people, and it was generally thought that the Government would feel bound to appease the public impatience by formally declaring its intention to resent the conduct of Prussia.[97]

(Palat): When the evening papers scattered the fateful news over the city, the explosion exceeded anything the best informed observers could have expected.[98]

(Special Police Report): A large crowd, which increased and diminished while on the march, coming from the Bastille, went up the boulevard with the flag carried in front, crying Long Live France!, singing the *Chant des Girondins* and the *Marseillaise*. Cries of Long Live the Emperor! Long Live the Army! Long Live France! were mingled with the singing. Applause from the cafes and private homes answered them. Some individuals who tried to object were manhandled. Boulevard Beaumarchais, Place du Château-d'Eau, Rue de Rambuteau, Place de Châtelet, Rue de Rivoli, Boulevard Saint-Michel, Boulevard du Palais, had the same demonstrations.[99]

(Kern of Switzerland): Last evening warlike demonstrations by large crowds [*par public nombreux*] on boulevards. Groups shouted Down with Prussia! in front of the Prussian embassy.[100]

(Prefect of Police): Last evening was very troubled, and prowar demonstrations occurred in several parts of Paris. Without waiting for the general report on these demonstrations, I believe I should immediately mention the one which took place, toward midnight, on the approaches to the Prussia embassy. Several crowds of between 600 and 1200 people approached the residence of M. de Werther, shouting: Long Live France! Long Live War! Down with Prussia! On to Berlin! Some of them even tried to scale the gates.

The police officer on duty, who had taken precautions, held them back, and lectured them on their behavior. They obeyed his admonitions. Count Daru and Marquis Villeneuve joined him in his efforts, and M. de Werther called him and thanked him.

The officer on duty said he had orders to protect the embassy and that a service had been established for that purpose.

During these incidents all the personnel of the Prussian embassy gathered in the courtyard of the building, a prey to acute excitement.[101]

Another police report told of traffic jams caused by the crowds. Omnibuses had to change their routes.[102]

All of this occurred with the news from about six papers, merely reproducing the curtailed Ems dispatch, and from the rumors circulating during the night and early morning. Lord Lyons gives us reason to suspect that this was in fact a culmination of the anti-Prussian sentiment stemming from anger over the "Father Anthony" renunciation. The Ems dispatch had picked up from where the inadequate withdrawal left off and swirled the feeling into the giant demonstrations of 14 July. The government had anticipated rightly, and Bismarck had calculated well his planted mine. Across the darkened sky of Paris a red rag had been flaunted; and the Gallic bulls had gone roaring into boulevard and square, charging head down against the very gates of the Prussian embassy.

Crescendo and Contretemps on 15 July

The day of the 15th dawned with all attention turned to the Palais Bourbon, seat of the legislative body, where the government would request a declaration of war by seeking approval of a war appropriation. Ollivier entered at one o'clock. His speech was given great applause and received with enthusiasm. There was no doubt that the great majority had been as aroused as the crowds, perhaps by the crowds of the night before. There was a minority, however, mostly on the left, but containing such men as Thiers, Favre, and

Gambetta, which refused to be stampeded. They wanted to see the documents (reports of Bismarck's insulting circular). Ollivier replied that they had been quoted in his declaration.[103] In closing his remarks, he tried to resort to a peroration, but after days and nights of crisis he was not at his best in choosing words. He said he accepted the decision "with a light heart," when he meant to say "with a clear conscience." His enemies badgered him with those words for years, but historians have since tended to accept his explanation. The chamber voted against demanding the documents but compromised by having the ministers appear with the documents before a committee. This delayed the deliberations until evening.

In the meantime the senate had moved faster, acclaiming Gramont's identical statement and proceeding to a quick vote of war. By now people were getting out of work and the crowds began to form for another night of demonstration.

Since the street manifestations were the main source for governmental information on opinion in these two critical days, considerable attention must be given them, particularly because some contemporaries and some historians have tried to belittle them or question the genuineness of their sentiments or spirit. Carroll definitely discounts them.

> The significance of the demonstrations on the boulevards [he wrote] during the evenings of the thirteenth and fourteenth as evidence of a general demand for war has been exaggerated. In view of the tension between the governments of France and Prussia, it was natural that crowds should gather and that chauvinists should make use of them.[104]

He then quotes Jules Simon and Thiers, two prejudiced antiwar contemporaries, to support his minimizing conclusions.

> (Simon): Everybody then believed that demonstrations were in fact organized by the police.
> (Thiers): The mass of the people disapproved of the demonstrations. I myself drove through the streets in an open carriage with MM. Daru and Buffet, and we were able to perceive the reality of things, it was that the people were far from wanting war.[105]

It is necessary, however, to examine a few other less prejudiced accounts to complete the picture of the night of 15-16 July.

> (Kern of Switzerland): Last evening, renewed manifestations took place on the streets of Paris. Only, along with prowar demonstrations, part of the public showed its sympathies for peace; these were in a very small minority. Hostile manifestations were made again before the building of the Prussian embassy, but this time they were stopped by the police.[106]
> (Princess Pauline Metternich of Austria): Paris was given over to unrestrained enthusiasm, and cries of On to Berlin! On to Berlin! resounded on all sides. People were elated, and don't let them try to tell me today, as they like to do, that nobody in France wanted war. *Everybody wanted it.* I speak of Paris at least, where young and old were literally mad. The old Duke of Caumont, on leaving the senate, screamed at the top of his lungs, On to Berlin!, not only as he climbed into his carriage, but he kept it up all the way from the Luxemburg to the Jockey Club. He waved his hat in the air and acted like a mad man. Instead of laughing at him, they admired his ardent patriotism! Everybody had lost his head.[107]

(Quadt of Bavaria): Even if the promises given by the Duke of Gramont [not to annex German territory] should be thought sincere, still I cannot refrain from noticing that from the chauvinism predominating here, it is not thinkable that a victorious France will show such an unusual disinterestedness when the day comes. . . . . Last night there took place here many disturbances of a republican character in which both peace and war parties demonstrated.[108]

(Beyens of Belgium): [After Ollivier's speech.] The people have also exhibited their joy by loud acclamations. . . . . The war will be very popular and the fury terrible.[109]

(Baroche [antiwar]): In Paris the enthusiasm is great and crowds are running through the streets and boulevards day and night, crying Long Live the Emperor! On to Berlin![110]

(Ollivier): [He gives much space to prowar demonstrations but admits counter-demonstrations.] However, on that day [15th] the Republicans organized a counter-demonstration in support of their orators in the chamber. From the Saint-Denis Gate, on the terreplein of the Gymnase, especially in front of the Café de Madrid, at the entrance to Faubourg Montmartre, big crowds were massed, howling Long Live Peace! Long Live Bismarck! All the public-meeting people were there as well as the editors of the demagogic press. For a moment, by their compactness and their discipline they seemed to have the upper hand over the opposing manifestations. But these [latter] manifestations were not long in making themselves felt, a collision took place, the Café de Madrid closed its doors, and the instigators disappeared. These miserable efforts only made more significant the passionate approval of the immense majority of the people of Paris.[111]

(La Gorce): [Describing the reassembled legislative body.] From time to time some newly arriving member passed about rumors from the city. They seemed made-to-order for the war party. On the boulevards and on the approaches to the Bastille they were hearing the *Marseillaise* sung, no longer intoned with caution [*à mi-voix*] but resounding with a provocative accent. Compact crowds were running the streets, shouting On to Berlin! Down with Prussia! The brilliance of the illuminations began to shine in the gathering darkness. That's what the news-mongers were reporting. Under these impressions the undecided began to give in; they let it be said, even repeated it themselves, that they were overwhelmed.[112]

Back in the legislative body the committee finally reported in favor of the government's war proposal, and around midnight the lower house approved it, 245-10.

It will be noticed that Kern, Quadt, and Ollivier all show that the demonstrations were not unanimous. Counterdemonstrations had taken place just as there had been opposition speeches in the legislative body. But almost every observer of these demonstrations conceded that the prowar crowds had definitely carried the day. Kern, Princess Metternich, Quadt, Beyens, Baroche, La Gorce, Rouher, Magne, Dréolle, Allain-Targé—and Ollivier whom we shall not count—testify to the preponderance of the war sentiment of the crowds.[113] Thiers's statement that "the people were far from wanting war" can hardly be sustained in the face of the testimony of other antiwar and foreign witnesses of the dramatic day of the 15th.

Opinion Post-Mortem

The charge of Simon still remains to be considered that "everybody believed . . . . these demonstrations . . . . were organized by the police," as well as the charge that the government even manufactured opinion rather than followed it.[114] As evidence of government prowar influence on the press Gramont's note to Ollivier of

3 July is cited, which said: "Starting tomorrow we will begin a cautious but effective campaign in the press."[115] What Gramont meant is shown by his later communications. To Mercier in Madrid he telegraphed: "This intrigue concocted by Prim with Prussia against France must be combatted effectively, and, to do it, you must use as much tact, prudence, and reserve as you do ingenuity and energy. Act on the press and through your friends without compromising yourself."[116] What Gramont had in mind here shows that he was thinking quite as much of the foreign (Spanish) press as of the French press, a common concern of all diplomats. We already know how the Prussians, Austrians, and Italians tried to influence the French press. Here Gramont was not trying to stir up war but merely to bring to the Spanish public the fact that France would combat the Hohenzollern candidacy. No fair-minded contemporary or historian has ever contested France's right to be opposed to the candidacy. Then Gramont turned to the *Constitutionnel*, which took inspiration from him and Ollivier, and suggested this tone for the first announcement: "But, while acknowledging the sovereignty of the Spanish people, the sole competent judge in such a matter, we could not repress a movement of surprise at seeing the scepter of Charles V confided to a Prussian prince."[117] Here is seen again that it was directed toward the Spanish people, who would be reading French newspapers or translations of them, to note French reactions. Also this merely registered French antipathy to a Hohenzollern on the Spanish throne—which was not an incitation to war. This was certainly cautious, whether effective or not.

What is more, other papers, obviously not under his control, were taking a stronger and not as cautious a stand as Gramont. Walsh, a consistent Legitimist opponent of the government, sent this telegraphic suggestion to the editor of the Legitimist *Gazette de France* on hearing the news: "Affirm and unmask this Prussian, Spanish, Portuguese intrigue."[118] The London papers, *Times, Standard, Daily Telegraph*, and *Pall Mall Gazette*, all denounced Prussia's conduct and the Hohenzollern candidacy in much stronger terms than Gramont's inspiration to the *Constitutionnel*.

This idea of governmental incitation to war seems completely torpedoed by the Anthony renunciation. Ollivier deliberately persuaded the *Constitutionnel* to advocate acceptance of the Anthony decision. Thus the two papers co-operative with the government, the *Constitutionnel* and the *Patrie*, found themselves in the opposite camp from that of the warlike newspapers between the 12th and the 14th— a strange inspiration if the government was trying to drum up a war. We know now that on the 13th the cabinet decided to accept the withdrawal without Prussia's participation, hoping that they might get Leopold's confirmation. Since this would have caused a furor in the

French public, it is inconceivable that the government would have incited the press and the mobs on those days. Then even after the Ems dispatch the cabinet decided initially to accept a conference rather than war. There would have been no purpose in inciting papers and mobs until that decision was changed. As we have seen, by the time the cabinet returned to the policy of declaring war, the papers and the people were already on the rampage. After the publication of the Ems dispatch, there were only five important papers which remained in the antiwar group: the *Temps, Siècle, Gazette de France, Journal des Débats*, and *Journal de Paris*.[119] That means that seven antiwar papers on 12 July had switched on 15 July to being prowar. That could not have been accomplished by the government, which was up to the last minute considering a peaceful conference. Actually, what every fair-minded student of these events must admit, the opinion which switched seven newspapers to favor war and which sent thousands upon thousands of Frenchmen surging into the streets had been manufactured, not by the government, but by a Prussian sitting in a dining room, rewriting a telegram.

The same arguments concerning the press apply to the accusation that the police stirred up the crowds to demonstrate for war. As has already been suggested, the government would have been considerably embarrassed to be accepting the Anthony (or Leopold) renunciation and a peace conference with one hand while whipping up the fury of the mobs with the other. It is almost inconceivable that the police would have done it in spite of the government. They were under the authority of the minister of interior, Chevandier, who was definitely antiwar in the cabinet.[120] He could not have done it himself, and he most surely would have known if someone else were doing it on such a large scale and would have put a stop to it.

Inspiring public demonstrations had been a common practice under the authoritarian empire. Hence it was natural for the public to suspect police incitation. But this was a responsible parliamentary cabinet with various shades of opinion within itself. There is little evidence beyond the carry-over of suspicion to sustain the charge. The foreign diplomats, who usually had a very good nose for intrigue, in all their reports took the demonstrations to be genuine and predominantly prowar. Jules Simon used the negative argument that the government only had to say the word and the demonstrations would have been stopped, another idea carried over from the authoritarian days.[121] But this innuendo comes with poor grace from Simon, the Republican who had always opposed the authoritarian government's repressive measures. And what a wholesale repression it would have to have been! By doing as Simon suggested, the government would have robbed itself of one of the two ways it still had to ascertain opinion in a fast-moving crisis. To have tampered

with the demonstrations either way would have left the government
in the dark. While still suspicious of government instigation, the
Times correspondent was fairer when he noted "the general impression that the government was not sorry to give the patriotic anti-
Prussian sentiment full play, partly to see what it was worth and
partly to make war popular."[122] According to this, the general impression was that the government was not instigating demonstrations
but leaving them the greatest freedom for the very best purpose—"to
see what it was worth." It would have been worthless if manufactured. There is considerable evidence, too, that the government
gave the peace demonstrations "full play" as well. If these did not
succeed so well, it was more because of the other free counterdemonstrations than because of police intervention. Indeed, the most important police interventions reported were against the prowar demonstrators at the gates of the Prussian embassy and before the residences
of Ollivier and Thiers.

Difficult as it was to obtain clear indications of opinion in Paris,
it was extremely difficult, if not impossible, to get any significant
sampling in the provinces during these last days. All the leaders
could have known was about the past, the dislike of France's position since 1866, the hatred of Prussia, the return to more peaceful
inclinations since 1867, and the revival of the war spirit in the
provinces the week before. Paris would have to be the barometer
for the rest of the country on the last two days, but in crises such
as 1792 and 1848 it had seemed as if Paris went further than the
country wanted. The government had good grounds for anticipating
that the provinces would want war under these very recent provocations, but it should have been somewhat wary about anticipating reactions similar to those in Paris. Yet the *Français*, a paper friendly
to the antiwar Thiers, seemed to confirm the prowar sentiments of
the provinces as expressed in the prefect reports:

> The news which arrives from the provinces is excellent; opinion welcomes the
> idea of the war against Prussia, not with that noisy effervescence which bursts out
> on the boulevards, but with a calm confidence and a virile resolution.[123]

The *Constitutionnel*, a peace paper four days before, also substantiates this:

> There has been in all France but one cry, but one single burst of enthusiasm.
> Yesterday, the declaration of the government, sent to the prefects in the afternoon,
> was posted up everywhere. It appeared sufficiently conclusive, and the people did
> not deliberate in order to take sides resolutely with the war. They report to us
> demonstrations in all the cities, with torchlight parades accompanied by national
> songs.
> The department seats where these unequivocal signs of French sentiment gave
> most energetic evidence are Perpignan, Nîmes, Tarbes, southern cities, patriotic
> centers from which heroes have come and will still come. Nancy has let her repug-
> nance of the foreigner be seen and has shown the energy that Lorraine will furnish
> to repulse him if he invades her territory. Lille was the scene of great popular
> demonstrations; Amiens is not behind Lille. On this side, as on all the others, the

frontier is well guarded. We have similar news from Dijon, le Havre, from the north, south, and center.[124]

There are, too, some prefect reports of August which describe provincial reaction to the outbreak of war. They come from other regions than those mentioned above in the *Constitutionnel* and therefore broaden the picture: (Manche) "The people of Manche unhesitatingly approved the policy of the government in the affairs of Germany." (Seine-Inférieure) "Never . . . . has agreement between public opinion and the government been more complete than in this circumstance." (Allier) "Opinion has ratified the attitude of the government in the Franco-Prussian dispute." (Haute-Vienne) "Revealing to public opinion the unworthy maneuvers of Bismarck has increased still more the popularity of the present war." (Bouches-du-Rhône) "The declaration of war was greeted with the greatest enthusiasm by the people. . . . . The dynastic, liberal, and Legitimist papers support the war and approve its justification."[125]

We can see that these reports portray about the same situation as in Paris: an overwhelming support for the government in the dispute and in the declaration of war that followed. These August reports also support the findings in the earlier special July reports from the departments.

From the beginning, then, the government was anticipating opinion and looking for subsequent confirmation. It does not seem from the evidence that it controlled appreciably the press or the demonstrations for the purpose of stirring up war feeling. However, either by anticipation or immediate participation, public opinion through the press, the prefect reports, the street demonstrations, and perhaps the legislative debates did play a definite role in moving events toward war. From the evidence at hand it seems to have opposed the Hohenzollern candidacy, blamed Prussia for its occurrence, rejected the Anthony renunciation, caught the implication of the Ems dispatch, and roared for war to defend France's honor. In the anticipation and evaluation of public opinion Gramont and the empress seemed closer to opinion than did Napoleon III and Ollivier, who were frequently seeking escapist alternatives. Opinion itself had alternated several times between peace and war since 1865. It ended on the note of war. Thus, on a July day in 1870, the "inevitable" war came to an ill-prepared France. Bismarck had willed it; the French government had declared it; but French public opinion, by its acts of commission and omission since 1865, had been an ever-present accessory before the fact.

CHAPTER XI

A VOICE CRYING IN THE WILDERNESS

There Was a Voice

A reading of the preceding chapters leaves no doubt that public opinion was an important factor in the formulation of French foreign policy in the middle of the nineteenth century. Even considered from the point of view of the shackled press, one is nonetheless convinced of the influence opinion played. The very circumstances which show that the press was censored, bribed, bludgeoned, and inundated with syndicated articles all bespeak the concern over opinion and its expression. But on the positive side, the systematic efforts made by the government to ascertain genuine opinion beneath the sham of press opinion by ordering the continuous sounding of opinion by the procureurs general, prefects, and prefects of police are convincing proof that there was not only a voice but also loud-speakers by which the voice could be heard in accents clear.

The chancelleries and embassies, however much they might be peopled by haughty nobles and aristocrats of the old school, no longer scorned the voice of the people. Foreign ministers inquired, embassy officials watched with eagle eye, budgets provided for secret funds to bribe and cajol, and ambassadors reported on opinion unendingly in their roles as the eyes and ears of a distant sovereign. Election results were analyzed; the galleries were filled during legislative debates; stock-market quotations were scanned, not so much in the interest of investments as for a barometric reading of the pressures of a certain class of the public.

Not only was great effort expended at the listening posts but also attention was turned to evoking expressions of opinion by trial balloons. Speeches were made, chance remarks uttered, articles written, documents presented, and pamphlets, especially, were published—all with the intent of eliciting responses. These devices were not in every instance to persuade the public, quite as often they were used as compasses to find directions or as registers to determine the amount and types of resistance to be overcome.

Among the various media by which opinion was given a chance to express itself, there were both poor ones and others more effective. The press was hopeless because of censorship, pressures, and bribery.

There were rare occasions, such as the Danish War, when the press and general opinion seemed almost identical. But more often, as in the Eastern question, the Rouher speech, the anti-Prussian sentiment during the Polish insurrection, the mediation announcement of 4 July 1866, the newspapers were far from reflecting the public as analyzed by the more systematic procureur and prefect reports. Any resemblance between press opinion and public opinion was largely coincidental. The rigged elections and the packed legislatures were not even taken seriously by Napoleon III himself as weathervanes of opinion.

On the other hand the intricate machinery set up by the procureurs general, the prefects, and the Paris prefect of police to ascertain and sample opinion, to check and countercheck it, to tally and analyze it, should evoke the admiration of such moderns as George Gallup and Elmo Roper. While it is regrettable that the reports of the prefect of police no longer exist, one must be thankful that the voluminous files of the procureur and prefect reports have given us ample and detailed evidence on the thinking of Frenchmen about their foreign affairs. A word should be said too for public demonstrations. Where they were spontaneous and not synthetic, they gave evidence of immediate and quick reactions to sudden events when the slower-moving administrative reports were not at hand. Besides, the parades, the cheering from the balconies, the illuminations, the bonfires, all not only registered reactions, they added a color and warmth so often missing in the drab reports of administrators.

"He That Hath Ears to Hear, Let Him Hear"

All of these arrangements for searching out opinion were not, like frequent administrative and military boondoggling, much ado about nothing. These reports, especially those of the procureurs general, were read, underscored, criticized, analyzed, summarized, and extracted. Rechecks on the surveys were made on critical occasions before both the Austro-Sardinian and Austro-Prussian Wars. If the reports had not been useful in more normal times, they would hardly have called for special reports in times of crises. Yet during the Austro-Sardinian War weekly reports were demanded of the procureurs general, and special reports were called for during the debate on the army bill and during the Spanish throne incident. At times the prefects were called in to Paris for direct reporting. The empress, La Valette, Cowley, Beyens, Rogier, Goltz, and Vautier all affirm the fact that the procureur and prefect reports were not only studied but actually studied at the highest level of the emperor and empress themselves.

Nor was the attention given to these reports just to satisfy idle curiosity. There is ample evidence that the information was weighed in determining policy and in choosing the means to use toward certain policies. In at least twelve known instances involving important policy do we see public opinion influencing decisions: hastening the peace in 1856, delaying the Austro-Sardinian War, contributing to the sudden armistice at Villafranca, preventing the government from abandoning the pope's temporal power, pressing the government to return to Rome in 1867, compelling it to protest in favor of the insurgent Poles, insisting on territorial compensations in the direction of the Rhine, and rejecting an effective army bill. In two instances opinion stood out as the strongest influence in determining major decisions: in swaying the emperor against forceful intervention after Sadowa and in forcing the government to take a firm stand on the Spanish throne question and to declare war after the Ems dispatch.

Yet it must be admitted that public opinion did not always have its way. In 1859 the emperor went right ahead with his plans to precipitate a war with Austria, knowing full well that opinion was against it. Again between 1861 and 1866 the government undertook and persisted in the Mexican expedition over the strong and continuous protests of the great majority of the people.

One aspect of public opinion that must not be overlooked by students is its influence before the fact. The anticipation by policymakers of what opinion would be is almost as important an opinion factor as opinion already expressed. After years of searching out opinion and studying its moods under certain circumstances the government was in a position to estimate the reactions of the immediate future. These calculations were just as valid opinion influences as the direct pressure from a developed opinion. It was quite a common occurrence for the empress to say that if such and such was done or not done, it would mean the end of the dynasty. The annexation of Savoy and Nice, the dismissal of Thouvenel and Drouyn de Lhuys, and the reoccupation of Rome in 1867 were all motivated by the anticipated effect it would have on opinion. The emperor's mediation announcement in the *Moniteur* of 5 July 1866 was clearly predicated on an anticipated expression of opinion. The expected result occurred instantaneously and precisely in the estimated direction. The only difficulty was its unexpected force. The sorcerer's apprentice had waved his wand, the waters gushed forth, but the poor apprentice was powerless to stem the tide. In the last months of the Second Empire anticipated opinion played an ever greater role in the rapid events of the two weeks prior to the declaration of war against Prussia. Here fatal decisions had to be made before the cumbrous machinery of administrative reports could give accurate accounts of opinion. The government leaders knew that the Paris press did not speak clearly for the rest of the country. They had to judge largely by their knowledge of past opinion reports. The later Paris responses to their antici-

pations merely confirmed them and encouraged the leaders to continue an endless chain of further anticipations. Here we do not have
a simple problem in cause and effect, it is a more devious one of the
effect anticipating the cause on the basis of prior causes.

"Interest Speaks All Sorts of Tongues"

There is no doubt that the voice of the people spoke and received attention, but of more fundamental importance, what did it
say? It was, of course, the noise of many waters, and not one clear
call for all of France. Yet, in a few instances it seemed to speak as
one voice. On the eve of every war except the last it spoke for peace;
on some occasions when war was avoided, it had also called for
peace, as in the Polish affair. On the question of preserving the pope's
temporal power sentiment, while not unanimous, was preponderant
for its preservation. Not just the clericals and Legitimists, not just
the wealthy bourgeoisie, concerned with temporal power as a property
right, not just the peasant who somehow felt that its loss would be
a sacrilege, but even the Protestants of Alsace stopped short of the
ultimate in lawlessness and confiscation. Frenchmen of the Second
Empire were not on the whole revolutionists, they were nationalists,
that is, French patriots. When it became a question of French honor
or French prestige, the voice spoke with little static. The proud ruler
and his noble peers had no monopoly on sense of honor, for from
the humblest cottage of the peasant to the smallest workshop of the
city came renewed homage to the fair name of France whenever
slight or insult was offered. And woe to him who would barter her
honor for a mess of pottage! On these things there could be little
doubt: peace, honor, and a modicum of reverence for their Holy
Father.

However, beyond these few clear tones, the voice of the people
spoke in many tongues. These divergencies may be seen better between classes than between political parties, because parties were
either submerged or blurred during most of the regime. Of all classes
the bourgeoisie and the peasants were the most influential. The bourgeoisie was by far the most insistent on peace, not primarily because
war was thought wrong; the struggle for survival and let the best
man win was the core of its laissez-faire or amoral philosophy. Rather
war interrupted the normal calculations of business, it increased the
taxes on the wealthy who would have to bear them, it decreased the
credit of the governments whose bonds they held, it exalted the
military whose power had more than once thwarted the power of the
business classes. The bourgeois stand on peace came nearer to being one of peace-at-any-price than that of any other group or class
in France. At this point honor and prestige took second place. Only
under one circumstance do we see the bourgeoisie falter on peace:

when the uncertainty of war or peace continued for so long as a deterrent to trade that they preferred war to the uncertainty.

However, France was predominantly agricultural. With the advent of universal suffrage the peasant's attitude was a basic consideration. Here too was an advocate of peace. War or military service took his sons from the work of the farm. Invading troops had time and again ravaged his fields and blocked the outlets to his markets. Stolid and courageous, his was not a coward's heart, but the plowshare and the pruning hook were his weapons against a grudging Nature in his peaceful fields and vineyards. Nevertheless the question of France's honor and prestige weighed more heavily on the countryman than on his bourgeois compatriot. In the rural community reputation, personal dignity, and self-respect counted for much where one was known to all his neighbors. His soil, too, was the soil of France. Therefore he was as concerned over the good name of France as he was for his own good name. There were times when the peasant and his sons would fight rather than have France submit.

On the question of the papacy Jacques the farmer was more realistic than he is usually given credit for. To him the religious hierarchy was mainly the local priest. The priest in prayer to him was natural, the priest in politics to him was ridiculous. For the pope to be priest and king did not suit his fancy enough to cause excitement. Thouvenel knew whereof he spoke when he said *"les vents ne sont plus aux croisades."* The peasant was delighted whenever the great landlords of France were forced to break up their estates; he had no qualms about seeing the pope bereft of most of his States of the Church. But when the Holy Father was reduced to a small plot of ground and to this remnant he held tenaciously as a small proprietor, this Jacques could understand. He supported this kind of temporal power as he would fight for his own landownership. Thus France as a whole never (Rouher's famous word) favored the disappearance of the last vestige of temporal power.

The city worker was almost an anomaly in French society. He existed in relatively small numbers in rather restricted areas of rare urban communities in a France which resisted industrialization right into the twentieth century. As a misfit he usually took the opposite side from that of other Frenchmen. In league with the lower bourgeoisie he could sometimes for short periods take over all of France from the central vantage point of urban Paris. He would proclaim republicanism, anticlericalism, chauvinistic nationalism, even socialism; but in the end the mills of provincial and rural Frenchmen, like those of the gods, would grind slowly but exceedingly fine. Monarchy, the church, a more reasonable patriotism, law and order, and private property would be re-established for the long haul.

Less stable and economically miserable the city proletariat was much more volatile. It sympathized with every revolutionary movement, be it republican, socialistic, or nationalistic. It fed on sensation and excitement. Hurrah for war! if it was to hurl itself against crowned tyrants or to liberate downtrodden peoples. Hurrah for war! if it would send France on a revolutionary crusade across Europe. It wanted war to vindicate the slightest reflection on France's good name. Here was the core of the war spirit in all the European wars of the Second Empire period. From the send-off they gave Napoleon III as he left for the battlefields of north Italy to the street demonstrations of those July days of 1870 the city workers were in the vanguard of the devotees of Mars. Hardly an armistice or a peace treaty received their wholehearted approval. But this voice was out of harmony with the big chorus of all France.

Likewise in their extreme anticlericalism the city workers were an exception to the general rule. French attitudes toward religion and the church went from extreme Christian fanaticism to extreme atheism, with the vast majority in the middle, mingling skepticism with outward perfunctory religious observance. All the forces of clergy and lay clericals could not move the peasantry and bourgeoisie. Yet all the imprecations and fulminations against pope and popery, against power temporal and spiritual, against the very institutions of church and Christianity, hurled by the city workers and their petty bourgeois allies, did not swerve the majority of Frenchmen from their middle course any more than did the fanatical clericals.

All this the government learned and knew as it sifted the voluminous reports of twenty years of surveys of opinion. In most cases its policy in the Near East, in Italy, and in Germany did not depart too far from these basic attitudes of bourgeois and peasant.

This Wilderness World

However, there is a haunting feeling which grows as one studies the foreign policy of the Second Empire, a feeling that perhaps public opinion is a failure as an initiator or supporter of a proper and successful foreign policy. Looked at from the point of view of contemporary private moral standards the French people seemed to be right. They believed in peace, disarmament, the conference method, help for the underdog, law and order, justice. But when these ideas were insisted on by the people and followed by their leaders in foreign affairs, they seemed to lead to wars, humiliations, defeats, disaster, unresolvable dilemmas, and an ever-weakening position in the world. It led also to a serious disagreement between the people and their leader, who saw more clearly than they the type of world with which he had to deal.

Yet it would have been hard for the man in the street to comprehend the state system on the highest level of the world community, indeed it still is today, so different is the state system from the regime of law and order established within national boundaries. For on this highest level there was not one authority keeping law and order and dispensing an even-handed justice, but rather a multitude of separate sovereign-state authorities, each working selfishly against the others for its own national interests. Each state reserved for itself the right to observe or violate the accepted rules of good conduct— misnamed international law; each state decided for itself whether to make or break treaty contracts, how it would interpret rules and treaties, what alliances it would make and adhere to; each state decided if and when it would attack its neighbor for its own profit or survival.

And the principal considerations in all these international situations were not right and justice but power and force. Population, resources, territory, armed might were the factors which counted on the chessboard of diplomacy. Not speeches and resolutions, said Bismarck, but blood and iron. There was but one god, Mars, and the threat of war, his prophet.

There was also the further complication in the nineteenth century, the coming of the industrial revolution. This gradually, almost imperceptibly, transformed the separate controlled national economies into one uncontrolled world economy. A civil war in far-off America crippled the French cotton industries for four long years. The factory women in the department of Aube who had had to turn to prostitution because of acute unemployment could not know that their lives had been changed and their morals undermined by a shot fired upon a place called Fort Sumter.[1] And so the frantic sovereign states, becoming yet more frantic, dashed about for more markets and scarce raw materials, equipping their armies with the new ingenious machines and clashing with their industrial and commercial rivals in ever more desperate wars for survival.

The world community is then still a wilderness jungle; the state system is a system of international anarchy. There the moral code is turned about upon its apex; might makes right, and to the strong go the spoils.

How could the French people understand all this as they insisted on a foreign policy based on civilized principles? They were the heirs of the Roman law and makers of the Napoleonic Code. Their courts dispensed justice on the basis of right. Their contracts were enforced by a legal system. Their police, who kept law and order, were among the best in the world. Their economy was still much more agricultural and artisan than industrial. How could they, in their little nooks and corners of France, conceive that the world system was still back in the primeval forests of brute men? Of course, they had no such conception. They judged the world arena by their national arena. They applied civilized rules of conduct and high private moral standards to the untamed wilderness of world affairs. And thus they faltered and failed.

Here we come face to face with an inevitable question: Should public opinion be allowed to influence foreign affairs? Can people ever be persuaded to the incredible belief that the world is a lawless wilderness? In a complex world of multiple economic factors, of international spying, of co-ordinating by intricate intelligence agencies the top-secret information from a thousand points of the globe, how can plain, honest Jacques know what should be done? More often he is faced with a *fait-accompli* of an Ems Dispatch or a Pearl Harbor. Jacques and his fellow compatriots cannot know enough about, nor make wise decisions on, foreign policy. They can only help in making blunders. More and more it is up to their leaders to know and decide. More and more Jacques has to do what he is told and die on some far-off, strange-named battlefield.

That is not democracy. But can democracy and the state system coexist any longer? The more we approach the study of world diplomacy from the direction of public opinion, the more the conviction grows that democracy and the industrialized state system are now incompatible. The world today is too small and too closely knit to be able to remain half civilized and half barbarian. Either the forces of democracy will establish a system of law and order on the highest level, or the brute forces on the highest level will impose monolithic, totalitarian dictatorships on the national level. Already we have had a preview of the latter alternative. Perhaps the only effective intervention of public opinion in foreign affairs will come at last when this ultimate decision has to be made.

NOTES

PREFACE

1. E. M. Carroll, *French public opinion and foreign affairs, 1870-1914* (New York, 1931).
2. For a more detailed description of these sources, see ch. i.
3. For other works dealing with French opinion on the Mexican Expedition and the American Civil War see W. R. West, *Contemporary French opinion of the American Civil War* (Baltimore, 1924); D. Jordan and E. J. Pratt, *Europe and the American Civil War* (New York, 1931); F. E. Lally, *French opposition to the Mexican policy of the Second Empire* (Baltimore, 1931); F. L. Owsley, *King Cotton diplomacy* (Chicago, 1931); and the more recent work of L. M. Case, *French opinion on the United States and Mexico, 1860-1867; extracts from the reports of the procureurs généraux* (New York, 1936).

CHAPTER ONE

Whence Comes The Voice?

1. The Franco-British allies had just recently won the Crimean campaign with the fall of Sebastopol.
2. *Débats,* 16 Nov. 1855.
3. *Débats,* 10 Feb. 1859.
4. Goltz to Bismarck, Paris, 3 March 1868, *Die auswärtige Politik Preussens,* ed. Historischen Reichs-kommission under the direction of Erich Brandenburg, Otto Hoetzsch, and Hermann Oncken (hereafter cited as APP) (Oldenburg, 1933-1939), IX, 757.
5. Autograph note of Napoleon III, published in R. Halt, ed., *Papiers sauvés des Tuileries* (Paris, 1871), p.25.
6. Cowley to Russell, Paris, 1 April 1861, V. Wellesley and R. Sencourt, *Conversations with Napoleon III* (London, 1934), p.196.
7. Among works showing this tendency are E. M. Carroll, *French public opinion and foreign affairs;* E. M. Carroll, *Germany and the great powers, 1866-1914* (New York, 1938); West, *French Opinion and Civil War;* Lally, *French opposition;* Jordan and Pratt, *Europe and Civil War;* O. J. Hale, *Germany and the diplomatic revolution* (Philadelphia, 1931).
8. L. M. Salmon, *The newpsapers and the historian* (New York, 1923), pp.439-440. Elaborating on the reasons why the press does not represent opinion, Salmon said: "The newspaper that is inherently weak and dishonest may yield to temptation . . . . and withhold news that is disadvantageous to its chief advertisers. . . . . It is often said that the editors, business managers, and the upper class of journalists are well paid, that they meet at social clubs and associate with capitalists, bankers, and men of wealth, and that they unconsciously reflect the views of this class; to this extent they do not represent the masses of the people" *(ibid.,* p.436).
9. Works which stress the role of the press in molding opinion are: Hale, *Diplomatic revolution;* Carroll, *French public opinion;* and S. B. Fay, *Origins of the World War* (New York, 1928).
10. Walter Lippmann, *Public opinion* (New York, 1929), pp.362,363. See also Salmon, p.252.
11. Georges Boris, "The French press," *Foreign affairs,* XIII (Jan. 1935), 322, 324, 326-327.
12. Carroll, *French opinion,* pp.43-46; C. Seignobos, *La Révolution de 1848 —Le Second Empire* in E. Lavisse, *Histoire de France contemporaine* (Paris, 1921), VI, 230-232.
13. Paris, 29 Aug. 1859, *Circulaires, notes et instructions du Second Empire (1851-1870)* (Paris, 1871), p.165.
14. Prefect report (F^{1c} III) from Bouches-du-Rhône 7, c. 7 Dec. 1867.

4—9

15. Same to same, 15 April 1867, *ibid.*, p.674.

16. Nigra to Cavour, Paris, 8 March 1680, *Il carteggio Cavour-Nigra del 1858 al 1861*, ed. Reale Commissione Editrice (Bologna, 1929), III, 154. See also F. L. Owsley, *King Cotton Diplomacy*, pp.179, 220-221, 305-306, 318-320; Jordan and Pratt, pp.220-222; Maurain, *Politique ecclésiastique*, p.158.

17. Prefect report (F^{1c} III), Manche 6, 10 Nov. 1866. See also Carroll, *French opinion*, p.9; Salmon, p.90; H. Avenel, *Histoire de la presse française depuis 1789 jusqu'à nos jours* (Paris, 1900), pp.540-541, 543-544; G. Weill, *Le journal, origines, évolution et rôle de la presse périodique* (Paris, 1936), p.226.

18. Minister of interior to prefects, Paris, 27 May 1857, *Circulaires*, pp. 166-167.

19. *Times*, 27 Sept. 1866. See also prefect report (F^{1c} III), Manche 6, 8 Oct. 1866. See also La Gorce (V, 341) who remarked on the use of syndicated articles to help the Army Bill.

20. Avenel, p.559; Paul de Cassagnac in *Pays*, 8 March 1868.

21. Beyens to Lambermont, [no date], Archives du Ministèrs des affaires étrangères, Brussels, MSS (cited hereafter as AEB), Beyens Papers.

22. Solms to Bismarck, Paris, 9 Dec. 1868, 8 Feb. 1869, APP, X, 327-328 (and footnote), 487 note.

23. Nigra to Cavour, Paris, 5 March 1859, CCN, II, 56. Other evidence of Italian bribery is found in *ibid.*, III, 187, 285.

24. Weill, p.227.

25. Hübner to Buol, Paris, 13 May 1857, Haus, Hof, und Staat Archiv, Vienna, MSS, Buol private papers, cited by Charles W. Hallberg in his yet unpublished study on *Franz Joseph and Napoleon III, 1852-1864*.

26. Until the annexation of Savoy in 1860 there were only twenty-seven courts of appeals. These court of appeals districts, usually made up of about three departments, were located in Agen, Aix, Angers, Amiens, Bastia, Besançon, Bordeaux, Bourges, Caen, Chambéry, Colmar, Dijon, Douai, Grenoble, Limoges, Lyons, Metz, Montpellier, Nancy, Nîmes, Orleans, Paris, Pau, Poitiers, Rennes, Riom, Rouen, and Toulouse.

27. Rouher circular to procureurs general, Paris, 24 Nov. 1849, Archives Nationales, Paris, MSS, series BB^{30}, carton 367.

28. Circulars of 27 Dec. 1852, 31 Dec. 1853, and 11 March 1859 in *ibid.*

29. Circular of 11 March 1859, *ibid.*

30. Procureur special reports, AN, BB^{30} 369, circular of 12 May 1859. Maurain, *Politique ecclésiastique*, p.334, n. 1.

31. Procureur report, Rouen, 3 Feb. 1859. A full description of this series of procureur reports will be found in the bibliography and later on in the footnotes of this chapter. Shortened references, however, will be used throughout this work in the manner of the beginning of this footnote.

32. Procureur report, Paris, 13 Feb. 1860.

33. Procureur report, Dijon, 11 Jan. 1864.

34. See L. M. Case, *United States and Mexico*, pp.309-436.

35. See chapter viii.

36. Procureur report, Besançon, 9 April 1859.

37. Procureur report, Dijon, 13 April 1867.

38. Procureur report, Metz, 10 March 1859.

39. Procureur reports: Montpellier, 5 July 1859; Chambéry, 29 June 1863.

40. Reports on crime and judicial matters are to be found in another separate series, BB^{18}.

41. The weekly reports during the Austro-Sardinian War tended to be shorter than ten pages.

42. The full citation of this collection is: Archives Nationales, Paris, MSS, Ministère de Justice, Rapports périodiques des procureurs généraux, series BB^{30} (hereafter cited as procureur reports, with place and date). When any other series of procureur reports are cited, the series designation will be given, i.e. BB^{18}; when no such designation is given in the footnotes, the citation refers to series BB^{30}. For detailed descriptions of this series see the bibliography at the end of this work as well as Maurain, *Politique ecclésiastique*, pp.xxii-xxiii.

43. Director of criminal affairs and pardons to procureur general at

9—16

Grenoble, Paris 17 Jan. 1860, AN, BB³⁰ 368.

44. AN, BB³⁰ 427-431, 450-451.
45. G. Vautier, "Au-delà et en deçà de nos frontières en 1866," *Révolution de 1848*, XXV (1928), 121-122.
46. *Memoirs of Count Horace de Viel Castel. A chronicle of the principal events, political and social, during the reign of Napoleon III from 1851 to 1864*, ed. Charles Bousfield (2nd ed., London, 1888), II, 258.
47. Carroll, *French opinion*, p.7.
48. Circular of Persigny, Minister of Interior, to the prefects, Paris, 13 Dec. 1860, Archives de l'Isère, Grenoble, MSS, Police générale, file 52 M 42.
49. Beyens to C. Rogier, Paris, 10 June 1866, Archives du ministère belge des affaires étrangères, Brussels, MSS, Correspondance politique (hereafter cited as AEB, CP), Légation française, XXIII, no.83.
50. Prefect reports (F¹ᶜ III), Ain 6, Paris, Dec. 1859.
51. The full citation of this series is Archives Nationales, Paris, MSS, series F¹ᶜ III, Administration générale. Esprit public et élections. Série départmentale. Comptes - rendus administratifs (hereafter cited as prefect reports [F¹ᶜ III]).
52. Goltz to Bismarck, Paris, 26 Oct. 1866; Solms to Bismarck, Paris, 30 Aug. 1867; APP,VIII, 117; IX, 198.
53. Maurain says: "Ce sont des cadres imprimés, où les préfets donnaient, pour chaque rubrique, une brève appréciation" (*Politique ecclésiastique*, p.xii).
54. After using them Maurain also notes that the prefect reports "are completely lacking after the third quarter of 1859" and that "then from November 1865 to the fall of the empire the monthly reports . . . . are almost all preserved" (Maurain, *Politique ecclésiastique*, pp.xi-xii). On the procureur reports Maurain says: "This series . . . . is complete with the exception of the reports from Angers, which are lacking except for 1864 and for 1868 and 1869" (*ibid.*, p.xxiii).
55. These departments were Ain, Allier, Bouches-du-Rhône, Finistère, Gironde, Haute-Vienne, Haut-Rhin, Indre-et-Loire, Isère, Manche, Meuse, Seine-et-Oise, Seine-Inférieure, Vendée.
56. Prefect report (F¹ᶜ III), Isère 7, 6 April 1868.
57. Procureur report from Lyons, 14 Oct. 1869, AN, BB³⁰ 389.
58 Cowley to Russell, Paris, 3 Sept. 1861, Public Record Office, London, MSS, Foreign Office, (hereafter cited as PRO, FO) France, 1396/1088. See also Cowley to Russell, Paris, 18 Jan. 1860, PRO, Russell Papers, G. D. 22/54.
59. Circular of 11 March 1859, AN, BB³⁰ 367.
60. Procureur report, Orleans, 9 Apr. 1864; *ibid.*, Pau, 10 April 1862; *ibid.*, Amiens, 1 Jan. 1863.

CHAPTER TWO

The Crimean War

1. For a discussion of these procureur and prefect reports see ch. i.
2. Procureur reports: Aix, 18 July 1853, and 27 Jan. 1854; prefect reports (F¹ᶜ III): Ain 6 (subprefect of Trévoux), 23 Nov. 1853; Ain 6 (subprefect of Nantua), 30 Dec. 1853; Seine-Inférieure 9, 7 Jan. 1854. Charles de Mazade in the *Revue des deux mondes* [hereafter cited as RDM] and J. B. O'Meagher, Paris correspondent of the London *Times*, both noted this public lack of concern (RDM, 15 Apr. 1853, p.412; 1 July 1853, p.195; *Times*, 23 Mar., 12 and 20 May, 24 June 1853).
3. For the mild, intelligent, and generally pro-British attitudes of business circles and most of the press see RDM (1853), 1 May, p.628; 1 June, pp.1060,1062-1063; 15 June, pp.1247,1251; 1 July, pp.195,197; 15 July, pp. 394-395,397; 15 Aug., pp.829-830; *Times* (1853), 24 Mar., 30 Apr., 30 May, 25 June, 5 July; *Pays* (1853), 27 May, 23 June, 15 July, 24 Sept.; *Journal des Débats* [hereafter cited as *Débats*] (1853), 30 May, 10 Aug., 26 Sept.; *Assemblée Nationale* (1853), 23 Mar., 5,7, 15 July; *Union* (1853), 25 June; *Constitutionnel* (1853), 4 June, 4-5 July; *Siècle* (1853), 18

July, 10 Aug., 24 Sept.; Sanford to Marcy, Paris, 30 June and 14 July 1853, National Archives, Washington, D.C., MSS, State Department Correspondence [hereafter cited as State Dept. Corr.], France, XXXV, nos.12,15; same to same, Paris, 13 June 1853, *ibid.*, French legation copy, Sanford No. 7; Alexandre de Hübner, *Neuf ans d'un ambassadeur d'Autriche à Paris sous le Second Empire, 1851-1859* (Paris, 1904), I, 157.

4. *Times* (report dated 12 Dec.), 14 Dec. 1853.

5. La Gorce, *Second Empire*, I, 199; Sir Spencer Walpole in *Cambridge Modern History* (New York, 1909), XI, 315.

6. For some expressions of press opinion on the Sinope incident see *Constitutionnel,* 10 Dec. 1853; RDM, 1 Jan. 1854, pp.185-186; *Siècle,* 2, 19, 30 Dec. 1853; *Assemblée Nationale,* 3 Jan. 1854.

7. *Times,* 23 Dec. 1853.

8. Cowley to Clarendon, Paris, 16 Dec. 1853, *British and Foreign State Papers,* LXIII (1855-1856), 359.

9. Napoleon III to Nicholas I, Paris, 29 Jan. 1854, Vicomte de Guichen, *La guerre de Crimée (1854-1856) et l'attitude des puissances européennes* (Paris, 1936), pp.114-115.

10. F. Rogier to Brouckère, Paris, 15 Dec. 1853, AEB, CP, Légation française, XVI, no.293.

11. Procureur report, Aix, 27 Jan. 1854.

12. Prefect reports (F^{1c} III), Manche 6, 5 Jan. 1854; Seine-Inférieure 9, 7 Jan. 1854; Isère 7, 1 Jan. 1854; Ain 6, subprefect reports from Nantua, 30 Dec. 1853; Gex, 1 Jan. 1854; Trévoux, 9 Jan. 1854.

13. Barman to Federal Council, Paris, 15 Dec. 1853, Archives Fédérales Suisses, MSS, Ministère des affaires étrangères, Rapports politiques, Légation de Paris [hereafter cited as AFS, RP], 1853. In a report five days later the minister, however, did note a little concern and uncertainty in opinion (Barman to Fed. Council, Paris, 20 Dec. 1853, *ibid.*).

14. La Gorce, *Second Empire,* I, 214.

15. Nassau Senior, *Conversations with M. Thiers and M. Guizot and other distinguished persons during the Second Empire, 1852-1860* (London, 1878), I, 212-213. For the press's constraint and caution in discuss-

ing war and peace see *Constitutionnel,* 9 Jan., 12 Feb. 1854; *Moniteur,* 5-11, 14 Feb. 1854; *Siècle,* 10 Jan., 12 Feb. 1854; RDM, 15 Feb. 1854, pp.830-831; *Débats,* 9 Feb. 1854; *Union,* 11 Jan. 1854; *Assemblée Nationale,* 10 Jan. 1854; *Times,* 13 Jan. 1854.

16. Prefect reports (F^{1c} III): Haut-Rhin 7, 19 Jan. 1854, 4 Feb. 1854; procureur reports, Dijon, 13 Jan. 1854; Metz, 23 Jan. 1854.

17. Procureur reports: Bordeaux, 3 Feb. 1854; Montpellier, 17 Jan. 1854; Toulouse, 2 Feb. 1854; Caen 26 Jan. 1854; Aix, 27 Jan. 1854; prefect reports (F^{1c} III): Gironde 6, 12 Jan. 1854; Indre-et-Loire 7, 18 Jan. 1854.

18. Senior, *Thiers and Guizot,* I, 212-213, 219, 231.

19. For the views of Faucher, Rivet, and Dumont see Senior, *Thiers and Guizot,* I, 206-207, 214, 222-223, 228-229, 231, 243, 281.

20. F. Rogier to Brouckère, Paris, 6, 7, 23 Jan., 14 Feb. 1854, AEB, CP, France, vols. XVI and XVII.

21. Sanford to Marcy, Paris, 9 Jan. 1854, State Dept. Corres., France, vol. XXXV; Barman to Federal Council, Paris, 24 Mar. 1854, AFS, RP, Paris, no.69.

22. Hübner, *Neuf ans,* I, 198, 203.

23. Poggenpohl to the Director of the Chancellery at St. Petersburg, 20 Mar. 1854, *Lettres et papiers du chancellier comte [Charles] de Nesselrode, 1760-1856,* ed. Count A. de Nesselrode (Paris, 1904-1912), XI, 38-39.

24. C. C. E. Greville, *The Greville Memoirs. Part III. A journal of the reign of Queen Victoria from 1852 to 1860* (London, 1887), I, 130-131.

25. Cowley to Clarendon, Paris, 28 Jan. 1854, *Secrets of the Second Empire. Private letters from the Paris embassy. Selections from the papers of Henry Richard Charles Wellesley, 1st Earl Cowley, ambassador at Paris, 1852-1867,* ed. F. A. Wellesley (New York, 1929), p.39.

26. Senior, *Thiers and Guizot,* I, 228-229.

27. *Siècle,* 24 Sept. 1853; RDM, 28 Feb. 1854, pp.1026-1027; *Débats,* 6 Feb. 1854.

28. Hübner, *Neuf ans,* I, 157; Mason to Marcy, Paris, 6 Mar. 1854, State Dept. Corr., France, no.9.

23—34

29. *Union*, 11 Jan. 1854; *Assemblée Nationale*, all during January 1854; *Times*, 13 Jan. 1854.
30. For all the confidences made to Senior see Senior, *Thiers and Guizot*, I, 212, 214, 222-223, 228-229, 231.
31. Baron Napoléon Beyens, *Histoire du Second Empire vu par un diplomate belge* (Paris, 1886), I, 98-99.
32. Cowley to Clarendon, Paris, 28 Jan. 1854, Wellesley, *Cowley letters*, p.39.
33. Hübner, *Neuf ans*, I, 203 (19 Jan. 1854); F. Rogier to Brouckère, Paris, 23 Jan. 1854, AEB, CP, France, XVII, no.19.
34. F. Rogier to Brouckère, Paris, 26 Jan. 1854, AEB, CP, France, XVII, no.24; account of Faucher in Senior, *Thiers and Guizot*, I, 207.
35. Cowley to Clarendon, Paris, 28 Jan. 1854, Wellesley, *Cowley letters*, p.39.
36. *Ibid.*
37. Hübner, *Neuf ans*, I, 205.
38. F. Rogier to Brouckère, Paris, 30 Jan. 1854, AEB, CP, France, no.28.
39. *Moniteur*, 5, 8-11 Feb. 1854; *Times*, 27 Feb. 1854.
40. RDM, 1 Mar. 1854, p.1050; *Débats*, 31 Mar. 1854.
41. *Siècle*, 2 Apr. 1854.
42. Underlining in the ministry of interior.
43. Prefect reports (F¹ᶜ III): Finistère 3, 15 Mar. 1854; Ain 6 (subprefects of Belley and Nantua), 22 Feb. 1854; Haute-Vienne 8, 28 Feb. 1854; Gironde 6, 9 Mar. 1854. Procureur reports: Besançon, 3 July 1854; Colmar, 1 June 1854.
44. Cowley to Clarendon, 16 Feb. 1854, Public Record Office, London, MSS, Foreign Office, France, 27, vol. 1007 (hereafter cited as PRO, FO, 27/1007).
45. Napoleon III to Nicholas I, Paris, 29 Jan. 1854, *Moniteur*, 14 Feb. 1854.
46. F. Rogier to Brouckère, 14 Feb. 1854, AEB, CP, France, no.40; Barman to Fed. Council, 15 Feb. 1854, AFS, RP, Paris, no.38.
47. Cowley to Clarendon, 16 Feb. 1854, PRO, FO, 27/1007.
48. Senior, *Thiers and Guizot*, I, 243.
49. *Constitutionnel*, 16 Feb. 1854.
50. Mason to Marcy, 19 Feb. 1854, State Dept. Corr., France, no.4.
51. Prefect reports (F¹ᶜ III): subprefects of Belley and Trévoux, Ain 6,

22 and 28 Feb. 1854; Meuse 8, 2 Mar. 1854; Manche 6, 7 Mar. 1854; Seine-Inférieure, 9, 14 Mar. 1854.
52. *Moniteur*, 3 Mar. 1854.
53. Mason to Marcy, 6 Mar. 1854, State Dept. Corr., Paris Legation, Mason no.9.
54. *Times*, 6 Mar. 1854.
55. *Univers*, 4 Mar. 1854.
56. *Assemblée Nationale*, 4 Mar. 1854.
57. *Times*, 6 Mar. 1854.
58. Mason to Marcy, 6 Mar. 1854, State Dept. Corr., Paris Legation, Mason no.9.
59. Prefect reports (F¹ᶜ III) of March 1854 from Isère, Seine-Inférieure, Manche, Finistère, Ain, Gironde, and Seine-et-Oise; procureur report from Grenoble, 20 July 1854.
60. La Gorce, *Second Empire*, I, 220-239.
61. RDM, 15 Aug. 1854, p.836.
62. *Ibid.*, 3 Oct. 1854.
63. *Ibid.*, 4 and 6 Oct. 1854.
64. A great hall leading to the court rooms in the Palais de Justice.
65. Henri Dabot, *Souvenirs et impressions d'un bourgeois du Quartier Latin (1854-1869)* (Paris, 1899), p.2.
66. RDM, 15 Oct. 1854, pp.398-399.
67. Taxile Delord, *Histoire du Second Empire* (Paris, 1870-1876), I, 581.
68. La Gorce, *Second Empire*, I, 328-329, 334-335.
69. Barman to Fed. Council, 23 Nov. 1854, AFS, RP, Paris, 1854, no.200.
70 Dabot, *Souvenirs*, p.3.
71. Procureur report, Bourges, 28 Dec. 1854.
72. *Ibid.*, Rouen, 1 Jan. 1855.
73. *Ibid.*, Dijon, 9 Jan. 1855.
74. *Ibid.*, Aix, 17 Jan. 1855.
75. See the procureur reports of January and February 1855 from Agen, Besançon, Bordeaux, Paris, Poitiers, and Rennes; and the prefect reports (F¹ᶜ III): Gironde 6, 19 Jan. 1855; Haut-Rhin 7, 24 Jan. 1855.
76. Delord, *Second Empire*, I, 607.
77. Senior, *Thiers and Guizot*, II, 5.
78. Procureur reports: Amiens, 28 July 1855; Orleans, 24 July 1855.
79. *Ibid.*, Paris, Aug. 1855.
80. Prefect report (F¹ᶜ III), Ain 6, 6 Apr. 1855.
81. La Gorce, *Second Empire*, I, 364.
82. Jean Maurain, *Baroche, ministre de Napoléon III* (Paris, 1936), pp. 161-162.
83. Wellesley, *Cowley letters*, pp.67,

69-70. Cowley wrote to Clarendon on 13 March 1855: "The Emperor's continual hankering after the Crimea has turned all minds here to peace as the only means of preventing the journey, and I believe that, if the Emperor's consent can be obtained, any terms will be accepted that will enable the French Government to bring their army away from the Crimea. Be sure that it is their only object at the moment for they feel that the Emperor's absence may be their doom" (Wellesley and Sencourt, p.75).

84. J. H. Harris, third Earl of Malmesbury, *Memoirs of an ex-minister* (London, 1884), II, 16; Maurain, *Baroche*, p.161.

85. Cowley to Clarendon, Paris, 26 April 1855, Wellesley and Sencourt, p.81.

86. La Gorce, *Second Empire*, I, 354; Hübner, *Neuf ans*, I, 313; Senior, *Thiers and Guizot*, II, 2-3.

87. Hübner, *Neuf ans*, I, 313 (2 Mar. 1855).

88. Barman to Fed. Coun., 3 Mar. 1855, AFS, RP, Paris, 1855, no.30; F. Rogier to Brouckère, Paris, 3 Mar. 1855, AEB, CP, France. See also Dabot, *Souvenirs*, p.7.

89. Procureur report, Nancy, 7 Aug. 1855.

90. *Times*, 6 Mar. 1855.

91. *Constitutionnel*, 12 Mar. 1855.

92. RDM, 15 Mar. 1855, pp.1304-1305.

93. Barman to Fed. Coun., 9 Mar. 1855, AFS, RP, Paris, 1855, no.37.

94. Prefect report (F^{1c} III): Vendée 5, 11 Apr. 1855.

95. La Gorce, *Second Empire*, I, 410-411.

96. *Ibid.*, p.410.

97. *Débats*, 24 June 1855.

98. *Constitutionnel*, 25 June 1855.

99. RDM, 1 July 1855, pp.228-229; *ibid.*, 15 July 1855, pp.452-454.

100. Greville, *Memoirs*, I, 263.

101. Rogier to Vilain XIIII, 23 June 1855, AEB, CP, France, XVII, no. 246.

102. Barman to Fed. Coun., 23 June 1855, AFS, RP, Paris, 1855, no.68.

103. Procureur report, Aix, 16 July 1855.

104. *Ibid.*, Besançon, 21 June 1855.

105. *Ibid.*, Nancy 7 Aug. 1855.

106. *Ibid.*, Amiens, 28 July 1855.

107. F. Rogier to Vilain XIIII, 20 July 1855, AEB, CP, France, XVII, no. 251.

108. Procureur report, Bordeaux, 11 July 1855.

109. Prefect report (F^{1c} III): Gironde 6, 14 July 1855.

110. Procureur report, Aix, 16 July 1855. Marseilles was the port of entry for most of the sick, wounded, and dead from the Crimea.

111. See the procureur reports of July and August 1855 from Douai, Caen, Amiens, Metz, Orleans, Besançon, Lyons, Riom, and Toulouse. For Tours, Limoges, Bar-le-Duc, and Rouen see prefect reports (F^{1c} III): Indre-et-Loire 7, 13 July 1855; Haute-Vienne 8, 1 July 1855; Meuse 8, 18 July 1855; Seine-Inférieure 9, 20 July 1855.

112. Procureur reports of July 1855 from Grenoble and Rennes. Prefect report (F^{1c} III): Manche 6, 14 July 1855.

113. La Gorce, *Second Empire*, I, 445.

114. F. Rogier to Vilain XIIII, 11 Sept. 1855, AEB, CP, France, XVII, no. 262.

115. Dabot, *Souvenirs*, pp.10-11. See also Mason to Marcy, 17 Sept. 1855, State Dept. Corr., France, Mason no.72.

116. Prefect report (F^{1c} III): Vendée 5, 13 Oct. 1855.

117. Prefect reports (F^{1c} III) of Oct. 1855 from Indre-et-Loire, Seine-et-Oise, Gironde, Seine-Inférieure, Manche, Ain, and Finistère; procureur reports of Jan. 1856 from Dijon, Toulouse, Caen, and Amiens; and of Feb. 1856 from Amiens, Nancy, and Aix.

118. Senior, *Guizot and Thiers*, II, 6 (4 Mar. 1855).

119. F. Rogier to Vilain XIIII, 11 Sept. 1855, AEB, CP, France, XVII, no. 262.

120. Mason to Marcy, 17 Sept. 1855, State Dept. Corr., France, Mason no.72.

121. *Débats*, 11 Sept. 1855; RDM, 15 Sept. 1855, p.1133; and *Assemblée Nationale* as reported in the *Times*, 20 Sept. 1855.

122. Prefect reports (F^{1c} III): Seine-et-Oise 9, 15 Oct. 1855; Gironde 6, 15 Oct. 1855.

123. Senior, *Thiers and Guizot*, II, 60-61 (1 Nov. 1855); Cowley to Clarendon, Paris, 24 Oct. 1855, Wellesley and Sencourt, p.94.

40—49

124. *Moniteur*, 16 Nov. 1855; *Débats*, 16 Nov. 1855.
125. *Times*, 19 Nov. 1855.
126. RDM, 1 Dec. 1855, p.1149.
127. Procureur reports: Besançon, 1 Jan. 1856; Toulouse, 23 Jan. 1856.
128. Cambridge to Victoria, 20 Jan. 1856, *Victoria letters*, 1st series, III, 212.
129. F. Rogier to Vilain XIIII, 11 Dec. 1855, AEB, CP, France, XVII, no. 288; Barman to Fed. Coun., 20 Dec. 1855, AFS, RP, Paris, 1855, no. 136; Mason to Marcy, 29 Dec. 1855, State Dept. Corr., France, Mason no.103.
130. *Times*, 18 Dec. 1855; RDM, 15 Dec. 1855, p.1378; *ibid.*, 15 Jan. 1856, p.451.
131. Prefect reports (F^{1c} III) : Seine-Inférieure 7, 15 Jan. 1856; Haut-Rhin, 7, 23 Jan. 1856; Ain 6, sub-prefect reports, Belley, 31 Dec. 1855, and Trévoux, 3 Jan. 1856; Vendée 9, 14 Jan. 1856. Procureur reports of Jan. 1856 from Caen, Metz, Nîmes, Orleans, Riom, Douai, Amiens (4 Feb. 1856), Rouen (8 Feb. 1856), Rennes, Bordeaux, Besançon, Dijon, and Toulouse.
132. Cowley to Clarendon, 18 Jan. 1856, Wellesley, *Cowley letters*, pp.90-91.
133. Hübner, *Neuf ans*, I, 382 (17 Jan. 1856).
134. *Courrier du Havre*, 18 Jan. 1856.
135. *Débats*, 18, 21 Jan. 1856; RDM, 1 Feb. 1856, pp.661-663; *Union*, 18 Jan. 1856; *Pays*, 18 Jan. 1856; *Constitutionnel*, 18 and 26 Jan. 1856; *Times*, 21 Jan. 1856; *Siècle*, 18 Jan. 1856.
136. Prefect report (F^{1c} III) : Manche 6, 24 Jan. 1856. Procureur reports: Amiens, 4 Feb. 1856; Rouen, 8 Feb. 1856; Orleans, 26 Jan. 1856; Riom, 29 Jan. 1856.
137. Senior, *Thiers and Guizot*, I, 233.
138. Mason to Marcy, 15 Feb. 1856, State Dept. Corr., France, Mason no. 116.
139. See above, pp.000.
140. For Brunnow's arrival see *Times*, 15 Feb. 1856; F. Charles-Roux, *Alexandre II, Gortchakoff, et Napoleon III* (Paris, 1913), pp.83-84; Dabot, *Souvenirs*, p.7.
141. Victoria to Napoleon III, 15 Feb. 1856, *Victoria letters*, 1st series,

III, 220. See also Charles-Roux, *Alexandre II*, p.84.
142. *Moniteur*, 19 Feb. 1856.
143. Clarendon to Victoria, 18 Feb. 1856, *Victoria letters*, 1st series, III, 223.
144. *Constitutionnel*, 18 Feb. 1856.
145. *Débats*, 18 Feb. 1856; *Siècle*, 19 Feb. 1856; *Moniteur*, 20, 22 Feb. 1856; *Constitutionnel*, 21 Feb. 1856; *Times*, 22 and 25 Feb. 1856.
146. Charles-Roux, *Alexandre II*, p.86.
147. *Moniteur*, 24 Feb. 1856; RDM, 1 Mar. 1856, pp.222-224.
148. Charles-Roux, *Alexandre II*, p.86.
149. *Moniteur*, 24 Feb. 1856.
150. Charles-Roux, *Alexandre II*, p.87.
151. Dabot, *Souvenirs*, p.15; Hübner, *Neuf ans*, I, 397; Barman to Fed. Coun., 26 Feb. 1856, AFS, RP, France, 1856, no.147; La Gorce, *Second Empire*, I, 460.
152. Charles-Roux, *Alexandre II*, p.84; La Gorce, *Second Empire*, I, 464.
153. Senior, *Thiers and Guizot*, II, 71-72 (9 May 1856).
154. *Ibid.*; Charles-Roux, *Alexandre II*, p.90-91; La Gorce, *Second Empire*, I, 464.
155. *Moniteur*, 2 Apr. 1856; *Times*, 3 Apr. 1856.
156. RDM, 1 Apr. 1856, p. 676.
157. *Moniteur*, 4 Mar. 1856.
158. Procureur report, Aix, 19 Feb. 1856.
159. *Ibid.*, Agen, 25 Jan. 1857.
160. Hübner, *Neuf ans*, I, 417 (12 Apr. 1856).
161. Clarendon to Victoria, 29 Mar. 1856, *Victoria letters*, 1st series, III, 232.
162. *Moniteur*, 31 Mar. 1856; *Times*, 2, 4 Apr. 1856; Dabot, *Souvenirs*, p. 16; Hübner, *Neuf ans*, I, 412, (30 Mar. 1856) ; Mason to Marcy, 31 Mar. 1856, State Dept. Corr., France, Mason no.132; Barman to Fed. Coun. 1 Apr. 1856, AFS, RP, France, 1856, no.121; F. Rogier to Vilain XIIII, 31 Mar. 1856, AEB, CP, France, XVIII, no.35.
163. The terms appeared in the *Moniteur* on 29 April and the protocol of the sessions on the 30th.
164. For these provincial reactions to the final peace see the procureur reports of July and August 1856 from Paris, Bordeaux, Grenoble, Col-

mar, Limoges, Toulouse, Aix, Lyons, Riom, Caen, Orleans, Metz, Agen, Amiens, Dijon, Poitiers, Rouen, Besançon, and Nîmes; and from the prefect reports [F^{1e} III] of April

1856 from Ain, Vendée, Gironde, and Seine-Inférieure; and from Manche in November, 1856.
165. La Gorce, *Second Empire*, I, 206-207.

CHAPTER THREE

An Italian War in the Making

1. Mme Cornu once said that Louis Napoleon "had two fixed ideas . . . . to become Emperor of France and . . . . liberator of Italy" (Senior, *Thiers and Guizot*, II, 212 [5 May 1859]).
2. Seignobos in Lavisse, *France contemporaine*, VI, 279.
3. Cavour to Victor Emmanuel, Baden, 24 July 1858, *Lettere edite ed inedite di Camillo di Cavour*, ed. Luigi Chiala (Turin, 1883-1887), II, 569-570.
4. *Ibid.*
5. Walewski knew of the emperor's war plans by the end of December (Walewski to Napoleon III, Paris, 28 Dec. 1858, G. Raindre, "Les papiers inédites du comte Walewski. Souvenirs et correspondance, 1855-1868," *Revue de France*, III [1925], 288).
6. *Presse*, 22 Nov. 1858; La Gorce, *Second Empire*, II, 373-374; Rogier to Vrière, 24 Nov. 1858, AEB, CP, France, XVIII, no 232.
7. Austria was technically allied to France in 1856 to guarantee the terms of the peace against Russia.
8. *Débats*, 26 Nov. 1858.
9. *Constitutionnel*, 29 Nov. 1858; Rogier to Vrière, 30 Nov. 1858, AEB, CP, France, XVIII, no.234.
10. *Moniteur*, 4 Dec. 1858.
11. Hatzfeld to Schleinitz, Paris, 6 Dec. 1858, APP, I, 96.
12. Rogier to Vrière, 12 Dec. 1858, AEB, CP, France, XVIII, no.239.
13. Prefect report (F^{1e} III): Bouches-du-Rhône 7, 3 Feb. 1859.
14. *Constitutionnel*, 4 Jan. 1859.
15. Baron Beyens, *Le Second Empire: vu par un diplomate belge*, ed. by his son (Paris, 1925-1926), I, 144.
16. Dabot, *Souvenirs*, p.48.
17. Viel Castel, *Memoirs*, II, 142; Reuss to Prince Regent, 4 Jan. 1859, APP, I, 145-146.
18. *Univers*, 5 Jan. 1859; *Times*, 7 Jan. 1859.

19. *Débats*, 7 Jan. 1859.
20. Rogier to Vrière, 7 Jan. 1859, AEB, CP, France, XIX, no.2.
21. Mason to Cass, 6 Jan. 1859, State Dept. Corr., France, XLV, no.370.
22. *Moniteur*, 7 Jan. 1859. The emperor ordered the insertion in a letter to Walewski of 6 Jan. 1859 (Raindre, *loc. cit.*, III, 292-293).
23. *Constitutionnel*, 8 Jan. 1859.
24. Rogier to Vrière, 15 Jan. 1859, AEB, CP, France, XIX, no.4. The Swiss minister telegraphed: "Hope for peace definitely confirmed. Bourse rises" (Kern to Fed. Coun., 15 Jan. 1859, AFS, RP, France, 1859, no. 7).
25. Malmesbury to Victoria, 18 Jan. 1859, *Victoria letters*, 1st series, III, 399.
26. Malmesbury to Cowley, 22 Jan. 1859, Earl of Malmesbury, *Memoirs of an ex-minister: an autobiography* (3rd ed.; London, 1884), II, 153.
27. RDM, 1 Feb. 1859, pp.732-733.
28. Rogier to Vrière, 14 Feb. 1859, AEB, CP, XIX, no.22. See also the prefect reports of January and early February (F^{1e} III), especially of Seine-Inférieure 9, 3 Feb. 1859.
29. Cowley to Palmerston, 25 Jan. 1859, Wellesley, *Cowley letters*, p. 174; Reuss to Schleinitz, 27 Jan. 1854, APP, I, 202.
30. Rogier to Vrière, 15 Jan. 1859, AEB, CP, France, XIX, no. 4.
31. Viel Castel, *Memoirs*, II, 143.
32. Greville, *Journal*, II, 220-221.
33. Walewski warned the emperor of hostile opinion on the marriage as early as 2 Jan. (Raindre, *loc. cit.*, III, 290-291).
34. Dabot, *Souvenirs*, p. 48.
35. *Constitutionnel*, 24 Jan. 1859; *Moniteur*, 25 Jan. 1859.
36. *Constitutionnel*, 25 Jan. 1859.
37. *Times*, 7 Feb. 1859.
38. Wellesley, *Cowley letters*, p. 175; Dabot, Souvenirs, p.48. See also Viel Castel, *Memoirs*, II, 144; and

58—65

Rogier to Vrière, 5 Feb. 1859, AEB, CP, France, XIX, no.15; Cowley to Clarendon, Paris, 6 Feb. 1859, Wellesley and Sencourt, p.159.

39. Procureur report, Aix, 22 Jan. 1859; prefect report (F¹ᵉ III): Haut-Rhin, 7, 11 Feb. 1859.

40. Napoleon III admtited his complicity in the pamphlet-writing when he told Walewski: "I requested M. de la Guéronnière to sign the pamphlet" (letter of 5 Feb. 1859, Raindre, *loc. cit.*, III, 295).

41. From the full account given by Rendu to Luigi Chiala in a letter dated Paris, 25 Aug. 1883, published in Chiala, *Cavour lettere*, III, 385-396. Walewski did protest in writing on the day the pamphlet appeared (Walewski to Napoleon III, Paris, 4 Feb. 1859, Raindre, *loc. cit.*, III, 295).

42. Dabot, *Souvenirs*, p. 49; *Times*, 7 Feb. 1859; Rogier to Vrière, 5 Feb. 1859, AEB, CP, France, XIX, no.15.

43. A. de la Guéronnière, *L'Empereur Napoléon III et l'Italie* (Paris, 1859).

44. *Times*, 7 Feb. 1859.

45. Rogier to Vrière, 5 Feb. 1859, AEB, CP, France, XIX, no.15.

46. Reuss to Schleinitz, 4 and 5 Feb. 1859, APP, I, 217-218.

47. Walewski was the illegitimate son of Napoleon I and Mme Walewska, and therefore cousin of Napoleon III.

48. Viel Castel, *Memoirs*, II, 145. Walewski used the same term "detestable effect" in a letter to the emperor of 5 Feb. 1859. (Raindre, *loc. cit.*, III, 295).

49. The procureur report from Agen, 7 Apr. 1859, is about the only one from that collection with a comment and it says: "Les révélations de la brochure *Napoléon III et l'Italie* n'ont pas produit grand effet. . . ."

50. *Moniteur*, 8 Feb. 1859.

51. *Ibid.*, 9 Feb. 1859.

52. Rogier to Vrière, 7 Feb. 1859, AEB, CP, France, XIX, no.17.

53. Prince Albert to Stockmar, 10 Feb. 1859, K. Jagow, ed., *Letters of the Prince Consort, 1831-1861*, translated by E. T. S. Dugdale (New York, 1938), pp.323-324.

54 Prefect reports (F¹ᵉ III): Ain 6, Feb. 1859; Maine-et-Loire 8, 2 Mar.

1859; Haut-Rhin 7, 3 Mar. 1859; Finistère 3, Apr. 1859; Haute-Vienne 8, 6 Apr. 1859; Vendée 5, 8 Apr. 1859. Procureur reports: Riom, 10 Apr. 1859; Colmar, 5 Apr. 1859; Pau, 6 Apr. 1859; Bourges, 7 Apr. 1859; Agen, 7 Apr. 1859; Nancy, 9 Apr. 1859; Grenoble, 11 Apr. 1859.

55. Rogier to Vrière, 23 Feb. 1859, AEB, CP, France, XIX, no.27; Delord, *Second Empire*, II, 434; La Gorce, *Second Empire*, II, 433.

56. Greville, *Journal*, II, 220-221.

57. Viel Castel, *Memoirs*, II, 145. Greville erred in saying that Fleury and Baroche were in favor of war (Maurain, *Baroche*, p.174).

58. Cte. Fleury, *Memoirs of Empress Eugenie* (New York, 1920), p.58; Beyens, *Second Empire*, I, 146-149.

59. Nigra to Cavour, 28 Feb. 1859, *Il carteggio Cavour-Nigra dal 1858 al 1861*, published by the Regia Commissione Editrice (Bologna, 1927), II, 44 (hereafter cited as CCN).

60. Prince Napoleon to Napoleon III, Paris, 5 Mar. 1859, E. D'Hauterive, "Correspondance inédite de Napoléon III et du Prince Napoleon," RDM, 1 Feb. 1924, p.520.

61. Napoleon III to Victor Emmanuel, 10 Feb. 1859, CCN, II, 9.

62. Within a few days the British foreign office had a copy of these instructions, which was later used by Theodore Martin in his study of the Prince Consort (Theodore Martin, *The life of His Royal Highness, the Prince Consort* [New York, 1879], IV, 313-314).

63. *Moniteur*, 5 Mar. 1859; A. Granier de Cassagnac, *Souvenirs du Second Empire* (Paris, 1882), III, 155.

64. Eugénie to Arese, 26 Aug. 1859, C. Pagani, "Napoleone III, Eugenia di Montijo e Francesco Arese in un carteggio inedito—L'Imperatrice Eugenia e l'Italia," *Nuova Antologia*, (1 Jan. 1921), pp.16-33.

65. Prefect reports (F¹ᵉ III): Finistère 3, Apr. 1859; Haute-Vienne 8, 6 Apr. 1859; Gironde 6, 17 Apr. 1859.

66. Rogier to Vrière, 12 Mar. 1859, AEB, CP, France, XIX, no.35.

67. Mérimée to Panizzi, 12 Mar. 1859, P. Mérimée, *Lettres à M. Panizzi, 1850-1870*, ed. by L. Fagan (Paris, 1881), I, 22.

68. Pourtalès to Schleinitz, 19 Mar. 1859, APP, I, 344.
69. Nigra to Cavour, 9 Mar. 1859, CCN, II, 76.
70. Procureur report from Metz, 10 Mar. 1859.
71. Procureur reports of March and April 1859 from Metz, Colmar, Pau, and Bourges.
72. Rogier to Vrière, 22 Mar. 1859, AEB, CP, France, XIX, no.39.

73. Procureur reports of April 1859 from Toulouse, Rennes, Riom, Aix, Metz, Orleans, Colmar, Bastia, Pau, Agen, Bourges, Nancy, Caen, and Grenoble.
74. Prefect reports (F^{1c} III) of April 1859 from Haut-Rhin, Vendée, Allier, Seine-Inférieure, Maine-et-Loire.
75. Procureur report, Besançon, 9 Apr. 1859.

CHAPTER FOUR

The Austro-Sardinian War

1. La Gorce, *Second Empire*, II, 443-447; Senior, *Thiers and Guizot*, II, 238,244.
2. Rogier to Vrière, 26 Apr. 1859, AEB, CP, France, XIX, no.60.
3. *Constitutionnel*, 4 May 1859.
4. On the reaction to the Austrian ultimatum see procureur special reports (369) of 21 May 1859 from Nancy (16 May), Agen, Angers, Colmar, Paris, Riom, Poitiers, and Rouen; and prefect reports (F^{1c} III) of 1859: Gironde 6, 30 Apr.; Isère 7, 4 May; Seine-et-Oise 9, 4 May; Seine-Inférieure 9, 4 May.
5. Senior, *Thiers and Guizot*, II, 242, 247 (3 May 1859).
6. Procureur special reports (369) of 1859: circular, 12 May; report from Rennes, 15 May; Maurain, *Politique ecclésiastique*, p. 334, n. 1.
7. Chambéry was later to make the twenty-eighth judicial district.
8. For the sudden change to belligerency in Paris and the provinces see the procureur reports of 1859: Paris, 2 May; and special reports (369) of May from Agen, Bastia, Bordeaux, Bourges, Caen, Dijon, Douai, Grenoble, Lyons, Montpellier, Nîmes, Orleans, Paris, Poitiers, Rouen, Rennes, Angers, Aix; of Pau, 2 July; Colmar, 8 July; and the prefect reports (F^{1c} III) of 1859: Gironde 6, 30 Apr.; Meuse 8, 30 Apr.; Ain 6, Apr.; Bouches-du-Rhône 7, 3 May; Isère 7, 4 May; Seine-et-Oise 9, 4 May; Seine-Inférieure 9, 4 May.
9. Rogier to Vrière, 23 Apr. 1859, AEB, CP, France, XIX, no.57; *Times*, 13 May 1859; Mérimée to Panizzi, 29 Apr. 1859, Mérimée, *Lettres à Panizzi*, I, 29-30.
10. Most of the second paragraph was underlined with pencil in the ministry of justice.
11. On the early attitude of the bourgeoisie see procureur special reports (369) of 21 May 1859 from Nancy, Douai, Grenoble, Limoges, Lyons, Metz, Paris, Pau, Amiens; of 28 May from Angers; of 1 and 8 June from Paris; from prefect report (F^{1c} III) from Isère of 4 May 1859; Senior, *Thiers and Guizot*, II, 242.
12. On the early opinion of peasants and urban workers see the procureur special reports (369) of 1859 from Nancy of 16 May; from reports of 21 May from Angers, Dijon, Douai, Grenoble, Limoges, Lyons, Paris, Rouen, Riom; of 28 May from Angers; of 1 June from Paris; and from the prefect reports (F^{1c} III) of 1859: Ain 6, Apr.; Seine-Inférieure 9, 4 May; and Senior, *Thiers and Guizot*, II, 247.
13. Maurain, *Politique ecclésiastique*, pp.327-344.
14. On the early attitude of the clergy see, in addition to Maurain, the procureur special reports (369) of 1859: of 21 May from Nancy, Aix, Agen, Angers, Besançon, Colmar, Douai, Grenoble, Pau, Rennes, Riom; of 24 May from Amiens; of 28 May from Angers, Bourges; of 2 June from Rouen; of 4 June from Angers; of 8 June from Paris; of 1 July from Orleans (382); of 6 July from Bordeaux (374); and from prefect report (F^{1c} III), Isère

72—80

7, 4 May 1859; Senior, *Thiers and Guizot*, II, 226-227.

15. Procureur report, Bordeaux (374), 6 July 1859.

16. For the early reaction of the Legitimists see procureur special reports (369) of 21 May 1859 from Nancy, Aix, Angers, Besançon, Douai, Grenoble, Limoges, Montpellier, Pau, Poitiers, Riom, Toulouse; of 24 May from Amiens; of 28 May from Aix, Angers, Lyons; of 4 June from Besançon; of 11 June from Aix and Besançon; and from Aix (370), 2 July; also Mérimée to Panizzi, Paris, 27 May 1859, Mérimée, *Lettres à Panizzi*, I, 38.

17. For early Republican prowar sentiment see the procureur special reports (369) of 21 May 1859 from Agen, Besançon, Bourges, Grenoble, Limoges, Lyons, Orleans, Pau, Riom, Toulouse; of 28 May and 4 June from Lyons; of 8 June from Paris; of 1 July from Orleans (382); of 2 July from Aix (370); and prefect reports (F¹ᶜ III): Isère 7, 4 May 1859; Calvados 9, 11 July 1859; and Beyens, *Second Empire*, I, 155.

18. Senior, *Thiers and Guizot*, II, 223, 229; Mérimée to Panizzi, Paris, 29 Apr. 1859, Mérimée, *Lettres à Panizzi*, I, 29-30; Delord, *Second Empire*, II, 457-458; La Gorce, *Second Empire*, II, 441-442.

19. On troop departures in the provinces see procureur special reports (369) of 21 May 1859 from Besançon, Grenoble, Montpellier, Riom, Toulouse; of 28 May from Aix; of 10 July from Lyons (379); of 11 July from Riom (386); and from prefect reports (F¹ᶜ III) of 1859: Bouches-du-Rhône 7, 3 May; Seine-et-Oise 9, 4 May; Seine-Inférieure 9, 4 May.

20. On Nepoleon III's departure for the front see Dabot, *Souvenirs*, pp.51-52; *Times*, 13 May 1859; *Constitutionnel*, 12 May 1859; Viel Castel, *Memoirs*, II, 154; *Débats*, 11 May 1854; Rogier to Vrière, 14 May 1854, AEB, CP, France, XIX, no.72; Mérimée to Panizzi, 10 May 1859, Mérimée, *Lettres à Panizzi*, I, 33; La Gorce, *Second Empire*, II, 448-449; Delord, *Second Empire*, II, 457-458; L. Chiala, *Pagine di storia contemporanea dal 1858 al 1892* (Turin, 1892-1893), I, 5.

21. On the increased interest in the war news see procureur special reports (369) of 21 May and 4, 11, 18 June from Besançon; of 28 May from Aix; of 28 May from Toulouse; of 4 June from Bordeaux; of 2 July from Lyons; of 8 July from Colmar (376); Fleury, *Memoirs*, II, 20-21.

22. On the battle of Montebello see procureur special reports (369) of 1859: of 28 May from Amiens, Angers, Bordeaux, Bourges, Lyons, Nancy, Toulouse, Paris, and Aix; of 4 June from Amiens and Toulouse; of 11 June from Nancy and Toulouse.

23. On the battle of Magenta see procureur special reports (369) of 1859: of 11 June from Aix, Amiens, A n g e r s , Besançon, Bordeaux, Bourges, Lyons, Nancy, Toulouse, and Rouen; of 15 June from Paris; of 18 June from Aix, Amiens, Besançon, Angers Bordeaux, Bourges, Nancy, Rennes, Toulouse, and Rouen; of 22 June from Paris; of 25 June from Aix and Bourges: of 5 July from Dijon (377); of 8 July from Colmar (376); and prefect report (F¹ᶜ III): Finistère 3, July 1859; and Viel Castel, *Memoirs*, II, 156; Fleury, *Memoirs*, II, 22-23; Granier de Cassagnac, *Souvenirs*, III, 160; Beyens, *Second Empire*, I, 158; *Constitutionnel*, 6, 15 June 1859; *Débats*, 6 June 1859; Rogier to Vrière, 7 June 1859, AEB, CP, Complément France; Mérimée to Panizzi, 9 June 1859, Mérimée, *Lettres à Panizzi*, I, 39.

24. On the battle of Solferino see procureur special reports (369) of 1859: of 25-29 June from Aix, Amiens, Besançon, Nancy, Rouen, Rennes, Toulouse, Bordeaux, Lyons, and Paris; of 2-3 July from Besançon, Lyons, Rennes, Toulouse, and Rouen; of 11 July from Rennes; and procureur regular reports of 1859: Bastia (372), 2 July; Douai (377), 2 July; Pau (384), 2 July; Agen (370), 7 July; as well as in *Constitutionnel*, 27 June 1859; and *Débats*, 27 June 1859.

25. La Gorce, *Second Empire*, III, 102, 109; A. Debidour in E. Lavisse and C. Rambaud, *Histoire générale* (Paris, 1899), XI, 273; Dabot, *Souvenirs*, pp.53-54; *Constitutionnel*, 8 July 1859; *Débats*, 13 July 1859.

26. Procureur report (369), Toulouse, 21 May 1859.
27. On the desire for peace before Solferino see procureur special reports (369) of 1859: of 11 June from Aix; of 22 June from Paris; and *Constitutionnel*, 6 June 1859; Cowley to Russell, 24 June 1859, PRO, Russell Papers, GD 22/53.
28. On the desire for peace before Villafranca see procureur special reports (369) from 25 June to 12 July 1859 from Amiens, Toulouse, Lyons, Rouen, and Rennes; and the procureur regular reports of 1859: Toulouse, 6 July; Agen, 7 July; Caen, 9 July; Metz, 10 July; Riom, 11 July; and prefect reports (F¹ᶜ III) of 1859: Vendée 5, 9 July; Gironde 6, 10 July; and *Débats*, 27 June 1859; La Gorce, *Second Empire*, III, 104-106.
29. From Rennes, Angers, Caen, Rouen, Amiens, Paris, Metz, Besançon, Dijon, Lyons, Bourges, Riom, Aix, Bordeaux, and Pau.
30. Fleury, *Memoirs*, II, 29-31.
31. Walewski to Napoleon III, 16 June 1859, Raindre, *loc. cit.*, IV, 90.
32. On the fear of a war with Prussia see procureur special reports (369) of 1859: of 16 May from Nancy; of 21 May from Besançon, Bourges, Lyons, Paris, and Rouen; of 28 May from Bourges; of 18-19 June from Besançon, Bordeaux, Nancy, and Rouen; of 22-26 June from Paris, Amiens, Besançon, Nancy, Rouen, Bordeaux, and Lyons; of 2-3 July from Besançon and Rouen; of 16 July from Aix; of 24 July from Nancy and Rennes; and procureur regular reports of 1859: Paris, 2 May; Pau, 2 July; Nancy, 2 July; Colmar, 8 July; Metz, 10 July; Lyons, 10 July; Riom, 11 July; Besançon, 8 Aug; and the prefect reports (F¹ᶜ III) of 1859: Gironde 6, 30 Apr.; Bouches-du-Rhône 7, 3 May; Seine-Inférieure 9, 4 May; Haut-Rhin 7, 9 July; and also *Constitutionnel*, 15 May, 3, 6 July 1859; *Débats*, 1 May 1859; Mérimée to Panizzi, 30 June 1859, Mérimée, *Lettres à Panizzi*, I, 44.
33. *Constitutionnel*, 4 May 1859.
34. Maurain, *Politique ecclésiastique*, p.329.
35. *Ibid.*, p.330.
36. *Legations* was another term for the Romagna, and Bologna was their principal city.

37. For the adverse reaction to the Romagna revolt before 2 July see procureur special reports (369) of 1859: of 11 June from Besançon; of 18 June from Bordeaux, Rennes, Toulouse, and Rouen; of 25-26 June from Nancy, Rouen, Bordeaux, and Lyons; of 2 July from Angers and Toulouse; and the procureur regular reports of 1859: Aix, 2 July; Douai, 2 July; Pau, 2 July.
38. Maurain, *Politique ecclésiastique*, p.343.
39. R. Halt, *Papiers sauvés des Tuileries* (Paris, 1871), p.265.
40. Cowley to Russell, 24 and 27 June 1859, PRO, Russell Papers, GD 22/53.
41. Fleury, *Memoirs*, II, 29.
42. Author's italics. *Ibid.*, p.33.
43. Walewski to Napoleon III, Paris, 17 and 22 June 1859, Raindre, *loc. cit.*, IV, 91-93.
44. A. Debidour, *Histoire diplomatique de l'Europe* (Paris, 1891), II, 197; Debidour in Lavisse and Rambaud, *Histoire générale*, XI, 468. Thomas insisted that it was the Catholic party more than Prussia or epidemics which brought about the armistice.
45. Eugénie to Napoleon III, Saint-Cloud, 16 June 1859, 1:35 P.M., Archives Nationales, MSS, F 90 365 980ᴮ, telegram No.5169.
46. Cavour to Prince Napoleon, 1 July 1859, Commandini, *Principe Napoleone*, p.175.
47. Hauterive, *loc. cit.*, p.538.
48. Cavour to La Marmora, 6 July 1859, Chiala, *Cavour lettere*, III, 106.
49. Cowley to Russell, 4 July 1859, PRO, Russell Papers, GD 22/53.
50. Same to same, 6 July 1859, *ibid.*
51. *Victoria letters*, 1st series, III, 458, footnote.
52. Cowley to Russell, 12 Aug. 1859, PRO, Russell Papers, GD 22/53.
53. Napoleon III to Pius IX, 31 Dec. 1859, *Moniteur*, 11 Jan. 1860.
54. On clerical opposition after 6 July see procureur special reports (369) for 1859: of 9 July from Angers and Toulouse; and procureur regular reports for July 1859 from Dijon, Montpellier, Toulouse, Bordeaux, Agens, Nancy, Colmar, Caen, Metz, Lyons, Nîmes, Riom, Grenoble, and Poitiers; and procureur regular reports: Besançon, 9 Sept. 1859; Orleans, 3 Oct. 1859; and prefect

89—94

reports (F^{1c} III) of 1859: Seine-Inférieure 9, 8 July; Allier 6, 9 July; Maine-et-Loire 8, 10 July; Haute-Vienne 8, 15 July.

55. *Constitutionnel* and *Moniteur*, 8 July 1859.

56. Reuss to Schleinitz, 9 July 1859, APP, I, 745.

57. On the cautious public reaction to the armistice news of 8 July see the procureur special reports (369) of 1859: of 9-16 July from Amiens, Angers, Besançon, Bourges, Nancy, Toulouse, Rouen, Rennes, Lyons, Paris, and Aix; and procureur regular reports of July 1859 from Lyons, Nîmes, and Grenoble; and prefect reports (F^{1c} III): Haute-Vienne 8, 15 July 1859.

58. On the celebrations at the first announcement of the signature of peace terms at Villafranca see procureur special reports (369) of 15-17 July 1859 from Lyons, Besançon, Bourges, Bordeaux, and Rouen; *Constitutionnel*, 13 and 14 July 1859; *Napoléonien* (Amiens), *Nouvelliste* (Rouen), *Courrier de Saint-Quentin, Courrier du Havre, Messager de la Manche, Napoléonien* (Troyes), *Progrès* (Compiègne), *Mémorial de Lille*, all of 13 July 1859; Quisard to Vrière, Lyons, 12 July 1859, AEB, CP, Consulats, VI, Lyons, no.6.

59. Procureur special report (369), Bourges, 16 July 1859.

60. For the press reaction to the Villafranca terms see *Moniteur*, 11 July 1859; *Constitutionnel*, 12, 13, 15 July 1859; *Débats*, 16, 17 July 1859; *Univers*, 15, 20 July 1859; *Ami de la Religion*, 14 July 1859; Maurain, *Politique ecclésiastique*, pp.345-346.

61. For the generally divided opinion over the peace terms see procureur special reports (369) of 16-19 July 1859 from Bourges, Toulouse, Bordeaux, Rouen, Rennes, and Paris; of 21-30 July from Angers, Besançon, Lyons, Nancy, Toulouse, and Aix; and procureur regular reports of 1859; Rouen, 20 July; Paris, 25 July; Besançon, 9 Sept.; Orleans, 3 Oct.; Colmar, 4 Oct.; Toulouse, 4 Oct.; Bastia, 6 Oct.; Agen, 7 Oct.; Riom, 7 Oct.; Besançon, 9 Oct.; Caen, 10 Oct.; Metz, 11 Oct.; Nîmes, 11 Oct.; Lyons, 12 Oct.; Rennes, 13 Oct.; Dijon, 14 Oct.; Nancy, 14 Oct.; and prefect reports (F^{1c} III) of 1859: Ain 6, 30

Sept., 1 Oct.; Allier 6, 8 Oct.; Seine-Inférieure 9, 10 Oct.; Gironde 6, 22 Oct.

62. For peasant approval of the peace terms see procureur special reports (369) of 18-24 July 1859 from Rennes and Nancy; procureur regular reports of 1859: Lyons, 12 Oct.; Dijon, 14 Oct.; and prefect report (F^{1c} III): Allier 6, 8 Oct. 1859. For clerical and Catholic approval of the peace settlements see procureur special reports (369) of 18-24 July 1859 from Rennes, Paris, and Nancy; and Maurain, *Politique ecclésiastique*, pp. 345-346. For Legitimist divided opinion on Villafranca see procureur special reports (369) of 16-23 July 1859 from Nancy, Besançon, Angers, Toulouse, Rouen, and Rennes; procureur regular reports of 1859: Rouen, 20 July; Douai, 3 Oct.; Grenoble, 16 Oct. For bourgeois mixed reaction to the peace terms see procureur special reports (369) of 16-19 July 1859 from Besançon, Nancy, Toulouse, and Paris; of 24-25 July 1859 from Nancy and Lyons; and procureur regular reports: Rennes, 13 Oct. 1859; Dijon, 14 Oct. 1859; and prefect report (F^{1c} III): Allier 6, 8 Oct. 1859. For Republican opposition to the peace of Villafranca see procureur special reports (369) of 1859: of 15-19 July from Lyons, Aix, Angers, Besançon, Toulouse, Rouen, Rennes, and Paris; of 21-30 July from Besançon, Lyons, Toulouse and Aix; and procureur regular reports of 1859: Grenoble, 12 July; Rouen, 20 July; Paris, 25 July; Orleans, 3 Oct.; Toulouse, 4 Oct.; Riom, 7 Oct.; Besançon, 9 Oct.; Lyons, 12 Oct.; Dijon, 14 Oct.; Nancy, 14 Oct.; and prefect report (F^{1c} III): Allier 6, 8 Oct. 1859.

63. On the emperor's return see La Gorce, *Second Empire*, III, 116-119; Cowley to Russell, 18, 25, 27 July 1859, PRO, Russell Papers, GD 22/53.

64. *Moniteur*, 20 July 1859; General Fleury, *Souvenirs du général Cte Fleury* (Paris, 1898), II, 132-134.

65. On the audience of the diplomatic corps see *Moniteur*, 22 July 1859; Rogier to Vrière, 21, 23 July 1859, AEB, CP, France, XIX, nos.93,96; Cowley to Russell, 21 July 1859, PRO, Russell Papers, GD 22/53.

66. Malmesbury, *Memoirs*, II, 206.
67. On the provincial reaction to the emperor's speeches, see procureur special reports (369) of 1859: Angers, 23 July; Besançon, 21 July; Rennes, 29 July; and procureur regular reports of Oct. 1859 from Colmar, Nîmes, Nancy, and Grenoble.
68. On the wave of resentment against Prussia see Thile and Reuss to Schleinitz, Paris, 9 and 19 July 1859, APP, I, 745, 761-762; Cowley to Russell, 24 June 1859, PRO, Russell Papers, GD 22/53; procureur special reports (369) of 1859 from Nancy, 16 May, 25 June, 24 July; Besançon, 21 May, 25 June, 2 July; Rouen, 21 May, 19 June, 25 June; Aix, 18 June, 16 July; Bordeaux, 18, 26 June; Paris, 22 June; Amiens, 25 June; Lyons, 26 June, 25 July; Rennes, 29 July; procureur regular reports of 1859: Pau, 2 July; Nancy, 2 July; Colmar, 8 July; Metz, 10 July; Lyons, 10 July; Riom, 11 July; Besançon, 8 Aug.; Dijon, 14 Oct.; and prefect report (F¹ᶜ III): Haut-Rhin 7, 9 July 1859.
69. On French resentment toward England · see Martin, *Prince Consort*, IV, 388-389; Cowley to Russell, 7 Aug. 1859, *ibid.*, pp. 389-390; procureur special reports (369) of 1859: Nancy, 16 May, 25 June, 24 July; Rouen, 19 June, 17 July; Angers, 23 July; Rennes, 29 July; and procureur regular reports of 1859: Besançon, 8 Aug., 9 Sept.; Douai, 3 Oct.; Aix, 5 Oct.; Nancy, 14 Oct.
70. On French postwar antipathy for Italians see Cowley letters to Russell, 24 June, 8 July, 11 July 1859, PRO, Russell Papers, GD 22/53; Albert to Prince Regent of Prussia, 15 June 1859, Jagow, *Prince Consort*, p.337; *Victoria letters*, 1st series, III, 458 (fn.); Eugénie to Arese, Sept. 1859, C. Pagani, "Napoleone III, Eugenia de Montijo e Francesco Arese in un carteggio inedite—L'Imperatrice Eugenia e l'Italia," *Nuova antologia*, (1 Jan. 1921), pp. 16-33; Mérimée to Panizzi, 15, 20 July 1859, Mérimée, *Lettres à Panizzi*, I, 51-53, 55-56; Reuss to Schleinitz, 19 July 1859, APP, I, 761-762; procureur special report (369), Rouen, 21 May 1859; procureur regular reports of 1859: Agen, 7 July; Besançon, 9 Sept.; Limoges, 3 Oct.; Nancy, 14 Oct.; Grenoble, 16 Oct.; prefect reports (F¹ᶜ III) of 1859: Ain 6, 7 Oct.; Bouches-du-Rhône 7, 19 Oct.
71. Maurain, *Politique ecclésiastique*, p.175.
72. For Catholic and clerical postwar disaffection see procureurs reports of Oct. 1859 from Orleans, Toulouse, Besançon, Caen, Metz, Nîmes, Lyons, Rennes, Nancy, Grenoble, Bordeaux, and Rouen; procureur special report (450), Poitiers, 5 Oct., no.48; prefect reports (F¹ᶜ III) of 1859: Ain 6, 7 Oct.; Allier 6, 8 Oct.; Vendée 5, 8 Oct.; Bouches-du-Rhône 7, 19 Oct.; Gironde 6, 22 Oct.
73. On the Republican trend toward supporting the Empire see procureur reports of 1859: Toulouse, 6 July; Bordeaux, 6 July; Angers, 9 July; Metz, 10 July; Grenoble, 12 July, 16 Oct.; Besançon, 8 Aug., 9 Oct.; Orleans, 3 Oct.; Riom, 7 Oct.; Nîmes, 11 Oct.; Lyons, 12 Oct.; Dijon, 14 Oct.; Nancy, 14 Oct.; Poitiers, 28 Oct.; Aix, 7 July 1860; prefect reports (F¹ᶜ III) of 1859: Allier 6, 9 July; Vendée 5, 9 July.

CHAPTER FIVE

Sardinian and French Annexations

1. La Gorce, *Second Empire*, III, 126-152.
2. *Ibid.*, pp.152-153.
3. On the early opinion concerning the Sardinian annexations of the duchies see procureur reports of Oct. 1859 from Douai, Limoges, Toulouse, Aix, Besançon, Caen, Nîmes, Lyons, Rennes, Dijon, Nancy, Grenoble, Poitiers and Rouen; prefect·reports (F¹ᶜ III) of 8 and 19 Oct. 1859 from Allier and Bouches-du-Rhône respectively.
4. La Gorce, *Second Empire*, III, 151-152.
5. The bishops of Beauvais, Châlons,

105—115

Evreux, Nantes, Nevers, Ajaccio, Angers, Autun, Belley, Coutances, Fréjus, Le Mans, Rodez, Saint-Flour, and Sens (Maurain, *Politique ecclésiastique*, pp.347-348).

6. *Moniteur*, 12 Oct. 1859.

7. On the growing protests of the French clergy see Maurain, *Politique ecclésiastique*, pp.344-348.

8. RDM, 15 Oct. 1859, pp.997-1006.

9. For opinion for and against the Romagna revolt and the proposed annexation of these Legations to Sardinia see the procureur reports of October 1859 from Aix, Besançon, Bordeaux, Douai, Grenoble, Lyons, Metz, Nancy, Nîmes, Orleans, Poitiers, Rennes, Riom, Rouen, Toulouse; and prefect reports (F^{1c} III) of October 1859 from Ain, Allier, Bouches-du-Rhône, Gironde, and Vendée.

10. Pagani, *loc. cit.*, pp.25-26.

11. Cowley to Russell, Biarritz, 5 Oct. 1859, PRO, Russell Papers, G.D. 22/53.

12. La Gorce, *Second Empire*, III, 154.

13. On the government action against the clerical press see Maurain, *Politique ecclésiastique*, pp.349-353.

14. *Ibid.*, p.353.

15. "L'Empereur m'a assuré qu' il plaidera leur [Modena's, Tuscany's, and the Romagna's] cause dans le congrès européen; qu' en attendant ils n'avaient qu'à ne pas permettre aux vieilles dynasties de rentrer" (Cavour to La Marmora, Turin, 16 July 1859, Chiala, *Cavour lettere*, III, 111).

16. *Constitutionnel*, 12 Jan. 1860.

17. In addition to the pamphlet itself, which can be found in the Bibliothèque nationale, summaries of it can be found in La Gorce, *Second Empire*, III, 174-175; and Maurain, *Politique ecclésiastique*, p.356.

18. On the appearance of the pamphlet see La Gorce, *Second Empire*, III, 173.

19. Cowley to Russell, Paris, 24 Dec. 1859, PRO, Russell Papers, G.D. 22/53.

20. On the initial reaction to the pamphlet see procureur reports of Jan. 1860 from Rennes, Rouen, Douai, Colmar, Besançon, Aix, Nîmes, and Agen; also a special report from Nancy of 28 Feb. 1860 in BB^{30} 450, no.9.

21. On the discussion over the emperor's role in the publishing of the pamphlet see La Gorce, *Second Empire*, III, 173-174; Cowley to Russell, Chantilly, 25 Dec. 1859, PRO, Russell Papers, G.D. 22/53; Martin, *Prince Consort*, V, 4. Even as early as 24 December Cowley wrote Russell that "the Emperor does not avow the authorship, but admits that he shares the author's views and opinions" (PRO, Russell Papers, G.D. 22/53). See also the procureur reports of Jan. 1860 from Rouen and Besançon and the special report from Nancy (BB^{30} 450) of 28 Feb. 1860.

22. "And Jesus said unto him [Judas]: Friend wherefor art thou come?" (*Univers*, 23 Dec. 1859).

23. Gramont to Walewski, Rome, 31 Dec. 1859, French Foreign Office Archives, Political Correspondence, as cited in Maurain, *Politique ecclésiastique*, p.357.

24. *Lettre de Mgr. l'éveque d'Orléans à un catholique sur le brochure le Pape et le congrès*.

25. Napoleon III to Pius IX, Paris, 31 Dec. 1859, *Moniteur*, 11 Jan. 1860.

26. On Walewski's resignation see *Moniteur*, 5 Jan. 1860; Desambrois to Dabormida, Paris, 5 Jan. 1860, CCN, III, 9-10; La Gorce, *Second Empire*, III, 182-183. Rogier, the Belgian minister, affirmed that the resignation was caused by the publication of the pamphlet without his (Walewski's) knowledge (Rogier to Vrière, Paris, 7 Jan. 1860, AEB, CP, France, XIX, no. 147).

27. Archives Nationales, Paris, MSS, Ministère de l'Intérieur, series F^{18}, carton 423, *Univers*, Decree no. 490, Paris, 29 Jan. 1860.

28. *Moniteur*, 30 Jan. 1860.

29. Rogier to Vrière, Paris, 11 Jan. 1860, AEB, CP, France, XIX, no. 148.

30. For an authoritative account of the open conflict between the Roman Catholic Church and the French state see Maurain, *Politique ecclésiastique*, ch. xiv.

31. *Ibid.*, p.397.

32. These districts, from north to south, were: Rennes, Caen, Rouen, Douai, Nancy, Poitiers, Riom, Lyons, Grenoble, Aix, Montpellier, Agen, and Bordeaux.

33. On the clergy's influence over the French people see the procureur reports of Jan. 1860 from Pau, Nîmes,

Besançon, Caen, Grenoble, Orleans, and Bordeaux; and the procureur reports of April 1860 from Aix, Douai, Montpellier, Rennes, Pau, Agen, Riom, Bordeaux, and Caen; and from procureur special reports (BB[30] 450) no.9 from Nancy, 28 Feb. 1860; no. 82 from Pau, 28 Feb. 1860; no.60 from Angoulème, 9 Mar. 1860; no.21 from Poitiers, 1 Feb. 1860; no.8 from Lyons, 27 Feb. 1860.

34. Penciled in the margin when read by officials in Paris.

35. The sixteen other districts with favorable sentiments were: Caen, Rennes, Douai, Paris, Orleans, Metz, Nancy, Colmar, Lyons, Grenoble, Riom, Nîmes, Aix, Agen, Toulouse, and Pau.

36. The twelve other districts with elements opposed to the pamphlet were Rennes, Douai, Limoges, Agen, Pau, Rouen, Colmar, Metz, Riom, Orleans, Paris, and Toulouse.

37. The eight districts noting some elements who were undisturbed or indifferent were: Lyons, Nancy, Limoges, Pau, Rouen, Besançon, Caen, and Nîmes.

38. The procureur reports of Dec. 1859 on the pamphlet were from Lyons and Rennes; of Jan. 1860 were from Lyons, Nancy, Aix, Douai, Limoges, Agen, Toulouse, Dijon, Pau, Rouen, Colmar, Nîmes, Besançon, Metz, Caen, Riom, Grenoble, and Orleans; and Paris (383), 13 Feb. 1860; and Poitiers (450), 1 Feb. 1860, no.21; Lyons (450), 27 Feb. 1860, no.8; Nancy (450), 28 Feb. 1860, no.9.

39. Maurain, *Politique ecclésiastique*, pp.381-397.

40. Cowley to Russell, Chantilly, 25 Dec. 1859, PRO, Russell Papers, G.D. 22/53.

41. The clerical press in Paris included the *Univers, Union, Correspondant, Ami de la Religion*, and the *Gazette de France*.

42. These included the *Constitutionnel, Patrie, Pays*, and *Opinion Nationale*.

43. On the press see *Gazette de France, Journal des Débats, Indépendance Belge, Siècle, Univers, Union*, of 24 Dec. 1859; also the *Journal des Débats* of 25 Dec. 1859 and 19 Jan. 1860; RDM, 1 Jan. 1860, pp.224-231; 15 Jan. 1860, pp.482-489.

44. Procureur report from Grenoble (378), 15 Jan. 1860.

45. On the agitation in Savoy see *ibid.*; La Gorce, *Second Empire*, III, 204-205, 210-212; R. Avezou, *La Savoie française sous le Second Empire, 1860-1870* (Chambéry, 1939), pp. 1-2; R. Avezou, *La Savoie depuis les réformes de Charles-Albert jusqu'à l'annexion à la France* (Chambéry, 1934); J. Trésal, *L'Annexion de la Savoie à la France, 1848-1860* (Paris, 1913); RDM, 1 Nov. 1859, pp.234-242.

46. Speech of Cowley to the house of lords, 23 April 1860 (Great Britain, *3 Hansard*, CLVII [1860], p.2127).

47. Metternich to Rechberg, Paris, 26 Nov. 1859, Wellesley and Sencourt, p.175.

48. Memorandum of Prince Albert, 14 Jan. 1860, Martin, *Prince Consort*, V, 20, fn.6.

49. Desambrois to Dabormida, Paris, 9, 10 Jan. 1860, CCN, III, 11, 13.

50. *Patrie*, 22, 25, 27 Jan. 1860.

51. Cowley to Russell, Paris, 3 Feb. 1860, PRO, Russell Papers, G.D. 22/54.

52. Cowley to Clarendon, Paris, 4 Feb. 1860, Wellesley, *Secrets*, p.197.

53. Arese to Cavour, Paris, 16 Feb. 1860, CCN, III, 72.

54. Thouvenel to Talleyrand, Paris, 24 Feb. 1860, *Moniteur*, 3 Mar. 1860.

55. *Moniteur*, 2 Mar. 1860.

56. Nigra to Cavour, Paris, 3 Mar. 1860, CCN, III, 137.

57. Pourtalès to Schleinitz, Paris, 3 Mar. 1860, APP, II (I), 177.

58. Cowley to Russell, Paris, 1 Mar. 1860, PRO, Russell Papers, G.D. 22/54.

59. Procureur reports of April 1860 from Rennes, Rouen, Riom, Lyons, and Nîmes. One other came from Riom, 5 July 1860.

60. Bixio to Cavour, Paris, 21 Mar. 1860, CCN, III, 206-207.

61. After the signature of the treaty Cavour turned to Talleyrand and said, "Et bien, monsieur le baron, désormais nous sommes complices." For the negotiation of the treaty and its aftermath see La Gorce, *Second Empire*, III, 209-212.

62. Cowley to Russell, Chantilly, 25 Dec. 1859, PRO, Russell Papers, G.D. 22/53.

63. The regions of France reporting, all of which showed unanimity or large majorities for the annexation of Savoy and Nice, were: Brittany, Normandy, Flanders, Lorraine, Or-

122—129

léanais, Franche-Comté, Burgundy,
Lyonnais, Poitou, Limousin, Au-
vergne, Dauphiné, Provence, E.
Languedoc, Guyenne, Béarn, and
Corsica.

64. The almost unanimous provincial
approval for the annexation of
Savoy and Nice will be found in
the procureur reports of April 1860
from Poitiers, Orleans, Aix, Douai,
Rennes, Pau, Agen, Dijon, Riom,
Corsica, Limoges, Nancy, Caen,
Rouen, and Grenoble; and in the
procureur reports of July 1860 from
Besançon, Douai, Montpellier, Dijon, Riom, Lyons, Corsica, Rennes,
Caen, Pau, Rouen, and Grenoble;
and from procureur reports of Oct.
1860 from Agen and Nancy.

65. For the Paris celebration see *Moniteur*, 15 June 1860; Dabot, *Souvenirs*, pp.70-71.

66. Guisard to Vrière, Lyons, 27 Aug.
1860, AEB, CP, Consulats, VI,
Lyons, no7. The consul added: "I
am speaking of this [visit] . . . .
with all the coolness and impartiality of a narrator."

67. Cowley to Russell, Chantilly, 14
Sept. 1860, PRO, Russell Papers,
G.D. 22/55.

68. For the amnesty see La Gorce,
Second Empire, III, 121-122.

69. *Constitutionnel*, 14 May 1860.

70. *Moniteur*, 21 May 1860.

71. *Constitutionnel*, 11 Sept. 1860.

72. Cavour to Nigra, Turin, 9 Aug.
1860, CCN, IV, 145; Metternich report to Vienna, 16 May 1860, as
cited in Salomon, *Metternich*, pp.
66-67.

73. RDM, 15 May 1860, pp.494-500; 15
Aug. 1860, p.994.

74. On the attitude of the *Débats* see
Débats, 27 July and 12 Nov. 1860;
Nigra to Cavour, Paris, 17 July
1860, Cavour to Nigra, Turin, 9
Aug. 1860, CCN, IV, 109, 145.

75. Senior, *Thiers and Guizot*, II, 329,
20 May 1860.

76. Opinion on the Garibaldi expedi-
tion can be found in the procureur
reports of July 1860 from Besan-
çon, Orleans, Montpellier, Dijon,
Riom, Toulouse, Aix, Agen, Lyons,
Bastia, Rennes, Pau, Bordeaux,
Nancy, Rouen, Nîmes, Limoges,
Grenoble, and Paris; of October
1860 from Agen, Aix, Limoges,
Toulouse, Riom, Amiens, Bastia,
Colmar, Pau, Rennes, and Caen.

77. C. Tivaroni, *L'Italia degli Italiani*:

*Storia critica del Risorgimento
italiano* (Turin, 1896), II, 248-249.

78. On another occasion Cialdini was
quoted as having said that the
parting remarks were: "Fatte, ma
fatte presto." On the Chambéry interview see La Gorce, *Second Empire*, III, 402-411; A. Debidour,
*Histoire des rapports de l'église et
de l'état en France de 1789 à 1870*
(Paris, 1898), pp.565-566; L. M.
Case, *Franco-Italian relations,
1860-1865: The Roman question
and the September Convention*
(Philadelphia, Pa., 1932), pp.10-14.

79. Napoleon III to Thouvenel, Toulon,
11 Sept. 1860, Archives du ministère des affaires étrangères, Paris,
MSS, Correspondance politique,
Italie, CCCL, 221.

80. Cavour to Nigra, Turin, 12 Sept.
1860, Chiala, *Cavour lettere*, IV,
2-4.

81. *Constitutionnel*, 15 Sept. 1860.

82. *Union*, 14 Sept. 1860.

83. *Debats*, 13 and 19 Sept. 1860.

84. By this time it was known that
General Cialdini was leading the
Sardinian forces into Umbria.

85. RDM, 15 Sept. 1860, p.484.

86. *Ibid.*, 1 Oct. 1860, pp.737-738; 15
Oct. 1860, p.999.

87. Bixio to Cavour, Paris, 14 Oct.
1860, CCN, IV, 249.

88. Gropello to Cavour, 15 Oct. 1860,
CCN, IV, 248.

89. Cowley memorandum on conversations with Thouvenel and Bour-
queney, Paris, 19 Oct. 1860, PRO,
Russell Papers, G.D. 22/55.

90. Cesare Cantù was an Italian deputy
in the lower house and a well-
known historian.

91. With the annexation of Savoy,
Chambéry became the seat of a new
court of appeals district.

92. This passage was marked by pencil in the margin by officials in
Paris.

93. The provinces where pro-Sardinian
groups appeared were Orléanais,
Flanders, Bordelais, P r o v e n c e,
Languedoc, Auvergne, Dauphiné,
Picardy, Corsica, Béarn, Lorraine,
Brittany, Poitou, and Ile de France.

94. The provinces with indifferent
groups were Orléanais, Picardy,
Limousin, Languedoc, Auvergne,
Béarn, western Normandy, Lyonnais, Lorraine, and Franche-Comté.

95. Groups in the provinces of
Languedoc, Orléanais, Flanders,

Picardy, Berry, Brittany, Bordelais, Guyenne, Provence, Auvergne, Alsace, Lorraine, Dauphiné, Béarn, Normandy, Ile de France, Lyonnais, and Franche-Comté.

96. Procureur report, Pau (384), 10 Oct. 1860.

97. Provincial opinion of all shades on the invasion of Umbria and the Marches may be found in the procureur reports of Oct. 1860 from Nîmes, Orleans, Douai, Bourges, Bordeaux, Agen, Aix, Limoges, Toulouse, Riom, Grenoble, Amiens, Corsica, Colmar, Pau, Montpellier, Metz, Rennes, Caen, Rouen, Lyons, Poitiers, Nancy, Paris, and Besançon.

98. On the annexation plebiscites see Tivaroni, *Italia degli Italiani*, II, 312-313, 342-344.

99. Similar anti-Italian views were held by some nonclerical groups in the districts of Rennes, Caen, Colmar, Dijon, Limoges, and Aix.

100. For opinion on the plebiscites and annexations in the Two Sicilies and in the Marches and Umbria see the procureur reports of Jan. 1861 from Lyons, Orleans, Bourges, Toulouse, Aix, Agen, Dijon, Douai, Bordeaux, Caen, Colmar, Pau, Limoges, Rennes, Besançon, Rouen, and Nancy.

101. "Le vent n'est plus aux croisades" (Thouvenel to Gramont, Paris, 23 Sept. 1860, Thouvenel, *Secret*, I, 221).

102. *Moniteur*, 25 Nov. 1860.

103. For a discussion of this new liberalization of legislative procedures see La Gorce, *Second Empire*, III, 442-447.

104. *Ibid.*, p.444.

105. Cowley's memorandum of a conversation with the emperor, 23 Nov. 1860, PRO, Russell Papers, GD 22/55.

106. "It is the fix in which H.M. finds himself in regard to the Italian question which has brought matters to a crisis," Cowley wrote to Russell on 30 Nov. 1860 (PRO, Russell Papers, GD 22/55). Pourtalès wrote Schleinitz, "Soit que le cabinet des Tuileries rentre dans les voies pacifiques . . . . , soit qu'il se lance dorénavant à bride abattue dans les voies aventureuses de la révolution, son action ne sera plus une et absolue" (1 Dec. 1860, APP, II [I], 740, fn. 3).

See also Gropello to Cavour, Paris, 28 Nov. 1860, CCN, IV, 278-279.

107. *Moniteur*, 5 Feb. 1861.

108. Thouvenel to Gramont, Paris, 4 Feb. 1861, Thouvenel, *Secrets*, I, 390; Cowley to Russell, Paris, 9 Feb. 1861, PRO, Russell Papers, GD 22/54.

109. On the emperor's throne speech see the procureur reports from Rennes, 5 Feb. 1861, 22 Mar. 1861; Lyons, 7 Feb. 1861, 8 Mar. 1861; Poitiers, Apr. 1861; Colmar, 1 Apr. 1861; Orleans, 3 Apr. 1861; Nancy, 10 Apr. 1861; Paris, 28 May 1861.

110. On the prince's speech and the debates in the senate see *Moniteur*, 2 Mar. 1861; La Gorce, *Second Empire*, III, 452-458; Delord, *Second Empire*, III, 97; Case, *Franco-Italian relations*, pp.56-59.

111. E. D'Hauterive, *Napoléon III et le prince Napoléon. Correspondance inédite* (Paris, 1925), pp.212-213; A. Comandini, *Il principe Napoleone nel risorgimento italiano* (Milan, 1922), pp.208-209.

112. For reactions to the speech of Prince Napoleon see procureur reports of March 1861 from Lyons; of April 1861 from Toulouse, Agen, Aix, Bordeaux, Limoges, Pau, and Amiens; and of May 1861 from Nîmes and Paris.

113. *Moniteur*, 14 Mar. 1861.

114. For debates in the legislative body see La Gorce, *Second Empire*, III, 457-466; and Delord, *Second Empire*, III, 109-111.

115. La Gorce, *Second Empire*, III, 463.

116. Pourtalès to Schleinitz, Paris, 22 Mar. 1861, APP, II (II), 266.

117. The report from Nancy said that "the cause of the Holy See had lost more supporters than it had gained by the debates."

118. For the direct reaction to the debates see the procureur reports of March 1861 from Rennes; of April 1861 from Colmar, Orleans, Nancy, Pau, Amiens, and Rennes; of May 1861 from Nîmes and Paris.

119. The procureurs general usually designated the following groups: Legitimists, Orleanists, Imperialists, clergy, businessmen (bourgeoisie), peasants, workers, Republicans, Socialists.

120. This total favorable to Italy includes 29 groups favorable to France's annexation of Savoy and Nice. This allocation seems justi-

137—143

fied, since it indicated that the
French people were willing to be
implicated in the Sardinian annexations in order to acquire the new
territory. It also measures the
countereffect Napoleon III sought
in injecting Savoy and Nice into
the picture. Without the question
of Savoy and Nice, the sympathy
for Italy would still stand at 63.

121. These indications were the poor responses to the call for volunteers
for the pope's army and to the
solicitations for the Peter's Pence.
An early report from Aix (7 July

1859) affirmed: "The emperor's
policy . . . . has more or less
openly elicited the support of a
goodly number of Republicans."

122. For the shift of political sentiment
in 1860 and early 1861 see the procureur reports of Jan. 1860 from
Orleans; of Apr. 1860 from Orleans, Montpellier, Toulouse, Bordeaux, and Metz; of July 1860
from Riom, Aix, Colmar, and
Nancy; of Jan. 1861 from Lyons;
of Apr. 1861 from Agen, Besançon,
and Aix.

123. La Gorce, *Second Empire*, III, 466.

CHAPTER SIX

The Roman Question

1. This change of emphasis is noted
in the procureur reports of 1861,
which now speak more often of the
Roman question rather than of the
Italian question. Indeed, the procureur general at Dijon in his report of 6 April 1861 remarked that
"the Italian question [has] become
the Roman question."

2. For these negotiations see Case,
Relations, ch. ii.

3. *Atti ufficiali del Parlamento italiano* (1860-1874), Chamber, 25
March 1861, pp.135-137; Case, *Relations*, pp.63-65.

4. *Atti ufficiali*, Chamber, 27 March
1861, p.144.

5. For the reactions to the Italian parliamentary debates of March 1861
see the procureur reports of April
1861 from Nancy, Metz, Besançon,
Riom, Limoges, Nîmes, and Corsica; and of July 1861 from Agen.

6. Recognition was given on 15 June
1861, but the public announcement was not made until 25 June.
See Thouvenel to Rayneval, Paris,
15 June 1861, Archives du ministère des affaires étrangères, Paris,
MSS, correspondance politique
(hereafter cited as AMAE, CP),
Italie, 351: 358-363; *Livre jaune*
(1861), pp.3-4; Case, *Relations*,
pp.108-111.

7. W. Grey to Russell, Paris, 6 June
1861, PRO, Russell Papers, GD
22/56; Beyens to Vrière, AEB, CP,
Légation française, XX, no.17.

8. It was also noted by Grey in his
letter to Russell of 6 June that

"many rejoice and see the 'Doigt
de Dieu' in this event."

9. For provincial opinion on Cavour's
death see the procureur reports of
July 1861 from Riom, Nîmes, and
Aix.

10. Dayton to Seward, Paris, 12 June
1861, enclosure, State Dept. Corr.,
France, L, no.11.

11. The seven districts where lack of
surprise was definitely noticed were
Besançon, Nancy, Lyons, Toulouse,
Bordeaux, Rouen, and Rennes.

12. Those districts favoring the recog-
nition (usually with the reserva-
tions) were Caen, Rouen, Douai,
Amiens, Nancy, Metz, Colmar,
Besançon, Lyons, Bourges, Riom,
Nîmes, and Toulouse.

13. Procureur report from Nancy, 6
July 1861.

14. For opinion on the recognition of
Italy see the procureur reports of
July 1861 from Rennes, Caen,
Rouen, Douai, Amiens, Nancy,
Metz, Colmar, Besançon, Lyons,
Bourges, Nîmes, Toulouse, Bor-
deaux, and Pau; and of 30 Oct.
1861 from Riom.

15. Cowley to Russell, Paris, 15 July
1861, PRO, Russell Papers, GD
22/56.

16. For the decline in interest in the
Roman question during the third
quarter of 1861 see the procureur
reports of October 1861 from
Rennes, Caen, Rouen, Douai,
Amiens, Paris, Orleans, Nancy,
Metz, Besançon, Dijon, Lyons,
Riom, Nîmes, Aix, Montpellier,

Toulouse, Agen, Bordeaux, and Bastia (Corsica).

17. For public indifference to the Roman question during the last quarter of 1861 see the procureur reports of Jan. 1862 from Rennes, Caen, Douai, Nancy, Colmar, Besançon, Dijon, Riom, Limoges, Nîmes, Toulouse, Agen, Bordeaux, and Pau.
18. *Moniteur*, 28 Jan. 1862.
19. *Ibid.*, 2 March 1862.
20. *Ibid.*, 4 March 1862.
21. For reaction to the debates on the Roman question in the early months of 1862 see the following procureur reports: Bordeaux, 6 March 1862; Amiens, 31 March 1862; Lyons, 1 April 1862; Toulouse, 4 April 1862; and Nancy, 5 April 1862.
22. The five districts were Riom, Paris, Amiens, Toulouse, and Bourges.
23. The three districts were Nancy, Lyons, and Toulouse.
24. On the continued indifference to the Roman question in early 1862 see the following procureur reports: Riom, 11 Feb. 1862; Paris, 18 March 1862; Amiens, 31 March 1862; and those in April 1862 from Bourges, Nancy, Lyons, and Toulouse.
25. Maurain, *Politique ecclésiastique*, p.606.
26. On court factions and activities see Reuss to Bernsdorff, Paris, 17 and 22 Oct. 1862, APP II (II), 16, note 5; Cowley to Russell, 28 Feb. 1862, PRO, Russell Papers, GD 22/57; Maurain, *Politique ecclésiastique*, pp.600-601; Maurain, *Baroche*, p.221; Robert Schnerb, *Rouher et le Second Empire* (Paris, 1949), pp.127-128.
27. Cowley was more easily taken in by the uneasiness caused by the legislative debates. He found Thouvenel "terribly out of spirits over the Italian question" because the clerical party seemed to be getting the upper hand and to be pushing the emperor hard through "the gentler sex." A week and a half later he was reporting the emperor as so disturbed that he even regretted having given the legislature "any liberty of speech" (Cowley to Russell, Paris, 28 Feb. and 10 March 1862, PRO, Russell Papers, GD 22/57).

28. Beyens to C. Rogier, Paris, 8 March 1862, AEB, CP, Légation française, XX, no.75.
29. Special report from the procureur general at Aix, 6 June 1862. See also Maurain, *Politique ecclésiastique*, p.608, note 3.
30. *Moniteur*, 11 June 1862; Maurain, *Politique ecclésiastique*, pp.614-615.
31. Maurain, *Politique ecclésiastique*, pp.612-615.
32. *Ibid.*, p.616. See also procureur report from Rennes, 4 July 1862.
33. Maurain, *Politique ecclésiastique*, pp.615-616, note 2.
34. Procureur report from Agen, 7 July 1862.
35. Procureur report from Besançon, 15 July 1862.
36. The districts of Caen, Amiens, Versailles (part of Paris district), Metz, Riom, Limoges, Nîmes, and Agen.
37. The districts of Douai, Lyons, Toulouse, Agen, Montpellier, Bordeaux, and Pau.
38. Maurain, *Politique ecclésiastique*, pp.615, 616.
39. On public reaction to the bishops' assembly in Rome in June 1862 see the procureur reports of July 1862 from Rennes, Caen, Rouen, Douai, Amiens, Nancy, Metz, Besançon, Lyons, Riom, Limoges, Nîmes, Aix, Montpellier, Toulouse, Agen, Bordeaux, and Pau; and of 26 Aug. 1862 from Paris; as well as Maurain, *Politique ecclésiastique*, pp.607-618.
40. For an account of these secret diplomatic maneuvers in the summer of 1862 see Case, *Relations*, pp.167-201.
41. Durando to representatives abroad, Turin, 10 Sept. 1862, *Libro verde*, 18 Nov. 1862, pp.1-3; AMAE, CP, Italie, 355; 128-130; *Livre jaune* (1862), pp.47-48.
42. *Gazzetta ufficiale del Regno*, 17 Sept. 1862.
43. Case, *Relations*, p.205.
44. Cowley to Russell, Paris, 26 Sept. 1862, PRO, FO, France, 1445/1136.
45. Napoleon III to Thouvenel, Paris, 20 May 1862; Thouvenel to La Valette, Paris, 30 May 1862; La Valette to Thouvenel, Rome, 24 June 1862; published in *Moniteur*, 25 Sept. 1862.
46. For press discussions see all the Paris papers between 31 Aug. and 24 Sept. 1862.

150—155

47. Baron Beyens reported the story that after the news of Garibaldi's defeat Prince Metternich, the Austrian ambassador, was said to have remarked to the papal nuncio in Paris: "You know, Monseigneur, if people saw our disheartened looks, they would take us for two Garibaldians" (Beyens to C. Rogier, Paris, 2 Sept. 1862, AEB, CP, Légation française, XX, no.152).

48. French public reaction to Aspromonte will be found in the procureur reports of Oct. 1862 from Rennes, Rouen, Orleans, Nancy, Metz, Colmar, Besançon, Bourges, Riom, Nîmes, Montpellier, Toulouse, and Bordeaux; and from Paris, 14 Nov. 1862.

49. See the Paris press between 21 and 23 Sept. 1862.

50. Procureur reports from Nancy, 20 Oct. 1862, and from Dijon, 8 Jan. 1863.

51. On the press reaction to the publication of the documents on 25 Sept. 1862 see all the Paris papers between 25 and 28 Sept. 1862.

52. Beyens to C. Rogier, Paris, 26 Sept. 1862, AEB, CP, Légation française, XX, no.157.

53. For public opinion on the documents in the *Moniteur* of 25 Sept. 1862 see the procureur reports of Oct. 1862 from Amiens, Nancy, Metz, Orleans, Bourges, Lyons, Nîmes, Montpellier, Bordeaux, and Bastia (Corsica); and of 14 Nov. 1862 from Paris.

54. Thouvenel to Flahault, Paris, 13 Oct. 1862, Thouvenel, *Secret*, II, 427-428.

55. It was said that Persigny with his sharp tongue contributed to the plain talking to the emperor by these words: "You're like me, you let yourself be governed by your wife: I only compromise my fortune, and I sacrifice it to keep peace in the family, while you sacrifice your interests as well as those of your son and of the whole country. You make it appear that you have abdicated, you are losing your prestige, and you discourage your remaining friends, those who serve you faithfully" (Ollivier, *Empire libéral*, V, 505-506).

56. For accounts of the dismissal of Thouvenel see Ollivier, *Empire libéral*, V, 505-510; Maurain, *Politique ecclésiastique*, pp.618-625;

Maurain, *Baroche*, pp.236-242; Schnerb, *Rouher*, pp.128-129; Thouvenel, *Pages*, pp.391-395; Case, *Relations*, pp.211-213.

57. *Moniteur*, 16 Oct. 1862.

58. Drouyn de Lhuys to French diplomatic representatives abroad, Paris, 18 Oct. 1862, *Livre jaune* (1862), p.15.

59. See the main Paris newspapers between 16 and 21 Oct. 1862.

60. These three districts were Aix, Besançon, and Paris. The American minister mentioned a strong demonstration at the Ecole de Médecine against the emperor's Italian policy in mid-November at the time classes were getting under way (Dayton to Seward, Paris, 21 Nov. 1862, State Dept. Corr., France, 53; Dayton no.228). For the general reaction to the replacement of Thouvenel by Drouyn de Lhuys see the procureur reports of Jan. 1863 from Caen, Rouen, Douai, Nancy, Metz, Colmar, Besançon, Dijon, Bourges, Grenoble, Nîmes, Aix, Montpellier, and Agen; and of 3 Feb. 1863 from Paris.

61. For continued indifference even after the publication of the letters and the dismissal of Thouvenel see the procureur reports of Oct. 1862 from Rennes, Caen, Amiens, Orleans, Nancy, Colmar, Lyons, Limoges, Aix, Toulouse, Agen, and Pau; of 14 Nov. 1862 from Paris; of Jan. 1863 from Rennes, Rouen, Metz, Dijon, Orleans, Bourges, Nîmes, Aix, Toulouse, Agen, and Bordeaux.

62. Count Arese, closest to Napoleon III of all Italians, wrote home that "the proximity of the elections explains why they want to show special consideration to the clergy" (Arese to Pasolini, Paris, 16 March 1863, P. D. Pasolini, [ed.], Giuseppe Pasolini, *Memorie raccolte da suo figlio* [Turin, 1887], I, 344-352).

63. Viel-Castel, *Memoirs*, II, 258.

64. Cowley to Russell, Paris, 17 Oct. 1862, PRO, Russell Papers, GD 22/58; Mulinen report, Paris, 14 Oct. 1862, Salomon, *Metternich*, p. 70; Maurain, *Politique ecclésiastique*, p.626.

65. For the shift of the clericals back toward the government after the appointment of Drouyn de Lhuys see the procureur reports of Jan. 1863 from Grenoble, Nancy, Agen,

Dijon, Montpellier, Aix, Caen, Metz, Rouen, Besançon, Colmar, Douai, Orleans, Toulouse, Riom, Rennes, and Bordeaux; and of 3 Feb. 1863 from Paris.

66. The seven bishops were the archbishops of Rennes, Tours, and Cambrai and the bishops of Nantes, Orleans, Chartres, and Metz.

67. On voting in the rural areas see Rivet's statement to Senior in Senior, *Thiers and Guizot*, II, 150.

68. Maurain, *Politique ecclésiastique*, p.665.

69. Ollivier, *Empire libéral*, VI, 260-261.

70. *Ibid.*, p. 261.

71. Maurain, *Politique ecclésiastique*, p.667.

72. Quoted by Seignobos in Lavisse, *France contemporaine*, VII, 32.

73. See the cartons BB³⁰ 427-431 concerning the elections of 1863.

74. The last two sentences were underlined in pencil by the officials in the ministry of justice. The two above quotations were in the procureur reports from Besançon of 13 July and 13 Oct. 1863.

75. For the indifference to the Roman question throughout 1863 see the procureur reports of 28 March 1863 from Orleans; of April 1863 from Lyons, Bordeaux, Agen, Montpellier, Riom, Dijon, Grenoble, Nancy, Toulouse, and Nîmes; of 18 May 1863 from Paris; of June 1863 from Lyons; of July 1863 from Dijon, Douai, Nancy, Colmar, Besançon, and Montpellier; and of Oct. 1863 from Douai, Nancy, Colmar, Besançon, Lyons, Orleans, and Riom.

76. The extracts can be found in the procureur reports, BB³⁰ 368, under the date of 28 June 1863.

77. Report by the minister of justice to the emperor, 28 June 1863, in the procureur reports, BB³⁰ 368.

78. Good accounts of the elections of 1863 may be found in La Gorce, *Second Empire*, IV, 179-240; Maurain, *Politique ecclésiastique*, pp. 634-667; Ollivier, *Empire libéral*, VI, 215-269; and Lavisse, *France contemporaine*, VII, 26-32.

79. For Napoleon III's embarrassing situation in early 1864 see Case, *Relations*, pp.263-266.

80. For a collection of pertinent extracts from the procureur reports on the Mexican expedition see

Case, *United States and Mexico*, pp.309-436.

81. Procureur report from Colmar, 16 Oct. 1863. See Case, *United States and Mexico*, p.351.

82. Grey to Russell, Paris, 2 Oct. 1863, PRO, FO, France, 1496/104.

83. For the growth of opposition sentiment in 1864 see the procureur reports of Jan. 1864 from Paris, Aix, and Bordeaux; of Apr. 1864 from Angers, Paris, Lyons, and Aix; of July 1864 from Aix. See also the reports on the local elections from Bordeaux, 17 Feb. 1864; from Orleans, 22 Feb. 1864 in Archives Nationales, Paris, MSS, series BB¹⁸ 1686-A⁴-161 and -218.

84. For continued indifference on the Roman question on the eve of the September Convention see the procureur reports of Jan. 1864 from Colmar and Besançon; of April 1864 from Angers, Nancy, Colmar, Lyons, Bordeaux, and Pau; and of July 1864 from Nancy, Besançon, Lyons, Aix, Montpellier, Toulouse, and Bordeaux.

85. Both Solms and Goltz, Prussian representatives in Paris, stressed the isolation factor in connection with the subsequent September Convention and the Roman question. Solms wrote Bismarck at the first news of the Convention: "Most opinions . . . . agree that the isolation in which France found herself may have been the most important cause for the rapprochement with Italy" (Solms to Bismarck, Paris, 22 Sept. 1864, APP, V, 216). Likewise Goltz wrote: "At this same time the interviews of the Northern sovereigns were worrying the Tuileries Court very much and prompted the desire to reconcile liberal opinion" (Goltz to Bismarck, Paris, 26 Sept. 1864, APP, V, 417).

86. Vimercati to Minghetti, Paris, 15 April 1864, M. Minghetti, *La Convenzione di settembre* (Bologna, 1899), pp.21-23.

87. For the negotiation of the September Convention see Case, *Relations*, pp.263-300; and Minghetti, *Convenzione*. For the text of the treaty see A. de Clercq, *Recueil des traités de la France* (Paris, 1880), IX, 129-130; *Livre jaune* (1864), pp.43-45; (English translation) Case, *Relations*, pp.299-300.

88. Case, *Relations*, pp.303-304.

162—169

89. *Constitutionnel,* 22 Sept. 1864. This was republished in the *Moniteur* the next day in order to give it more authenticity.

90. Drouyn de Lhuys to Sartiges, Paris, 12 Sept. 1864, *Moniteur,* 2 Oct. 1864.

91. These were Aix, Amiens, Besançon, Bourges, Caen, Colmar, Dijon, Douai, Grenoble, Limoges, Lyons, Montpellier, Nancy, Orleans, Paris, Rennes, Riom, and Toulouse.

92. The sixteen districts favoring the temporal power were Aix, Amiens, Besançon, Bordeaux, Bourges, Colmar, Dijon, Grenoble, Lyons, Metz, Montpellier, Nancy, Nîmes, Paris, Rennes, and Toulouse.

93. For opinion on the September Convention see the procureur reports of Oct. 1864 from Rennes, Caen, Amiens, Nancy, Metz, Colmar, Besançon, Dijon, Lyons, Angers, Bourges, Riom, Limoges, Chambéry, Aix, Nîmes, Montpellier, Toulouse, and Bordeaux; of 14 Nov. 1864, from Paris; of Jan. 1865 from Rennes, Caen, Amiens, Nancy, Metz, Colmar, Besançon, Lyons, Riom, Grenoble, Aix, Montpellier, Toulouse, Agen, and Bordeaux; of April 1865 from Rennes, Orleans, Nancy, Metz, Besançon, Dijon, Bourges, Riom, and Montpellier; of 11 May 1865 from Paris. See also the prefect reports (F^{1c} III): Bouches-du-Rhône 7, 15 Oct. 1864; Seine-et-Oise 9, 15 Oct. 1864; Meuse 8, 15 Oct. 1864; Indre-et-Loire 7, 17 Oct. 1864; Manche 6, 18 Oct. 1864; Vendée 5, 18 Oct. 1864; Allier 6, 18 Oct. 1864; Gironde 6, 31 Oct. 1864; Meuse 8, 1 Nov. 1864; Haute-Vienne 8, c. 1 Nov. 1864; and Allier 6, 2 Nov. 1864.

94. Nigra to Visconti-Venosta, Paris, 15 Sept. 1864, AMAE, CP, Italie, 360: pp.392-394.

95. La Marmora to Nigra, Turin, 7 Nov. 1864, *Gazetta Ufficiale,* 7 Nov. 1864. See also Case, *Relations,* pp. 320-323.

96. For public reaction to the publication of interpretative documents on the September Convention see the procureur reports of 14 Nov. 1864 from Paris and of Jan. 1865 from Douai, Nancy, Besançon, and Montpellier.

97. For the reaction of French opinion to the encyclical and *Syllabus* see the procureur reports of Jan. 1865 from Chambéry, Riom, Limoges, Toulouse, Besançon, and Caen; of 17 Feb. 1865 from Paris; of 30 Mar. 1865 from Chambéry; of April 1865 from Bourges, Orleans, Aix, Rennes, Caen, Metz, Montpellier, and Besançon; of 11 May 1865 from Paris; and the prefect report (F^{1c} III): Gironde 6, 1 Feb. 1865.

98. Maurain, *Politique ecclésiastique,* p.721.

99. It will be noticed that the emperor usually avoided the term "temporal power."

100. By reference to Saint Louis, Napoleon III wished to link the resistance of the secular state to a ruler canonized by the church and to one of the forefathers of the line supported by the clerical Legitimists.

101. Maurain, *Politique ecclésiastique,* pp.728-734.

102. Opinion on the debates and votes in the legislature concerning the September Convention may be found in the procureur reports of April 1865 from Orleans, Rennes, Besançon, and Montpellier; of 11 May 1865 from Paris; and of July 1865 from Douai, Nancy, Metz, Riom, and Pau. Lord Cowley affirmed that the emperor's speech "had certainly made a good impression in Paris" (Cowley to Russell, Paris, 17 Feb. 1865, PRO, Russell Papers, GD 22/61).

103. Maurain, *Politique ecclésiastique,* p.735.

104. Ollivier, *Empire libéral,* VII, 390-392.

105. For the hostile reaction to the Ajaccio speech see the procureur reports of July 1865 from Rennes, Caen, Douai, Orleans, Besançon, Lyons, Riom, Aix, Toulouse, and Pau.

106. For opinion in 1865 on evacuation see the procureur reports of Oct. 1865 from Amiens, Besançon, Riom, Grenoble, Montpellier, Toulouse, and Bordeaux; of Jan. 1866 from Rennes, Besançon, Poitiers, Limoges, Montpellier, Bordeaux, Pau, and Paris; and prefect report (F^{1c} III), Manche 6, 1 Dec. 1865.

107. The districts decidedly in favor of the temporal power in 1866 and 1867 were: Rennes, Douai, Seine-et-Oise, Nancy, Metz, Besançon,

Lyons, Riom, Chambéry, Grenoble, Montpellier, Toulouse, Agen, and Bordeaux; those which indicated prevailing indifference were Limoges and Pau.

108. For French opinion on papal temporal power, 1865-1867, see procureur reports of Oct. 1865 from Nancy, Paris, and Riom; of Jan. 1866 from Rennes and Besançon; of April 1866 from Nancy, Besançon, Riom, Chambéry, Montpellier, and Bordeaux; of Oct. 1866 from Rennes and Toulouse; of Jan. 1867 from Lyons, Agen, Douai, Metz, Limoges, Grenoble, Pau, Aix, Bordeaux, Nancy, and Rennes; of July 1867 from Nancy; of Oct. 1867 from Douai, Nancy, and Grenoble; of Jan. 1868 from Rennes; and prefect report (F^{1c} III), Seine-et-Oise 9, c. 1 Sept. 1866.

109. *Moniteur*, 23 Jan. 1866.

110. Quoted in Maurain, *Politique ecclésiastique*, p.739.

111. For French opinions holding Napoleon III accountable for the pope's safety after evacuation see the procureur reports of Oct. 1865 from Nancy, Besançon, Riom, and Bordeaux; of Jan. 1866 from Rennes, Nancy, Besançon, and Pau; of April 1866 from Douai, Nancy, and Bordeaux; of Oct. 1866 from Rennes, Besançon, Bourges, Riom, Poitiers, Chambéry, Montpellier, Toulouse, and Agen; of Jan. 1867 from Rennes, Douai, Nancy, Metz, Lyons, Grenoble, Montpellier, Agen, and Bordeaux; of 14 Feb. 1867 from Paris; of Oct. 1867 from Rennes, Douai, Nîmes, and Bastia (Corsica); and from the prefect report (F^{1c} III) from Ain 6, late Oct. 1866.

112. Cowley to Stanley, Compiègne, 11 Dec. 1866, Wellesley and Sencourt, *Conversations*, p.317.

113. Drouyn de Lhuys, now out of office, had already written the emperor that he must not abandon the pope (Drouyn de Lhuys to emperor, 16 Aug. 1867, quoted in Maurain, *Baroche*, p.391, note 1).

114. Strangely enough Baroche, as minister of justice, and La Valette, as minister of interior, had full knowledge of the opinion reports from their subordinates, the procureurs general and the prefects, in which the public was shown to be insistent on protecting the pope.

115. L. Chiala, *Pagine*, p.27.

116. These districts, covering all sections of France, were: Rennes, Caen, Rouen, Amiens, Nancy, Metz, Colmar, Dijon, Lyons, Bourges, Riom, Poitiers, Limoges, Chambéry, Nîmes, Montpellier, Toulouse, Bordeaux, and Pau.

117. For French opinion on Garibaldi's expedition against Rome see the procureur reports of Oct. 1867 from Chambéry, Limoges, Lyons, Nîmes, Dijon, Bourges, Riom, Bordeaux, Rouen, Metz, Amiens, Colmar, Caen, Rennes, Poitiers, Nancy, and Montpellier; of Jan. 1868 from Nancy, Pau, Toulouse, and Dijon; and the prefect report (F^{1c} III), Vendée 5, 4 Oct. 1867.

118. Maurain, *Politique ecclésiastique*, pp.821-822; *Times*, 1 Nov. 1867.

119. For press opinion on the expedition and Mentana see (in 1867) *Débats*, 27 Oct., 4 Nov., 6 Nov., 11 Nov.; *Siècle*, 28 Oct., 5 Nov., 7 Nov., 12 Nov.; *Temps*, 4 Nov.; *Liberté* 4 Nov.; *Opinion Nationale*, 4 Nov., 11 Nov.; *Univers*, 31 Oct., 5 Nov., 10 Nov.; *Union*, 6 Nov.; *Gazette de France*, 11 Nov.; *France*, 31 Oct.; *Etendard*, 31 Oct.; *Monde*, 7 Nov.; *Avenir National*, 11 Nov.; *Patrie*, 31 Oct., 6 Nov.; *Constitutionnel*, 5 Nov., 6 Nov.; *Times*, 1 Nov., 2 Nov., 12 Nov.

120. Beyens to C. Rogier, Paris, 4 Nov. 1867, AEB, CP, Légation française, XXIV, no.79.

121. Grenoble and Versailles at first reported some opposition, but later reports showed preponderant support. Likewise, Paris, Limoges, and Aix noted small hostile minorities.

122. French overwhelming approval of the reinstitution of the occupation of the Papal States and the action at Mentana may be found in the procureur reports of 26 Oct. 1867 from Montpellier; of Nov. 1867 from Lyons and Paris; of 31 Dec. from Chambéry; of Jan. 1868 from Nancy, Bordeaux, Douai, Grenoble, Amiens, Orleans, Agen, Metz, Bourges, Poitiers, Riom, Pau, Rennes, Aix, Limoges, Toulouse, Dijon, Rouen, Besançon, Montpellier, and Caen; and of 15 Feb. 1868 from Paris; and in the prefect reports (F^{1c} III) from Haut-Rhin 7, c. 30 Nov. 1867; Allier 6, 30 Nov. 1867; Seine-Inférieure 9, 1 Dec. 1867; Finistère 3, 2 Dec.

172—180

1867; Isère 7, 6 Dec. 1867; Seine-et-Oise 9, 13 Dec. 1867.

123. *Moniteur*, 19 Nov. 1867.

124. *Ibid.*, 6 Dec. 1867.

125. "Sire, il n'y a pas eu moyen de faire autrement." See Maurain, *Politique ecclésiastique*, pp.821-832; La Gorce, *Second Empire*, V, 314; Pinard, *Mon journal* (Paris, 1892), I, 236.

126. The seventeen districts favoring Rouher's "Never" speech were: Rennes, Rouen, Metz, Colmar, Orleans, Poitiers, Riom, Besançon, Lyons, Grenoble, Chambéry, Aix, N î m e s, Montpellier, Toulouse, Agen, and Pau.

127. For opinion on Rouher's "Never" speech see the procureur reports of Dec. 1867 from Lyons and Chambéry; of Jan. 1868 from Grenoble, Nîmes, Orleans, Agen, Metz, Poitiers, Riom, Pau, Rennes, Toulouse, Dijon, Besançon, and Montpellier; and the prefect reports (F^{1e} III): Bouches-du-Rhône 7, c. 7 Dec. 1867; Haut-Rhin 7, c. 31 Dec. 1867; Seine-Inférieure 9, 31 Dec. 1867; Allier 6, 1 Jan. 1868; Finistère 3, 3 Jan. 1868.

128. *Débats, France, Etendard, Siècle, Avenir National, Opinion Nationale, Liberté*, and *Temps*.

129. For press opinion on Rouher's "Never" speech see: *Débats*, 6, 7 Dec. 1867; *France*, 6 Dec. 1867; *Etendard*, 6 Dec. 1867; *Siècle*, 7, 8 Dec. 1867; *Avenir National*, 7 Dec. 1867; *Univers*, 7 Dec. 1867; *Union*, 7 Dec. 1867; *Liberté*, 7 Dec. 1867; *Temps*, 7 Dec. 1867; *Opinion Nationale*, 7 Dec. 1867.

130. French opinion on Prussia and Germany will be taken up more in detail in subsequent chapters.

131. *Débats*, 18 Sept. 1867; Solms to Bismarck, Paris, 18 Sept. 1867, APP, IX, 245.

132. For opinion comment on the Prussian implications of Mentana see the procureur reports of Oct. 1867 from Dijon, Lyons, Poitiers, Nîmes, Montpellier, and Bastia; of 14 Nov. 1867 from Paris; of Jan. 1868 from Rennes, Caen, Nancy, Montpellier, and Agen.

133. For the declining interest in the Roman question after Mentana see the procureur reports of April 1868 from Nancy, Besançon, Lyons, and Bordeaux; of 4 July 1868 from Aix.

134. 10 May 1869.

135. On the elections of 1869 see Maurain, *Politique ecclésiastique*, pp. 902-949.

CHAPTER SEVEN

The Polish Insurrection and the Danish War

1. Cowley to Russell, Fontainebleau, 15 June 1860, PRO, Russell Papers, GD 22/54.

2. Reuss to Schleinitz, Paris, 3 May 1861, APP, II (II), 322-323.

3. Pollone to Cavour, Paris, 23 June 1860, CCN, IV, 34-35.

4. Beyens, *Second Empire*, I, 313. See also Oncken, *Rheinpolitik*, I, 14-15.

5. H. von Sybel, *The founding of the German Empire by William I*, based chiefly on the Prussian state documents, trans. M. L. Perrin (New York, 1891), II, 415.

6. Procureur report from Rouen, 15 July 1860.

7. See all the procureur reports between April 1863 and January 1864.

8. Stanislas Lesczynski, who had been driven from the Polish throne in the War of the Polish Succession (1733-1735) in which he had been aided by France, was given the duchy of Lorraine as a consolation prize by his son-in-law, Louis XV. Here, as an enlightened ruler, he had done a great deal for the progress and welfare of his adopted people.

9. Procureur report from Nancy, 12 April 1863.

10. Goltz to Bismarck, Paris, 10 March 1863, APP, III, 388-389.

11. Cowley to Russell, Paris, 20 Feb. 1863, PRO, Russell Papers, GD 22/60.

12. F. Rogier to C. Rogier, Paris, 28 Feb. 1863, AEB, CP, Légation française, XXI, no.8.

13. Metternich to Rechberg, Paris, 26 Feb. 1863, Oncken, I, 8. See also same to same, Paris, 22 Feb. 1863, Haus, Hof, und Staat Archiv (Vienna), cited in H. Salomon,

L'ambassade de Richard de Metternich à Paris (Paris, 1931), p.88.

14. Dayton to Seward, Paris, 23 Feb. 1863, *Papers relating to foreign affairs* (Washington, 1863), pp.713-714.

15. Dabot, *Souvenirs*, p.121, 6 March 1863.

16. La Gorce, *Second Empire*, IV, 448.

17. The report from Angers, 5 Apr. 1864, alone failed to insist on peace in its expression of sympathy for the Poles.

18. Procureur report from Paris, 5 Aug. 1863.

19. For brief but characteristic opinions opposing a war for the liberation of Poland see the procureur reports of 28 March 1863 from Orleans; of April 1863 from Douai, Lyons, Colmar, Rouen, Caen, Nancy, Besançon, and Toulouse; of July 1863 from Bourges, Riom, Montpellier, Poitiers, Aix, and Bordeaux; of 30 Sept. 1863 from Chambéry; of Oct. 1863 from Agen, Amiens, Metz, Pau, Limoges, and Grenoble; of Jan. 1864 from Nîmes, Rennes, and Dijon.

20. Reuss report on an interview with Napoleon III, Fontainebleau, 8 June 1863, Oncken, I, 19-20. For an English translation see Wellesley and Sencourt, pp.219-221.

21. For public approval of Billault's speech see the procureur reports of 28 March 1863 from Orleans; of April 1863 from Bordeaux, Colmar, Agen, Dijon, Riom, Metz, Rouen, Caen, Besançon, Toulouse, and Nîmes.

22. For sentiment against Gorchakov's replies see the procureur reports of Oct. 1863 from Rouen, Douai, Nancy, and Agen; and of 5 Jan. 1864 from Nancy.

23. Haus, Hof, und Staat Archiv (Vienna), Varia, 5 Aug. 1863, cited in Salomon, *Metternich*, p.90.

24. F. Rogier to C. Rogier, Paris, 5 Nov. 1863, AEB, CP, Légation française, XXI, no.57.

25. Goltz to Bismarck, Paris, 5 Nov. 1863, APP, IV, 109.

26. Approval of the congress proposal may be found in the procureur reports of Dec. 1863 from Lyons and Chambéry; of Jan. 1864 from Douai, Orleans, Besançon, Bordeaux, Bourges, Riom, Rouen, and Dijon; and of Feb. 1864 from Colmar, Paris, and Poitiers.

27. For the decline of sympathy and interest concerning Poland see the procureur reports of Jan. 1864 from Nîmes, Nancy, Rouen, Aix, Besançon, and Colmar; of Apr. 1864 from Lyons, Chambéry, Angers, Metz, Nancy, Bordeaux, Limoges, Colmar, Douai, and Lyons; of July 1864 from Besançon, Dijon, Aix, Nancy, Bordeaux, and Colmar.

28. Goltz to Bismarck, Paris, 5 Aug. 1863, APP, III, 704-705.

29. For French bitterness toward England on Poland and the congress see the procureur reports of 3 April 1863 from Bordeaux; of July 1863 from Montpellier and Bordeaux; of Oct. 1863 from Bourges, Rouen, Limoges, and Nancy; of 31 Dec. 1863 from Chambéry; of Jan. 1864 from Nancy, Douai, Amiens, Bourges, Toulouse, Metz, Bordeaux, and Besançon; of 2 Feb. 1864 from Colmar.

30. For revival of friendliness toward Russia see the procureur reports of Jan. 1864 from Rouen and Bordeaux.

31. Goltz to Bismarck and William I, Paris, 15, 16, 20 Feb. 1863, APP, III, 247, 253-254, 273-277.

32. Procureur report from Colmar, 16 Oct. 1863.

33. For the discrepancies between press and public opinion on going to war for Poland see the procureur reports of Oct. 1863 from Paris, Orleans, Colmar, Besançon, and Limoges; and of Jan. 1864 from Rennes and Pau.

34. Procureur report from Amiens, 7 July 1864.

35. The year 1847 was just one year before the overthrow of Louis Philippe.

36. Beyens to C. Rogier, Paris, 16 Dec. 1863, AEB, CP, Légation française, XXI, no.81.

37. Russell to Cowley, London, 24 Jan. 1864, France, Ministry of Foreign Affairs, *Les origines diplomatiques de la guerre de 1870-1871* [hereafter cited as *Origines*], I (Paris, 1910), 186-188.

38. Drouyn de Lhuys to La Tour d'Auvergne, Paris, 26 Jan. 1864, *Origines*, I, 197-200.

39. Metternich to Rechberg, Paris, 19 Jan. and 3 Feb. 1864, Haus, Hof, und Staat Archiv (Vienna), cited in Salomon, *Metternich*, p.92.

40. Beyens to C. Rogier, Paris, 3 Feb.

188—193

1864, AEB, CP, Légation française, XXI, no.128.

41. Goltz to William I, Paris, 21 Feb. 1864, Oncken, I, 32-33.

42. Beyens to C. Rogier, Paris, 22 Feb. 1864, AEB, CP, Légation française, XXI, no.134.

43. Goltz to Bismarck, Paris, 26 April 1864, APP, IV, 741; same to same, Paris, 30 April 1864, APP, V, 58. A consultation of all the Paris papers during this period will confirm Goltz's grudging admission.

44. Solms to Bismarck, Paris, 22 Sept. 1865, APP, VI, 385. For other evidence of outside influences on the Paris press see APP, IV, 151-152, 356, 434, 602; V, 74, 295, 296, 315-316, 320, 345, 647, 654, 684, 704; VI, 53, 57, 73, 121, 361 (footnote); Wellesley and Sencourt, p.235.

45. For the difficult comprehension of the Schleswig-Holstein question see the procureur reports of March 1864 from Chambéry and Lyons; and of April 1864 from Metz and Pau.

46. For French sympathy for Denmark see the procureur reports of April 1864 from Dijon, Bordeaux, Limoges, and Colmar; of July 1864 from Lyons, Agen, Douai, Montpellier, Angers, Toulouse, Besançon, Metz, Dijon, Pau, Nancy, Bordeaux, and Aix; of Oct. 1864 from Dijon, Amiens, Bourges, Riom, and Toulouse.

47. Procureur report from Nancy, 14 April 1864.

48. For unanimous French opinion favoring a peaceful policy on the Danish War see the procureur reports of Jan. 1864 from Nancy, Rouen, Dijon, Besançon, Limoges, and Bordeaux; of 26 March 1864 from Lyons; of April 1864 from Riom, Toulouse, Caen, Dijon, Nancy, Limoges, Colmar, Douai, and Pau; of 3 May 1864 from Paris; of July 1864 from Douai, Angers, Toulouse, Riom, Besançon, Pau, Nancy, and Bordeaux; of 18 Aug. 1864 from Paris; of Oct. 1864 from Lyons, Amiens, Bourges, Toulouse, Nancy, and Colmar; of Jan. 1865 from Dijon, Bordeaux, Nancy, and Amiens.

49. Cowley to Russell, Paris, 13 June 1864, Wellesley and Sencourt, p. 227.

50. Bismarck to Werther, Berlin, 14 June 1864, APP, V, 224.

51. Goltz to Bismarck, Paris, 29 July 1864, APP, V, 345.

52. See the procureur reports of April 1864 from Metz and Colmar.

53. For the French reaction to the London Conference of 1864 see the procureur reports of July 1864 from Riom, Bordeaux, Colmar, Lyons, Agen, Montpellier, and Besançon; of 18 Aug. 1864 from Paris; and of 7 Oct. 1864 from Lyons.

54. For strong public support of the government's abstention policy in the Danish War see the procureur reports of March 1864 from Chambéry and Lyons; of April 1864 from Toulouse, Angers, Amiens, Caen, Rouen, Nancy, Colmar, Douai, and Pau; of July 1864 from Lyons, Agen, Douai, Montpellier, Riom, Besançon, Metz, Pau, Bordeaux, and Colmar; of 18 Aug. 1864 from Paris; of Oct. 1864 from Dijon, Bourges, Rouen, Toulouse, Nancy, and Colmar; and of 15 Jan. 1865 from Bordeaux.

55. Goltz to Bismarck, Paris, 11 July 1864, APP, V, 298.

56. See APP, IV, 505, 652; V, 230, 274, 294, 296, 320, 417; VI, 335.

57. For provisional concern over an anti-French alliance see the following procureur reports: Lyons, 26 March 1864; Rouen, 10 April 1864; Nancy, 14 April, 15 Oct. 1864.

58. See especially *Pays*, 4 Aug. 1864; *Constitutionnel*, 7 Aug. 1864; *Débats*, 5 Aug. 1864; *Siècle*, 5, 6, Aug., 24 Sept. 1864; also Prussian comments on the press in APP, V, 320, 568.

59. The weak and indifferent reaction of French opinion to the peace terms ending the Danish War may be found in the following procureur reports: Douai, 4 Oct. 1864; Bourges, 8 Oct. 1864; Nancy, 15 Oct. 1864, 15 Jan. 1865; Colmar, 27 Oct. 1864; Bordeaux, 15 Jan. 1865.

60. Drouyn de Lhuys circular, Paris, 29 Aug. 1865, *Origines*, VI, 453-454.

61. For French reaction to the Gastein Convention see the Prussian reports in APP, VI, 335, 353, 361; the various Paris newspapers between 15 Aug. and 3 Sept. 1865; and the procureur reports of Oct. 1865 from Douai, Chambéry, Limoges, Amiens, Besançon, Bordeaux, Grenoble, and Nancy; and of 15 Nov. 1865 from Paris.

62. For favorable reactions to Drouyn de Lhuys' circular of 29 Aug. 1865 see the procureur reports of Oct. 1865 from Chambéry, Besançon, Grenoble, and Nancy; and of 15 Nov. 1865 from Paris.

63. Cowley to Russell, Paris, 24 Feb. 1864, Wellesley and Sencourt, p.226.

64. Goltz to Bismarck, Paris, 20 Apr. 1864, APP, IV, 748.

65. For French opinion on Rhine compensations see the following procureur reports: Bordeaux, 20 Jan. 1864, 16 Jan. 1865, 18 Jan. 1866; Nancy, 15 Oct. 1864, 15 Oct. 1865; Douai, 5 Oct. 1865.

66. See Constitutionnel, 25 June 1864.

67. Cowley to Russell, PRO, FO, France, 27/1525.

68. For anti-British sentiment during the Danish War see the procureur

reports of Jan. 1864 from Besançon and Bordeaux; of 2 Feb. 1864 from Colmar; of April 1864 from Riom, Angers, and Rouen; of 30 June 1864 from Chambéry; of July 1864 from Agen, Angers, Toulouse, Besançon, Metz, Nancy, Bordeaux, and Colmar; of Oct. 1864 from Amiens, Bourges, Rouen, and Nancy.

69. For opinion finally advocating a rapprochement with England see the following procureur reports: Nancy, 14 April 1864, 16 Oct. 1865; Paris, 3 May 1864; Toulouse, 8 July 1864; Amiens, 10 Oct. 1865; Grenoble, 16 Oct. 1865.

70. For press suggestions of a rapprochement with Prussia see Siècle, 29 Sept. 1864; Goltz to Bismarck, Paris, 4 March, 29 Aug. 1865, APP, V, 708; VI, 361.

CHAPTER EIGHT

The Austro-Prussian War

1. See G. Roloff in Cambridge Modern History, XI, 447.

2. This aim of Napoleon III to expand French territory along the Rhine is particularly stressed, probably overstressed, by Oncken (Rheinpolitik, Introduction).

3. For early opinion demanding peace see the procureur reports of April 1866 from Lyons, Amiens, Douai, Bordeaux, Metz, Dijon, Besançon, Nancy, Colmar, Aix, Riom, and Pau; and of 5 May 1866 from Paris.

4. Wächter to Varnbuler, Paris, 11 April 1866, Oncken, Rheinpolitik, I, 132.

5. Beyens to C. Rogier, Paris, 29 March 1866, AEB, CP, Légation française, XXIII, no.23.

6. Metternich to Mensdorff, Paris, 1 May 1866, telegram, Oncken, Rheinpolitik, I, 145.

7. Nigra to La Marmora, Paris, 23 April 1866, A. La Marmora, Un po' più di luce sugli eventi politici e militari dell' anno 1866 (2nd ed.; Florence, 1873), pp.170-171.

8. Constitutionnel, 15 April 1866; Patrie, 6 April to 2 May 1866.

9. Siècle, 9, 13, 17 April and 2, 3 May 1866.

10. Nigra to La Marmora, Paris, 1 May

1866, La Marmora, Più di luce, p. 189.

11. Moniteur, 4 May 1866.

12. Ibid.

13. Kern to Federal Council, Paris, 3 May 1866, telegram, AFS, RP, Légation de Paris, 1866, no.14.

14. Beyens to C. Rogier, Paris, 3 May 1866, AEB, CP, Légation française, XXIII, no.51. La Gorce also tells us (Second Empire, V, 612-613) that "almost all hands were extended to the orator of the opposition and for more than fifteen minutes there was a confused murmur of approving remarks."

15. G. Rothan, Les origines de la guerre de 1870: La politique française en 1866 (1st ed.; Paris, 1883), p.126.

16. His hopefulness concerning support for intervention is reflected in his remarks to Goltz on 1 May when he expressed the opinion "that the eyes of France are directed towards the Rhine" (Goltz to Bismarck, Paris, 1 May 1866, Wellesley and Sencourt, p.256).

17. Moniteur, 7 May 1866.

18. Metternich to Mensdorff, Paris, 8 May 1866, Oncken, Rheinpolitik, I, 178.

19. Oncken, Rheinpolitik, I, 165, quot-

200—205

ing Radowitz. Napoleon III in his Bordeaux speech of 1852 had said, "The Empire means peace."

20. See the issues of these papers on 8 May 1866.

21. All of these views are found in the number of 8 May 1866. See also the *Siècle* of 9 and 10 May and the *Pays* of 12 May. Raymond Guyot says (*Histoire diplomatique, 1815-1870; cours sténographié* [Paris, 1930], p.633): "The Auxerre speech made a very profound impression. Within a few days almost all the nongovernmental press came out against war, especially war on the side of Prussia." Guyot leaned on the slender reed of the Paris press, but now the administrative reports and those of foreign diplomats confirm these same attitudes of the public in general.

22. Beyens to C. Rogier, Paris, 9 May 1866, AEB, CP, Légation française, XXIII, no.54.

23. Beyens to C. Rogier, Paris, 7 May 1866, *ibid.*, no.52.

24. Cowley to Clarendon, Paris, 8 May 1866, Wellesley and Sencourt, p.259.

25. Goltz to Bismarck, Paris, 8 May 1866, *ibid.*, pp.264-265.

26. For opinion on the Auxerre speech see the procureur reports of June 1866 from Orleans and Lyons; of July 1866 from Douai, Amiens, Metz, Riom, Nîmes, and Toulouse; and the prefect reports (F¹ᶜ III) of 1866: Seine-et-Oise 9, 2 June; Meuse 8, 2 June; Allier 6, 5 June; Isère 7, 6 June; and Bouches-du-Rhône 7, 31 May.

27. Cowley to Clarendon, Paris, 9 July 1866, PRO, FO, 27/1620.

28. Rothan, *Politique de 1866*, p.142.

29. Napoleon III to Drouyn de Lhuys, 11 June 1866, *Moniteur*, 13 June 1866.

30. Beyens to C. Rogier, Paris, 27 May 1866, AEB, CP, Légation française, XXIII, no.66.

31. Hansen, *Coulisses*, p.80.

32. Cowley to Clarendon, Paris, 9 July 1866, PRO, FO, France, 27/1620.

33. Bigelow to Seward, Paris, 14 June 1866, State Dept. Corr., France, LXI, no.335.

34. Nigra to La Marmora, Paris, 14 June 1866, La Marmora, *Più di luce*, p.328.

35. Fane and Cowley to Clarendon, Paris, 14 and 15 June 1866, PRO, FO, 27/1618.

36. Oberst Kiss de Memeskér to Bismarck, Paris, 22 June 1866, Oncken, *Rheinpolitik*, I, 282.

37. Magne to Napoleon III, Paris, 20 July 1866, Rothan, *Politique de 1866*, pp.459-460. Although the emperor did not receive this information until after 5 July, still it confirms the other testimony available to him by that date.

38. See the *Constitutionnel, Presse, Opinion Nationale, Journal des Débats*, and *Siècle* from 13 to 15 June 1866; *Revue des deux mondes*, 1 July 1866; and the reports of J. B. O'Meagher, Paris correspondent of the London *Times*, in *Times*, 16 and 24 June 1866.

39. For antiwar opinion during the war see the procureur reports of June 1866 from Orleans, Lyons, and Chambéry; of July 1866 from Amiens, Douai, Caen, Metz, Colmar, Bourges, Dijon, Grenoble, Aix, Riom, Nîmes, Montpellier, Toulouse, and Agen; of 5 Aug. 1866 from Paris; prefect reports (F¹ᶜ III): Manche 6, 7 June 1866; Finistère 3, 4 July 1866; Seine-et-Oise 9, 2 June, 4 July 1866; Meuse 8, 2 June, 4 July 1866; Vendée 5, 8 June 1866; Allier 6, 4 July 1866; Indre-et-Loire 7, 2 July 1866; Haute-Vienne 8, 2 July 1866; Isère 7, 6 June 1866; Gironde 6, 30 June 1866.

40. The prefect of police in Paris was also in the habit of gathering information on public opinion, even from the provinces. None of these reports exists now in the archives of the prefecture of police, since they were presumed to have been destroyed by fire during the Communard revolt. It is also possible that what Beyens thought were police reports were, in this instance, actually the reports of the prefects and procureurs general.

41. Beyens, to C. Rogier, Paris, 10 June 1866, AEB, CP, Légation française, XXIII, no.83.

42. There was, however, a small faction made up of the emperor's cousin, Prince Napoleon, and some of his pro-Italian friends who advocated French entrance in the war against Austria if she should invade Italy. The *Opinion Nationale* and the *Liberté* reflected their views

but without much enthusiasm. While there was pro-Italian sentiment in some parts of France, this group of the Palais Royal, as it was sometimes called, and their papers had no apparent success in persuading the public in Paris and the provinces to favor going to war to aid Italy. From the administrative reports and the diplomatic dispatches, including some from the Italian minister, we see that this group was a negligible quantity in the great sea of general sentiment. For mentions of the existence of this group see E. Bourgeois, *Manuel historique de politique étrangère* (5th ed.; Paris, 1919), III, 689; E. Ollivier, *L'empire libéral* (Paris, 1902), VIII, 176-177; Metternich in Oncken, *Rheinpolitik*, I, 254; *Times*, 24 May 1866; and J. Doutenville, "La France, la Prusse, et l'Allemagne au lendemain de Sadowa," *Nouvelle revue*, LI, (1921), 122-131.

43. La Gorce, *Second Empire*, V, 12-13.
44. Paris report of 4 July 1866 in *Times*, 5 July 1866.
45. Cowley to Clarendon, Paris, 1 July 1866, Wellesley and Sencourt, p. 283.
46. Reuss to William I, Paris, 10 July 1866, Oncken, *Rheinpolitik*, I, 330; Wellesley and Sencourt, p.291.
47. La Gorce, *Second Empire*, V, 14.
48. Heinrich von Sybel, *The Founding of the German Empire by William I* (New York, 1890-1898), V. 246.
49. *Ibid.*, p.247; *Moniteur*, 5 July 1866.
50. Dabot, p.202.
51. For this premature rejoicing see La Gorce, *Second Empire*, V, 20; Kern to Federal Council, 5 July 1866, AFS, RP, Paris, 1866, no.32; Rothan, *Politique en 1866*, p.192; Goltz to Bismarck, Paris, 6 July 1866, Oncken, *Rheinpolitik*, I, 309; Metternich to Mensdorff, Paris, 7 July 1866, *ibid.*, p.317.
52. Procureur report, Rouen, 10 July 1866.
53. On the exultation over the news of French mediation see the procureur reports of July 1866 from Colmar, Dijon, Rennes, Riom, Grenoble, Nîmes, and Pau; and the prefect reports (F¹ᶜ III) of July 1866 from Bouches-du-Rhône,

Isère, Ain, Meuse, and Vendée; and of 13 Aug. 1866 from Gironde.
54. See *Siècle, Journal des Débats, Avenir National, Opinion Nationale, Temps, Union, Monde,* and *Gazette de France*, 6, 7 July 1866.
55. See *Constitutionnel, France Politique,* and *Patrie* of 6 July 1866. See also Goltz to Bismarck, Paris, 6 July 1866, Oncken, *Rheinpolitik*, I, 309; La Gorce, *Second Empire*, V, 20.
56. Goltz to Bismarck, Paris, 6 July 1866, Oncken, *Rheinpolitik*, I, 309.
57. For accounts of this discussion see Doutenville, *loc. cit.*, pp.122-131; La Gorce, *Second Empire*, V, 15-20; Sybel, *Founding*, V, 248-251; G. Vautier, "Au delà et en deçà de nos frontières en 1866," *Révolution de 1848*, XXV (1928), 112; Ollivier, VIII, 424-425; J. Maurain, *Baroche, ministre de Napoléon III* (Paris, 1936), p.311.
58. Rothan, *Politique de 1866*, p.209.
59. Guyot, *Histoire diplomatique*, p. 642; Oncken, *Rheinpolitik*, I, 38, 318; H. Oncken, *Napoleon III and the Rhine* (New York, 1938), p.26; Sybel, V, 250; Doutenville, *loc. cit.*, pp.122-131; Vautier, *loc. cit.*, p.112; R. C. Binkley, *Realism and Nationalism* (New York, 1935), p. 270.
60. Bourgeois, *Manuel historique*, III, 685-689; Ollivier, VIII, 425; A. Thomas in *Cambridge Modern History*, XI, 480.
61. Metternich to Mensdorff, Paris, 7 July 1866, Oncken, *Rheinpolitik*, I, 317; Ollivier (*Empire libéral*, VIII, 425) also stated that "il [Napoléon III] était en ce moment très frappé de ce qu'on lui racontait de la satisfaction du peuple de Paris."
62. Rothan, *Politique en 1866*, p.313.
63. This remark was reported by Olózaga to the Swiss minister, Kern (J. Conrad Kern, *Souvenirs politiques* [Paris, 1887], p.205).
64. For early indecisive opinion on the belligerents see RDM, 1 July 1866; *Times*, 4 July 1866; procureur reports: Lyons, 28 June 1866; Toulouse, July 1866; Colmar, 12 July 1866; and the prefect report (F¹ᶜ III) of Haut-Rhin 7, 1 July 1866.
65. The cities from which anti-Prussian reports came were Chambéry, Toulouse, Rouen, Limoges, Douai, Saint-Lô, Versailles, Quimper, Aix, Mont-

211—217

pellier, Caen, Dijon, Lyons, Nancy, Paris, and Pau.

66. Nigra to La Marmora, Paris, 23 June 1866, L. Chiala, *Ancora un po più di luce sugli eventi politici e militari dell' anno 1866* (Florence, 1922), p.366.

67. For French opinion on the belligerents during the Austro-Prussian War see the procureur reports of June 1866 from Lyons and Chambéry; of July 1866 from Toulouse, Douai, Bourges, Aix, Montpellier, Caen, Dijon, Colmar, Bastia, Lyons, Nancy, and Rouen; of 5 Aug. 1866 from Paris; of Oct. 1866 from Poitiers, Rouen, Nancy, Dijon, Agen, and Pau; the prefect reports of 1866 (F^{1c} III): Bouches-du-Rhône 7, 30 June; Haut-Rhin 7, 1 July; Seine-Inférieure 9, 1 July; Haute-Vienne 8, 2 July; Manche 6, 4 July; Seine-et-Oise 9, 4 July; Finistère 3, 4 July; Allier 6, 4 July; and Isère 7, 6 July. For some press opinion see *Constitutionnel*, 16 June 1866; *Siècle*, 20 June 1866; *Débats*, 21 June 1866; *Times*, 22 June 1866; *France Politique*, 21 June 1866; RDM, 15 June 1866, pp.1035-1036; (1 July 1866), in Chronique politique. Other references may be found as follows: Metternich to Mensdorff, Paris, 17 June 1866, Oncken, I, 278; Beyens to Lambermont, Paris, 22 June 1866, AEB, Beyens Papers; Beyens to C. Rogier, Paris, 26 June 1866, AEB, CP. Légation française,

XXIII, no.89; same to same, Paris, 2 July 1866, *ibid.*, no.95; Nigra to La Marmora, Paris, 23 June 1866, Chiala, *Ancora*, p.366.

68. For French hostility to the peace terms see the procureur reports of July 1866 from Nancy; of Aug. 1866 from Paris; of Sept. 1866 from Aix and Chambéry; of Oct. 1866 from Agen, Rennes, Limoges, Orleans, Toulouse, Bourges, Metz, Caen, Grenoble, Besançon, Montpellier, Riom, Colmar, Rouen, Bordeaux, Nancy, and Aix; of Nov. 1866 from Paris, Agen, and Poitiers; of Dec. 1866 from Lyons; of Jan. 1867 from Toulouse, Douai, Orleans, Montpellier, Besançon, Limoges, Rouen, Bordeaux, Nancy, and Rennes; the prefect reports (F^{1c} III) of 1866: Indre-et-Loire 7, 1 Aug.; Seine-Inférieure 9, 1 Aug.; Seine-et-Oise 9, (4) Aug.; Manche 6, 4 Aug.; Isère 7, 7 Aug.; Ain 6, late Aug.; Seine-et-Oise 9, c. 1 Sept.; Allier 6, 5 Sept.; Isère 7, 5 Sept.; Manche 6, 6 Sept.; Haut-Rhin 7, 1 Oct.; Seine-et-Oise 9, 6 Oct.; Isère 7, 8 Nov.; and Ain 6, late Dec.

69. For examples of these press attitudes see *Siècle*, 4 Aug. 1866; *Opinion Nationale*, 3, 7 Aug. 1866; *Temps*, 17 Aug. 1866; *Presse*, 17 Sept. 1866; *Constitutionnel*, 29 July 1866; *Patrie*, 20 Aug. 1866; *Times*, 9, 20, 22 Aug. 1866.

70. Rouher to Conti, Cerçay, 6 Aug. 1866, Rothan, *Politique de 1866*, pp.467-468.

CHAPTER NINE

Compensations and Armaments

1. Magne to Napoleon III, Paris, 20 July 1866, Rothan, *Politique de 1866*, pp.460-461.

2. Metternich to Mensdorff, Paris, 26 July 1866, Oncken, I, 379-380; Salomon, p.144.

3. Beyens to C. Rogier, Paris, 14 July 1866, AEB, CP, Légation française, XXIII, no.115.

4. Cowley to Stanley, Paris, 10 Aug. 1866, Wellesley and Sencourt, pp. 303-304.

5. On the reversal of opinion from satisfaction to dissatisfaction over France's mediation role see the procureur reports of Oct. 1866 from

Toulouse and Riom; of Nov. 1866 from Paris, Agen, and Poitiers; of Jan. 1867 from Orleans, Toulouse, Dijon, Montpellier, Grenoble, Rouen, and Rennes; and the prefect reports (F^{1c} III): Isère 7, 7 Aug. 1866; Manche 6, 10 Nov. 1866; Ain 6, late Dec. 1866.

6. Rothan, *Politique de 1866*, p.461.

7. For the shift from peace to war sentiment in 1866 see the procureur reports of July 1866 from Colmar; of Sept. 1866 from Aix and Chambéry; of Oct. 1866 from Agen, Orleans, Toulouse, Metz, Besançon, Montpellier, Bastia, Pau, and Aix;

of Nov. 1866 from Agen; of Dec. 1866 from Lyons; of Jan. 1867 from Toulouse, Grenoble, Limoges, Metz, Rouen, Colmar, Nancy, and Rennes; and the prefect reports (F^{1c} III): Isère 7, 7 Aug. 1866; Haut-Rhin 7, 1 Sept. and I Oct. 1866; Allier 6, 9 Oct. 1866; Manche 6, 10 Nov. 1866.

8. Magne to Napoleon III, Paris, 20 July 1866, Rothan, *Politique de 1866*, p.461.

9. For early press discussions on'compensations see *France*, 6, 11 July 1866; *Opinion Nationale*, 24 July 1866; *Temps*, 25, 27 July 1866; *Patrie*, 26 July 1866; *Siècle*, 30 July, 4 Aug. 1866; *Débats*, 31 July 1866.

10. For early provincial demands for compensation see the procureur reports of July 1866 from Douai, Colmar, Lyons, and Nancy; and the prefect reports (F^{1c} III): Indre-et-Loire 7, 1 Aug. 1866; Haut-Rhin 7, 1 Aug. 1866.

11. Metternich to Mensdorff, Paris, 7 July, two dispatches of 26 July 1866, Oncken, I, 319, 377-380.

12. Drouyn de Lhuys to Benedetti, Vichy, 29 July 1866, *Origines*, XI, 281-282.

13. Benedetti to Drouyn de Lhuys, Berlin, 6 Aug. 1866, *ibid.*, p.399.

14. Rothan, *Politique de 1866*, pp.358-359, 391; *Siècle*, 10 Aug. 1866.

15. Note found in the emperor's papers, Rothan, *Politique de 1866*, pp.469-470.

16. Cowley to Bloomfield, Paris, 15 Aug. 1866, Wellesley and Sencourt, p.305.

17. Rouher to Benedetti, Paris, 16 Aug. 1866. [Cerçay Papers], *Origines*, XII, 116-117.

18. Benedetti to Rouher, Berlin, 23 Aug. 1866 [Cerçay Papers], *ibid.*, pp.170-171.

19. Rouher to Benedetti, Paris, 26 Aug. 1866, [Cerçay Papers], *ibid.*, p.195.

20. La Valette to Moustier, telegram, Paris, 3 Sept. 1866, *ibid.*, p.256.

21. Cowley to Stanley, Paris, 14 Sept. 1866, Wellesley and Sencourt, p. 313.

22. Goltz to William I, Paris, 11 Sept. 1866, APP, VIII, 71.

23. Michel Chevalier was the French negotiator of the low-tariff treaty with England in 1860.

24. There is no doubt about Napoleon III's responsibility for statements of French foreign policy nor about his participation in the preparation of the circular. There is some difference of opinion over whether the emperor or Rouher originated the main ideas in the state paper. Rothan pointed out that the idea of large agglomerations was a part of the Saint Helena observations of Napoleon I, to whose Legend his nephew was supposed to be devoted (*Politique de 1866*, p.366); Doutenville said, "the emperor drew it up in agreement with Rouher" (*loc. cit.*, p.365); and the Belgian chargé reported that the part guaranteeing the pope's sovereignty "was written in the emperor's own hand on the draft" (d'Anethon to C. Rogier, Paris, 18 Sept. 1866, AEB, CP, Légation française, XXIII, no.170). The emperor's own story was: "I had several long conversations with . . . . La Valette. . . . . Among other things, I said to him. . . . ." In these later reminiscences Napoleon may be trying to save face for La Valette. What he told him may have already been written up by Rouher (Fleury, *Memoirs*, II, 157). On the other hand Cowley ignored the role of Rouher when he said, "It is the joint concoction of His Majesty and La Valette" (Cowley to Stanley, 18 Sept. 1866, Wellesley and Sencourt, p.313); while Schnerb affirmed that "Rouher therefore drew up the note, after having consulted Michel Chevalier, and had it published by La Valette in the *Moniteur*" (R. Schnerb, *Rouher et le Second Empire* [Paris, 1949], pp.191-192), and Hansen was of the opinion that the circular was drawn up by Rouher and approved by the emperor (Hansen, *Coulisses*, pp.123-124).

25. Bigelow to Seward, Biarritz, 19 Sept. 1866, *Papers relating to foreign affairs*, (1866-1867), p.353. As confirmation of this preparatory press effort, Rothan said, "The semiofficial press tried in vain to calm opinion by showing that the government had not departed from our great national traditions" (*Luxemburg*, p.52); and Solms reported to Bismarck: "With the exception of the *Presse* the attitude of the French newspapers is becoming more restrained. Minister

221—229

Marquis de la Valette, to whom I made a few appreciative remarks about it, repeated to me what he had already told our royal ambassador [Goltz]: 'That shall be taken care of; the hostile tone shall cease immediately'" (Solms to Bismarck, Paris, 6 Sept. 1866, APP, VIII. 61); while on almost the same day Bigelow noted "the obviously constrained silence of the French press upon the subject [of Drouyn de Lhuys' retirement]" and described it as "an attempt . . . . to deprive his retirement of political importance in the estimation of the public" (Bigelow to Seward, Paris, 7 Sept. 1866, State Dept. Corr., France, Despatches, LXI, no.365). See also *Constitutionnel*, 13 Aug. 1866.

26. The circular was dated the 16th but was published on the 17th. Some authorities erroneously state that it appeared in the *Moniteur* of the 16th.

27. Eighty-four years later Russia (the USSR) had 200,000,000 and the United States, 150,000,000.

28. La Valette to French diplomatic representatives abroad, Paris, 16 Sept. 1866, *Moniteur*, 17 Sept. 1866; *Origines*, XII, 301-306; *Livre jaune* (1867): *L'Allemagne et l'Italie*, pp.101-107; *Archives diplomatiques*, IV (1866), 335-340.

29. *Times*, 18 Sept. 1866.

30. For the Paris press reaction to the La Valette Circular see the *Constitutionnel*, *Temps*, *Liberté*, *Débats*, *Patrie*, *Union*, *Gazette de France*, and *Avenir National* of 18 Sept. 1866; the *Opinion Nationale*, *Siècle*, *Pays*, and *France Politique* of 19 Sept. 1866.

31. D'Anethon to C. Rogier, Paris, 18 Sept. 1866, AEB, CP, Légation française, XXIII, no.170; Cowley to Stanley, Paris, 18 Sept. 1866, PRO, FO, France, 27/1622.

32. For the system of government-syndicated articles see *Union de la Sarthe*, week of 24 Sept. 1866; *Times*, 27 Sept. 1866.

33. For public reaction to the La Valette circular see the procureur reports of Sept. 1866 from Aix and Chambéry; of Oct. 1866 from Agen, Douai, Limoges, Orleans, Toulouse, Bourges, Metz, Caen, Nîmes, Grenoble, Montpellier, Riom, Bordeaux, Rouen, Nancy, Bastia, Pau, and

Aix; of Nov. 1866 from Agen and Poitiers; of Jan. 1867 from Dijon, Riom, and Rouen; and from the prefect reports (F^le III) of Sept. 1866 from Bouches-du-Rhône; of Oct. 1866 from Seine-Inférieure, Meuse, Haute-Vienne, Haut-Rhin, Indre-et-Loire, Seine-et-Oise, Manche, Allier, Isère, and Ain.

34. *Débats*, *Temps*, and *Liberté* of 18 Sept. 1866.

35. Procureur reports: Nancy, 22 Oct. 1866; Rouen, 12 Jan. 1867.

36. These dissatisfied districts were Rennes, Caen, Rouen, Nancy, Colmar, Besançon, Dijon, Lyons, Grenoble, Toulouse, Limoges, and Bordeaux.

37. For continued demands for compensations after the La Valette Circular see the procureur reports of Dec. 1866 from Lyons; of Jan. 1867 from Toulouse, Dijon, Besançon, Grenoble, Limoges, Metz, Rouen, Bordeaux, and Nancy; of Feb. 1867 from Colmar; of April 1867 from Caen; and of Oct. 1867 from Rennes.

38. Pietri to Napoleon III, Rothan, *Luxembourg*, pp.61-62. Halt (Vieu) attributes the last part of this document to de Maupas (dated 8 May 1857) (*Papiers sauvés des* Tuileries [Paris, 1871], p.197), but Rothan, who presumably saw the manuscripts in the archives, attributes both the first half and last half to Pietri, and, while mentioning no date, includes it in his text dealing with the aftermath of the Circular.

39. Vautier, *loc. cit.*, XXV (1928), 121-122.

40. Fleury, *Memoirs*, II, 168.

41. Rothan, *Luxembourg*, pp.112-114.

42. Private letter, Moustier to Benedetti, Paris, 7 Jan. 1867, *Origines*, XIV, 49.

43. Ollivier, IX, 232-233.

44. Beyens to C. Rogier, Paris, 14 Feb. 1867, AEB, CP, Légation française, XXIV, no.14. Vaillant's notebook (14 Feb. 1867) says: "L'empereur lit mal; il est un peu embarrassé de l'espèce de froideur avec laquelle ce qu'il dit est accueilli; le papier tremble dans sa main" (Ollivier, IX, 237).

45. Beyens to C. Rogier, Paris, 14 Feb. 1867, AEB, CP. Légation française, XXIV, no.14; Goltz to Bismarck,

Paris, 15 Feb. 1867, APP, VIII,
397; Ollivier, IX, 237.

46. "Il n'y a plus une seule faute à
commettre" (Ollivier, IX, 270-280).

47. *Ibid.*, pp.290-295.

48. *Ibid.*, pp.309-310.

49. Goltz to Bismarck, Paris, 23 Mar.,
5 July 1867, APP, VIII, 501; IX,
137.

50. Hostile sentiment toward Rouher's
"Three Segments" speech and the
German alliances may be found in
the procureur reports of March
1867 from Lyons and Chambéry; of
April 1867 from Bordeaux, Nancy,
Dijon, and Rennes; of July 1867
from Agen, Dijon, Orleans, Besan-
çon, and Colmar; of Oct. 1867
from Metz, Rennes, and Nancy; of
Jan. 1868 from Toulouse and
Rouen; of July 1868 from Pau and
Nancy; of Oct. 1868 from Dijon;
of Jan. 1869 from Nancy; in the pre-
fect reports (F¹ᵉ III): Meuse 8, 1
Oct. 1867; Allier 6, 30 Nov. 1867.

51. Cowley to Stanley, Paris, 8 April
1867, PRO, FO, France, 27/1659.

52. *Moniteur*, 9 April 1867.

53. For provincial opinion on the London Treaty settling the Luxemburg
dispute see the procureur reports
of June 1867 from Chambéry; of
July 1867 from Agen, Douai,
Bourges, Toulouse, Nîmes, Grenoble, Dijon, Metz, Rouen, Riom,
Orleans, Poitiers, Colmar, Aix,
Rennes, and Nancy; of Aug. 1867
from Paris; of Oct. 1867 from
Dijon, Riom, and Nîmes; the prefect reports (F¹ᵉ III) of May 1867
from Allier and Ain; of June 1867
from Meuse, Haute-Vienne, Haut-
Rhin, Seine-Inférieure, Finistère,
Manche, Isère, and Seine-et-Oise;
of Aug. 1867 from Gironde.

54. *Constitutionnel, Patrie, France
Politique, Débats, Siècle, Presse,
Temps, Etendard,* and *Semaine
Financière.*

55. *Gazette de France* and *Avenir National.*

56. The press opinions were revealed
particularly in the issues of 15 and
16 May 1867.

57. For universal peace sentiment in
1867 see all procureur and prefect
reports for that year.

58. *Times*, 17 May 1867.

59. Hansen, *Coulisses*, pp.144-145.

60. For the countervailing expressions
of opinion, indirectly adverse to the
London Treaty, see all the pro-

cureur and prefect reports from
June to December 1867.

61. A considerable part of this section
is based upon the excellent study
by Dr. Gordon Wright of the University of Oregon ("Public opinion
and conscription in France, 1866-
1870," *Journal of modern history,*
XIV [1942], 26-45). Dr. Wright has
used many of the same original
sources that the present author has
used and has come to substantially
the same conclusions as the latter.
The footnotes of this section will
indicate any additional material
used by the present writer.

62. *Times*, 5 July 1866.

63. Cowley to Stanley, Paris, 1 Sept.
1866, PRO, FO, France, 27/1622;
Claremont to Fane, Paris, 10 Sept.
1866, *ibid.*; Solms to Bismarck,
Paris, 3 Sept. 1866, APP, VIII,
59-60.

64. *Patrie*, 9 Sept. 1866; Claremont to
Fane, Paris, 10 Sept. 1866, PRO,
FO, France, 27/1622.

65. For provincial reactions to the military passage of the La Valette Circular see the procureur reports of
Sept. 1866 from Aix and Chambéry; of Oct. 1866 from Orleans,
Toulouse, Bourges, Riom, Colmar,
Rouen, Bordeaux, and Aix.

66. Wright, "Conscription," *loc. cit.,*
p.28.

67. *Ibid.*, p.29.

68. Prefect of Loire-Inférieure to subprefects, 13 Dec. 1866, Archives dé-
partmentales (hereafter cited as
AD), Loire-Inférieure, M, cited in
Wright, "Conscription," *loc. cit.,*
p.30.

69. For the prefect reports see Wright,
"Conscription," *loc. cit.*, p.30.

70. For the procureur reports on provincial reaction to the commission's
army bill see those of Dec. 1866
from Agen, Chambéry, and Lyons;
of Jan. 1867 from Douai, Dijon,
Montpellier, Grenoble, Metz, Riom,
Colmar, Aix, and Besançon. See
also Wright, "Conscription," *loc.
cit.*, p.30.

71. Author's italics.

72. Ollivier, IX, 236-237.

73. AD, Nièvre, M, 22 March 1867,
cited in Wright, "Conscription,"
loc. cit., p.31.

74. For all these petitions see Archives
Nationales, Paris, MSS, series C
1120 (Wright, "Conscription," *loc.
cit.*, p.32).

237—242

75. The small body which prepared all imperial legislation for presentation to the two houses.
76. La Gorce, *Second Empire*, V, 341.
77. Fleury, *Memoirs*, II, 176. The Prussian, Thile, in a memorandum to his foreign office said that he had heard that M. Saint-Paul of the French interior ministry admitted "that the French press, in order to make armaments popular, has for a long time had to adopt a warlike attitude" (Berlin, 25 Feb. 1868, APP, IX, 727).
78. Wright, "Conscription," *loc. cit.*, pp.35-36; *Liberté*, 22 Sept. 1866.
79. Procureur reports on sentiment concerning the revised army bill: of March 1867 from Lyons; of April 1867 from Douai, Caen, Grenoble, Nîmes, Bastia, Besançon, Pau, and Colmar; of July 1867 from Toulouse, Orleans, Limoges, and Aix; of Oct. 1867 from Limoges, Metz, Rouen, Caen, and Poitiers; of Dec. 1867 from Chambéry; of Jan. 1868 from Nîmes, Bourges, Limoges, Montpellier, and Caen.
80. Wright, "Conscription," *loc. cit.*, p.37.
81. Procureur report, Limoges, 15 Jan. 1868.
82. Prefect reports (F^{1c} III), Basses-Pyrénées, 4 Dec. 1867, 28 Jan. 1868, cited in Wright, "Conscription," *loc. cit.*, pp.37-38.
83. La Gorce, V, 343; Wright, "Conscription," *loc. cit.*, p.38.
84. La Gorce, V, 336-344; Wright, "Conscription," *loc. cit.*, pp.37-39.
85. For the generally favorable reception given the final version of the Army Law see the procureur reports of Jan. 1868 from Bourges, Metz, Poitiers, Limoges, Montpellier, and Caen; of March 1868 from Lyons; of April 1868 from Douai, Caen, Riom, Limoges, Metz, Montpellier, Rennes, Nancy, and Grenoble; of July 1868 from Douai, Bourges, Caen, and Nancy; of Oct. 1868 from Grenoble, Toulouse, Angers, and Poitiers; of Jan. 1869 from Paris.
86. Religious bigotry, strangely enough, played some part in the attitude toward Prussia. It was sometimes found that French orthodox (Fundamentalist) Protestants looked upon the King of Prussia as a sort of patriarch of European Protestantism and therefore did not share in the suspicions of and animosity toward Prussia (procureur reports: Colmar, 17 July, 12 Oct. 1867; Toulouse, 1 April 1868).
87. For the open demonstrations against the early enrollments see the regular procureur reports of March 1868 from Toulouse, Montpellier, and Bordeaux; of Apr. 1868 from Bordeaux and Toulouse; special procureur reports (BB^{18} 1765) from the following districts: Bordeaux, 19, 20, 21 March, and 4 April 1868; Dijon, 17 March 1868; Poitiers, 26 Feb. 1868; Angers, 14 March 1868; Rennes, 6 April 1868; AD, Gironde, M 1185, 22, 25, 28 March 1868; prefect report (F^{1c} III), Tarn-et-Garonne 5, 1 April 1868 (all cited in Wright, "Conscription," *loc. cit.*, pp.39-43).
88. See procureur reports: Poitiers, 15 April 1868; Grenoble, Oct. 1868.
89. Wright, "Conscription," *loc. cit.*, p.44.
90. The reports are so unanimous and repetitious on this theme that, to save unnecessary detail of reference, the author can refer the reader with confidence to most procureur reports between January 1867 and January 1868.
91. Procureur reports: Caen, 8 Apr. 1867; Rouen, 10 Oct. 1867.

CHAPTER TEN

The Last Straw

1. Robert H. Lord, *The origins of the War of 1870* (Cambridge, Mass., 1924).
2. *Bismarck, the man and statesman*, a translation of his *Gedanken und Erinnerungen* by A. J. Butler (New York, 1899), II, 57-58.
3. See ch. ix.
4. APP, IX, 728.
5. Lord, pp.16-18.
6. See ch. x.
7. *Bismarck, man and statesman*, pp. 87-89.
8. *Ibid.*, p.88.
9. Lord, p.7.

10. Authenticated and quoted by Lord (pp.23-24).

11. *Ibid.*, p.9.

12. E. M. Carroll, "French opinion on war with Prussia in 1870," *American historical review*, XXXI (1926), p.685-687.

13. The passages reproduced by Ollivier (XIV, 41-47) from the issues of 5-7 July are: *(Pays):* "This affair . . . . is the drop of water which makes our cup of bitterness overflow. . . . . Impose on us a Prussian king at Madrid? No, we will not permit it." *(Soir):* "But we are thirty-eight million prisoners if this news is not false. It has to be false; it will be if we want it to be. But is the French government still able to will it?" *(Siècle):* "France, encircled on all borders by Prussia or by nations under her influence, would be reduced to an isolation like that which formerly caused the long struggles . . . . against the house of Austria." *(Gaulois):* "If we have to choose once again between our country, diminished and reduced, and war, we will not hesitate!" *(Charivari):* "France looks without being able to act. Do you think that is something for a Frenchman to be proud of?" *(Temps):* "If a Prussian prince were placed on the Spanish throne, we would not be put back just to Henry IV but back to Francis I [two periods of war against Spain.]" *(Centre Gauche):* "We are surrounded. Bismarck has made his marriage contract with Spain. But the army? The French army. It must mark time, arms stacked . . . . poor France!" *(Français):* "[It] would be reviving at their pleasure a formidable preponderance against which our fathers fought for two centuries." *(Réveil):* Those who love Prussians can regale themselves. They can find them everywhere. . . . . If that is revenge for Sadowa, well, it's complete." *(Gazette de France):* "Prussia would crowd us and menace us on all sides."

14. Werther to William I, Paris, 5 July 1870, Lord, pp.126-127; Beyens to d'Anethan, Paris, 5, 6 July 1870, AEB, CP, Légation française, XXV, nos.138, 139; Kern, *Souvenirs*, p.203; Metternich to Beust, Paris 15 July 1870, Ollivier, XIV, 35.

15. *Times,* 6 July 1870.

16. Carroll, *loc. cit.,* p.685.

17. *Times,* 8 July 1870.

18. Duke of Gramont, *La France et la Prusse avant la guerre* (Paris, 1872), pp.40-41.

19. Those favoring Gramont were the *Gaulois, Figaro, Univers, Correspondant, Constitutionnel, Pays, Soir, Presse, Opinion Nationale, Moniteur Universel,* and *Liberté;* those opposed were the *Français, Temps, Siècle, Réveil, Electeur Libre, Public, Rappel, Avenir National,* and *Revue des deux mondes* (Carroll, *loc. cit.,* pp.687-689; Ollivier, XIV, 118-122).

20. Solms to William I, Paris, 8 July 1870. Kern, *Souvenirs,* p.208. Kern saw and copied this message. The same wording is not found in the telegrams published by Lord. Lord uses the text sent to the foreign office (Lord, p.153), but Kern copied a supposed duplicate sent to William.

21. Lyons to Granville, Paris, 7 July 1870, *British and Foreign State Papers,* LX (1869-1870), 792. Sorel's interpretation of public opinion at this time was that the war sentiment was "superficial" and that the government should have toned down the press excitation. Consequently, in commenting on Lyons' dispatch, he says: "On voit à quel point l'opinion publique était déjà faussée par les ministres et par les journaux, puisqu'un observateur aussi clairvoyant s'y trompait" (Albert Sorel, *Histoire diplomatique de la guerre franco-allemande* [Paris, 1875] I, 68-69, 79, note 1). But now, with access to the archives of continental countries, we see that if Lyons misjudged opinion, he did so along with his colleagues from Prussia, Austria, Belgium, and Switzerland as well as the *Times* correspondent and the Paris police. In fact the estimates of all of these keen observers were confirmed by the prefect reports on the reaction to Gramont's speech in the provinces (see below), Sorel's views to the contrary notwithstanding. It should be noted that the prefect reports (*Journal Officiel,* 2 Oct. 1870) were available to Sorel in 1875, but he either overlooked them or declined to use them.

246—250

22. Kern to President Dubs, Paris, 9 July 1870, AFS, RP, Légation de Paris, 1870, no.71.
23. Beyens to d'Anethan, Paris, 9 July 1870, AEB, CP, Légation française, XXV, no.147.
24. Vitzthum tells about the day of 11 July 1870 in a letter to Andrassy of 16 Jan. 1873, Wellesley and Sencourt, p.366.
25. Police reports of 7 and 8 July 1870, quoted by Ollivier (XIV, 115-117).
26. In his reply the prefect of Hautes-Alpes wrote: "J'ai reçu le 8 juillet votre circulaire télégraphique invitant les prefets à vous adresser des rapports sur l'effet produit par la déclaration du Gouvernement (du 6) et par les affaires d'Espagne" (letter to the minister of interior, 10 July 1870, published in *Journal Officiel*, 2 Oct. 1870). See also report of the prefect of Haute-Saône, 11 July 1870, in *ibid*.
27. No report seems to be extant for the department of Haute-Savoie. Extracts of all of the others were published by the Republican minister of interior in the *Journal Officiel*, 2 Oct. 1870.
28. Carroll, *Opinion and foreign affairs*, p.29, note 68.
29. The departments could be listed as follows: *Approving:* Ain, Allier, Aisne, Alpes-Maritimes, Ardennes, Aube, Aude, Aveyron, Bas-Rhin, Basses-Alpes, Basses-Pyrénées, Bouches-du-Rhône, Calvados, Cher, Corrèze, Corse, Côte-d'Or, Côtes-du-Nord, Dordogne, Doubs, Drôme, Eure, Eure-et-Loire, Gironde, Haute-Loire, Haute-Marne, Hautes-Alpes, Haute-Pyrénées, Haute-Vienne, Haut-Rhin, Isère, Jura, Landes, Loire-Inférieure, Loir-et-Cher, Loiret, Lot-et-Garonne, Lozère, Maine-et-Loire, Marne, Mayenne, Meurthe, Morbihan, Oise, Orne, Puy-de-Dôme, Pyrénées-Orientales, Sarthe, Savoie, Seine-Inférieure, Tarn, and Vendée; *disapproving:* Ardèche, Cantal, Charente-Inférieure, Creuse, Deux-Sèvres, Haute-Garonne, Haute-Saône, Hérault, Indre, Indre-et-Loire, Loire, Lot, Meuse, Moselle, Rhône, Saône-et-Loire, Seine-et-Marne, Seine-et-Oise, Somme, Var, Vaucluse, Vienne, Vosges, and Yonne; *noncommittal:* Ariège, Charente, Finistère, Gard, Gers, Ille-et-Vilaine, Manche, Nièvre, Nord, Pas-de-

Calais, and Tarn-et-Garonne (*Journal Officiel*, 2 Oct. 1870).
30. *Journal Officiel*, 2 Oct. 1870.
31. Jules Pointu, *Histoire de la chûte de l'empire, 6 juillet-4 septembre 1870* (Paris, 1874), pp.3, 55.
32. Pointu, pp.61-62. Pointu accounts for only 86 reports; there were 87.
33. Prefect report from Eure-et-Loire, 10 July 1870, *Journal Officiel*, 2 Oct. 1870.
34. Pointu, p.61.
35. Prefect report from Gironde, 8 July 1870, *Journal Officiel*, 2 Oct. 1870.
36. See the texts of the reports in *Journal Officiel*, 2 Oct. 1870.
37. Prefect report from Rhône, 8 July 1870, *ibid*.
38. Prefect report from Charente, 9 July 1870, *ibid*.
39. Prefect special report from Haute-Loire, 13 July 1870, *Journal Officiel*, 2 Oct. 1870.
40. Prefect report from Pyrénés-Orientales, 8 July 1870, *ibid*.
41. Pointu actually gave a total of only 15 prowar departments: "quinze sur quatre-vingt-six" (p.62). He neglected to count the two prowar reports which he had quoted on the previous page (p.61). Carroll and the present author have raised Pointu's evaluation to 18 prowar by just an examination of his own tallies.
42. The present author's evaluation of the departments is as follows: *prowar:* Ain, Allier, Aisne, Alpes-Maritimes, Ardèche, Ardennes, Aube, Aude, Aveyron, Bas-Rhin, Basses-Alpes, Bouches-du-Rhône, Calvados, Charente, Charente-Inférieure, Cher, Corrège, Corse, Côte-d'Or, Côtes-du-Nord, Creuse, Deux-Sèvres, Dordogne, Doubs, Drôme, Eure, Eure-et-Loire, Gard, Gers, Gironde, Haute-Garonne, Haute-Loire, Haute-Marne, Hautes-Alpes, Hautes-Pyrénées, Haute-Vienne, Hérault, Ille-et-Vilaine, Isère, Landes, Loir-et-Cher, Loire, Loire-Inférieure, Loiret, Lot, Lozère, Maine-et-Loire, Manche, Marne, Mayenne, Meurthe, Nord, Oise, Orne, Pas-de-Calais, Pyrénées-Orientales, Rhône, Saône-et-Loire, Seine-et-Oise, Tarn, Tarn-et-Garonne, Vendée, and Vosges; *antiwar:* Cantal, Haute-Saône, Haut-Rhin, Indre, Indre-et-Loire, Jura, Lot-et-Garonne, Meuse, Moselle, Puy-de-Dôme,

Sarthe, Seine-Inférieure, Seine-et-Marne, Somme, Var, Vaucluse, and Vienne; *noncommittal:* Ariège, Basses-Pyrénées, Finistère, Morbihan, Nièvre, Savoie, and Yonne (*Journal Officiel*, 2 Oct. 1870).

43. See note 21, above.

44. C. Nigra, *Poesie originali e tradotti: aggiuntovi un capitolo dei sui ricordi diplomatici,* ed. Alessandro d'Ancona (Florence, 1914), pp.101-102; Ollivier, XIV, 241.

45. Lord, p.78.

46. Ollivier, XIV, 232, 235, 252.

47. Nigra, *Poesie*, p.103.

48. The real term was stronger and more vulgar—*la paix foireuse*—which literally meant the diarrheic peace, or figuratively the white-feather peace.

49. Beyens to d'Anethan, Paris, 13 July 1870, AEB, CP, Légation française, XXV, no.158.

50. Hansen, *Coulisses*, p.210.

51. Metternich to Beust, Paris, 12 July 1870, Oncken, III, 428.

52. It must be remembered that opinion in Paris and the provinces for the few days preceding 12 July (see above) was demanding and expecting satisfaction from *Prussia.*

53. Lyons to Granville, Paris, 12 July 1870, Wellesley and Sencourt, p. 368.

54. Fleury, *Memoirs*, II, 252.

55. Gramont to Benedetti, (Paris), 12 July 1870, *Origines*, XXVIII, 255.

56. Carroll, *Opinion and foreign affairs*, p.30.

57. Lord, p.79.

58. The Spanish ambassador's announcement was not really official. He was not the agent of Anthony. His official announcement would only come from Spain, and that had not yet arrived.

59. Leopold had finally signed a renunciation to be sent to Spain, but the French government only knew of Anthony's renunciation. Gramont was stretching a point here.

60. Gramont, p.149.

61. Ollivier, XIV, 293-299.

62. Gramont, pp.148-149.

63. Carroll, *loc. cit.*, p.690.

64. *Ibid.*, note 67.

65. *Gazette de France*, 2 July 1870.

66. *Ibid.*, 13 July 1870.

67. *France*, 13 July 1870; see also *Times*, 14 July 1870.

68. Carroll, *loc. cit.*, p.690, note 67; Ollivier, XIV, 272.

69. The line-up of papers was: against demands on Prussia: *Débats, Temps, Avenir National, Siècle, Journal de Paris, Français, Cloche, Réveil, Rappel,* and *Histoire;* for demands on Prussia: *Soir, Presse, Liberté, Pays, Figaro, Gazette de France, Univers,* and *France.*

70. Beyens to d'Anethon, Paris, 13 July 1870, AEB, CP, Légation française, XXV, no.158; Kern to Dubs, Paris, 13 July 1870, AFS, RP, Légation de Paris, 1870, no.74; Werther to German foreign office, Paris, 13 July 1870, Lord, p.223.

71. Ollivier, XIV, 337.

72. Metternich to Beust, Paris, 14 July 1870, Oncken, III, 437.

73. Ollivier, XIV, 337-341.

74. *Times*, 14 July 1870.

75. Lord, pp.83-92.

76. *Bismarck, the man and statesman,* II, 95.

77. *Ibid.*, p.101.

78. See above, ch. x.

79. *Bismarck, man and statesman,* II, 98.

80. Ollivier, XIV, 355-356.

81. Ollivier, XIV, 373.

82. There was also an additional breach of international courtesy in the fact that Prussia published information on a negotiation which the French did not consider to have been concluded.

83. Carroll, *loc. cit.*, p.692.

84. Actually the Prussians did not call up all their forces until 16 July, but Ollivier says that the French minister of war, Le Boeuf, had been erroneously informed that Prussian full mobilization had already begun (Ollivier, XIV, 400).

85. Lord, pp.82-83.

86. Carroll, *Opinion and foreign affairs*, p.30. Italics are the present author's.

87. See ch. ix for an elaboration of these.

88. It would be difficult here to cite separately every individual item. I refer the reader to most of the procureur reports between March 1867 and Oct. 1869. The exceptional procureur reports showing a resigned attitude toward Prussia's position were: Poitiers, 10 Oct. 1868; Caen, 18 Jan. 1869. Also reporting hostility to Prussia were the prefect reports (F^{1c} III) from Ain 6, April 1867; Allier 6, 29 May 1867; Seine-et-Oise 9, 10 June 1867.

260—277

89. See ch. ix.
90. For confirmation I refer the reader to all the procureur reports from March 1867 to October 1869 and to the prefect reports (F^{1c} III) of April 1867 from Ain and Seine-Inférieure; of May 1867 from Allier, Indre-et-Loire, Gironde, Meuse, Haut-Rhin, Isère, and Seine-et-Oise; of June 1867 from Allier (29 May), Ain, (late May), Haut-Rhin, and Finistère; and of Sept. 1867 from Seine-et-Oise.
91. It is presumed that what the ambassadors saw and heard were seen and heard by Gramont or his informants.
92. Metternich to Beust, Paris, 15 July 1870, Oncken, III, 446.
93. Carroll, *loc. cit.*, p.693.
94. La Gorce, *Second Empire*, VI, 298.
95. *Constitutionnel*, 15 July 1870 (actually distributed in the late evening of the 14th, as was customary).
96. La Gorce, *Second Empire*, VI, 298.
97. Lyons to Granville, Paris, 14 July 1870, *British and foreign state papers*, LX (1869-1870), p.5.
98. B. E. Palat, *Les origines de la guerre de 1870* (Paris, 1912), p. 524.
99. Special police report on events of the night of 14-15 July, dated 15 July 1870, Ollivier, XIV, 384-385.
100. Kern to Federal Council, Paris, 15 July 1870, AFS, RP, Légation de Paris, 1870, no.79, telegram.
101. Report of the prefect of police, forwarded to Gramont, Paris, 15 July 1870, *Origines*, XXVIII, 385-386.
102. Police report, Paris, 15 July 1870, Ollivier, XIV, 384.
103. Ollivier could not present the texts of the documents at that time because they would have revealed the confidential channels through which the French diplomats abroad obtained such information.
104. Carroll, *loc. cit.*, p.690.
105. *Ibid.*, pp.690-691.
106. Kern to Dubs, Paris, 16 July 1870, AFS, RP, Légation de Paris, 1870, no.80.
107. Pauline Metternich, *Souvenirs de la Princesse Pauline de Metternich,* ed. Marcel Dunan (Paris, 1935), p.208.
108. Quadt to Bray, Paris, 17 July 1870, Oncken, III, 451.
109. Beyens to d'Anethon, Paris, 15 July 1870, AEB, CP, Légation française, XXV, no.169.
110. Baroche to Alphonse Baroche, Paris, 17 July 1870, Maurain, *Baroche*, p.489.
111. Ollivier, XIV, 494-495.
112. La Gorce, *Second Empire*, VI, 311.
113. On Rouher, Magne, Dréolle, and Allain-Targé see Schnerb, *Rouher*, p.275.
114. Carroll, *loc. cit.*, p.679.
115. Gramont to Ollivier, Paris, 3 July 1870, Ollivier, XIV, 23 (not p.27), cited in Carroll, *loc. cit.*, p.685 and note 34; *Origines*, XXVIII, 21, note 3.
116. Gramont to Mercier, Paris, 3 July 1870, *Origines*, XXVIII, 22.
117. Gramont for the *Constitutionnel*, Paris, 3 July 1870, *Origines*, XXVIII, 22, note 2; Ollivier, XIV, 27-28. It was published in *Constitutionnel*, 4 July 1870.
118. Walsh to Saint-Chéron, 2 July 1870, *Origines*, XXVIII, 19, note 2. Walsh heard indirectly of the news a day before it broke in Paris and informed Gramont immediately.
119. The *Times* correspondent mentioned only the *Temps*, *Débats*, and *Gazette de France* as being opposed to the war (*Times*, 18 July 1870).
120. Ollivier, XIV, 392-393.
121. J. Simon, *Souvenirs du quatre septembre 1870 et la chûte du Second Empire* (Paris, 1876), p.145.
122. *Times*, 16 July 1870.
123. Quoted in Ollivier, XIV, 498.
124. *Constitutionnel*, 17 July 1870.
125. Originally the author has selected fourteen representative and evenly scattered departments for a sampling of prefect reports. For August there are in the Archives Nationales reports on war sentiment from five of these departments. See the prefect reports (F^{1c} III) of August 1870 from Manche, Seine-Inférieure, Allier, Haute-Vienne, and Bouches-du-Rhône.

CHAPTER ELEVEN
A Voice Crying in the Wilderness

1. Report of Brière-Valigny, assistant of the procureur general, Paris, 28 Aug. 1862, Case, *United States and Mexico*, p.82.

BIBLIOGRAPHY

ARCHIVE SOURCES

Archives de la préfecture de police. Paris.
  Series A^A 434. Notes sur les événements, politiques: complots, conspirations, mouvements populaires, etc., 1852-1870.
    This designated series was consulted but was very fragmentary. It contained nothing on the secret reports on opinion made by the prefect of police to the minister of interior. It was believed by the archivist that such material had been destroyed during the fires of the Commune uprising of 1871.
Archives départementales de l'Isère. Grenoble.
  Series 52 M 42. Police générale.
    This contained a copy of the circular of the minister of interior to the prefects, dated 13 December 1860.
Archives du ministère des affaires étrangères. Brussels. (Cited as AEB.)
  Correspondance politique. Légations. France.
    Volumes XVI to XXV (1854-1870).
  Consulats. France. Volume VI.
  Beyens' private correspondence with Lambermont, secretary-general in the Belgian foreign ministry.
Archives du ministère des affaires étrangères. Paris. (Cited as AAE.)
  Correspondance politique.
    The files of correspondence with Great Britain, Sardinia, and Italy were those principally used.
Archives fédérales. Bern. (Cited as AFS.)
  Rapports politiques. Légation de la Suisse à Paris.
    Volumes 1859 to 1870.
Archives nationales. Paris.
  Series BB^{18}. Ministère de la justice. Division criminelle.
    This collection includes reports from the procureurs general on the elections of 1857 and 1869.
  Series BB^{30}. Ministère de la justice. Rapports périodiques des procureurs généraux. (Cited as procureur reports, without the carton number when the district cartons are used.)
    This series contains the main reports of the procureurs general on public opinion and economic conditions. The numbers and contents of the cartons are indicated as follows:
    370 (Agen, Aix)
    371 (Angers [mostly for 1864] and Amiens)
    372 (Bastia [Corsica])
    373 (Besançon)
    374 (Bordeaux, Bourges)
    375 (Caen, Chambéry)
    376 (Colmar)
    377 (Dijon, Douai)
    378 (Grenoble, Limoges)
    379 (Lyons)
    380 (Metz, Montpellier)
    381 (Nancy)
    382 (Nîmes, Orleans)
    383 (Paris)
    384 (Paris, Pau)
    385 (Poitiers)
    386 (Rennes, Riom)
    387 (Rouen)
    388 (Toulouse)

368 Summaries of reports.
369 Weekly reports during the Austro-Sardinian War.
389 Reports from October 1868 to October 1869.
　　These were not put in the separate district files.
395-423 Political affairs.
425 Inventory of Series BB[30].
427-443 Elections of 1863
450-451 Agitation on the Roman question, 1860-1861.
Series F[1e] III. Ministère de l'Intérieur.
　　Administration générale. Esprit public et élections.
　　Série départementale. Comptes-rendus administratifs.
　　(Cited as prefect reports [F[1e] III].)
　　　　This series contains the main reports from the prefects concerning
public opinion and is divided into separate cartons, one for each depart-
ment. Almost all the reports from 1859 to 1865 are missing.
　　　　In the preparation of this study fourteen departments were selected,
including rural and urban areas and locations in all parts of France. They
were: Ain, Allier, Bouches-du-Rhône, Finistère, Gironde, Haute-Vienne,
Haut-Rhin, Indre-et-Loire, Isère, Manche, Meuse, Seine-et-Oise, Seine-Infér-
ieure, and Vendée.
Series F[18]. Administration de la Presse.
　　Each newspaper has its own file. The files of the *Univers* (423) and the
Siècle (417) were the ones particularly consulted.
Series F 90 365 980[B].
　　This collection contains telegrams from the government to the emperor
in Italy in 1859.
National Archives. Washington.
　　Correspondence of the Department of State. (Cited as State Dept. Corr.)
　　　　The material consulted in this collection was the reports of the Ameri-
can ministers to France during the Second Empire.
Public Record Office. London.
　　Foreign Office Correspondence. (Cited as PRO, FO.)
　　　　The reports of Cowley and Lyons from Paris were used and are found
in the series 27, France.
Russell Papers. G. D. 22.
　　　　This contained the bulk of Cowley's private correspondence with Lord
John Russell during the period of the Second Empire.

PRINTED SOURCES

Ami de la Religion. (Ultramontane clerical newspaper.)
Archives diplomatiques. Recueil mensuel international de diplomatie d'histoire. Pub-
　　lished under the auspices of the French Ministry of Foreign Affairs. Paris,
　　1861 ff.
　　　　A monthly publication of official documents issued by the French and
　　other foreign governments.
Assemblée Nationale. (A Fusionist monarchist newspaper.)
Atti ufficiali del parlamento italiano, 1860-1874. Chamber. Turin, Florence, Rome,
　　1861-1874.
　　　　Official report of debates in the Italian parliament.
Avenir National. (Moderate Republican newspaper.)
Beyens, Baron Napoléon. *Histoire du Second Empire vu par un diplomate belge*
　　(Baron Eugène Beyens). 2 v. Paris, 1924-1926.
Bismarck, the man and statesman. Translated from Bismarck's *Gedanken und Erin-
　　nerungen* by A. J. Butler. 2 v. New York, 1899.
British and foreign state papers. Compiled by the librarian and keeper of the papers
　　of the Foreign Office. London, 1836 ff.
　　　　An annual publication of official documents issued by the British and
　　other foreign governments.
Cavour, Camillo di. *Lettere edite ed inedite di Camillo di Cavour.* Ed. by Luigi Chiala.
　　6 v. Turin, 1883-1887.

Chiala, Luigi. *Ancora un po' piu di luce sugli eventi politici e militari dell' anno 1866.* Florence, 1922.

Circulaires, notes et instructions du Second Empire, 1851-1870. Paris, 1871.

Clercq, A. J. H. de, and Clercq, E. F. S. de. *Recueil des traités de France depuis 1713 jusqu'à nos jours.* 23 v. Paris, 1864-1917.

Comandini, A. *Il principe Napoleone nel risorgimento italiano.* Milan, 1922.

Constitutionnel. (A semiofficial Imperialist newspaper.)

Correspondant. (An ultramontane clerical newspaper.)

Courrier du Havre. (Newspaper of le Havre.)

Cowley, Henry Richard Charles, 1st Earl. *Secrets of the Second Empire. Private letters of Henry Richard Charles Wellesley, 1st Earl Cowley, ambassador at Paris, 1852-1867.* Ed. by F. A. Wellesley. New York, 1929.
> Extracts from Cowley's private correspondence mainly with Lord John Russell.

Dabot, Henri. *Souvenirs et impressions d'un bourgeois du Quartier Latin (1854-1869).* Paris, 1899.

Die auswärtige Politik Preussens. Edited by the Historischen Reichskommission under the direction of Erich Brandenburg, Otto Hoetzsch, and Hermann Oncken. 10 v. Oldenburg, 1933-1939. (Cited as APP.)
> An excellent edition of the Prussian diplomatic documents to 1869. Volume VII, on the middle of 1866, has not yet been published.

Documents diplomatiques (Livres jaunes).
> Published by the French Ministry of Foreign Affairs. Paris, 1861 ff.

Fleury, Comte. *Memoirs of the Empress Eugénie.* 2 v. New York, 1920.

Fleury, Comte Emile F. *Souvenirs du général comte Fleury.* 2 v. Paris, 1898-1899.

France Politique. (A nonofficial Imperialist newspaper.)

Gazette de France. (Legitimist and moderately clerical newspaper.)

Gramont, Duc de. *La France et la Prusse avant la guerre.* Paris, 1872.

Granier de Cassagnac, A. *Souvenirs du Second Empire.* 3 v. Paris, 1882.

Greville, Charles C. F. *Greville memoirs, a journal of the reigns of King George IV, King William IV, and Queen Victoria.* Ed. by Henry Reeve. 8 v. New York, 1896-1899.

Guichen, Vicomte E. de. *La guerre de Crimée (1854-1856) et l'attitude des puissances européennes.* Paris, 1936.
> Contains a selection of official documents from the French and other foreign ministry archives.

Halt, Robert. Ed. *Papiers sauvés des Tuileries.* Paris, 1871.
> Contains some of the papers found in the Tuileries Palace in 1871.

Hansard's parliamentary debates, 3rd series.
> The records of the debates of the British house of lords and house of commons.

Hansen, Jules. *Les coulisses de la diplomatie. Quinze ans à l'étranger (1864-1879).* Paris, 1880.

Hauterive, Ernest de. *Napoléon III et le prince Napoléon. Correspondance inédite.* Paris, 1925.

Hübner, Alexander von. *Neuf ans d'un ambassadeur d'Autriche à Paris sous le Second Empire, 1851-1859.* Paris 1904.
> A French translation of Hübner's reminiscences of his mission to Paris.

Il Carteggio Cavour-Nigra dal 1858 al 1861.
> Edited by the Reale CommissioneEditrice. 3 v. Bologna, 1929. (Cited as CCN.)
> An excellent collection of Sardinian diplomatic documents.

Jagow, K. Ed. *Letters of the Prince Consort, 1831-1861.* Translated by E. T. S. Dugdale. New York, 1938.

Journal des Débats. (A liberal Orleanist Paris paper, cited as *Débats.*)

Journal Officiel.
> The official journal of the French government after 1869 for debates and official acts.

Kern, J. Conrad. *Souvenirs politiques.* Paris, 1887.
> Kern was Swiss minister to Paris in the last half of the Second Empire.

La Guéronnière, A. de. *L'Empereur Napoléon III et l'Italie.* Paris, 1858.

La Guéronnière, A. de. *Le pape et le congrès.* Paris, 1859.

La Marmora, Alfonso. *Un po' piu di luce sugli eventi politici e militari dell'anno 1866*. 2nd ed.; Florence, 1873.
> Revelations by a general and prime minister of Victor Emmanuel II of Italy.

Les origines diplomatiques de la guerre de 1870-1871. Published by the French Ministry of Foreign Affairs. 29 v. Paris, 1910-1930. (Cited as *Origines*.)
> Official documents from the archives of the French ministry of foreign affairs from 1863 to 1870, containing some of Rouher's Cerçay Papers.

Malmesbury, J. H. Harris, 3rd Earl of. *Memoirs of an ex-minister*. 2 v. London, 1884.

Martin, Theodore. *The life of His Royal Highness, the Prince Consort*. 5 v. London, 1875-1880.
> This work contains extracts from British public documents as well as from Prince Albert's private correspondence.

Mérimée, Prosper. *Lettres à M. Panizzi, 1850-1870*. Ed. by L. Fagan. 2 v. Paris, 1881.

Metternich, Pauline. *Souvenirs de la Princesse Pauline de Metternich*. Ed. by Marcel Dunan. Paris, 1935.
> Pauline Metternich was the wife of the Austrian ambassador in Paris (1859-1870).

Minghetti, Marco. *La Convenzione di settembre*. Bologna, 1899.

Monde. (Ultramontane clerical newspaper.)

Moniteur Universel. (Cited as *Moniteur*.)
> The official journal of the French government during the Second Empire until 1869. It contains not only the official texts of the parliamentary debates but also the official publication of current diplomatic documents and government statements.

Nesselrode, Comte Charles de. *Lettres et papiers du chancellier comte de Nesselrode, 1760-1856*. Ed. by Count A. de Nesselrode. 11 v. Saint Petersburg, 1904-1912.

Nigra, Costantino. *Poesie originali e tradotti; aggiuntovi un capitolo dei sui ricordi diplomatici*. Ed. by Alessandro d'Ancona. Florence, 1914.

Ollivier, Emile. *L'Empire libéral*. 18 v. Paris, 1895-1912.
> While this is a detailed history of most of the Second Empire, it is quite as much the re-enforced recollections of the author.

Oncken, Hermann. *Die Rheinpolitik Kaiser Napoleons III von 1863 bis 1870 und der Ursprung des Krieges von 1870-1871*. 3 v. Stuttgart, 1926.
> This contains a selection of diplomatic documents from Prussia, Austria, and other German states. The introduction and the selections suggest a pro-German bias.

Opinion Nationale.
> For a long time this was the paper reflecting the liberal Imperialist views of Prince Napoleon.

Pagani, C. "Napoleone III, Eugenia di Montijo e Francesco Arese in un carteggio inedito—L'Imperatrice Eugenia e l'Italia," *Nuova antologia*, (1 Jan. 1921), pp. 16-33.

Papers relating to the foreign relations of the United States (1861-1870). Washington, 1862-1871.
> Official documents submitted annually to the United States Congress.

Papiers et correspondance de la famille impériale. 2 v. Paris, 1870.
> Papers found in the Tuileries Palace in 1870 after the fall of the Second Empire.

Patrie. (Semiofficial Imperialist newspaper.)

Pays. (Semiofficial Imperialist newspaper.)

Phare de la Loire. (Republican newspaper of Nantes.)

Pinard, Ernest. *Mon journal*. 2 v. Paris, 1892.

Presse. (Independent liberal newspaper.)

Raindre, G. "Les papiers inédits du comte Walewski. Souvenirs et correspondance, 1855-1868," *Revue de France*, 1925: I, 74-104, 485-511; II, 39-56; III, 281-305; IV, 82-96, 311-326.

Revue des deux mondes. (Cited as RDM.)
> A liberal Orleanist semimonthly magazine whose section, *Chronique politique*, contains very good discussions of foreign policy.

Senior, Nassau. *Conversations with distinguished persons during the Second Empire, 1860-1863*. 2 v. London, 1880.

Senior, Nassau. *Conversations with M. Thiers and M. Guizot and other distinguished persons during the Second Empire, 1852-1860.* 2 v. London, 1878.

Siècle. (A moderate Republican newspaper.)

Simon, Jules. *Souvenirs du quatre septembre 1870 et la chûte du Second Empire.* Paris, 1876.

Temps. (Moderate Republican newspaper.)

Times (London).
> The news articles sent from Paris by J. B. O'Meagher often contain excellent analyses of public and press opinion.

Union. (A Legitimist and clerical newspaper.)

Union de la Sarthe. (A provincial newspaper.)

Univers. (An ultramontane clerical newspaper.)

Victoria, Queen. *The letters of Queen Victoria.* 1st Series, 1837-1861, ed. by Arthur C. Benson and Viscount Esher. 2nd series, 1861-1885, ed. by George E. Buckle. 6 v. London, 1908, 1927.

Viel Castel, Horace de. *Memoirs of Count Horace de Viel Castel. A chronicle of the principal events, political and social, during the reign of Napoleon III from 1851 to 1864.* Edited by Charles Bonsfield. 2nd ed. 2 v. London, 1888.

Wellesley, Victor, and Sencourt, Robert. *Conversations with Napoleon III.* London, 1934.
> Extracts from the private correspondence of Lord Cowley, principally with Lord John Russell and Lord Clarendon.

PUBLISHED HISTORICAL STUDIES

Avenel, H. *Histoire de la press française depuis 1789 jusqu'à nos jours.* Paris, 1900.

Avezou, Robert. *La Savoie depuis les réformes de Charles-Albert jusqu'à l'annexion à la France.* Chambéry, 1943.

Avezou, Robert. *La Savoie française sous le Second Empire, 1860-1870.* Chambéry, 1936.

Binkley, Robert C. *Realism and nationalism.* New York, 1935.

Boris, Georges. "The French press," *Foreign affairs,* XIII (1935).

Bourgeois, Emile. *Manuel historique de politique étrangère.* 5th ed. 3 v. Paris, 1919.

Cambridge Modern History. Vol. XI. New York, 1909.

Carroll, E. Malcolm. "French opinion on war with Prussia in 1870," *American historical review,* XXXI (1926), 679-700.
> While this study utilized the prefect reports for the year 1866, it is based largely on press opinion for the year 1870. Carroll concludes that opinion, far from pushing the French government into the war, was actually opposed to war.

Carroll, E. Malcolm. *French public opinion and foreign affairs, 1870-1914.* New York, 1931.
> A pioneer work on French opinion, based largely on the press.

Case, Lynn M. *Franco-Italian relations, 1860-1865.* Philadelphia, 1932.
> The sections dealing with public opinion are based on a selection of procureur reports.

Case, Lynn M. "French opinion and Napoleon III's decision after Sadowa," *Public opinion quarterly,* XIII (1949), 441-461.
> The editors of this journal have kindly permitted the author to incorporate this article into Chapter IX of this book.

Case, Lynn M. Ed. *French opinion on the United States and Mexico, 1860-1867.* New York, 1936.
> A reproduction of the texts of the procureur reports dealing with French opinion on the American Civil War and the Mexican expedition as well as with the economic conditions in France affected by the American Civil War. The introductory chapter describes the collections of the procureur and prefect reports.

Case, Lynn M. "New sources for the study of French opinion during the Second Empire," *Southwestern social science quarterly,* XVIII (1937).

Charles-Roux, F. *Alexander II, Gortchakoff, et Napoléon III.* Paris, 1913.

Chiala, Luigi. *Pagini di storia contemporanea dal 1858 al 1892.* 3 v. Turin, 1892-1893.

Debidour, Antonin. "Formation de l'unité italienne," Ch. VII in Vol. XI of E. Lavisse and A. Rambaud, *Histoire générale du 4ᵉ siècle à nos jours*. 12 v. Paris, 1893-1901.

Debidour, Antonin. *Histoire des rapports de l'église et de l'état en France de 1789 à 1870*. Paris, 1898.

Debidour, Antonin. *Histoire diplomatique de l'Europe*. Series I. 2 v. Paris, 1891.

Delord, Taxile. *Histoire du Second Empire*. 6 v. Paris, 1869-1875.

Doutenville, J. "La France, la Prusse, et l'Allemagne au lendemain de Sadowa," *Nouvelle revue*, LI (1921), 122-131.

Fay, Sidney B. *Origins of the World War* (I). 2 v. New York, 1929.

Guyot, Raymond. *Histoire diplomatique, 1815-1870; cours sténographié*. Paris, 1930.

Hale, Oron J. *Germany and the diplomatic revolution*. Philadelphia, 1931.

Hale, Oron J. *Publicity and diplomacy with special reference to England and Germany, 1890-1914*. New York, 1940.

Jordan, D. and Pratt, E. J. *Europe and the American Civil War*. New York, 1931.
        Based primarily on press opinion.

La Gorce, Pierre de. *Histoire du Second Empire*. 7 v. Paris, 1894-1905.
        One of the best histories of the Second Empire. The author inclines toward the liberal monarchist point of view.

Lally, F. E. *French opposition to the Mexican policy of the Second Empire*. Baltimore, 1931.
        Based mainly on newspaper sources.

Lippmann, Walter. *Public opinion*. New York, 1929.

Lord, Robert H. *The origins of the war of 1870*. Cambridge, Mass., 1924.
        A scholarly study tending to the view that Bismarck bears considerable responsibility for the outbreak of the Franco-Prussian War. Half of the volume contains texts of German documents.

Maurain, Jean. *Baroche, ministre de Napoléon III*. Paris, 1936.

Maurain, Jean. *Histoire ecclésiastique du Second Empire*. Paris, 1930.
        A thorough study, including the use of procureur and prefect reports in dealing with public opinion.

Newton, Thomas W. Legh, Baron. *Lord Lyons. A record of British diplomacy*. 2 v. London, 1913.

Owsley, Frank L. *King Cotton diplomacy*. Chicago, 1931.

Pointu, Jules. *Histoire de la chûte de l'empire, 6 juillet-4 septembre 1870*. Paris, 1874.
        A prejudiced Republican book which distorts evidence to make it appear that French opinion was mostly antiwar in July 1870.

Rothan, Gustave. *Les origines de la guerre de 1870: La politique française en 1866*. 1st ed.; Paris, 1883.

Rothan, Gustave. *Souvenirs diplomatiques. L'affaire du Luxembourg*. 4th ed. Paris, 1884.

Salmon, Lucy M. *The newspaper and the historian*. New York, 1923.
        An excellent critique of the press as an historical source.

Salomon, Henry. *L'ambassade de Richard de Metternich à Paris*. Paris, 1931.
        The author has made use of the Haus, Hof, und Staat Archiv in Vienna.

Schnerb, Robert. *Rouher et le Second Empire*. Paris, 1949.

Seignobos, Charles. *La révolution de 1848-le Second Empire*, Vol. VI in E. Lavisse, *Histoire de France contemporaine*. Paris, 1921

Sorel, Albert. *Histoire diplomatique de la guerre franco-allemande*. 2 v. Paris, 1875.
        A work written soon after the events and taking the view that the prevailing opinion was opposed to resort to war in 1870.

Sybel, Heinrich von. *The founding of the German Empire by William I*. Translated by M. L. Perrin. 7 v. New York, 1890-1898.
        This account is pro-Prussian but based on the Prussian state documents.

Trésal, J. *L'annexion de la Savoie à la France, 1848-1860*. Paris, 1913.

Tivaroni, Carlo. *L'Italia degli Italiani: storia critica del Risorgimento italiano, 1735-1870*. 9 v. Turin, 1888-1897.

Vautier, G. "Au-delà et en deçà de nos frontières en 1866," *Révolution de 1848*, XXV (1928), 112-122.

Weill, Georges. *Le journal, origines, évolution et rôle de la presse périodique*. Paris, 1936.

West, W. R. *Contemporary French opinion of the American Civil War.* Baltimore, 1924.

Based primarily on press opinion.

Wright, Gordon. "Public opinion and conscription in France, 1866-1870," *Journal of modern history,* XIV (1942), 26-45.

An excellent study based upon procureur and prefect reports.

INDEX